Delightful Horrors
Early Gothic Novels 1764-1809

Delightful Horrors

Early Gothic Novels 1764-1809

Maria Teresa Marnieri

Acknowledgements

No amount of thanks could be enough to express my gratitude for my family, who inspired and supported me. I wish to express my deepest esteem and thankfulness to Maria José Solé Sabater for supervising the doctoral program with attention and rectitude. I am deeply indebted to Didac Pujol, John Stone and Joan Curbet for their precious suggestions concerning my research. I am forever grateful to Sara Martín Alegre, Jordi Coral and Carme Font for their illuminating teachings. I would like to mention Andrew Monnickendam and Stuart Gillespie for their remarkable academic modus operandi.

Love all, trust a few, do wrong to none (William Shakespeare)

Presentation

This book represents a further development of a PhD thesis, which proposed to study the early Gothic, with its sublime beauty and powerful horror. I presented some parts of this book, especially the ones concerning the classical mould in the early Gothic, in seminars, conferences and articles in Mexico, Costa Rica, Great Britain and Europe starting from 2014 when the hypothesis of classical, medieval and renaissance sources in the Gothic had not been explored thoroughly and still seemed purely speculative. Despite initial setbacks, academic volumes, papers, articles and dissertations have reprised and used topics and ideas formulated in my doctoral thesis after its publication in 2016, even though a generalised form of amnesia prevented their authors to cite the original source.

The limited timespan explored in this text is inversely proportional to the authors' inventiveness and literary syncretism. This in-depth study does not follow the Gothic chronology rigorously and every chapter is independent from the others. After two pseudo-propaedeutic introductory chapters about the genre, the book starts with Horace Walpole's publication of *The Castle of Otranto* in 1764, analyses major early Gothic novels and ends with the appearance of the novel *Manfroné* in 1809. It analyses the works by William Beckford, Ann Radcliffe, Matthew Lewis, Mary Robinson, Charlotte Dacre and other early Gothic authors. The ideas presented in this book highlight the impact of literary translation, the importance of comparative literature, the influence of philosophy and, most of all, the pervasiveness of classical (in particular), medieval and renaissance themes merging with sources from the enlightenment and the long eighteenth century, which led to the rise of the literature of horror. The text also analyses tropes connected to the Gothic (Sublime and Picturesque in Nature, Architectures and Iconographies). Dedicated to all the lovers and researchers of the Gothic, *Delightful Horrors* represents an original reinterpretation of the genesis of the genre.

I have been imitated so well, I've heard people copy my mistakes
(Jimi Hendrix)

Contents

Early Gothic's Different Souls

Let me tread
Its neighb'ring walk of pines, where stray'd of old
The cloyster'd brothers: thro' the gloomy void
That far extends beneath their ample arch
As on I tread, religious horror wraps
My soul in dread repose. But when the world
Is clad in Midnight's raven-colour'd robe,
In hollow charnel let me watch the flame
Of taper dim, while airy voices talk
Along the glimm'ring walls, or ghostly shape
At distance seen, invites with beck'ning hand
My lonesome steps, thro' the far-winding vaults.
(Thomas Warton. *The Pleasures of Melancholy*)

The passion caused by the great and sublime in *nature,* when these causes operate most powerfully, is Astonishment; and Astonishment is that state of the soul, in which all its motions are suspended, with some degree of Horror.
(Edmund Burke. *A Philosophical Enquiry into the Origins of our Ideas on the Sublime and the Beautiful*)

Thus, while he strays, a thousand rural scenes
Suggest instruction, and instructing please.
And see betwixt the grove's extended arms
An Abbey's rude remains attract thy view.
(William Shenstone. *The Ruined Abbey*)

In 1764, a text that was to generate a lasting interest was printed anonymously in Italy. After eighteen months *Dei Delitti e delle Pene* had already been reprinted six times and had been translated into French by

André Morellet, while Italian printers, Giovan Claudio and Pietro Molini, printed Italian versions in Paris and London (Annamaria Loretelli 2017). The copies by Pietro Molini sold out in London, indicating that the reception of Italian texts was still remarkably high and the language well known. The English translation, *An Essay on Crimes and Punishments,* published in 1767, was attributed to Voltaire, and ten years later, the 1775 English edition still bore Voltaire's name on the frontispiece, as the French philosopher had in all probability written the commentary to the text. The anonymous English translator, identified as the journalist and liberal politician John Wilkes, claimed that "perhaps no book, on any subject, was ever received with more avidity, more generally read, or more universally applauded" (Beccaria 1775: iv). The real author, Marquis Cesare Beccaria, was quite eager for anonymity during a period when the Austrian government, in control of Venice, Milan and northern Italian territories, used the ruthless secret police to banish dangerous books and suffocate any form of revolt, and the Inquisition could still exert its universally abhorred power. In effect, the Spanish Inquisition condemned and prohibited the book from 1777 until 1820 after Juan Antonio de las Casas' translation was issued in 1774 in Spain (Raffaella Tonin 2010).

One of the best jurists of the epoch, and a member of the Milanese Enlightenment, he was the friend of philosophers, historians and literati such as Pietro and Alessandro Verri, with whom he exchanged ideas about freedom and justice. Beccaria, who was in contact with French, European and American philosophers, intellectuals and politicians, described different typologies of crimes and forms of punishments. In particular, the part of his essay on punishments aroused an incredible amount of attention. It concerned the description of tortures used to obtain confessions from suspects. Beccaria's accounts of inflicted sufferings were so vivid that they provoked a marked impression on readers. The violent methods used to obtain confessions were thoroughly described, and the horrors of torture were depicted with realistic details. Beccaria, however, did not intend to be morbid or indulge in violent and gory scenes. His idea was to denounce the inhumanity and the uselessness of torture in a fair legal system. The surprising popularity of the text, known by a vast public, was also due to the author's rigorous and transparent legal language. A genuine admirer of the praiseworthy English dissemination of knowledge, Beccaria advocated the development of science and reason as well as the promotion of just laws for social improvement, thus reflecting the influx of the Enlightenment:

Let Liberty be attended with knowledge. As knowledge extends, the disadvantages which attend it diminish, and the advantages increase. A daring impostor, who is always a man of some genius, is adored by the ignorant populace, and despised by men of understanding. Knowledge facilitates the comparison of objects, by showing them in different points of view. When the clouds of ignorance are dispelled by the radiance of knowledge, authority trembles, but the force of the laws remains immovable. Men of enlightened understanding must necessarily approve those useful conventions, which are the foundations of public safety. (*An Essay on Crimes and Punishments:* 167–168)

To promote enlightened societies Beccaria needed to describe the appalling atmospheres of various forms of inhuman punishments, the cruelty of which was directly proportional to their uselessness, no matter if a prisoner was guilty or not. Beccaria's gloomy descriptions of unjustified tortures create a sharp antithesis of darkness and light that prefigures the cultural contrasts of the epoch that several scholars identify as an ideal Romantic period of multiple dichotomies, stretching between 1750 and 1850 (Miriam Wallace 2009). *An Essay on Crimes and Punishments* was also influential in the circles of the American Founding Fathers and inspired revolutionary ideals (Loretelli 2017; John Bessler 2014). The interaction between Italy and English Romanticism, a topic recently attracting scholars' attention (Frank O'Gorman and Lia Guerra 2013), is analysed by Charles P. Brand (1957), who foregrounds Beccaria's extraordinary success in Europe and in England. Beccaria provided the collective imagination with real-life tales of horror that were soon to be transposed into the most terrifying stories in the early Gothic novels that we intend to analyse in this book.

A few years before the publication of Beccaria's *Essay*, an anonymous German artist painted a portrait, now at the Royal Castle Museum in Warsaw, depicting a person sitting under a tree surrounded by an Italian landscape dotted with ancient ruins and dominated by hovering clouds in a stormy sky. Even though he is encompassed by a menacing nature, the character enjoys his position in the middle of the wilderness. The painting seems a compendium of the different ideals dominating the period, namely the love for lush landscapes and the attraction to classical antiquity: it is a portrait of the famous art historian and archaeologist Johann Joachim Winkelmann, who spent part of his life in Italy discovering the secrets of ancient art and architecture. The renowned Swiss-turned-cosmopolitan painter Angelika Kaufmann captured an iconographic portrait of Winkelmann in 1764 after the revered German scholar had completed two texts on the recent archaeological discoveries in Pompeii and Herculaneum. As C. W. Ceram narrates in *Gods, Graves and Scholars. The Story of Archaeology*, first published in 1949, Winkelmann's tragic and violent death four years later made an intellectual, such as Lessing, exclaim that he would have offered years of his life to that incomparable genius, equally exalted by Goethe and Schiller.

While Winckelmann was a successful promoter of Greek models, his contemporary Giovanni Battista Piranesi highlighted the importance of Roman Antiquity. A painter and engraver, Piranesi etched phantasmagorias of ancient Roman monuments that were acclaimed in Italy as well as in Great Britain and Europe. His artworks on Roman Antiquity, together with Winckelmann's theories on classical art, were essential in determining renewed classical sensibilities, whereas his descriptions of nightmarish and labyrinthine imaginary architectures, responsible for forging new iconographies of terror, were universally commended. Richard Wendort (2001: 162) highlights that "Piranesi's views of Rome had such a profound influence on the cultural imagination of the late eighteenth century, in fact, that the images themselves became yet another superimposition with which the modern eye would have to contend". Wendort explains that in his *Italian Journey*, written in the 1780s and published in 1816, Goethe confessed that his first sight of the ruins of Rome had failed to measure up to Piranesi's views of them. Horace Walpole, moreover, urged his contemporaries to "study the sublime dreams of Piranesi, who seems to have conceived visions of Rome beyond what it boasted even in the meridian of its splendour. Savage as Salvator Rosa, fierce as Michael Angelo, and exuberant as Rubens, [Piranesi] has imagined scenes that would startle geometry" (Wendort: 163). While Beccaria was publishing different editions of his remarkable study on crime and punishment in the 1760s, and Piranesi was mesmerising art lovers with his etchings of improbable geometries in the same years, Winckelmann gave his influential *History of Ancient Art* to the press a few months before Walpole published his Gothic sensation in 1764. Like Beccaria's and Walpole's books, and Piranesi's works, Winkelmann's text, *Anmerkungen über die Geschichte der Kunst des Alterthums* in the original version, was popular and recurrently reprinted. Winckelmann was fascinated by Italy, its majestic past and its classical vestiges. His *Gedanken über die Nachahmung der Griechischen Werke in der Malerei und Bildhauerkunst* (1755) had been equally important for establishing a new viewpoint on Antiquity. The visionary painter Henry Fuseli considered Winkelmann's text revolutionary and translated it into English to spread the German scholar's novel ideas that he reputed to be crucial for every artist. Fuseli's translation, known as *Reflections on the Painting and Sculpture of the Greeks: with Instructions for the Connoisseur, and an Essay on Grace in Works of Art,* was published in London in 1767. Winkelmann and Piranesi were among the many figures that influenced artistic reception and ideas on Classicism in Europe and also contributed to the diffusion of the image of Italy as a place of ancient ruins, luxuriant nature and surrounded by mystery.

Winkelmann and Piranesi conveyed the soul of Classicism, a complex soul polarised between contrasting images of ethereal beauty and latent horrors, both features representing an intrinsic part of Greek and Roman literary and iconographic traditions. Classicism and other sources from the literary past were essential throughout the eighteenth century, and elements from Antiquity were introduced where they were least expected. David Hopkins (2007) convincingly posits that interactions with the ancients function at various levels in many eighteenth-century works. Dafydd Moore (2016) highlights the profusion of examples from Homer, Virgil and the Classics in an epic meant to exalt northern traditions in opposition to the ancient epic of classical southern poets. Published a few months after *The Castle of Otranto,* James Macpherson's *The Works of Ossian* (1765) contains records of Homer's and Virgil's Classical examples, taken from the original versions of John Dryden's and Alexander Pope's translations. Despite their insertion in the poem with a different objective in mind (that is, the contrastive exaltation of medieval epic in Gaelic), they reveal the significant, unrelenting effect of Classicism. According to Moore, Macpherson's omission of explanatory notes in subsequent editions may be thought-provoking. In the beginning, Macpherson may have chosen to add paratextual details to juxtapose *Ossian* to ancient Classical masterpieces, thus reinforcing its epic value. On the contrary, their elimination betrays a preoccupation with avoiding the recognition of evident hypotexts (or earlier texts) behind his collection.

An eclectic writer and a scandalous celebrity, active in the last three decades of the eighteenth century, Mary Robinson created multifaceted works offering further examples of Classical influence and cultural syncretism. She was a child prodigy writing poetry from the age of seven. She became a teacher, then a popular actress when still an adolescent to support her family. She was a Romantic poetess (probably, the first Romantic altogether), a successful playwright, a novelist and a Gothic author, oftentimes ignored or despised by critics. Robinson wrote odes, sonnets and plays, interspersed with images of love and nature, and the preoccupation with women's position in society. Tim Fulford (1999) provides an interesting insight into the political value of Robinson's correspondence with Coleridge, a sincere admirer of her poetic rhythm and musicality in spite of his general idiosyncrasy for women writers. Notwithstanding her literary value, the poetess was one of Richard Polwhele's explicit targets, together with Mary Wollstonecraft, in his 1798 caustic poem against women writers. *The Unsex'd Females: A Poem addressed to the Author of the Pursuits of Literature*, which Polwhele dedicated to James Mathias, aimed at discouraging the reading of female writers. Despite the prevalently Romantic nature of her works, Robinson is an interesting author, mirroring the duality of her times, as she was deeply inspired by the Classics, but at the same time was attracted to authors from the Middle Ages and the Renaissance and experimented new forms of literature. A successful imitator of Sappho and Greek poets, she dedicated some of her dramatic dialogues in verse to Petrarch and his lover Laura and wrote poems with Gothic nuances inherited from Ann Radcliffe. Robinson's eclecticism demonstrates the co-existence of both classical roots and medieval influences forging new currents and ideas in the mutability of literature during the enlightenment and at the end of the eighteenth century.

The title of this book is an oxymoron derived from Edmund Burke's theory of the sublime published in 1757. *Delightful Horrors* intends to explore the different souls and the multiple forms of literary genius converging within early Gothic novels, which featured an original blend of various sources, frequently unrecognisable in the whirlwind of creativity, shaping romances and horror stories published during the last decades of the eighteenth century. Mary Favret (1994) postulates that the popular eighteenth-century epistolary novel generated the sentimental novel, the Jacobin novel, the Gothic novel and the historical novel. If, on the one hand, this idea is sustainable, on the other hand, it is an over-simplification, as it cannot adequately justify the incredible richness of literary sources hidden in the early Gothic novels. Contexts and iconographies in the Gothic novel did not originate as an impromptu output but were the consequences of Classical, Medieval, Renaissance, and Enlightenment ideas and images that became part of the rich substratum of early Gothic literary productions. The most relevant novels published in Britain during the last four decades of the eighteenth century enclosed inner voices representing a dialogue with a majestic past, both recent and distant, autochthonous and cosmopolitan, harmonious and intimidating. The apparent oddities of the works by Horace Walpole, William Beckford, Ann Radcliffe, Matthew Gregory Lewis and a number of their Gothic contemporaries that this study intends to analyse were the conscious and semi-conscious manifestations of the multiple influences the authors had absorbed, manipulated, and adapted to their stories.

The shadows cast on the Gothic by several critics and contemporary writers at the time of their publication established lasting prejudices against them. Preconceptions were mostly dissipated by positive and articulated critical analyses during the last two decades of the twentieth century, with David Punter, Robert Miles, Emma Clery, Maggie Kilgour, Anne Williams and Michael Gamer being among the most important scholars to acknowledge the literary value of early Gothic novels and the Gothic genre in general. Critical literature on Gothic fiction published at the turn of the twentieth century and in the new millennium has carried out an ongoing rehabilitation of the Gothic in general and of the early Gothic novel in particular, a literary phenomenon that still offers intriguing hidden meanings, without considering its innumerable proliferations in subsequent decades and centuries. *Delightful Horrors* is a journey of discovery of the prismatic essence of early Gothic novels. The convergence of fundamental works played an important role both in the characterisation of the long eighteenth century and in the genesis of the Gothic. However, the attraction for terrifying and supernatural contexts did not start with the Gothic novel. The love for the gloomy and the mysterious had manifested before the rise of the Gothic. One of Joseph Addison's aesthetic meditations about the supernatural had appeared in the *Spectator* in 1711, in which he had praised the introduction of the supernatural to provoke contrasting feelings of pity and terror in the manner of playwrights. Shared by John Dryden and John Dennis, Addison's ideas were innovative, even though he might have conceived them by reading Boileau, as he suggested relying on "the authority of the classical past" (Clery 1995: 34–35). To justify the birth of the Gothic, Clery also posits that individuality, inscribed in subjective fruition of novels, brought about the need for private forms of mystery, an idea shared by Christy Desmet and Anne Williams (2007), who link the solitary enjoyment of reading with the individualistic appreciation of the Gothic. Whereas pinpointing the origin of the early Gothic remains a difficult task, it is possible to argue that the beginning of its manifestations was brought about decades before its flowering, as Addison's idea of horror as well his meditation on Longinus's sublime in literature substantiate. Although horror and fear seem to represent the Gothic's main features, Williams (1995: 11) provides a soothing definition, describing the Gothic as "the supposedly common fantasy, which is the desire to escape the reality", even though Williams is against categorising such an ambiguous literary current and creating boundaries for it. In her *Perils of the Night*, Eugenia

DeLamotte (1990: 13) argues, "[a] thoughtful analysis of 'Gothic' should challenge the kind of literary history that organises, delineates, and defines: a literary history that also confines us within some inherited literary concepts, particularly ideas about genre, that can be as confusing as Udolpho's amazing structures". The Gothic novel was young but already differentiated by the end of the eighteenth century. After the single cases of Walpole in the 1760s and Clara Reeve in the 1770s, Sophia Lee, William Beckford and Charlotte Smith, among others, dominated the decade of the 1780s. The 1790s saw the beginning (and the apparent end) of Radcliffe's creations, Robinson's experiments and the publication of Lewis's scandalous novel. These successful authors were imitated by a constellation of semi-unknown and anonymous writers, whose horror novels did not generally possess relevant literary qualities and were often written as a means of subsistence for their creators. Imitators of Gothic novels were less interested in lofty literary sources to insert in their stories and more intent upon contexts of suspense, echoing the pages of more famous writers. Although Beckford, Radcliffe and Lewis showed forms of mutual influences together with their borrowings from Walpole, each author was characterised by a specific style, not replicated by other novelists. The early Gothic writers provided examples of intertextuality, a notion of literary echoes conceived by Thomas S. Eliot (1923) after William Butler Yeats had partially outlined it at the end of the nineteenth century. Eliot demonstrated that literary and artistic creations were the consequence of ideal dialogues between authors either belonging to different epochs or contemporary periods, an idea further developed by post-modern philosopher Jacques Derrida (1980), who asserted literary works' impossibility of belonging to a single genre or category, due to continuous linguistic and cultural reverberations at play. In the case of the early Gothic novels, we can trace both unidirectional and mutual influences.

A reluctant beginner of the genre, Walpole initiated new themes and narrations, and his 1764 romance is a literary mixture uniting classicism, horror, suspense and the supernatural. Walpole influenced Reeve, who, in her turn, provided a basic model for Gothic writing, which developed in two different directions, one towards the historical novel and one towards the romance. Sophia Lee and Martha Harley adopted the former and Radcliffe, Robinson, Regina Maria Roche, Francis Lathom and Mary Ann Radcliffe preferred the latter, whereas Lewis (and also Charlotte Dacre) tended to exacerbate Gothic horrors. Beckford created an elegant form of Gothic masqueraded as an Oriental tale. Radcliffe borrowed themes and devices from all her Gothic predecessors, including Charlotte Smith. Lewis used Radcliffe's ideas in *The Monk* (1796) emphasising the contexts of horror, and Radcliffe later reproduced some of Lewis's dark images by transposing them into *The Italian* (1797), filtering out gory details.

These multifaceted writing modes reflected each writer's cultural knowledge and literary tastes. This text investigates early Gothic horror stories published at the end of the eighteenth century. *Delightful Horrors* intends to demonstrate that the difference between genuine Gothic authors and the mass of their Gothic imitators is that Walpole, Beckford, Radcliffe and Lewis were intellectually rich and complex, absorbed cultural influences from different periods and were motivated by the desire for cultural recognition. It is difficult to ascertain whether they were conscious of the impact their inventions had or if they were aware of the possible proliferation of *a posteriori* Gothic. It may be plausible to infer that each and every one of them wanted to create lofty forms of narratives that became exemplary, and consistently imitated, even though they were despised by much of the mainstream culture and literary criticism of the late eighteenth century and the nineteenth century. Some authors peripherally used variegated Gothic styles to pass on their ideas or to obtain more success as is the case with Frances Fanny Burney and her work *Camilla* (1796). Smith was remarkably experimental in her writing and introduced Gothic atmospheres to attract a wider public. Others, such as William Godwin and Mary Wollstonecraft, used the Gothic mode to make their socio-political messages more alluring. Robinson somehow reproduced the Radcliffean mode in her Gothic texts *Vancenza* (1792) and *Hubert de Sevrac* (1796). Roche and Dacre, respectively famous for *Clermont* (1798) and *Zofloya* (1806), intended to sublimate stories of Radcliffe and Lewis respectively, albeit with mixed results. Like Smith, Eliza Parsons exploited the trend to earn economic independence during the 1790s. Meanwhile horror stories from national and foreign authors invaded the market. Although less popular authors could not compare with Walpole, Beckford, Radcliffe and Lewis, the propagation of their innumerable and widely read Gothic replicas contributed to the creation of a durable bias toward the early Gothic novel and the literature of terror. Cheap and low-quality imitations of Gothic novels, distributed by Minerva Press and circulating libraries, provoked a sense of growing animadversion for the genre. The concentration of romances, tales of horror, and stories of ghosts set in mysterious castles and sinister abbeys between the 1790s and the first decade of the nineteenth century is astonishingly high. Many of them were issued as chapbooks (cheap and normally anonymous pocket versions of popular novels), advertised in bluebooks, namely the marketing tokens of the time–inexpensive catalogues–used by circulating libraries to keep their readers apprised about available titles. Anonymous as well as popular authors exploited the frenzy for Gothic mysteries. Lewis published collections of romantic tales and horror narratives that he had translated or adapted from previous stories or foreign authors (*The Bravo of Venice*, 1805; *The Wood Daemon, or the Clock has struck*, 1807; *Romantic Tales*, 1808). The semi-unknown Martha Harley wrote six popular Gothic novels between 1786 and 1798 before being almost entirely forgotten (*St. Bernard's Priory, an old English Tale*, 1786; *The Castle of Mowbray, an English Romance*, 1788; *The Prince of Leon. A Spanish Romance*, 1794). After *Caleb Williams* (1794), Godwin published a historical Gothic story (*St. Leon, A Tale of the Sixteenth Century*, 1799). John Moore, famous for publishing *Zeluco* in 1789, turned to the Gothic (*Grasville Abbey: A Romance*, 1797; *The Heirs of Villeroy. A Romance*, 1806). The author of *The Recess* (1797), Sophia Lee penned a horror story (*Almeyda, Queen of Granada*, 1797). Eliza Fenwick, famous for her children's books, experimented with the Gothic genre (*Secrecy, or the Ruin of the Rock*, 1795). In imitation of Radcliffe and Lewis, some women writers acquired notoriety at the end of the century such as Roche (*Clermont. A Tale*, 1798; *Nocturnal Visit. A Tale*, 1800), Dacre (*Confessions of the Nun of St. Omer*, 1805; *Zofloya*, 1806), prolific Mary (also known as "Mrs.") Meeke, with several formulaic novels (*The Abbey of Clugny*, 1795; *Count Saint Blanchard*, 1796; *The Sicilian*, 1797) and Robinson (*Vancenza; or, the Dangers of Credulity* 1792; *Hubert de Sevrac. A Romance*, 1796). Eliza Parsons turned to Gothic tales to solve her financial problems (*The Castle of Wolfenbach*, 1793; *The Mysterious Warning*, 1796; *The Valley of Saint Gotthard*, 1799). Lathom, a versatile novelist, imitated Radcliffe and published Gothic stories full of blood and horror (*The Castle of Ollada*, 1795; *The Midnight Bell*, 1798; *Mystery. A Novel*, 1800; *The Fatal Vow*, 1807). The mysterious Mary Anne Radcliffe exploited her surname, and Radcliffe's silence, to publish novels of terror that may have attracted readers for their Radcliffean themes (*The Veiled Picture, or the Mysteries of Gorgono*, 1802; *Manfroné: or, the One-handed Monk*, 1809). An Eliza Ratcliffe published a single novel: *The Mysterious Baron* (1808). Henry Mackenzie, an otherwise sentimental author, conceived the terror novel *The Neapolitan* (1796). About forty anonymous Gothic novels and romances were published between 1797 and 1807. Louisa Stanhope, Sarah Wilkinson, Mrs. R.M.P. Yorke and William Ireland compiled a profusion of terror and horror stories in the first decade of the nineteenth century while a myriad of authors used pseudonyms or pen names and produced countless volumes of Gothic stories. Moreover, innumerable novels were printed anonymously (Peter Garside, James Raven, and Rainer Schöwerling 2000). Eighteenth-century critics' impatient rejection of the Gothic may have been justifiable, after all.

The increase in the disparaging terminology that was invented to define the Gothic after 1796 was equally remarkable: some of the definitions were "modern romance", "the terrible school", "the terrorist system of novel writing", "terrorist novel writing", or "hobgoblin romance" (Clery 1995: 148). As a result, the Gothic was relegated to an inferior literary niche in the decades to come. Burlesque versions of the Gothic reinforced the idea that stories of terror were risible. Moreover, renowned writers' and eminent critics' ironic responses conveyed lasting prejudices. Clifford Siskin (1988) posits that the stereotypes created by the so-called Romantic authors entrapped both readers and critics into forming a false idea about the Gothic while, on the other hand, they elevated and glorified their own movement by basing it on the concept of timeless imagination, pretending to have elements in common with illustrious literary forms throughout all times. Just as Stephen Greenblatt (2011) redefines the notion of the Renaissance, Siskin's neo-historical criticism casts a different light on the literary and poetic creations of the early nineteenth century. The chronological contiguity of the early Gothic with Romanticism created opposing ideas concerning analogies and distinctions between the two apparently contrasting movements. Whereas some scholars consider them antithetical, others have identified a single mainstream uniting the Gothic and the Romantic. Williams (1995: 7) assumes that there cannot be any distinction, as "Gothic and Romanticism are one", while Gamer (2000: 7–9) observes that there is no synthesis between the two movements because of Romantic "dismissiveness and hostility" towards the Gothic, although their connections run deep. Besides, readers' and critics' negotiations tend to settle clichés of literary categories and periodisation. Gamer (2000: 11) also underlines the problematic dialectics between the Gothic and Romantic because of their "adjacency and overlapping" and that the "Gothic perpetually haunts, as an aesthetic to be rejected, Romanticism's construction of high literary culture". In recent times, scholars have tended to identify many more analogies between supposedly conflicting literary movements. Wallace's collection of miscellaneous essays (2009) identifies multiple links between the Augustan Age, the Enlightenment, Pre-Romanticism, Romanticism and the Gothic, which are parts of an uninterrupted flow in spite of conventional literary classifications tending to separate them rigidly. Influenced by the bias of Romantic superiority, Robert Hume (1969: 285) emphasised the analogies between Gothic and

Romantic, even though he did not consider them part of a single entity: "That Gothicism is closely related to Romanticism is clear, but it is easier to state the fact than to prove it tidily and convincingly. There is a persistent suspicion that Gothicism is a poor and probably illegitimate relation of Romanticism, and a consequent tendency to treat it that way". He also assumed that (286):

[A]mong the novels of the period 1764–1820 a distinction seems necessary between the novel of 'terror' and the novel of 'horror'. This distinction has its origin in the aesthetics of the mid-eighteenth century: as Mrs Radcliffe puts it, terror and horror are so far opposite, that the first expands the soul, and awakens the faculties to a high degree of life; the other contracts, freezes and nearly annihilates them [...]. Neither Shakespeare nor Milton by their fictions, nor Mr Burke by his reasoning, anywhere looked to positive horror as a source of the sublime, though they all agree that terror is a very high one. In short, terror opens the mind to the apprehension of the sublime, while (according to Mrs Radcliffe) the repugnance involved in horror closes it.

Contrary to what R. Hume opined, Romantic works contain considerable traces of Gothic. Not to mention the improbable, but steadily adopted, separation between terror and horror, as postulated by Nathan Drake in 1798 and then apparently embraced in a posthumous essay by Radcliffe (1826) the paternity of which, or, better, maternity, so to speak, cannot be verified. The polarity between terror and horror turns out to be an unconvincing stratagem to identify loftier works from low-quality imitations. Making such a distinction is a rather feeble way of determining the literary value of a Gothic story and its strategy of fear, as Burke's oxymoron "delightful horror" clearly suggests. The separation between Gothic and Romantic as well as terror and horror may not be so mechanical. In his first preface, Walpole claims that "Terror, the author's principal engine, prevents the story from ever languishing" (*The Castle of Otranto*: 4) and is used as a literary device. It is interesting to note that Conrad's dramatic death in the first pages is a "spectacle of horror" (17), thus confirming the interchangeability of the two terms in the early Gothic. The protagonists of Radcliffe's and other novelists' Gothic romances experience feelings of terror and horror that are sometimes interchangeable, contrasting Drake's, R. Hume's and some critics' suppositions. Reiterating the incongruous and slavish divergence between horror and terror betrays an old-fashioned scholarly examination of the Gothic based on truism rather than on real knowledge. The formulaic distinction is an unconvincing stereotype, which is due more to a superficial reading of the early Gothic–or, better, to a very poor analysis of the genre–than to observable literary elements. Reeve mostly adopted the distinction that she theorized and used it in her censored form of horror, which turned out to be rather unappealing. Minor Gothic authors such as Martha Harley, an aspiring literary clone of both Reeve and Lee's historical Gothic, reiteratively emulated it. Some editors' redundant essay in the umpteenth text about the Gothic (published in the 2020s) unconvincingly resurrected this outdated and unnecessary distinction between horror and terror, which does not help improve our knowledge of the early Gothic, being a simple repetition of superficial clichés.

Undoubtedly, 1764 was a cultural breakthrough because of the momentous publications that were issued in that year, among which *The Castle of Otranto* incontrovertibly remains a milestone in the path of the Gothic. However, determining the dating of the early Gothic seems to be a difficult task due to its embryonic manifestations before its *terminus a quo*. Clery dates the beginning of the Gothic trend to 1762, whereas Miles slightly widens the Gothic by starting it in 1750. The inauguration of early Gothic narratives of terror is sometimes positioned in a nebulous period, corresponding to so-called Pre-Romanticism, a conventional definition of a literary anticipation of original themes and images promoting new sensibilities. In some cases, Pre-Romanticism is seen as the incipient manifestation of the Romantic Movement, which became dominant at the beginning of the nineteenth century. William Blake is an example of the ambiguity surrounding this literary current, as some scholars include him amongst the Romantics, while others consider him a Pre-Romantic either for being about a decade older than William Wordsworth and Samuel T. Coleridge or for the difficulty of categorising his unique poetic creations, introducing latent Gothic elements.

Like several scholars of Gothic fiction, R. Hume defined the chronological limits of the Gothic as starting in 1764 and ending in 1820, choosing *Melmoth the Wanderer* (1820) as the grand finale of the Gothic genre. A number of scholars consider Charles Robert Maturin's novel the last example of the early Gothic phase. However, Hume does not follow his delimitation, as he extends the Gothic chronology to other periods. The scholar (289) concludes, "the early Gothic novels are precursors of Romanticism in their concern with sensibility, the sublime and the involvement of the reader [even though] in its highest forms Romantic writing claims the existence of higher answers where Gothic can find only unresolvable moral and emotional ambiguity". The critic expressed a prejudice that perfectly mimicked Wordsworth and Coleridge's assumptions meant to reiterate Gothicists' inferior position in literature. As Gamer (2000) has extensively demonstrated, Wordsworth's frequent and subtle dismissal of "frantic novels" moulded a negative critical viewpoint of the Gothic for decades to come. Coleridge unceasingly belittled the importance of the Gothic in both his reviews and works, while Lord Byron expressly ridiculed Gothic authors. Ironically, and despite their apparent rejection of the Gothic, the very same Coleridge, Wordsworth and Byron, together with Percy B. Shelley and John Keats, among others, made extensive use of Gothic symbolism in their Romantic compositions. Those Romantic authors intending to distance themselves from the clear matrix of their imagery carried out the attack against the Gothic. Gamer (2001: 93) convincingly claims:

> [T]he language of influence between writers, whether of direct borrowing or wilful misreading, cannot adequately represent the mediating forces at work, let alone capture the richness of the appropriations that do occur. While Gothic may be a notoriously shifting and complex object of study for any literary historian interested in the genre, its rapid changes and instability at the end of the eighteenth century, rather than frustrating us, should form part of our definition of the term.

The Romantics intended to preserve their high profile and aura of originality while simultaneously being acknowledged as the beginners of a new poetic model. Stuart Gillespie (2011) reveals that they also produced imitations of Antiquity, both Greek and Latin, but they tended to camouflage Classical influences in their works, while Wordsworth ambiguously eliminated his studies and translations of the Classics. Despite their Romantic camouflage, Wordsworth, Coleridge, Byron and other contemporary poets were harshly criticised by Thomas Love Peacock in 1820 because their "poetry was absurdly derivative of ancient models of inspiration and composition" (Nick Groom 2009: 35). Gamer (2001: 98) uses the words "attraction and repulsion" to describe the strange relationship between the Romantics and the Gothic. Substantiating his assertions, he convincingly maintains that Romanticism may have scattered from a form of literary opportunism. Initially oriented towards legitimising their unsuccessful forms of Gothicism, the Romantics not only distanced themselves from it but also systematically ventilated its inferiority. Coleridge started Lewis's ruin and Byron completed it. Jane Austen was pitiless with Smith and Radcliffe, her favourite targets. In *Emma* (1815), she ridiculed *The Romance of the Forest* (1791), while

Northanger Abbey (1817) was partly a parody of *The Mysteries of Udolpho* (1797). Austen's *Sense and Sensibility* (1811) was a pessimistic remake of Smith's novel *Celestina* (1791) aimed at spotlighting her female forerunner's narrative weaknesses. Austen also ironized the so-called "horrid novels" that were initially thought to be the result of her creative imagination. Among them are Parsons's *The Castle of Wolfenbach* (1793) and *The Mysterious Warning* (1796), and Roche's *Clermont* (1798). Austen's *Northanger Abbey* allowed literary critics to discover that a series of "horrid novels" had been effectively printed. Notwithstanding this derision, the Gothic resisted criticism and persisted, offering the building blocks for further developments.

Reactions to early Gothic fiction were heterogeneous, starting from its first appearance with the publication of *The Castle of Otranto* in 1764. Afraid of negative opinions, Walpole decided to publish anonymously. He used a literary device to give credibility to the story by presenting the novel as a translation of an Italian text—originally a manuscript, written by "Onuphrio Muralto, Canon of the Church of St. Nicholas at Otranto" between 1095 and 1243. The elegant Italian incunabula, published in Naples in 1529 and translated into English by "William Marshal" (*WO*: 1), was later found in the library of an aristocratic family in Northern England. William Marshal is also the apparent author of the "preface", providing some clues about the story.

In the preface to the novel's second edition published a few months later, Walpole unveiled the truth and explained that his choice was due to the novelty of the innovative "attempt to blend the two kinds of romance, the ancient and the modern". Caught by surprise, contemporary critics tried to find reasonable motivations for the public's enthusiastic reception of horror stories imbued with supernatural elements. Fred Botting (2008) compares negative critical opinions on phantasmagoria with critical analyses of the Gothic meant to denounce its apparent absurdities. With the passing of time and the creation of shallow Gothic duplications, critics hoped for the approaching end of this kind of narrative, though it never came. Although Walter Scott only partially appreciated Gothic literature, he contributed to raising awareness of the genre, to which other authors and poets became indebted, despite their reluctance to admit its influence.

A lifelong collector of all things Walpolian and instrumental in the creation of the Walpole Lewis Library at Yale University, Wilmarth Lewis is the author of an illuminating introduction to *The Castle of Otranto*. W. Lewis (1969: viii) quotes Scott's presentation of the 1811 edition of *The Castle of Otranto*, in which the Scottish writer affirmed that the novel was "remarkable not only for the wild interest in the story but as the first modern attempt to found a tale of amusing fiction upon the basis of the ancient romances of chivalry". Walpole's story was paramount in the development and further propagation of the Gothic, as he admitted in his correspondence some thirty years later when Radcliffe published *The Mysteries of Udolpho* (1794), even though he was an unwilling progenitor of the genre. Despite the success of the literature of terror, scholars considered the Gothic as a secondary form of literature, or even as non-literature, especially when several writers, many among them women, followed Walpole's example. The Gothic became the object of negative scrutiny in different periods, starting from its development at the end of the eighteenth century until the present day. Gamer (2000: 204), for instance, reckons that "probably the most emblematic of Modernists' dismissals of Gothic was Virginia Woolf" in her article "Gothic Romance" published in 1921. With the exclusion of several articles in specialised reviews, literary historians in the nineteenth century and during the first half of the twentieth century either minimised the importance of the Gothic or did not even consider it worth mentioning in their anthologies and studies. Influential for his comprehensive studies on English literature, David Daiches considered the Gothic as "a dilettante interest in the Middle Ages" in *A Critical History of English Literature* (1960). The American scholar Samuel Chew completely ignored it. Williams (1995: 1) showed how twentieth-century eminent critics such as F. R. Leavis, Wayne Booth and Ian Watt, famous for exalting the realistic tradition in fiction, definitely excluded Gothic authors from their critical analyses. The late Italian scholar Elio Chinol compiled various anthologies of English literature with minimum explanations of the Gothic. Williams provokingly suggests, "twentieth-century keepers of the House of Fiction have always treated Gothic as a skeleton in the closet". It was necessary to wait for Northrop Frye (1963) and Devendra Varma (1966) to obtain a revaluation of the genre.

Michael Munday (1982) investigates the attention that early critical reviews paid to the Gothic. Even if only some writers, such as Samuel Richardson, acclaimed author of the epistolary novels *Pamela* (1740) and *Clarissa* (1748), Henry Fielding and Laurence Sterne, were generally recognised as accomplished men of letters, literary magazines took Gothic novels and romances into consideration even though the reputation of the novel, in general, and the Gothic, in particular, was rather poor. Critics tended to "hit out at the Gothic novel, the *bête noire* of both the *Edinburgh* and the *Quarterly*" while the scholar John Wilson Croker expressed the desire to "expose the raving nonsense which novel readers are content to receive as sublimity and pathos" (Munday: 205–206). Critics reprehended authors and their avid readers alike, both instrumental in the survival of the abhorred Gothic genre, and their remarks exposed circulating libraries' scarce cultural contents as well. The critic John Gibson Lockhart, active at the beginning of the nineteenth century, dismissed Godwin's *Caleb Williams* for its "gliding phantoms and unearthly horrors" (211). Similar judgements were usually directed towards Gothic works published during the same decade while scholars and critics became increasingly sceptical of the success of the Gothic trend. Miles (1993) defines the phenomenon as "the effulgence of Gothic" because of the mind-blowing bulk of Gothic publications that occurred in a relatively short period. Despite frequent rebukes by critics, the interest aroused in the public by the new form of literature based on frightful and mysterious events was immediate and continued over time. Gothic novels were different from previous forms of fiction, and highly esteemed authors appeared to be exempt from any Gothic contamination. However, even if from a slightly ironic point of view in his *Rise of the Novel*, Ian Watt (1987: 27) identifies the first element of fictional Gothic architecture in one of Fielding's most famous novels, declaring that: "Fielding is some way from Richardson's particularity. He gives no full interiors, and his frequent landscape descriptions are conventionally stereotyped. Nevertheless, *Tom Jones* (1749) features the first Gothic mansion in the history of fiction".

Gothic is problematic stylistically, but it also introduces a series of linguistic posers. The cultural value of the word Gothic is semantically complex for its multiple meanings. Scholar Alfred E. Longueil (1923: 453–455) traces the story of the term and credits Walpole for the beginning of a new linguistic and literary nuance of "Gothic", thanks to his choice to define his novel, *The Castle of Otranto*, "a Gothic story". Longueil formulates a theory about the multiple meanings of the word "Gothic":

Critical terms, like other speculations, have their ups and downs. So it has been with the adjective gothic. The term had its inception humbly enough as a Germanic race name. But because the Goths, being Teutons, conceived and built upon an ideal of beauty foreign to the world they overset; and because mediaeval men, fashioning their new world, rebuilt it nearer to the Teutonic than the classic heart's desire; and because to Renaissance sceptics the Gothic ideal, wrought in castle and cathedral, seemed dark and thwarted beside the measure of a Parthenon, it came to pass, in the early Renaissance, that the term Gothic took on a new and coloured meaning, a meaning that masked a sneer. To the Renaissance,

Mediaeval or Gothic architecture was barbarous architecture. By a trope all things barbarous became Gothic.

Wittily summarised and historically pertinent, Longueil's history of the designation of "Gothic" underlines its complexity. The word Gothic conveys different and contrasting semantic ideas that can be historical, artistic and literary. The Goths that had been the first wave of people to invade and conquer the Roman territory represented the last drop that caused the collapse of the Empire. Specialised in the forging of arms and handicraft, they did not build several monuments but limited themselves to imitating, using (or abusing) existing Roman structures. Moreover, the architectures that were medieval, namely Romanesque and Gothic, were not the works of the long-gone Goths, disappeared in the sixth century. The term Gothic, therefore, contains an inner anachronistic contradiction, which perpetuated throughout the centuries. Longueil also traces a history of the different nuances of the word. Geoffrey Chaucer and William Shakespeare employed the term, which still bore derogatory connotations in the seventeenth century. Longueil provides evidence by citing Edward Waterhouse's work on the great fire of London, published in 1667, one year after the disaster. Waterhouse had used the expression "Gottish and Vandalique fire", two adjectives that were synonyms of the words "destructive" and "violent". The ambiguity of the term was remarkable. Constantly examining and comparing the meanings of terms in order to define their validity (John Stone 2012), the revered lexicographer, essayist and critic Samuel Johnson considered a "Goth" as "one not civilised, one deficient in general knowledge, a barbarian", an idea that had been espoused by Dryden, who considered the "Gothique manner" as a synonym for "barbarous". Interestingly, Walpole's real opinion about the term has not been clearly ascertained. His Gothic taste was the result of a form of enlightened antiquarianism made of an idealised medieval past blended with his eighteenth-century sense of modernity. Walpole certainly dissented with the nationalist use of gothic, as his 1785 letter to John Pinkerton reveals. He implicitly rejected "proto-nationalist appropriations of medieval literature that are instantiated by Pinkerton's work, which is best remembered now for its early assertions of the inherited biological superiority of Germanic, 'Gothic' races" (Stephen Yeager 2019: 152).

After the publication of several Gothic novels describing an infinity of pseudo Gothic abodes and ruins, Sir James Hall's *An Essay on the Origins, History, and Principles of Gothic Architecture* appeared in 1797 and exalted the superiority of Northern and Germanic medieval forms.

According to the author, the flamboyant Gothic was an example of perfection, especially when compared to the less elaborate Italian Gothic. The text intended to instil order on a miscellany of architectural depictions in early Gothic novels. After carrying a negative halo for centuries, the word Gothic acquired another connotation and "began to be invested with a set of different and contradictory values in both aesthetic and political terms. This resulted from the reclamation of a native English past that played a crucial role in the eighteenth century of literary and political nationalism" (Glennis Byron and David Punter 1999: 4). Byron and Punter also indicate that, "like the Goths themselves, Gothic as a term is endlessly mobile" and we can verify its levels of ambiguity in the different declinations of the idea in the various novels written at the end of the eighteenth century.

The Gothic novel prospered in parallel with the diversification of literary genres. Multiple hypotheses exist regarding both the incipience of Gothic fiction and its sources. Robert Rix (2014) has identified the presence of Norse mythology in British literature at the turn of the century. He suggested that Lewis was among the authors influenced by northern myths and Danish epic legends, especially in his later productions. In his "Advertisement" to his novel *The Monk,* Lewis mentions that his novel's poetic interlude "The *Water-King,* from the third to the twelfth stanza, is the fragment of an original Danish ballad" (*The Monk*: 6), a fact that seems to validate Rix's hypothesis. However, the clues Lewis provides about his novel are generally misleading and do not clearly specify their provenance and, as we will see in the chapters dedicated to *The Monk*, the sources that he exploits are innumerable and difficult to detect. As a consequence of the effects of both Goethe's extraordinary success and of the translations of German novels that invaded Britain in the 1790s, Maurice Lévy (1995) deduces that the growing number of ghost stories was partially due to the effects of German literature, an opinion adopted by James Watt (1999: 71–72):

Any treatment of the impact of German writing in this period must begin by acknowledging the extent of its popularity, at least after the first rendering in 1779 of Goethe's *Sorrows of Young Werther* (written in 1774). [...] The influx of German *romances* began in 1794 with the translation of Carl Kramer's *Herman of Unna*, succeeded most famously by translations of Schiller's unfinished work *The Ghost Seer* and Cajetan Tschink's *A Victim of Magical Delusions* in 1795, and two versions of Carl Grosse's *The Genius* in 1796 (also translated as *Horrid Mysteries*).

Considering the chronology of German horror stories and their English renderings, it is, however, plausible to think that they had a rather belated effect, and their influence was probably more effectual at the very end of the century or the beginning of the next when most early English Gothic novels had already been published. Rictor Norton (1999) asserts that the translators of German works used Radcliffe's language prevalently; therefore, the German influx does not seem to be substantial, even though Lewis exploited German material for his literary achievements after *The Monk*, and Eliza Parsons subtitled *The Castle of Wolfenbach* "A German Story". The fever for German novels, however, diminished when a series of pamphlets and articles divulged conspiracy theories. Abbé Augustin Barruel, a French publicist living in exile in England, accused the German Illuminati and French philosophers, such as Voltaire and Rousseau, of being responsible for the beginning of the French Revolution and its atrocities (Amos Hofman 1993). Other documents blamed the Rosicrucian and various secret societies that had flourished in Germany before 1789 for the extreme political unrest that shook nations in the last years of the eighteenth century. After these publications, Germany began to be seen as the cradle of dangerous conspiracies and no longer the picturesque setting of Faustian legends.

Apart from Addison's postulations about the rhetorical necessity of the supernatural, Clery (1995) also traces roots of the captivation of mystery back to the seventeenth century, while Lévy reports that the mysterious life of the alchemist Cagliostro inspired fictional creations and played a considerable role in establishing the foundation for horror stories, including German horrid fictions. In his *Idée sur les romans* (around 1800), De Sade justified the Gothic genre as the natural consequence of revolutionary events. Ronald Paulson (1981: 534–535, 537) made a distinction between the novels written before and after the Revolution, a period of extreme political and social unrest degenerating through the episodes of the French Terror:

The Gothic did, in fact, serve as a metaphor with which some contemporaries in England tried to come to terms with what was happening across the Channel in the 1790s. [...]The popularity of Gothic fiction in the 1790s and well into the nineteenth century was due in part to the widespread anxieties and fears in Europe aroused by the turmoil in France finding a kind of sublimation or catharsis in tales of darkness, confusion, blood, and horror.

In Paulson's words, Walpole's Manfred and Lewis's Ambrosio might be the embodiments of Revolutionary oppressors, whereas the Gothic castle is but a metaphor for the horrors taking place inside the Parisian Bastille. While Paulson's vision might be adapted to the literature produced after the 1790s, it cannot explain the changes in taste that developed at the outset of the Gothic genre, started decades before the traumatic outcome of the French Revolution. Neo-Marxist critics, such as Raymond Williams (1983) and Terry Eagleton (2004), interpret the birth of Gothic fiction as a signal of tension within the Georgian period, as society was changing in response to the Industrial Revolution. On the contrary, while analysing the prefabricated myth of the sublime, Thomas Weiskel (1986) deems the Gothic more orthodox and conservative than revolutionary for its façade of sentimental exaggerations. The American writer and literary critic Edmund Wilson, among others, insisted on British writers' rejection of the French Revolution in his article "A Treatise on the Tales of Horror", included in the *New Yorker* on 27 May 1944. Wilson gave an ironically negative opinion of the Gothic genre and wondered about its unpredictable survival: "One had supposed that the ghost story itself was an obsolete form; that it had been killed by the electric light", he hopelessly exclaims. It had not. After its apparent conclusion in the 1820s, the Gothic novel was revived various times during the nineteenth century. It continued to prosper and expand its focus on horror, and fear was incorporated into new multimedia horrific stories in multiple geographic contexts and different chronologies. Wherefore critical appreciation of the controversial phenomenology of horror and terror dialectically multiplied.

One of Umberto Eco's most occult and esoteric novels, swarming with mysteries and featuring an ambiguous ending, *Foucault's Pendulum*, was published in 1988. In his explanatory essay, the Italian scholar Ruggero Puletti (2000) underlines how Eco's novel, amply imitated by Dan Brown in his 2003 *Da Vinci Code*, reflects the general growing taste for the gloomy, the mysterious and the horrifying, typical of any fin de siècle in the last four hundred years and more. Eco's story, along with other contemporary works written at the end of the twentieth century, seems to confirm the existence of a cyclic attraction to fear, which revives curiosity for inexplicable dark events. A trend that is linked to the rebirth of millennial theories associated to the doctrine of the Millennium in the *Book of Revelations*. Byron and Punter (1999) also explore the influence of the Millennium theory extensively as far as the literature of horror is concerned, confirming the latent preoccupations emblazoning the early Gothic. Coincidentally, a growing number of essays taking into consideration the Gothic genre flourished in the early 1980s, and this trend is still valid. Despite renewed critical attention, the Gothic remains inherently mysterious, and George Haggerty (2008: 383) rightfully observes, "Gothic resists any attempts to explain it". From psychoanalytical perspectives to post-modern interpretations, from gender literary theories to social analyses, from queer studies to historical research, Gothic literary criticism has provided numerous alluring hypotheses concerning the genre. Kilgour (1995: 221) maintains, "Gothic criticism swelled with increasing rapidity". Suzanne Rintoul (2004: 702) identifies "the problem of defining the Gothic in the face of its ever-expanding criticism", whereas Jerrold Hogle (2001), despite producing several essays on the Gothic, provocatively argues that Gothic fiction is hardly Gothic at all. Chris Baldick and Robert Mighall (2012: 269) believe that Gothic criticism emerged from the confluence of two "antithetical strands of modern Romanticism in the 1930s: on the one side, the reactionary medievalism of Montague Summers, and on the other the revolutionary modernism of the surrealists". The problems Baldick and Mighall detect in contemporary Gothic criticism also reflect an excess of post-modernism and an anti-realist stance. In his introduction to *The Monk*, Nick Groom (2016: vii) confirms the tendency to "narrativize anxieties" in critical terms (Rintoul: 704). Groom's description of the guillotine and the tortures imposed on a Savoyard noblewoman (Maria Teresa Carignano-Savoia, known as Princesse de Lamballe) are far more disquieting than Lewis's and other Gothic novelists' narrations and corroborate what critics such as Rintoul, Kilgour, Baldick and Mighall highlight about Gothic criticism:

On 3 September 1792, the Princesse de Lamballe, one of Queen Marie Antoinette's closest friends, was summarily tried before a revolutionary tribunal. She refused to swear an oath to liberty and equality, and declare her hatred for the king and queen, and was immediately given up to the Parisian mob. She was lynched and decapitated, and her head was paraded on a pike before the window of the queen, who duly fainted. There were also darker rumours that she had been stripped naked, raped repeatedly, both alive and dead, that her breasts had been bitten off to revive her, that she had been eviscerated and her guts wrenched out and used as belts, and that her genitals had been mutilated.

In a similar way, Markman Ellis (2000: 1) starts his study on Gothic fiction by introducing a macabre anecdote of the French natural philosopher Barthélemy Faujas' visit to the cabinet of a London surgeon,

John Seldon, while travelling in England in 1799. The shocking epiphany of the event concerns the scientist's late fiancée. In fact, the surgeon had embalmed the body of his young lover, which lay naked under a glass frame, to show to his visitors. These examples demonstrate how Gothic fiction has a mesmerising power that creates extra-textual contaminations of its dominant atmospheres in critical texts. Kilgour (1995: 221) underlines "the monstrous dimension of Gothic criticism", while Baldick and Mighall (2012: 210) write, "Gothic criticism is condemned to repeat what it has failed to understand so reproduces in its own discourse what we call the trope of Gothicising the past", an idea supported by Lauren Fitzgerald (2003: 44), who finds "striking resemblances" between the language of Gothic novels and the language of Gothic criticism. This may seem a further confirmation of the difficulty of understanding the Gothic's mysterious different souls.

> Though [the castle] was now lighted up by the setting sun, the
> gothic greatness of its features, and its mouldering walls of dark
> grey stone, rendered it a gloomy and sublime object. [...] The
> light died away on its walls, leaving a melancholy purple tint,
> which spread deeper and deeper, as the thin vapour crept up
> the mountain, while the battlements above were still tipped
> with splendour.
> (Ann Radcliffe, *The Mysteries of Udolpho*)

The expansion of the Gothic in the nineteen and the twentieth centuries
has sparked critical attention. Several scholars have tended to erase its
terminus ad quem and broaden the early Gothic chronologically by
reversing its traditional time limits. Both Punter and Botting have
reconsidered the subject several times, with their focus on the
multiplication and diversification of the Gothic after 1820. Their interest,
along with that of other critics, has widened to include contemporary
variations in multiple media. However, an exhaustive analysis of the vast
ambit of the Gothic is difficult to carry out because of the growth of the
horror mode outside of specific Gothic literature per se. The intermingling
of genres and media in the culture of post-modernism has further
complicated the definition of the Gothic genre. A conspicuous part of the
critical effort on the Gothic has concentrated on a multiplicity of
apparently recurring themes. Some studies concern the meaning of
geographical locations, the function of architectures and the peculiarity of
landscape descriptions. The tendency is to generalise these *topoi*, turning
them into stereotypes. Early Gothic plots are generally thought to be set
in Italy, a country traditionally associated with mystery and crime
according to an Anglo-Saxon viewpoint. However, the percentage of
Gothic novels written during the second half of the eighteenth century
featuring Italian settings is curiously low. While *The Castle of Otranto, A
Sicilian Romance* (1790), *Hubert de Sevrac* (1796), *The Italian* (1797),

24

Zofloya (1806) and *Manfroné* (1809) are set in Italy, several novels belonging to the early Gothic are not. Reeve's *The Old English Baron* (1778), Lee's *The Recess* (1785), Beckford's *Vathek* (1786), Smith's *Emmeline* (1788), Harley's *The Castle of Mowbray* (1788), Radcliffe's *The Castles of Athlin and Dunbayne* (1789), *Gaston de Blondeville* (1826) and *The Romance of the Forest* (1791), Parsons's *The Castle of Wolfenbach* (1793), Lewis's *The Monk* (1796), Lathom's *The Midnight Bell (1798)* and Roche's *Clermont* (1798), just to mention the most famous ones, take place in non-Italian locations such as England, Scotland, France, Germany, Switzerland, Spain, or in the Far East. Even a supreme symbol of Gothicism as *The Mysteries of Udolpho* (1794) is mostly set in France—even though horrifying events take place in the titular Italian castle.

Italian locations were numerous in travel journals. Poets, novelists, essayists, diarists, geographers and historians, among others, regularly published travel literature during the eighteenth century to describe a vast typology of journeys, in particular on the Continent. The flow of detailed descriptions of distant places provided a cornucopia of precious material for literary inventions and Gothic tales. A vast phenomenon associated with travelling and travel literature was the Grand Tour, usually followed by the publishing of travel diaries, letters collections, fictionalised travel tales or literary descriptions. Painters and artists moved to other countries to refine their techniques, whereas affluent and cultivated people went to mainland Europe for culture and entertainment. Young aristocrats could travel more easily than women to various countries without the danger of ruining their reputations. One of the first women to describe the Grand Tour and the journey to Italy was Samuel Johnson's friend and intellectual socialite Hester Lynch Piozzi on the occasion of her second marriage to an Italian music teacher. She collected the records of her experience in a text that became popular in her circle and probably attracted Radcliffe's interest. Mrs Piozzi's two-year-long journey offered long descriptions of landscapes and towns, though they expressed patronising attitudes towards the country on many occasions—a characteristic shared by several British travellers. Eager for originality and uniqueness, she admired lesser-known works of art but often ignored important monuments (Camillo Von Klenze 1909). As a woman traveller, Mrs Piozzi was an exception, protected as she was by her Italian husband, helping her with the language, and her intellectual coterie of British travel companions, with whom she invented the Della Cruscan poetic exchange. While other aristocratic women travelled, they did not commonly write their memoirs as men did. Susan Lamb (2009: 352) remarks that some "prominent women went to the Continent" and apparently committed "sexual improprieties" they understandably preferred to censor.

Despite occasional salacious episodes, which were concealed with the utmost care, the Grand Tour was generally the crowning of a long intellectual pilgrimage that took wealthy families' heirs to different countries and places of interest. Englishmen's journeys on the Continent provoked either enthusiasm or extreme loathing, as Attilio Brilli (2006) and Jeremy Black (1992; 2003) explain in their studies on the Grand Tour. Ever since the Renaissance, the opinions of Italy included two opposing ideas. The former described Italy as a land blessed by a mild climate, offering natural and artistic beauties, whereas the latter saw the country as the place of vice, infested with criminals. These were better known as banditti and *lazzaroni*–idlers who made their living by begging in Naples, as per the definition in the Merriam Webster dictionary, or "(in Naples) a homeless person living by begging or by doing odd jobs", in the entry of Collins Dictionary. Moralists had warned against the dangers of sending young men abroad where they would soon become acquainted with vice, while enthusiasts described the Grand Tour as the soul-inspiring discovery of culture and history. Despite its gloomy reputation, Italy was the favourite destination for the Grand Tour on account of its beauty, mild climate and rich culture, but it remained the abhorred place of perdition, populated by vicious papists in the Protestant mentality.

Tracing the history of the Italian journey from the Renaissance to the twentieth century, Brilli explains that a relevant number of aristocrats, academics and literati visited Italy in the eighteenth century, either for leisure or for cultural interests. Among them were writers such as Tobias Smollett, Laurence Sterne, Beckford, Walpole and his friend Thomas Gray. Famous painters including Richard Wilson, Joshua Reynolds, Joseph Wright of Derby and Alexander Cozens spent a lot of time in Italy. These writers and artists represent emblematic examples among the many opting for Italy as their cultural destination. Francis Bacon had underlined the pedagogical value of travelling abroad in the sixteenth century and had been among those intellectuals positively impressed by this opportunity. However, many writers were against travelling to the Continent and especially to Italy. Roger Asham was probably the initiator of the "Italophobic" attitude in 1570. In 1592, he was followed by Thomas Nashe's definition of Italy as "the academy of murder", stressing the analogies between Machiavellian Italians and the Elizabethan theatrical villains. Bishop Joseph Hall wrote in 1617 that journeys to Italy were not necessary and, in 1670, Richard Lassels warned parents about the risks of visiting Italy. In his *Thoughts concerning Education* of 1693, John Locke looked favourably on journeys to Italy, provided they were excluded at a young age. The vignettes described by Smollett showed sordid individuals of all kinds populating the Italian Peninsula, and Adam Smith stated that Italy turned young sensible Englishmen into madcap hedonists. Bishop Richard Hurd, illustrious author of *Letters of Chivalry and Romance* (1762), asserted that travel had a cosmopolitan value and had to be expanded all over the world. In his opinion, travelling to Italy was beneficial, as Englishmen could tangibly demonstrate their superiority in comparison to "inferior" Italian people. According to Brilli, Edward Gibbon thought that travellers had to become cultural interpreters of the different world that Italy presented to them. Scholar George S. Rousseau (1991) introduces the notion of the Grand Tour as a form of homosexual secret arrangement allowing greater freedom than in the travellers' countries of origin.

During the eighteenth century, semi-fictional renderings of journeys were not completely realistic, oscillating between the acid descriptions of Smollett's *Travels through France and Italy* (1766) or improbable adventures, such as those found in Sterne's *A Sentimental Journey through France and Italy* (1768), actually a response to Smollett's exaggerated contempt. The dangers of the journeys on the Continent were emphasised by the descriptions of extreme geographies where uncommon adventures took place. Unless travellers made long detours in France, the crossing of the Alps, compulsory for all those travelling from the North, was a sublime as well as an objectively dangerous enterprise. Carried by five strong men, Gibbon admitted in his autobiographical notes, published posthumously in 1796, that the crossing of the Mont Cenis was not only arduous but also extremely dangerous. As Simon Schama (1995: 463–464) narrates, during the crossing of the same pass, Walpole had to face a rather difficult situation: "It was when his lapdog, Tory, got eaten by a wolf that Horace Walpole began to have serious reservations about Mont Cenis. Swathed in beaver furs, he had been lumbering up the mountain path on a chaise carried by four sweating porters" when he saw his dog taken away by a young wolf. Schama asserts that Walpole's shock was understandable. Equally shaken, Walpole's travelling companion and best friend, Gray, commented that perhaps Mont Cenis "carried the permission that mountains have of being frightful rather too far". Walpole decided that the cursed mountain was a devilish place. Others, like James Boswell, described fewer monuments and sites of interest than their amatory adventures (Brilli: 35–37). The "representation of Italy in eighteenth-century fiction was largely shaped by the knowledge of Italy" provided by writers generally unfamiliar with the country, such as Richardson. "On the contrary, having travelled through and written about

Italy, John Moore was less acquainted with the country's geography and history" than many others (Massimiliano Demata 2006: 7). Patrick Brydone and Henry Swinburne gave original accounts of less widely known places, such as the south of Italy and Sicily, in particular, with its majestic volcano–mythical Mount Etna. The former wrote a text dedicated to William Beckford, the writer's father, published in 1773 (*A Tour through Sicily and Malta*). The latter, Swinburne, explored the regions during the reign of the Bourbons, and his experience was published with an abundance of details in 1790 (*Travels in the Two Sicilies*). Both authors were successful and probably influenced Radcliffe's *A Sicilian Romance* and *The Italian* with their settings in Southern Italy. Cited by Robinson in her novels, John Smith's *Select Views of Italy with Topographical and Historical Descriptions* (1792) provided an ultra-detailed compendium of Italy accompanied by a remarkable number of etchings and prints of the peninsula that could help writers in forming better images of the country.

Despite not being a united nation at the time, Italy was, however, visualised as a single identity. Scholars and historians, both Italian (Ernesto Galli Della Loggia 1998; Aurelio Lepre 2008) and non-Italian (Denis Mack Smith 1997), have studied the issue of Italian identity. They have concluded that Italy is a nation not only for its present situation but also for its physical position protected by a crown of mountain chains, its notable silhouette, the common ancient past of its different regions, and its language, spoken along the entire Peninsula. On the contrary, the Austrian minister Metternich stated that Italy was simply a geographical notion, with no right of ever being a nation, just when his Austro-Hungarian government politically controlled and policed the northern territories in the 19th century. Notwithstanding its beauty, the country was also the imaginary place of terrible misdeeds, unfathomable mysteries and unspeakable horrors, a hind-thought that was only in part due to the direct experience of few unfortunate travellers. In many cases, negative prejudices derived from literary knowledge acquired through Machiavelli, Shakespeare, Webster, Milton and other relevant writers. A further possible explanation for this duality of vision, made of aesthetic attraction and horror, lies partly in the impact of the Inquisition. Originally created in the twelfth century, it acquired major strength in Catholic countries after the long and unsuccessful Council of Trent, or Trento, in Northern Italy, in the second half of the sixteenth century. The Council had been supposed to settle the differences between the Church of Rome and the Lutheran creed, but the dramatic clash simply worsened. Even if it had originally developed in the Middle Ages to fight against different forms heresy, the Inquisition turned into a frightening and everpresent entity after the Council's failure. The Holy Tribunal's methods of the Inquisition were abhorred, especially in Protestant and Anglican countries, who identified the Inquisition and Catholicism as one single dangerous body. As the Inquisition was described in some early Gothic novels, it might be argued that Beccaria's accounts had reinforced the fear provoked by the violent and secretive methods of the Catholic Church's tribunal, regarded with repugnance by Protestant countries and dreaded in nations where Catholicism was dominant.

A recurrent character in many horror stories is the terrifying edifice, be it a castle, a dungeon, an abbey, a cathedral or a dark crypt. Complex architectures are sometimes portents of mystery or doom when inserted into Gothic fiction. Architecture (and the castle, in particular) has long been defined as a metaphorical labyrinth and a system of symbolic values in early Gothic novels. Sometimes interpreted as a psychoanalytical device representing the inside of the human soul, or as a symbol of powerful patriarchy, imposing architecture plays an important role in the development of a number of Gothic plots. Kate Ferguson Ellis (1989) interprets the Gothic castle as the symbol of the dramatic struggle of women imprisoned in patriarchal structures. On the other hand, Claudia Johnson (1995: 76) rejects social analyses or psychoanalytical interpretations of the castle as "an inward landscape sealed off from history", representing unresolved anxieties and traumas. On the contrary, she regards architectures as "actual, material features of the European countryside inscribing the still surviving feudal past", connected with the objective preoccupation of property and inheritance. Nevertheless, not all early Gothic novels feature labyrinthine castles. By looking into stereotypes associated with the early tales of horror, it is possible to realise, strangely and unexpectedly, that the architectures featured in Gothic romances rarely belong to the historical gothic period. In some cases, architectures are even inessential and no description of structures is provided. When tortuous mansions are part of the narration, they exert a peculiar sense of mystery and recall Piranesi's unusual geometries or Salvator Rosa's capriccios. Architectural structures playing important roles in some Gothic plots seem to be a consequence of two elements. On the one hand, they reflect the love for unusual constructions and their frequent iconographic reproductions. The eighteenth century showed a predilection for the creation of artificial architectures and instant ruins, imitating an imaginary past, mostly classical, which became fashionable in the gardens of aristocratic mansions, in theatrical *mise-en-scènes* and illustrations, all enriched with illusive structures. On the other hand, they seem to be linked to a different kind of ruins, scattered over the British countryside even since the medieval period, which were a memento of dark ages. Deborah Kennedy (2001) identifies the ruins of medieval abbeys and monasteries as a symbol of acquired freedom after the abhorred oppressive feudal past embodied by the Catholic Church in England. As far as the proliferation of artificial ruins, especially after 1745, David Stewart (1996, 400) claims that they did not precisely correspond to an aesthetic need, but they were rather "attacks on England's Catholic and baronial past". A more complex and nuanced interpretation is provided by a recent study, which takes different perspectives into consideration, such as the motif of picturesque sensations and romantic feelings that these ruins offered especially when they were in the context of a luxuriant landscape (James McKean, 2020). McKean asserts for example that a latent dichotomous essence can be detected in William Shenstone's *The Ruin'd Abbey, or the Effects of Superstition*, written in 1743, but published posthumously in 1764. Started as a historical composition to celebrate the freedom from superstition, the poem progressively modifies the initial fierce criticism and features pleasant nocturnal atmospheres in the manner of Graveyard poets. Johnson and Gray did not completely appreciate Shenstone's works, but the author contributed to the development of poetic nostalgic mood and the appreciation of medieval ruins. The comparison between medieval architecture–a cultural emblem of northern countries–and Romanesque and Gothic structures in southern countries conveyed the sense of superiority of the former and the limitations of the latter. Per contra, some Gothic settings of horror stories are placed in southern architectures and Mediterranean countries, whose gothic buildings were not, however, as impressive as their northern real-life counterparts.

The French philosopher Montesquieu had already noticed the social and cultural differences between the North and the South in his *Spirit of the Laws* (1748). He had delineated his foundational theory on the influence of climates bringing about clear-cut differences between Northern and Southern populations–an opposition that had been partly interrelated to the so-called *Quarrel of the Ancients and the Moderns* in literary terms. Curiously, dark Gothic contexts and northern atmospheres were applied to Mediterranean countries in Gothic novels. Generally reproduced in picturesque representations, non-fictional Italy, on the contrary, offered brilliant, sunlit colours and peaceful images, and was painted, especially during the eighteenth century, by innumerable artists, who reproduced or invented a variety of Italianate scenes, creating in this way a cultural oxymoron and a literary antithesis. The early Gothic persistent obsession with architectures, which oddly became as important as characters in flesh and blood, is one of the great enigmas of the genre. Historically, genuine architectural mania became a truism at the end of the 18th century. A notable contributor in Great Britain had been Walpole both physically, with the creation of his pseudo Gothic mansion, Strawberry Hill, and ideally, with his original Gothic tale, *Otranto*, in which the title-character is not a person but the castle itself, a feature typically imitated by Parsons, Radcliffe and Lathom, among others. Only apparently indifferent to Gothic literary atmospheres, Beckford frequently describes intriguing majestic architectures. Sandro Jung (2011) convincingly claims that *Vathek's* architectural richness was responsible for Gothic writers' focus on architecture, and Smith and Radcliffe were among them. The vast catalogue of sumptuous dwellings, towers, and richly adorned mansions convey an atmosphere of lightness and beauty in Beckford until the moment when the characters explore the subterranean vaults of a mysterious palace that cannot compare to any known architectures.

In apparent imitation of Walpole, Beckford transformed his paternal mansion, Fonthill Abbey, in a bewildering Gothic building in parallel and competition with his illustrious antecedent, whom he secretly despised. However, the huge amount of money for Fonthill Abbey was badly spent, as the central tower collapsed several times until it was necessary to dismantle part of the structure, now almost completely lost (Caroline Dakers 2018).

Hall's text on gothic architecture (1797) put some order in a miscellany of descriptions in early Gothic novels and gave dignity to a style, which he reputed a symbol of northern inventiveness and strength. The text was written after three decades of terrifying descriptions of quasi-Gothic vaults, dungeons, secret galleries and labyrinths, populated with distressed characters trying to escape their destiny in sinister plots. One of the novelists to emphasise architectures a few years after Walpole was the inventive Charlotte Smith. Her detailed architectural descriptions created a horde of Gothic imitators of her ideas. Smith published the second volume of *The Banished Man* in 1794. The preface was probably written after the astoundingly successful publication of Radcliffe's *The Mysteries of Udolpho*, and unequivocally showed the resentment that Smith felt for the novelist whom she considered an imitator, if not a plagiarist, of her style (*The Banished Man*: iii):

For my own part who can now no longer build *châteaux* even *en Espagne*. I find that Mowbray Castle, Grasmere Abbey, The Castle of Rock-March, the Castle of Hauteville, and Rayland Hall, have taken so many of my materials to construct, that I hardly have a watch tower, a Gothic arch, a cedar parlour, or a long gallery, an illuminated window, or a ruined chapel, left to help myself. [....] But my ingenious contemporaries have fully possessed themselves of every bastion and buttress–of every tower and turret–of every gallery and gateway, together with all their furniture and ivy mantles, and mossy battlements; tapestry, and old pictures, owls, bats and taverns.

Through irony, Smith is mocking contemporary writers and, at the same time, draws attention to her powerlessness in relation to multiple plagiarisms of her ideas. Imitating successful authors was a common praxis among writers of popular tales, a strategy involving little effort and more success, but Smith's accusation may cast a shadow of doubt on Radcliffe's creativity. Although the severe scholar James Mathias was ready to recognise the genius in Smith, her revolutionary comments on the social situation, similar in spirit to Wollstonecraft's outcry denouncing injustice against women, was not easily accepted by an increasingly conservative reading public, frightened by the excesses of the French Revolution. Despite her merits, Smith was overshadowed by the works of more popular writers and almost completely forgotten. Whether Radcliffe had plagiarised Smith's architectural inventions consciously or had been under the influx of intertextual echoes providing material for her novels, it is not possible to know with certainty. However, it is true that Radcliffe not only specialised in the description of buildings of all kinds but also gave a special relevance to her architectural inventions, as if they were real characters. The architectural variety in her novels is remarkable, for her descriptions and for the symbolism that the various buildings acquire in her stories. The castle is a relevant entity in the plots of *Otranto* (1764), Radcliffe's *The Castles of Athlin and Dunbayne* (1789), *A Sicilian Romance* (1790), *The Mysteries of Udolpho* (1794), Robinson's *Hubert de Sevrac* (1796) and Mary Ann Radcliffe's *Manfroné* (1809) by virtue of its contrast to the exterior world. On the other hand, *The Romance of the Forest* (1791) introduces an interesting sequence of places, symbolising the phases of the novels and the improvement in the protagonist's situation. We move from an undefined style of the buildings in Paris to a perfect image of the pseudo-Gothic abbey and the ruins where the characters find a safe refuge. The abbey and the ruins represent the privileged locus of the story's narrative universe. In the second part of the novel, a modest castle ("chateau") in the mountains represents peace and happiness and becomes the metaphor of a blissful life. Left as such, the descriptions of different architectures may seem a simple narrative device in Radcliffe, Walpole, Beckford, Smith, Robinson and other Gothicists. A more attentive reading reveals strange mutable qualities in the buildings that may be ascribed to Piranesi's visual impact and, in particular, to his series of etchings called *Prisons of Invention* (*Le Carceri d'invenzione*), endowed with multiform daunting structures, which inspired mysterious abodes in Walpole's novel and early Gothic stories. Nevertheless, Piranesi's influence is far from explaining Radcliffe's narrative technique, which tended to expand and contract spaces in a sort of fluid and hallucinatory vision, not only transforming castles, mansions and ruins into labyrinths but also mysteriously altering entire architectures. These strange edifices seem to become themselves living structures, a phenomenon that is relevant in Radcliffe's *The Romance of the Forest* and her other novels– and, partially in Mary Ann Radcliffe and Robinson. Radcliffe's narrations appear to transform architectural elements into protean entities. The following long description of the ruins and abbey in the second chapter of *The Romance of the Forest* (*RF* in quotations) is a remarkable example of Radcliffe's narrative skill:

When he unclosed the door, the dismal aspect of the place revived the apprehension of Madame de la Motte, and extorted from Adeline an inquiry whither they were going. Peter held up the light to shew the narrow stair-case that wound round the tower; but de la Motte, observing the second door, drew back the rusty bolts, and entered a spacious apartment, which, from its style and condition, was evidently of a much later date than the other part of the structure: though desolate and forlorn, it was very little impaired by time; the walls were damp, but not decayed, and the glass was yet firm in the windows. They passed on to a suite of apartments resembling the first they had seen, and expressed their surprise at the incongruous appearance of this part of the edifice with the mouldering walls they had left behind. These apartments conducted them to a winding passage that received light and air through narrow cavities, placed high in the wall and was at length closed by a door barred with iron, which being with some difficulty opened, they entered a vaulted room. [...] The room appeared to have been built in modern times upon a Gothic plan. Adeline approached a large window that formed a kind of recess raised by one step over the level of the door; she observed to de la Motte that the whole floor was inlaid with mosaic work; which drew from him a remark, that the style of this apartment was not strictly Gothic. He passed on to a door which appeared on the opposite side of the apartment, and, unlocking it, found himself in the hall by which he had entered the fabric. He now perceived, what the gloom had before concealed, a spiral stair-case, which led to a gallery above, and which, from its present condition, seemed to have been built with the more modern part of the fabric, though this also affected the Gothic mode of architecture: de la Motte had little doubt that these stairs led to apartments, corresponding with those he had passed below, and hesitated whether to explore them. (*RF*: 20–21)

This lengthy extract can help better understand the novelist's technique. The first narrative aspect is the strategy used to create suspense and expectation. The remotest recesses of the ruin are slowly uncovered while the characters, initially moved by curiosity, enter a state of agitation, also transmitted to the reader. Accompanied by their servant, de la Motte, his wife and Adeline are exploring their refuge. The characters' slow progression along the partially decaying walls is ominous and every corner seems to hide an unpredictable danger or horrible secrets. The "door barred with iron" is unusual for its excessive "strength" and its presence is apparently inexplicable. It leads to "a large vaulted room", provoking fears for its uncommon aspect and position. The second aspect is Radcliffe's strategy combining reality with illusory architectures. The characters observe structures, passages and rooms magically multiplying. The abbey becomes a protean element, fluidly augmenting its framework in the form of self-reproductive fractals that confuse, frighten but also, enigmatically, protect the characters. This characteristic is common to the majority of buildings that Radcliffe describes, but the ruin of *The Romance of the Forest* features this ambiguous mutability reiteratively. The third factor is Radcliffe's insinuating meditation on the nature of literature. The fact that the author describes the style of the galleries and the apartments as not genuinely "Gothic" is a form of meta-literary irony. Radcliffe herself underlines that the Gothic on display is artificial, like Philip James de Louthenbourg's trompe-l'oeil effects, or a scenery in an opera by Handel, or a vision of Piranesi's imaginary *Prisons of Invention*. Radcliffe's changeable architectures transmit a variety of meanings. They are theatrical stages of suspense or reflections of visual arts inevitably reflecting the mystery of the plot. Radcliffe's word-painting of labyrinthine dwellings and alluring descriptions of landscapes are unparalleled narrative prerogatives. Similarly, concealed or subterranean labyrinths, vaults, dark chapels, dungeons and crypts hide horrible secrets and dark mysteries in Walpole, Beckford, Lewis, Mary Anne Radcliffe and other Gothic novelists.

However, the introduction of secret locations may also have a protective function for some characters, as we can verify in Radcliffe's novels. The dichotomy between negative/positive architectures is present in *The Castle of Otranto* in which buildings seem to change their original function depending on the characters that inhabit them. In Lewis, strange subterranean structures come to represent the monolithic reign of devilish forces (Hogle 2004). "The labyrinthine catacombs in *The Monk* reflect Ambrosio's dilemmas. […] The labyrinth, like the shifting optical illusions of Piranesi's *Prisons*, disorganises boundaries between inside and out, marking an inescapable and reciprocal entanglement of internal and external worlds" (Eva Kosofsky Sedgwick 1980: 25). Williams (1995) interprets Lewis's horrid underground galleries as metaphors of dark patriarchal rules (87) and Catholicism's obscure duplicity inasmuch as many architectural structures in Gothic novels belong to religious buildings (117). Hence, a number of scholars identify forms of latent criticism of Catholicism in tales of horror, an aspect that, however, existed before the rise of the Gothic novel. Laurence Sterne's satire of Catholicism in *Tristram Shandy* (1767), intended to ridicule the French, confirms his anti-Catholic stance. Peter Walmsley (2009) underlines how Sterne's various characters criticise Catholicism and its connotations of "murder, rapine [and] bloodshed", claiming that the novel is a further example of a text that "is about national self-fashioning against the Continent and the Catholic other". Deeply intent upon haranguing papism, Hogle (2014) and Groom (2016) claim that the Gothic novel is to be inscribed in this agenda, as they strictly interpret Lewis's and Radcliffe's works as manifestos against the negative effects of Catholic superstition. Expanding Kosofsky Sedgwick's ideas, Botting (1993: 262) interprets the Gothic labyrinth as a form of "heterotopia", the Foucauldian multiple space of human geography, either physical or mental. "As heterotopias, the labyrinth becomes doubly other: literally constituted of detours, repetitions, and duplications which traverse the same space with an interminable criss-crossing of differences and divergences, a space that is other to, constitutive of and resistant to, the known limits of society and subjectivity". The prevalence of dungeons is *The Monk*'s architectonic characteristic, with the exception of the narrative subplot set in Castle Lindenberg where Raymond experiences supernatural events. Therefore, the castle does not acquire in Lewis the importance it has in Walpole, Reeve, Smith, Harley, Radcliffe, Parsons, Lathom, Mary Anne Radcliffe and others. Although feminist criticism posits that the castle stands for patriarchal symbolism and domestic violence in horror stories, symbolic connotations in mansions can be found before the Gothic novels. A pre-Gothic character such as Richardson's Pamela "can bring purity to the fallen aristocratic castle and make it a home worthy of the name" (Ferguson Ellis 1989: 8) because the emerging middle class can change the decadence, which has been hovering over the aristocracy and their abodes for centuries. Even if the dungeon is part of the structure, it is not the actual building. It is the most hidden and secretive part where darkness reigns and crimes are committed. In *Manfroné, or the One-handed Monk* (1809), a Gothic novel generally attributed to Mary Anne Radcliffe—whose identity remains a mystery (Rictor Norton 2000a)—the dismal castle secretly connected to an old monastery is the sombre symbol of dark powers menacing Rosalina, the young female character. The *topos* of the castle, essential in Walpole's Gothic story, is not however relevant in *The Monk*, *Vathek*, *The Romance of the Forest*, or *Zofloya* a fact that foregrounds the problematic value of univocal statements about early Gothic literature, even though intertextuality is at play in the development of the genre.

Interactions and contrasts between castles, abbeys and ruins, and surrounding natural settings are another relevant element in some late eighteenth-century Gothic novels. Like architecture, nature is reputed to be an important ingredient in early Gothic fiction, as it might represent "the outside", the place surrounding the inner self, embodied by the castle or any majestic or fearful building. However, descriptions of nature were not an invention of the Gothic. Nature and landscape were included in masterpieces of previous epochs. In particular, Classical masterpieces abounded with descriptions of nature. Between the end of the Middle Ages and the beginning of Humanism, picturesque natural surroundings acquired a new status. Giovanni Boccaccio's *Decameron* (1351) features a nature that does not represent divine presence, but becomes an allegorical place, a locus *amoenus,* where suggestive settings and peaceful agricultural activities are the inspiring frames for narration. Boiardo's *Orlando Innamorato* (1495), Ariosto's *Orlando Furioso* (1516), Edmund Spenser's *The Fairies Queene* (1590), Shakespeare's *As You Like It* (1598) and *A Midsummer Night's Dream* (1595) introduce actions that take place in forests both beautiful and strange, and oftentimes interspersed with magic. Renaissance painters provided works of art that improved the hitherto stylised portrayal of nature, typical of gothic paintings. Although the Renaissance exalted symmetry, harmony and the human form, it introduced the focus on nature and unknown landscapes that are to be found in Leonardo, Titian, Giorgione, Raphael and other conspicuous artists of the period. Landscapes became the leading elements in seventeenth-century Dutch paintings, which influenced Italian Salvator Rosa and Italianate paintings by Nicolas Poussin and Claude Lorrain. It also dominated the settings of French Rococo painters a century later. Nature entered narrations in English novels during the eighteenth century, although protagonists were interested in its practical aspects at first. Critical awareness regarding nature increased during the century, as landscapes were exalted in descriptions of inspiring natural surroundings, later defined as Pre-Romantic, in particular by the Graveyard Poets, Rousseau and Goethe. The growing prominence of sublime atmospheres and the love for mysterious locations in literature have been associated to the depiction of landscapes in art. Eric Hirsch (1995: 2) highlights how "the word landscape was introduced in the English language in the late sixteenth century as a technical term used by painters. It came from the Dutch *Landschap*". Therefore, landscape was acknowledged and appreciated as a form of art. Hirsch further notes that "[t]his ideal or imagined world depicted in various genres of landscape painting by artists such as Poussin, Lorrain, and Rosa was linked to the perception of countryside scenery and its subsequent improvement: the goal was to achieve a correspondence between the pictorial idea and the countryside itself". An interesting example is Shenstone's pioneering landscape gardening. The poet, who originally intended to create pastoral scenes taken from the Classics, was able to transform his Leasowes farm into a beautiful picturesque garden, characterized by luscious corners and a romantic "carefully calculated naturalness" (John Dixon Hunt 1989), based on the free expansion of the vegetation in contrast with the restricted and geometrical *jardin à la française*. Fulford (1996: 101) indicated the political importance of any discourse connected with landscape in the eighteenth century, including the poetic works of James Thomson and William Cowper, Samuel Johnson's generalisations, Edmund Burke's text on the sublime, William Gilpin's essays on the picturesque (1782) and Uvedale Price's comparative study of sublime and picturesque (1794):

Samuel Johnson did not only use eighteenth-century conceptions of sublimity in language as a standard by which to criticise Shakespearian disorder. He also used the vocabulary of landscape description as a strategy, a means of persuading his readers by emotion as well as reason of the rightness of his views when he could not triumph by logic [...] Like Johnson, the picturesque writers wished to uphold the power of the landed gentleman, like Cowper, they wished to recall him to his traditional paternalist role. For Gilpin, as for Johnson, it was in his confrontation with an older rural culture that his rhetorical self-assertion became associated with local speech. And that speech resisted codification by the traditional rules of taste and eluded subordination to the social and political judgements of the gentlemanly classes.

Fulford's (1996: 3) hypothesis is intriguing, as he provides a special justification for the growing importance of landscape and nature in various forms of art and explains that (105):

Through landscape-gardening, through painting, and through the descriptions of prose-writers and poets, views of the landscape owned by gentlemen became representations of the legitimacy of their power and the benefits it brought the nation. [...] Eighteenth-century writers were able to rework the Virgilian epic and georgic into a panegyric on the national benefits deriving from a landscape 'naturally' productive of wealth, viewed from the commanding position of the noblemen and gentlemen who owned it.

In *Robinson Crusoe* (1719), Daniel Dafoe underscored the pragmatic aspect of wild nature and completely excluded any picturesque value from the narration for the sake of a utilitarian use of the environment. Fulford's idea could easily be applied to Beckford, an elegant writer and an affluent landowner, ravished to describe natural landscapes he was proud to own. A different case is represented by his contemporary Richard Payne-Knight, an aristocrat with a large estate known for his libertine free-thinking expressed in a scandalous publication dedicated to Priapus, A*ccounts of the Remains of Priapus* (1786), featuring a pagan vision of nature. His most influential text was *An Analytical Enquiry into the Principles of Taste,* published in 1805, which summarised his studies of the picturesque and sharply contrasted with previous authors, as he considered nature the ideal place where a gentleman's sensuality found inspiration. The development of industrialisation puzzled various intellectuals, sensitive to the dramatic changes in the environment. Cowper's case is particularly noteworthy. A humanitarian idealist imbued with neo-classical and Augustan themes and a steady admiration for Homer, he was one of the first authors shrinking from the Industrial Revolution's iniquitous effects on nature, as he could perceive the dangerous consequences of industrialisation from its early development. His poems expressed love for the natural world and had a strong impact on Radcliffe. *The Task* (1785) contains a mixture of echoes from Classical, Medieval and Renaissance authors. The beginning of the section entitled "The Garden" is worth noticing for its striking resemblances with Dante Alighieri's difficulty in the *Inferno*'s opening lines and relief in its final lines, also influenced by the *Comedy*, a work that was to shape early Gothic in more than one way, as we will see in the next chapters:

As one who, long in thickets and in brakes
Entangled, winds now this way and now that
His devious course uncertain, seeking home;
Or, having long in miry ways been foiled,
And sore discomfited, from slough to slough
Plunging, and half-despairing of escape;
If chance at length he finds a greensward smooth
And faithful to the foot, his spirits rise,
He chirrups brisk his ear-erecting steed,
And winds his way with pleasure and with ease.
(*The Task*: 48)

Written after the Gothic trend had already started, *The Task* shows how eighteenth-century authors were deeply affected by a miscellany of sources, manifested forms of Romantic sensibility before the beginning of canonical Romanticism and more often than not expressed appraisal of nature in its many forms.

The feelings that inspired Burke in his foundational essay (1757), written thirty years before *The Task*, were the sublime, astonishment and horror. Like early Gothic novels, the manifestations of the sublime are the object of critical commentaries and explanations that, as Martin Price (1969) notes, make it difficult to find a categorical meaning for it. The concept of the sublime was in direct connection with the growing importance of landscape, and while the discourse on the sublime can be traced through different epochs back to the Classics, it acquired greater importance during the entire eighteenth century in Great Britain and Europe. The sublime is prominent in Dante's horrific vision of nature and the underworld depicted at the commencement of the *Divine Comedy* (1320). In spite of having been created almost four hundred years before the development of Gothic novels, *The Comedy* is interspersed with horrid images that provoked feelings of terror: its first lines convey a sense of fear, correlated with the sublime described by Burke (Extract from Princeton Dante Project):

Midway in the journey of our life
I came to myself in a dark wood,
For the straight way was lost
Ah, how hard it is to tell
The nature of that wood, savage, dense and harsh—
The very thought of it renews my fear!
It is so bitter death is hardly more so.

(*Inferno*: Canto I, lines 1–7)

Burke's *A Philosophical Enquiry into the Origin of our Ideas of the Sublime and Beautiful* (1757) was more than an essay containing theories on perception. Published seven years before *Otranto*, the text represented a literary landmark, absorbing ideas from a classical past and, at the same time, fashioning new tastes in literature. Burke was a cultural *Janus Bifrons*, the Roman god of duality. He looked backwards towards emotions of awe, fear and horror that were deeply rooted in Classical poets such as Homer and Virgil, while simultaneously re-inventing the classical notion of the sublime inherited from Antiquity to be passed on to future generations, imbued with new sensibilities. Burke's operation was, in a way, strategic and insightful. He not only created a compendium of the ideas from a classical treatise on rhetoric attributed to the mysterious figure known as Pseudo-Longinus but also absorbed the teachings of the French Nicolas Boileau and his *Art Poétique* (1674). Dennis's and Addison's respective promotion of the sublime during the late seventeenth century and in the first decades of the eighteenth century probably prompted Burke to create his foundational essay (Robert Doran 2015). However, Boileau, Addison and Dennis had not been the first scholars to display the importance of the sublime. The attraction to the sublime had become popular again during the Renaissance, when one of the many Italian humanists, Francesco Robortello, found, translated and commented on a Greek manuscript of Longinus's *Peri Hýpsous* in 1554 (Renato Ricco and Susanna Villari 2016). Robortello's Latin translation became instrumental in the propagation of sublime ideals. Even though the German philosopher Immanuel Kant is celebrated as a great theorist of the sublime, it should be noted that his monumental essay *Critique of Judgment* (1790) was published after British anticipations and reasoning on the subject, which had paved the way for the early Gothic trend in novels. Greek and Latin authors originally propounded the sublime. Together with Pseudo-Longinus, Dionysius of Halicarnassus, Lucretius and Virgil were aware of the sublime, and they either described its effects or used its rhetorical potential to compose impactful descriptions, still memorable after centuries since their creation. Schama (1995: 443–445) finds that the sense of Burkean horror, anticipated by Walpole and Gray when they described their dramatic passage through the Alps in 1737, is intriguing because it shows how, in a period dominated by Augustan measure and enlightened rationalism, there was a lurking need for dramatic events to excite both body and mind. When post-adolescent Walpole and Gray rejoiced in the terrifying and dangerous chasms in the

Alps, the tumults and the horrors of the end of the century were not even conceivable, as Schama (445) clarifies, "What they were interested in, along with the high mountain passes, was not a true epiphany with the omnipotent Almighty, but an experiment in sensation. [...] Where earlier mountain travellers had recoiled from mountain terror, Walpole and Gray revelled in it".

Starting with the sense of Burke's "delightful horror" and the desire for terror, this book intends to proceed to capture the primeval spirit of the early Gothic. With the exception of Radcliffe and Beckford, nature is not always a predominant factor in the early Gothic novel, but the sublime can be equally obtained through the sense of horror and anguish depicted by Walpole, Reeve, Lee, Harley, Lewis, Dacre and other writers, who had generally excluded nature from their narratives with only rare exceptions. David Durant (1982: 529) provocatively posits that the Gothic is not part of Radcliffe's works because of her use of nature as her special constituent: "against the chaotic universe, [she offers] the lost world of the pastoral. Her ideal is much more pleasant than the Gothic underworld or the modern world that it symbolises". Directly interwoven with the protagonists' feelings and with the sublime, narrative visions of landscapes took up symbolic roles during climatic events in Radcliffe's novels, as Jayne Elisabeth Lewis clarifies (2006: 378):

Neither the earliest reviews of her novels nor the critical inquiries of the present day have much managed to separate the fruits of her literary labours from contemporary theory and practice of the visual arts. Predictably, attention focuses on the landscapes so compulsively rendered in all of her major novels– ostensibly natural scenes whose extreme detail and even more extreme conventionality stamp Radcliffe as a "pictorialist" in the manner of the great landscape artists of her century and the one preceding it. Though these artists–conventionally listed as Poussin, Claude, and Rosa, whose imaginativeness was essential in Radcliffe's inspiration–diverged rather dramatically in style, Radcliffe appears to have mediated effortlessly among them.

An essential part of Radcliffe's Gothic narratives, nature encyclopaedically incorporated literary tendencies, different landscapes and multifaceted iconographies. Undeniably, iconographies of different epochs together with seventeenth-century landscape paintings were instrumental in the creation of early Gothic literature. Paintings by eighteenth-century French painters François Boucher and Jean-Honoré Fragonard abounded with descriptions of natural settings, and their

Rococo style was decorative and idyllic, filled with mythological and bucolic themes in pleasant surroundings. It was their latent erotic streak, however, which entered early Gothic narratives. Active during a large part of the eighteenth century, Italian painters Canaletto and Francesco Guardi preferred city views and townscape painting. However, their mysterious capriccios, uniting architectural ruins and unusual landscapes, became popular because their pictorial approach conveyed picturesque and melancholy impressions and a sense of Romantic nostalgia. The view painter Giovanni Paolo Panini, active in Rome, introduced the capriccio technique in the seventeenth century. The capriccio generally featured ruined architectures within an urban context or surrounded by a landscape. The famous Galli da Bibiena family, scenic artists, perfected capriccios in order to create startling theatrical settings. Their technique was improved by Italian expat Marco Ricci, periodically residing in England. Rosa's and Claude's dramatic scenes encased in majestic landscapes, together with Piranesi's disquieting visions, complemented picturesque paintings of landscapes. Painters played a remarkable role in the formation of taste and the development of mysterious Gothic atmospheres. According to Yang-feng Wu (2009), impressive and dramatic Baroque paintings were instrumental in determining narratives in Radcliffe and Lewis. Eighteenth-century painters, equally itinerant in various European countries, such as Francesco Casanova, brother of the more famous Giacomo, de Louthenbourg, Cozens, Claude Joseph Vernet and Hubert Robert–creators of imposing landscapes–influenced taste and artistic reception. Their works became attainable by a vast public thanks to reproductions and prints. Contemporary and past artists, both British and European, were widely known thanks to a growing number of etchings and engravings that made massive amounts of replicas of famous paintings available to larger audiences. Several British painters influenced the appreciation of nature. Richard Wilson was significant for his role in connecting the English picturesque ideal with an Italianate landscape. As great admirers of art, both Walpole and Beckford owned extensive art collections that included paintings by Renaissance artists, Salvator Rosa as well as seventeenth- and eighteenth-century artworks and their paintings could provide interesting sources of inspiration for their writing. While the Grand Tour provided an occasion to discover antiquities, painting workshops in Italy–especially in Rome–attracted painters from all over Europe, eager to learn new techniques and observe landscapes and architectures they later reproduced in their countries of origin, increasing artistic awareness.

The "long eighteenth century" was an overflowing and culturally challenging period, when literature, art, philosophy and science progressed admirably. Originally centred on British history (1688–1815), Frank O'Gorman's chronological expansion of the century is now applied to both British and European literature. Many ideas flourished and spread to different countries, and the search for knowledge was accompanied by a strong will to classify, catalogue and arrange learning to make it available for both experts and the less intellectual masses. The French Encyclopaedia was one of the first attempts to universally explain science and culture and make them accessible to humankind. A great novelty of that time was the idea of popularising art, and the first museums were opened to show the public paintings and artistic objects that had for the most part been a prerogative of private *Wunderkammern*, the so-called curiosities cabinets, in private aristocratic mansions. After the opening of the Capitoline Museums in Rome in 1734, the *Uffizi*, a prominent art gallery in Florence, was inaugurated in 1743, attracting widespread interest for the richness of its collections. It was during the second half of this culturally superabundant century that the Gothic novel bloomed. The Enlightenment and Pre-Romanticism, antithetical in spirit, chronologically coexisted and developed mutual influences. Embedded in the cultural flux of the Age of Reason, the Gothic extended into the Romantic zone, essentially determining its expansion. The year 1798 saw the publication of Wordsworth and Coleridge's *Lyrical Ballads*, a work that became synonymous with Romanticism and was to attract the literary elite. However, it was also the year of the release of Roche's *Clermont* and Lathom's *Midnight Bell*–dark Gothic stories abounding with terror and suspense about victimised young characters and avidly read by a large public.

The focus of this research is concentrated on the relevant manifestations of the Gothic genre in the decades that followed the novelty Walpole introduced with *The Castle of Otranto*. The restricted eighteenth-century's *fin de siècle* chronology of the early Gothic is inversely proportional to its high levels of creativity and inventiveness. After some years of apparent calm following *The Castle of Otranto*, a new wave of Gothic novels appeared in the last two decades of the century. Along with *Otranto*, this book includes an analysis of early Gothic novels published between 1786 and 1809 and successfully absorbed into the Gothic category notwithstanding their utmost differences. The novels that are analysed here were created before, during and after the French Revolution, taken by many as a point of reference for the Gothic genre. However, its links to the French Revolution are a critical convention a quo, which does not take into consideration Gothic peculiarities that already existed before the dramatic events from 1789 onwards. Therefore, the influence of revolutionary events should be exclusively applied to the Gothic production belonging to the 1790s. Even so, the French Revolution per se cannot alone explain the expansion of the sublime, the supernatural, the Gothic or the taste for strange architectures and dramatic landscapes. The attraction for horrid and terrifying contexts existed before the tragic revolutionary events took place, as the epigraphs to the first chapter testify–taken as they were from works published in 1747, 1757 and 1764, respectively.

Delightful Horrors uses a critical perspective that looks backwards in time, ignoring *a posteriori* knowledge, trying to adapt to the authors' viewpoints and creating a critical tabula rasa to discover new elements in their works. The intent is to establish what influences Walpole, Beckford, Radcliffe, Lewis and other Gothic authors may have received from their education, readings and contextual cultural experiences that could lead to the birth of the Gothic. Gillespie and Hopkins's (2005) analysis of literary reception and translations can help understand conscious and unconscious cultural dissemination through the tradition of literary translation, which played a fundamental role in the development of literature and the adaptation of cultural influences, both diachronic and synchronic. This research intends to read Walpole's *Otranto* with a different perspective, extrapolate new elements in Beckford's *Vathek* (1786), unveil sources behind Radcliffe's novels and *The Romance of The Forest* (1791), investigate cultural echoes in Lewis's *The Monk* (1796) and analyse some narrative devices in Robinson's *Hubert de Sevrac* (1796) and other minor novels of the period. Existing critical hypotheses were crucial for starting this study before proceeding towards new research fields to identify unusual aspects of the early Gothic's mysterious genesis. Not all Gothic works are the same, but a distinctive trait that helps to recognise a higher form of Gothic is the use of Classical, Medieval, Renaissance sources as well as influences from the Enlightenment and the long eighteenth century. Evidence is provided by the scope and pervasiveness of themes from the Classical past, both Greek and Latin dominating the early Gothic novels, whereas references to great Medieval and Renaissance models denote that early Gothic novelists absorbed the cultural messages of the past while reflecting the cultural atmosphere of the eighteenth century and the power of the Enlightenment. They absorbed, in fact, echoes of eighteenth-century poets, novelists and philosophers, which reveal a profound love for knowledge in the enlightened tradition of their time. Although their novels became popular for the mechanisms of suspense and the use of the supernatural, they provided elegant narratives with eclectic and composite cultural implications, which a highly cultivated minority could perceive and common readers could enjoy. Both the implicit and explicit scandalous contents in early Gothic novels may have been responsible for the less than tepid recognition of their cultural value. Prose works before Walpole, Beckford, Radcliffe and Lewis featured different kinds of narratives related to stereotyped ways of writing, and distinct prose styles were a characteristic of authors belonging to previous generations. The authors chosen for this study are relevant for their special narrative forms. Beckford, Walpole, Radcliffe, Lewis as well as Robinson and other early Gothicists exhibited richly flexible forms of prose that could include different registers and styles, thus injecting originality into a way of writing that was supposedly less dignified than other mainstream literary or poetic works. Some peculiar characteristics, which make their writing original and distinguishable, give them literary dignity. The first is the rich quality of their prose. The second aspect is the poetic value of their language, competing with poetry and elevating the formal level of their writing. Early Gothic authors show a penchant for poetry, either reproducing passages of famous poems or inserting poetic images into their narrations, meant to be idyllic, romantic and dramatic at the same time. The third important feature is that all early Gothic novelists played with the notion of genre. Whether it was Walpole's pastiche, Beckford's pseudo Oriental tale, Radcliffe's word-painting or Lewis's melange of genres, any definitive categorisation turns out to be virtually impossible because of their experimental narrative modes going in multiple directions: early Gothic's reverberations opened doors for narratological possibilities. The fourth important element is an interrelation with iconographies that demonstrates the pictorial qualities of each of these writers' prose. Their novels represented a cultural and intellectual *aperçu* of the long eighteenth century and the previous epochs, blended into new narrative and narratable systems.

Mystery lingers on early Gothic writers. Like Radcliffe's obstinate silence, Walpole's, Beckford's and Lewis's verbose letters, or Robinson's memoirs cannot be deciphered. Inscrutability and secrecy also characterised their novels, as they introduced thrilling narratives of suspense anticipating modern crime stories. The places they depicted transcended reality and acquired a legendary halo. They reproduced human desire to recreate mythical regions, an idea emphasised in Umberto Eco's *Book of Legendary Lands* (2014). Their highly inventive romances and Gothic stories also conceived complex universes, where different influences and images, partially hidden, proliferated under a gloomy surface. Together with their constant allusions to Antiquity, Medieval romance and Renaissance beauty, early Gothic authors shared an even stranger feature, as their conclusions are oftentimes unusual, unexpected and, in a way, incomplete, interspersed with imperceptible forms of existential anguish. Uncertain finales are open and liable to multiple interpretations. Eco's *Open Work* (2000) is not only the title of one of his most famous essays but also one of the bases of his aesthetic philosophy that appears to be connate with the enigma of early Gothic literature.

Oh! Guard the marvels I relate
Of fell ambition scourg'd by fate
(Horace Walpole. *The Castle of Otranto*)

While Prime Minister Robert Walpole had dedicated most of his life to politics, his youngest son Horace, an eclectic intellectual, preferred plunging into art, architecture and literature. Walpole's pedigree, so to speak, was very similar to that of Beckford and Lewis, as each descended from important families holding a respectable place in politics and endowed with remarkable fortunes, even if Walpole was reputed to be the real aristocrat among the three of them. However, the legendary halo surrounding Walpole's ancestry is not completely true. Equally, the mythical beginning of his novel is based more on imagination than facts, as the study of the Gothic "has been shaped by its powerful myth of origins, the oft-told tale of Horace Walpole, Father and Great Original, a tale which is itself a full-fledged Gothic narrative" (Williams 1995: 8). The genesis of *The Castle of Otranto* (henceforth *WO* in quotations), Williams comments, is generally described in mythical terms, repeating and amplifying Walpole's well-known story of his sudden inspiration after a strange dream, leading to the rapid composition of the novel. In Williams's opinion (9):

Few books about the Gothic fail to repeat this wonderfully appropriate story. It provides an aristocratic and vaguely 'supernatural' lineage worthy of any Gothic hero. At the same time, it is a fundamentally bourgeois fantasy; the Walpoles had not been born aristocrats, but elevated to the peerage within living memory, just as Strawberry Hill was made, not born, a Gothic castle. Like those lords of great estates whose holdings contained no authentic ruins, Walpole had to build his own Gothic pile.

Even though the legendary aura progressively built around the figure of Walpole is overemphasised, his Gothic romance acquired an indisputable monumental importance. *The Castle of Otranto* (1764) is a watershed text in English literature and the development of the Gothic genre. Some of its relevant features have been critically observed from various perspectives. However, it is worth taking into consideration some devices, such as fake historical contexts, blatant anachronisms, ambiguous architectural descriptions and the bizarre use of landscapes and grottoes. Despite their frequent implausibility, some of these features would become essential in subsequent romances and novels in the decades to come, all sharing the common denominator of the Gothic tale of horror. Walpole's literary endeavour was characterised by a form of cultural hybridism, created using a sort of post-modern intuition mixed with narrative techniques of suspense responsible for a drastic change in the history of prose writing. As we have seen before, Walpole's unusual masterpiece was coincidentally published in the same year as Winkelmann's and Beccaria's foundational works. These key texts offer a variety of literary facets and cultural sources belonging to the long eighteenth century (also reflecting previous epochs), and are essential to the formation of the Gothic genre and taste. Winkelmann reiterated the importance of classicism confirming that culture was still imbued–both consciously and unconsciously–with examples from Antiquity. Beccaria provided gloomy and ghastly images, even though his intent had been to expose legal injustice, and Walpole created a basic compendium of horror for future Gothicists.

Recent critical analyses have highlighted that the separation of cultural currents is difficult to maintain (Wallace 2009). A number of scholars note that traditional delimitations of literary waves become less clear-cut insofar as research progresses and discovers new, unexpected analogies between apparently incompatible authors, or authors belonging to different cultural movements. A further confirmation of the deep connection between supposedly distant literary movements is provided by an analysis of articles in *The Spectator*. Expanding Clery's intuitions, Peter Walmsley (2009: 45) highlights how Addison's and Steele's articles, in issues 411 to 421, are dedicated to the exploration of imagination, seeking to build an aesthetic, derived from Locke's precepts, based on the constant concern for death and ghosts. Both a philosophical development and a common literary device in the Classics, imagination dominates the eighteenth century, and the Gothic is one of the most evident consequences of that latent passion for mystery, imbued with Classicism. The British Augustan Age and the French Enlightenment not only brought about new scientific, philosophical, cultural and literary masterpieces but also simultaneously promoted the appreciation of great works belonging to Antiquity and other important periods, such as the Middle Ages and the Renaissance. Dante, Boccaccio and Ariosto were recognised as great literary role models belonging to an ideal past era, still viewed as a single period without distinctions. This lack of periodisation, a cultural practice that was not established until the late nineteenth century, shaped a fluid vision of the past. Its only demarcation was the contrast between the Ancients and the Moderns. This indefinite historical distinction of epochs was probably one of the causes of the blurred chronology of Walpole's story and Gothic romances, in general. Jo Tollebeek (2001) highlights that William Roscoe's *The Life of Lorenzo de Medici, Called the Magnificent* (1795) cast a new light on historical periods. The creator of a sort of agricultural utopia in Tuscany, where he lived for the most part of his life, the Swiss economist and historian Jean Charles Léonard Simonde de Sismondi had a special intuition. His sixteen-volume collection, *Histoire des républiques italiennes au moyen âge* (1807–1826), about the history of Italian Republics during the Middle Ages, represented the first in-depth study to introduce a clear division of historical periods. The French historian Jules Michelet, the inventor of the Renaissance concept in his 1855 *History of France* (*Histoire de France*), later developed the distinction between the Middle Ages and subsequent historic and literary movements. A routinely overlooked aspect in Gothic criticism is that the lack of a clear determination of bygone epochs may have caused the usually disparaged historical vagueness in Walpole, and later in Radcliffe, Lewis and other Gothic adepts. This different perspective could lead to an alternative way of looking at their early Gothic tales. Instead of betraying intellectual ignorance, they reflect a cultural aspect of their time.

The following lines are interesting as they convey sentimental and nostalgic portrayals, immersed in a gloomy atmosphere recalling Gothic narratives:

> In these deep solitudes and awful cells
> Where heav'nly-pensive contemplation dwells,
> And ever-musing melancholy reigns;
> What means this tumult in a vestal's veins?

The phrases "deep solitudes", "ever-musing melancholy" and "awful cells" form a chain of *topoi* that were typical of the Gothic. However, one of the Augustan Age most fervent classicists created such a Gothic feeling. The style of the imagery described here was to become prominent seventy years after the classicist Alexander Pope penned these verses. The lines are taken from the beginning of Pope's *Eloisa to Abelard* (1717). Written in heroic couplets, the epistle imitated the Ovidian style of *Amores* and *Heroic Epistles*, dated back to the first century BCE. The desolate and melancholy images of the dark cells are anticipations of themes that Gothic writers would absorb and amplify some five or six decades later. Summers (1969) was the first scholar to notice Pope's sorrowful atmospheres in his *Gothic Quest*. Williams (1995) further develops this intuition to demonstrate *The Castle of Otranto* was not a "parthenogenesis", or the unprecedented creation of a new form of literature that did not previously exist, but, in reality, it had some remarkable antecedents, which Walpole astutely absorbed and re-elaborated. In order to demonstrate his evident debt to Pope and his unexpected Gothic and Romantic features, Williams cites Walpole's words in a letter to Sir Horace Mann. Walpole describes the progress in the building of his gothic architectural ideal, Strawberry Hill, on 12th June 1753: "My house is so monastic, that I have a little hall decked with long saints in lean arched windows and with taper columns, which we call the Paraclete, in memory of Eloise's cloister" (Williams 1995: 49–50). Walpole's education and eclecticism enabled his construction of original literary forms (and architectures) through the assimilation of lofty works from the past.

The Castle of Otranto was presented as a translation of a manuscript of "the darkest ages" (*WO*: 3), composed during the Middle Ages and printed during the Renaissance. The subtitle was "A Story", as the frontispiece of the first edition demonstrates. Walpole then made some significant changes to the second edition, which was issued after a few months in 1765. As a first step, after the successful reception of the very first edition, Walpole added a second preface to the original shorter one, in which he unveiled the mystery behind his authorship and justified the use of a pseudonym (William Marshal, the "translator" of the pseudo manuscript/incunabula), motivating his decision with a certain fear that the public might not accept his novel. That he was afraid of possible negative reactions is confirmed by his resolve not to use his private printing press at Strawberry Hill. He used an external publisher instead (James Lilley 2013). After considering the unexpected enthusiasm caused by the novel, Walpole decided to declare his paternity of the book. Secondly, he added the word "Gothic" to the subtitle "A Story" and this choice was the turning point for the birth of the Gothic genre. Interestingly, as Yeager (2019: 148) remarks, the original first preface already contained indirect hints at Gothic, especially with the mention of the "black letter" (*WO*: 3), characterising the original Italian text, which is synonymous of "Gothic letterform". An anomaly and an anachronism, as this lettering would have been justifiable in a medieval illuminated text, but was improbable in Italian Renaissance incunabula (as *The Castle of Otranto* was supposed to be, after probably being passed on orally and/or as a manuscript for centuries). However, the notion of black lettering conveys a visual idea of the text, which is not only Gothic for its contents but also for its form and appearance. Most importantly, Walpole justified the creation of a tale of fantasy, perhaps reprising Hurd's recent work about romance published in 1762, which must have influenced some of his literary preferences. Walpole claims that he attempted to create a harmonious mélange of different forms of romance (WO: 7).

The very first edition of Walpole's novel was published on 24th December 1764. William Bathoe and Thomas Lownds of London published the second edition in April 1765, in which the word "Gothic" was added to the subtitle, a foray into an ambiguous linguistic field that would bear remarkable consequences. However, during the same year, J. Hoey of Dublin published the novel without adding the word "Gothic" to the subtitle, showing that the term Gothic might still convey problematic impressions. Moreover, a front page of an edition dating 1765 is still printed with the subtitle "A Story", as can be seen in W. Lewis's 1969 introduction to the novel. Whereas intellectuals started using and commenting on the term "Gothic" enriching it with new cultural and political nuances during the eighteenth century, Walpole had not initially conceived the idea of the "Gothic" as a definition of the story. And the Gothic still did not exist as a literary genre. Walpole's addition of the term "Gothic" had important repercussions that helped recognise the rise of a new trend in literature, as Markman Ellis (2000: 17) explains:

It is clear that to eighteenth-century readers, the term 'gothic' identified a complicated and slippery topic connoting some related but distinct judgments about medieval culture, national history, civic virtue and the enlightenment. Judgments about the propriety and value of the gothic lay behind Horace Walpole's decision to rename the second edition of his novel, *The Castle of Otranto*: when it had first appeared on 24th December 1764, the anonymous novel was subtitled 'A Story' [...] In later decades, the other writers followed Walpole by identifying their work as 'gothic', such as Clara Reeve's *The Old English Baron: A Gothic Story*.

Walpole introduces other important changes in the second edition, the most relevant of which is the insertion of an epigraph in Latin from

Horace. Defining his authorship implied adding a loftier sense to his work including a Classical quotation. As W. Lewis suggests after Clarence W. Mendell's remark, the epigraph is not correct and the sense of the original test is reversed in Walpole, who "frequently misquoted" (1969: xii–xiii), but might have altered the Horatian couplet on purpose to justify the strangeness of the story. Conceived as a divertissement–"a matter of entertainment" in the words of the pseudo medieval chronicler of the story (*WO*: 4)–the novel was to play a monumental role in the decades to come. Despite the remarkable amount of critical literature dedicated to Walpole and *The Castle of Otranto*, some of its fascinatingly contradictory features and hidden sources are worth exploring. In the first preface, the author ("translator") had explained that the original manuscript of the events narrated in his novel, supposedly found in the library of an ancient family in the north of England, had been printed in the year 1529 in Naples, when the Renaissance was in full swing in Italy. However, Walpole later specifies that the story may have taken place between 1095 and 1243, a time span of almost two hundred years between the first and the last Crusade. Considering actual events, the story of *Otranto* could have developed during different kingdoms and historical contexts. It may have taken place under the Salian Franks' rule, or under the House of the Hohenstaufen, all Germanic families, who, in turn, took power and ruled over the Holy Roman Empire in Germany and in that part of Italy, which lay either north or south of the Papal State and Rome. Currently a laid-back seaside resort, famous for its crystalline waters with nuances of emerald and turquoise, the real Otranto was located (and still is) in the South Eastern part of the Italian Peninsula on what we call the heel of the metaphorically boot-shaped Italy. The periodisation Walpole included concerning his story may also have coincided with the Norman conquest of Sicily and the South (for decades under the Arab rule between the tenth and eleventh centuries). The Normans later expanded to conquer the whole of Southern Italy, as historian Massimo Montanari (2002), among others, summarises when describing the different phases of the Middle Ages and the various layers of populations settling in Italy after conquering it. After settling permanently in the northwest of France and invading Britain in 1066, the Normans carried out the conquest of the Peninsula's southern territory. The colonisation of Southern Italy was the Norman expansion's phase in the Continent outer territories to oppose both Frank and Germanic control in the central parts of Europe.

Interestingly, there were no longer traces of the Goths when Walpole's story took place. Despite having given the fatal blow to the Roman Empire and after separating into two violent tribes, known as the Ostrogoths and

Visigoths, the Goths had disappeared from the Italian territory by the time Byzantine emperor Justinian won back part of the Roman Empire in the sixth century, several centuries before the setting of *The Castle of Otranto*. Walpole's invention of a manuscript conveyed a realistic sense of the events, whereas his turbid periodisation created an antithetical effect, namely a vagueness surrounding legendary past events. Despite the literary device of the manuscript, historical facts are indefinite and the atmosphere of the novel recalls a fairy tale rather than a chronicle. However, similar scenarios—the discovery of ancient parchments unveiling strange stories—have often been used to create a semblance of credibility. Eco employed the manuscript device in many of his novels. Published in 1980, the mediaeval story of the novel *The Name of the Rose* was long thought to have been copied from a genuine manuscript detailing real events in fourteenth-century Northern Italy until the Italian author himself decided to reveal the truth. Ruth Mack's (2009: 128) sees Walpole as an antagonist of the Enlightenment for his interpretation of history and the supernatural: "Far from simply opposing realist truth, [*The Castle of Otranto*] is deeply invested in interrogating the terms for that truth to support the possibility of real historical representation on grounds others than those empiricist philosophy was willing to offer". Jonathan Dent (2004) contends that *Otranto* was in part the consequence of Walpole's careful reading of David Hume's volumes of history. In reality, Walpole's private correspondence with friends and his exchanges with Hume concerning his *History of England* (1754–1762) reveal how sceptical Walpole was about reliable historiographic narration.

As far as art and architecture, the period of Walpole's story may be characterised by proto-Romanesque, Romanesque and/or Norman styles. The Gothic style was not called "Gothic" until the Renaissance when Giorgio Vasari, among the first commentators of that architectural development, wrote that it originated with the Goths, which is, in fact, an incorrect statement. This new form of architecture started with the improvement and development of pointed arches, ogives, ribbed vaults and flying buttresses during the thirteenth century. These new architectural characteristics allowed for a remarkable vertical expansion and greater luminosity, in comparison to the Romanesque style, from which Gothic style originated. Vasari appreciated some Italian manifestations of Gothic style, even though he admired the symmetrical perfection of the Renaissance.

The author of the essay on Gothic art in 1797, Hall was of a different opinion and provided an appreciation of the Northern Gothic canon in contrast with both Classical structures of the past and Mediterranean versions of the Gothic architectural style. The church of Saint-Denis in France is supposed to represent the actual beginning of the new architectural trend in the twelfth century. The Metropolitan Museum of Art, New York, organised a symposium on the church of Saint-Denis and the Abbot Suger, probably the mind behind the project introducing a new form of architecture (Paula Lieber Gerson 1986), which exploited the insertion of majestic windows to obtain extreme verticality. The Gothic progressively developed as an elegant expansion of the Romanesque style, impressive for its imposing structures, staggering verticality and bright painted-glass windows. Later Gothic architecture would expand all over Europe with different regional characteristics. On the other hand, the Italian Gothic developed towards the end of the thirteenth century as a mere extension of the existing Romanesque (locally described as *Romanico*) and did not include certain characteristics of the Northern Gothic, such as buttresses and flamboyant arches. The simplicity of Italian Gothic is especially evident in the south of the Peninsula. Verticality was used for town hall towers in medieval city-states, such as in Siena's *Palazzo dei Priori* (the seat of the city's governors), or in high towers belonging to aristocratic palaces. Such vertical expansion was a status symbol of the town's wealthy families—as in the little borough of San Gimignano in Tuscany. Flamboyant arches were sometimes built in the north of the Italian Peninsula, more receptive to foreign northern influences in transalpine countries, as the majestic and elaborated Milan cathedral, the *Duomo*. Hall's essay on Gothic architecture exalted the superiority of northern and Germanic medieval forms adding that the flamboyant Gothic was an example of perfection, especially when compared to the poor Italian Gothic that "only Vasari, who had never crossed the Alps", could describe in positive terms. Hall's enthusiastic exaltation of Gothic architecture was in contrast not only with what Vasari had claimed but also contradicted a common negative bias, still valid for British literati and scholars during the first half of the eighteenth century, namely its supposed barbarous nature. According to Longueil, the term "Gothic" seemed to convey a lack of proper civilisation and had mostly negative connotations until the publication of *Otranto*. The creation of Walpole's pseudo-Gothic mansion Strawberry Hill should have reproduced the Gothic style, but it was a composite form, representing his eccentric ideals. It was more a hybrid structure than a genuine gothic building. W. Lewis explains that, as Walpole himself admitted later, the library of Trinity College in Cambridge was also responsible for his Gothic characterisations (1969: xi). Walpole's *Otranto* was halfway between a common derogatory prejudice, inherited from a conventional linguistic and historical use, and the growing enthusiastic exaltation of the northern tradition in literature and art, which was changing the perspective on the gothic. Walpole's story, which had to convey dark times, was partly moulded on the Classics, since he adapted some of Shakespeare's plays to his plot. Ironically, Walpole is likely to have invented the Gothic genre while having different cultural, architectural and literary archetypes in mind. He considered his mansion and the vast collection of artefacts inside as representative of the Gothic, even though they included disparate objects belonging to various cultures, from ancient Greece to the Renaissance (Lilley 2013).

An interesting architectural contradiction of Walpole's Gothic romance lies in the fact that the castle of Otranto is not a real castle, but a fortified citadel. Otranto is a town surrounded by battlements on defensive walls in the easternmost part of Italy projecting between the Adriatic and the Ionian Seas towards the Mediterranean, Greece and the Middle East. Its strategic position had forced its inhabitants to protect the area by constructing a fortress on the city walls. It acquired its final form in the sixteenth and seventeenth centuries under the kingdom of Aragon, when the Spaniards managed to conquer and take possession of most parts of the Italian Peninsula after a series of grisly wars with France, fought on Italian territory. Only expert historians and geographers probably knew the silhouette of the city's bastions reflected in the beautiful, transparent Adriatic Sea. Walpole might have had the chance to see the place directly during his Grand Tour in 1737 or maybe later in life, even though it is quite improbable, as the place was quite distant from the beaten track of the Grand Tour. In the 1780s, he admitted choosing the name "Otranto" while looking at a map of Southern Italy. In her analysis of Walpole's Italian journey, Williams (2006: 22) reveals, "Walpole would confess to Sir William Hamilton that he had chosen the word 'Otranto' [because] the word was well-sounding, suitable for his gothic story". Walpole's fortunate choice may be a further example of "serendipity", the propitious coincidence in a series of events, a term he had invented after reading *The Three Princes of Serendip*. The legend was the English translation of *Peregrinaggio di tre giovani figliuoli del re di Serendippo* "a novella translated and adapted into Italian from Persian by a Cristoforo Armeno, and published in Venice in 1557 by Michele Tramezzino" (Lilley 2013: 103).

Williams also analyses some of Walpole's experiences as a supposed spy in Southern Italy, unequally ruled by the Bourbon kings. When he arrived in Calabria, nowadays a luxuriant region of Italy, part of Magna Graecia in ancient times, Walpole was so appalled by the general poverty and people's awful conditions–imputable to the corrupt Spanish rule–that he decided to abandon the place and return to his aristocratic circles of friends and parties in Rome and Florence. Although many critics have identified the castle in the novel with the writer's extravagant mansion, and even though Walpole refers in his correspondence to his neo-Gothic dwelling as a source of inspiration, it is not possible to detect concrete analogies to Strawberry Hill, as the descriptions provided in the novel are not sufficient to recognise the place. The castle itself is not described in detail and its parts are time and again defined as "the court", "the steps", "the stairs", "the window", "the trap-door", "the black tower", etc., all architectural items that may belong to any place, not necessarily to a castle, or to a Gothic castle, or even to Walpole's Neo-Gothic mansion. The Gothic building in *The Castle of Otranto* was probably in the author's mind, but it could not be deciphered as Gothic in style. Lee Morrissey (1999: 124) concludes that the introduction of "architectural technical terms such as 'subterraneous passages, several intricate cloisters, battlements in the tower' increase the possibility of the castle's existence". This idea is not substantiated by any clear description of Otranto, of which the form and nature remain vague and undefined. Walpole used terms indicating cultural and architectural knowledge, but did not provide any concrete description of a specific castle. What Walpole described was probably a personal, idealised idea of Gothic. Although the identification of the novel's setting is virtually impossible because of its haziness, the narrative importance of the castle in the economy of the story is undeniable. The characters are claustrophobically enclosed inside spaces and do not seem to move freely. Exiting the castle involves precariousness and peril. Traditionally, according to Walpole's admission, *The Castle of Otranto* originated from a dream, or, better, a nightmare the author had one night in Strawberry Hill (Clery 1996: viii), a memory that cannot be corroborated but has become part of the legends surrounding the first Gothic novel.

Two years before publishing his original novel, Walpole started compiling *Anecdotes of Painting in England*, a series of essays collected in five volumes, completed in 1771, in which Walpole praised Piranesi's etchings and engravings for their remarkable creativity and admirable inventiveness. In all probability, the castle that he described was not inspired by a real edifice but was an imaginary invention mostly based on Piranesi's intriguing representations, which Walpole thoroughly enjoyed. Several etchings describing majestic interiors of prisons, towers, and palaces seem to be the perfect settings for the development of the story. The different versions of *The Staircase with Trophies* (Piranesi 2011: I,

132–133), created between 1749 and 1750, belonging to Piranesi's phantasmagorical collection named *Imaginary Prisons,* now at the Metropolitan Museum of New York, is a spectacular illustration of grandiose architectural structures, where stairs, corridors, towers, vaults, arches, and passages form a harmoniously mysterious ensemble. That Piranesi's *Prisons* may have influenced Walpole is an idea shared by art historian Orietta Rossi Pinelli (2003). The art expert remarks that Piranesi's architectural inventions, which may be the results of his direct observation of Venice's Arsenal, with its gigantic structures, and his appreciation of the now popular architectural capriccios, had become quite common in the second part of the eighteenth century. As other structures conceived by Piranesi, the image of majestic and gloomy *Staircases with Trophies* could perfectly embody *The Castle of* Otranto's mysterious setting. Characters move, hide, spy, run for safety, commit crimes or meet their terrible destiny within these nightmarish structures. Despite the lack of precise descriptions of the various locations in the story, Walpole conveyed a sense of architectural anguish and oppression he had been able to observe in Piranesi's etchings, a painter and engraver that he had exalted and promoted. Walpole was aware of the sublime and dreamlike nature of Piranesi (Wendort 2001: 162). Piranesi's ancient ruins, frightening vaults, and gloomy prisons were intricate and surreal labyrinths imbued with a sense of latent danger, which bewildered and bewitched viewers. Ergo, the mysterious Castle of Otranto was less a geographical entity than the result of Walpole's architectural fantasy mingled with his original reinterpretation of Piranesi's dismal geometries inspiring astonishment, anguish and awe, some of the feelings Burke considered a fundamental source of the sublime.

At the very beginning of the story, after a gigantic supernatural helmet outside the castle smashes Conrad, the first lines of the novel introduce Manfred, his father, Hippolita [sic], his mother, and Matilda, his sister, who are in great shock. Instead of going into the courtyard in the aftermath of the tragedy, they remain inside the building as if they were captives. When Matilda retires, we learn that she goes to "her chamber", while Manfred, the story's most important character, muses on his son's death in his own chamber. The author does not give any factual or realistic descriptions of furniture, styles or structures and architectural accounts are vague, an aspect that leads to a restricted and cramped view of the castle interior. This oppressive sense of confined space obliges the reader to remain in constant contact with the characters' limited perspective. Whereas other characters start to be moving freely, the castle becomes an impediment for Manfred. Even his secluded and passive wife Hippolita, despite having been ordered by her tyrannical husband to remain in her room, wanders freely and goes to the monastery to meet the mysterious Father Jerome, the other character free to move to and fro all the locations in the story with an unusual, and almost supernatural, rapidity. Once the limits of spaces are trespassed, other dire events take place, such as tragic deaths outside the castle walls, or the manifestation of a ghost exiting the frame of a painting.

Walpole supplies some elements about the mysterious chronology of the story in his first preface to *The Castle of Otranto*. He adds that "the Spanish names of the domestics seem to indicate that this work was not composed until the establishment of the Aragon kings in Naples had made Spanish appellations familiar in that country" (*WO*: 4). However, the characters' names do not always follow the rule that Walpole anticipates in his preface. A literary Gothic-related aspect is the interchangeability of Italian and Spanish names, settings, and even words, and Walpole's *Otranto* is no exception. A similar example is in Lewis's *The Monk,* in which characters use Italian words when in distress despite living in Spanish locations and contexts. In *The Castle of Otranto*, the characters' names curiously sound Teutonic in Manfred's family (Manfred, Conrad, Matilda). In particular, the name "Manfred" recalls the Hohenstaufen heir living during the mid-thirteenth century. Redbeard's grandson, the historical Manfred died at a relatively young age in 1266, the last king of his dynasty. Like the protagonist of *The Castle of Otranto*, he was a usurper and sat on the throne of his nephew Conradin, the legitimate heir, who mysteriously died when he was still an adolescent, like *Otranto*'s Conrad. According to a legend, Manfred's father, Frederick II Hohenstaufen, suddenly fell ill in the prime of his life and succumbed to a strange and incomprehensible death, perhaps caused by a poison supposedly prepared by Manfred himself. It was an intricate event in medieval history that might have provided narrative material for many an author of horror stories. A history enthusiast, Walpole probably had some knowledge of these events. In the novel, ruthless Manfred's archenemy, Frederic, can sound either Mediterranean or Germanic, a duplicity that reflects the strange personality of the character, initially a formidable enemy, and then an improbable ally. Other characters' names sound Italian (Isabella, Bianca), or even Greek (Theodore, Hippolita). Potential antagonists sound French and Spanish (Gerome, Jaquez, and Diego). The two worlds, Northern and Southern, are blended in a form of bizarre onomastics, which Walpole probably inherited from Shakespeare. This sort of exotic tendency was to influence Walpole's imitators in the process of defining the protagonists' names in most horror stories.

A contradiction tending to paradox dominates the exordium of Gothic literature. The perspective of the term gothic changed and started to express typical northern culture and translate the positive values of its superiority, which had become evident after the publication of *Otranto* and *Ossian*. For this reason, it is unclear why southern and Mediterranean places were chosen as Gothic locations in many of the stories, or why northern countries, connected to lofty Germanic ideals, presented dark and cruel shadows when settings of Gothic novels were in the North. Clara Reeve (*The English Baron*), Sophia Lee and Charlotte Smith produced Gothic stories one or two decades after the publication of *The Castle of Otranto*, but they chose to set them in the North. Like her Gothic imitators Eliza Parsons and Francis Lathom, Radcliffe herself opted for a northern atmosphere for her first novel (*The Castles of Athlin and Dunbayne*).

The atmosphere in *The Castle of Otranto* may not be genuinely Gothic as far as history, art, and architecture are concerned. However, the constant fear, the supernatural occurrences and the horror dominating the scenes were to become the basis of Gothic narratives. Longueil added that Walpole's novel introduced a new and lasting nuance of the word Gothic, linked to gloomy atmospheres and inexplicable mysteries. Mark Madoff (1979) justifies the lack of historical accuracy in *The Castle of Otranto*, counterbalanced as it is by the functional use of the past. On the other hand, Samuel Kliger (1952) writes, in stark contrast to Longueil, that the mythology of the Gothic had started as a political term in the seventeenth century when the supporters of parliamentary monarchy interpreted the Gothic-Saxons and their common assemblies as a proto-example of democratic discussions. Undoubtedly, the word Gothic acquired a completely new linguistic and cultural nuance after Walpole's *Otranto*, but its different meanings remained ambiguous, oftentimes contradictory, or even antithetical. Walpole's blatant anachronisms and the lack of precision have also been interpreted as a form of rupture between a mythical past based on a system of alliances dictated by paternal functions, embodied by Manfred and the unsettling aspects of modern romantic desire, reflected in Theodore.

Published two years before *Otranto*, Hurd's (1762: 193) work had not only exalted the dignity of the gothic ideals connected to ancient northern tribes but had also fervently praised the value of ancient romances: "The ages, we call barbarous, present us with many a subject of curious speculation. What for instance is more remarkable than the Gothic CHIVALRY. Or than the spirit of ROMANCE, which took its rise from that singular institution? Nothing in human nature, my dear friend, is without its reasons". Hurd's foundational text, organised in philosophic-literary letters exchanged between great authors of the past develops two original ideas: the new meaning of the term gothic, complementary to an ideal period of heroic values embodied in chivalry, and the exaltation of the literary form of *"Romance"*, generated by stories of chivalry with a moral message. Hurd gives dignity to romance as an expression of art inspired by enchanted narrations:

The Spirit of Chivalry was a fire that soon spent itself: but that of *Romance*, which was kindled at it, burnt long, and continued its light and heat even to the politer ages. The greatest geniuses of our own and foreign countries, such as Ariosto and Tasso in Italy, and Spenser and Milton in England were seduced by these barbarities of their forefathers; were even charmed by the *Gothic* Romance. Was this caprice and absurdity in them? Or, may there not be something in the *Gothic* Romance peculiarly suited to the views of a genius, and to the ends of poetry? [...] The circumstances of the *Gothic* fictions and manners must be pointed out (195–196).

If the "greatest geniuses" of the past were fascinated by romance, Hurd comments, this form of literature must certainly be superior. However, the romances created in France in the seventeenth century are not worth mentioning, while Medieval and Renaissance literary endeavours, known as romances and containing a mixture of heroism, magic and love, are for Hurd evidence of great forms of art. In all probability, Walpole absorbed Hurd's considerations and adroitly captured the new spirit of the times by choosing the subtitle "A Gothic Story" and developing the idea of romance. After explaining the definition of romance–and the distinction between old and new romance–in his second preface, he justified the use of this literary construction for the development of his novel, based on "the powers of fancy" (*WO*: 7). After Hurd had underlined the higher significance of romance, which influenced Walpole, both Radcliffe and Lewis rejected mundane forms of realism and remained attached to an old style in the tradition of Dante, Ariosto and the mythical legends of the Middle Ages, trying to give a new form of dignity to their romances. They were frustrated in their intent by hordes of imitators, busy at creating inflationary numbers of popular terror novels, inevitably devaluing their personal efforts. Gothic imitators transformed the newly revived genre in a second-hand literary production. That romance was deemed an important form of literary creation is demonstrated in Nathan Drake's essay on *Gothic Superstition* (1798), which he included in the collection entitled *Literary Hours* published in 1800. Arthur Cooke (1951: 24) indicated that romance was highly encouraged and claimed, "Drake pointed out that the eighteenth century *romance* writers had made use of one branch of the Gothic supernatural, employing only those effects which were productive of horror and terror. There was, he added, an entirely different branch of medieval superstition, which had so far been disregarded by contemporary writers". Chaucer, Spenser, Ariosto and Shakespeare had used this literary form, which included magical beings such as "elves" and "fairies" that Cooke defines as "sportive", or, in the contemporary sense, fantasy creatures. On the other hand, Botting (1996: 26) uses James Beattie's essay *On Fable and Romance* (1783) to draw a distinction between novel and romance. According to Botting, "[Beattie's] essay argues that Cervantes's *Don Quixote* signals the end of the old or medieval *romance* and the emergence of the modern *romance* or novel [...] Novels are divided into serious and comic forms. However, Beattie's essay concludes in a cautionary way, describing *romance*s as a dangerous recreation", a prejudice pervading the literary criticism of the time, which partly contrasts Hurd's study on romance and ideally rejects an infamous text by Ferrante Pallavicino published in 1642 that we analyse in the chapter dedicated to Radcliffe. Both terms, gothic and romance, pervade an indefinite territory and oscillate between the grandiose and the undignified, a dichotomy that still seems to persist.

Some incongruous aspects in Walpole's story are worth exploring: ineffective communications and limited perspectives are among his narrative strategies to convey high levels of suspense. Notwithstanding all the various plausible hypotheses about the creation of the early Gothic as a new literary genre, the first Gothic narrative starts with an intrinsic imprecision. *Otranto* reflects, on the one hand, the general preference of the reading public for exotic narrations and locations while, on the other hand, it tends to create an Italianate background reproducing a stereotyped and fabricated idea of Italy and the South, filtered by a British perspective, which does not fully reflect reality. As Williams (2006: 22) puts it, the reading public was eager for "otherness" and "exoticism", and Italy could provide both. "Walpole's choice seems so suitable that critics have seldom ventured beyond a few generalizations about these continental places as the obvious 'other' for late eighteenth-century Britain: absolutist and long-standing feudal governments in contrast to English 'liberty', 'superstitious' Roman Catholicism in contrast to enlightened Protestantism. [...] Fantasies of 'otherness' are historically contingent", but are determined by "a private dimension as well".

A further aspect is the increasing need, not new in literature, for strong emotions, generally satisfied through images of fear and terror. Clery (1995) justifies the development of contexts of mystery and fear in eighteenth-century England with a greater demand for spirituality. She also highlights how Addison and other literati had welcomed the use of the supernatural in dramatic stories, provided they imitated the Classics. Concerning the supernatural and ghostly latencies, the literature of Antiquity offers many examples of horror. Ghosts and the supernatural were copious in Greek and Latin literature and can be found in a relevant number of works by Aristophanes, Euripides, Aeschylus, Hesiod, Herodotus, Homer, Plutarch, Apuleius, Lucan, Horace, Ovid, Macrobius, Plautus, Tacitus and Seneca. Even the bucolic Virgil dedicated some of his verses to the horrid descriptions of supernatural events. One of the few authors apparently rejecting any form of magic or superstition was Cicero: *De Divinatione* (44 BCE), treated supernatural themes with irony and contempt, even though Cicero himself used horror as a literary device to effectively convey some of his ideas. Thanks to his classical education, and his journeys through Italy, Walpole was a connoisseur of Latin and Greek literature, and his works show evident traces of Antiquity.

Investigating the "development of the emotion of fear" characterising the 1760s in Britain, Clery (1995) starts her analysis from the 1762 "case of the Cock Lane Ghost", just two years before the publication of Walpole's novel. According to Clery, however, the presence of the supernatural in literature dates back to the seventeenth century. The increase in the apparitions of ghosts and the proliferation of their descriptions supposedly undermined atheism and created a connection with the after-world. Conversely, ghosts and the supernatural in Walpole do not reveal a theological need to connect with spiritual entities. Using the presence of ghosts in *Otranto* is rather a narrative strategy that he admittedly borrowed from Shakespeare, whose reputation had been increasing ever since the 1737 Licensing Act, and whose plays were represented at frequent intervals. Walpole affirmed he mostly borrowed from the tragedies of *Hamlet* and *Macbeth*, even though the sources of *Otranto* are wider. One of the sources for Shakespeare's bloodiest and most intense tragedies is the first-century Roman philosopher, historian and playwright Seneca (Jordi Coral Escolá 2007). Based on extreme violence and horror, Seneca's stories were powerfully tragic examples and provided material for *The Castle of Otranto*'s strange events. Revenging ghosts and megalomaniac tyrants are a frequent dramatic strategy in Senecan drama, as Susanna Braund (2013) has highlighted. Their presence is horrifying, meant to destroy guilty and innocent characters alike.

Interestingly enough, tyrants and ghosts become an essential part in the construction of Walpole's novel. The first ghostly presence appears in the form of the giant helmet, a synecdoche for the ancient legitimate king, striking the usurper's doomed heir. Similarly, Seneca's ghosts generally inaugurate the story, and are sometimes part of the chorus announcing tragic events as in *Thyestes* (64 CE), a tragedy with some similarities with *Otranto*. Originated from a Greek myth, the story introduces Tantalus' ghost, called by the Furies from his tomb to haunt his cruel and revengeful heirs, guilty of atrocities carried out to usurp the throne, and destined to gruesome technophagy (inspiring *Titus Andronicus*'s horrors). Whereas Seneca's figure of a vengeful and ruthless tyrant is moulded on the historical persona of Emperor Nero, fictional Manfred, a real master of deceit in his own view, embodies Walpole's emblem of the tyrant yearning for power. He is, au contraire, turned into an inept figure, doomed to succumb to events instead of controlling them, even though he inexorably becomes a filicide. The Classical mould is latent, but conspicuous and it highlights Walpole's respect for the Classics, also confirmed in his next oeuvres and the problematic play *The Mysterious Mother* (1768). Williams (1995) points up the reverence that Walpole had shown for the tragic Greeks that he wanted to celebrate by writing *The Mysterious Mother*, a dark story of incest following Aeschylus's example of the unnatural, however unconscious, love between a mother and her son.

Confirming his respect for classical canons, Walpole organised *The Castle of Otranto* in five chapters, reproducing a standard dramatic structure used for classical plays, following the Aristotelian unities. Walpole declares that his work is a "romance", but also a "drama". The events take place in three distinct settings, the castle, the monastery, and the nearby church of Saint Nicholas. Their proximity denotes the unity of place, whereas the chronological brevity of the story, lasting less than twenty-four hours, honours the unity of time. The unity of action is not clearly delineated, even though Manfred's paroxysm seems to represent the main action in the plot. After Conrad is killed by the supernatural helmet before reaching the chapel where his "hasty" wedding should be celebrated (*WO*: 15), frenzy begins and Manfred's obsessive behaviour is unchained. He stalks the other characters while he is himself incessantly haunted by horrid visions of death. As Elisabeth Napier (1987: 88–89) claims:

The tonal instability of the *Castle of Otranto* leads an air of recklessness to the novel that is intensified by the story's pace. [...] There are no digressions, unseasonable descriptions, or long speeches. Every sentence carries the action forward. The excitement is constantly renewed. [...] The pace of Walpole's tale begins to escalate immediately after the introduction of the main characters and the relation of the prophecy [concerning] his family and his power.

What Napier calls "recklessness in the story's pace" is justified by William Marshal, Walpole's pseudonym, in the first Preface, "There is no bombast, no similies, no flowers, digressions, or unnecessary descriptions. Everything tends directly to the catastrophe" (*WO*: 4). After the short-lived shock of his son's inexplicable death, Manfred becomes the main character of the story. He decides to act immediately, but his frenzied activities are under the sign of futility. The more he frets, the less he can accomplish any action or obtain any concrete results. He is incapable of acting effectively to change the turn of events, and all his desires remain frustrated. Sentencing a young peasant, Theodore, to death simply because he was a witness to Conrad's violent end, divorcing his wife, Hippolita, making an alliance with his enemy, Frederic, trying to seduce Isabella (the girl engaged to his son) and, most important of all, saving his usurped kingdom are all projects included in his secret agenda, which he is nonetheless incapable of carrying out. He moves around the castle, turned into a suffocating space that he cannot fully control and where he is virtually entrapped. His incestuous desire and his fatal crime involving his innocent heirs is a Senecan vestige in a story that is indebted to various authors for its development. The power of Shakespearean influence is particularly strong in some sections of the novel, which is a sort of re-visitation of Hamlet's tragedy, in consideration of the emotional paralysis that characterises Manfred. However, the role of the son revenging his father is reversed in the figure of a father, desirous to honour his son's memory—an action that he can never accomplish, or that he does not really want to pursue.

On a linguistic level, the story proceeds through a lack of convincing communication: Manfred orders his servants to do things for him, but their linguistic interaction is not complete, as they are taken by a sort of aphasia, blocking their verbal exchanges, especially when the situation is on the brink of drama. The servants' dialogic interventions should serve as an interlude in the narration, in imitation of Shakespeare's farcical intermezzos meant to release some of the distressing tension, but their function is not exclusively comic. Their words are broken and communication is imperfect on three different occasions, causing frustration and rage in Manfred. His patriarchal power and his irrational violence are diluted by his servants' inefficiency, ineptitude and linguistic inertia. The first time verbal interaction stagnates is when the frightened servants are unable to speak and explain what they witnessed outside the castle a few moments before. Once they are inside the castle, they cannot utter the words to describe Conrad's horrible death, "clashed to pieces" by the helmet fallen from the sky. The second time that the dialogue is incomplete is when Manfred asks his servants if they were able to find Conrad's bride-to-be, Isabella, now a fugitive, trying to escape from Otranto: the two servants continue delaying their answers, motivating their incapacity with extreme fear. The third time, the dialogue between Manfred and Bianca–his daughter's maid–does not proceed because of the servant's ambiguity and cunning reluctance in answering Manfred's questions. Manfred is frustrated, enraged and offended. Because of these obstacles, he gradually seems to lose all authority, as he does not have access to essential knowledge, shared by other characters instead. Walpole motivates the insertion of these pseudo comic intermissions to add realism as well as irony to the various scenes, in the same way as Shakespeare was able to mix genres in his works. Manfred can only communicate smoothly with his servants once, but the disclosure he obtains tragically makes him commit a fatally irreversible act.

The characters' limited perspective is one of Walpole's most salient narrative aspects together with oppressive obscurity. "In much early Gothic fiction, darkness is the locus of torment, punishment, mystery, corruption and insanity" (Cavallaro 2002: 26) and darkness becomes an interesting aspect of the narration in *The Castle of Otranto*. When Isabella, pursues her flight from lustful Manfred, intent upon trying to seduce and eventually marry her to secure his dynasty, she finds herself in a vault surrounded by darkness, again a possible memory of Piranesi's architectural nightmares. She can hear a voice, but she cannot see the person come to her aid. Similarly, Matilda eavesdrops on a person's lament through her window at night, but she cannot see the young man uttering sweet words of love for her, a clear echo of the balcony scene in Shakespeare's *Romeo and Juliet*. Characters walk through darkness when Theodore and Isabella meet again while escaping from the castle for different reasons. They are together in the forest among "gloomiest shades". Darkness is equally dominant in the story when Manfred takes action for the first time and goes out of the castle, or at least, this is the first time that the reader can see him go outside his mansion:

In the gloominess of the night, [...] Manfred, whose spirits were inflamed, and whom Isabella had driven from her on his arguing his passion with too little reserve, did not doubt but the inquietude she had expressed had been occasioned by her impatience to meet Theodore. Provoked by this conjecture, and enraged at her father [Frederic], he hastened secretly to the great church. Gliding softly between the aisles, and guided by an imperfect gleam that shone faintly through the illuminated windows, he stole towards the tomb of Alfonso. (*WO*: 104)

Indifferent to the soft light of the moon that may help him see, Manfred is blinded by the flames of his passion and the pangs of his jealousy, which lead him to the murder of an innocent and his inevitable destiny. Walpole has also astutely inserted a political idea in his gory drama. It might be worth mentioning Chapter VII of the Renaissance political essay *The Prince* (1513) in relation to Manfred's useless strategies to preserve his usurped throne. The chapter is dedicated to those rulers able to acquire their position thanks to favourable coincidences, or by means of violence and wars. The well-known author, Nicolò Machiavelli, explains that this form of power might be extremely volatile and dangerous, as those who govern by virtue of violent action, not through hereditary succession, face higher risks of losing their power. Manfred belongs to the category of usurpers and is keenly aware of the impending danger. No matter how much effort he puts into his actions, he cannot hold his position and is doomed to lose both his power and his kingdom. However, whereas for Machiavelli the reasons for defeat belong to the consequences of human miscalculations and/or adverse events, in Manfred's case he is ousted by supernatural intervention and the presence of vindictive ghosts.

The Castle of Otranto displays a recurring feature that makes the scenes appear claustrophobic. This limited vision conveys high levels of insecurity and fear and the characters cannot explain or see what is happening during the most crucial events, especially when Theodore, Isabella, and Matilda are concerned. When they hear mysterious sounds, when they are in danger, when they are trying to escape, and on various other occasions, they are constantly in the dark and unable to decipher their environment. Despite their predicament, they manage to explore different spaces inside the castle and the surrounding territory. On the contrary, Manfred appears cloistered in his labyrinthine castle, a place of metaphorical seclusion and immobility. This seems to reverse the trope of the castle as a labyrinth to entrap powerless women, envisaged by Ferguson Ellis (1989), as it imprisons the male character, instead. The tyrannical protagonist is in perpetual but ineffective motion and his agitation is inconclusive: there is no real movement, no control over the territory, and no power over the other dramatis personae in the story. As a result of his suffocating confinement and his constant rage, the protagonist reproduces the repetitive movements of wild animals inside a cage. The pervasiveness of darkness is a constant factor in the development of the story in *The Castle of Otranto*, a narrative device that becomes recurrent in Gothic novels, even though the Gothic did not precisely invent this particular preference for obscurity. Paulette Choné (2001) and Pascal Quignard (2015) have demonstrated through iconographic analyses how darkness and gloomy contexts were invariably chosen to express themes of anguish and/or sensuality in both painting and literature before the advent of the Gothic. The night and its darkness represent an important trope commonly exploited during the eighteenth century. The protagonists of libertine novels act during the night, and obscurity becomes the preferred setting for Pre-Romantic and Graveyard Poets. Seven years before *Otranto* was printed, Burke's essay analysed the importance of darkness and its deep connections with sublime feelings. The century was dominated by the Enlightenment, the cultural light of the epoch that had a mysterious counterpart in literary scenes of nocturnal shadows. Darkness in *Otranto* is a dense metaphor with multiple meanings. It is the emblem of dark political machinations, a metonymy for mysterious events, an allegory of the different characters' sexual desires, both latent and manifest, and a symbol of Manfred's patriarchal attitudes and dangerously predatory character.

Walpole does not use landscape in his text, which is, on the contrary, a prerogative characterising Beckford, Radcliffe and Robinson. There is only a single and bizarre exception, as the romance includes one unclear mention of the sea and the coast, basic features of the real Otranto, built on and surrounded by water. Apart from this and other misrepresentations, the text contains only one allusion to the landscape. The novel includes the episode of the forest where two characters, Theodore and Isabella, have flown to escape the dangers menacing them. A simple peasant, whose real identity is about to be discovered, Theodore is unjustly condemned to death for witnessing Conrad's final moments, whereas Isabella, late Conrad's fiancée, absconds from Manfred's dangerous courtship, and tries therefore to abandon the castle in secret. The two elements of the landscape are the forest and the grotto. The forest is "to the east" of the castle. Behind "that forest is a chain of rocks, hollowed into a labyrinth of caverns" (*WO*: 71). Theodore escapes with a heavy heart from the castle, forced to abandon his newfound love, Manfred's mistreated daughter Matilda. Instead of hiding, as Father Jerome has suggested, he starts "hovering between the castle and the monastery [...] determined to repair to the forest that Matilda had pointed out to him" (WO: 70). Theodore's solitary wandering precedes the autobiographical *Reveries of a Solitary Walker* by Jean-Jacques Rousseau, published almost twenty years later in 1782. An outsider, and an unwilling witness of the young prince's bizarre death, Theodore slowly acquires importance within the story. First, he becomes a victim of Manfred's ire and risks his life to help Isabella and protect Matilda. Facing an unjust predicament for witnessing a supernatural event, which does not depend on him, Theodore unchains Manfred's unjustified wrath because he secretly represents his nemesis. Turned into a fugitive, he soon becomes Matilda's love interest and Isabella's champion. A pivotal element in the denouement of Walpole's Gothic romance, a deep sense of inexplicable melancholia oppresses Theodore and, in spite of his heroism, his romantic involvement and the partially positive dénouement that revolutionises his life, sadness dominates his soul. Like some male characters in Shakespeare's *Love Labour Lost* (1598) and other plays, Theodore manifests a deep but incomprehensible sense of grief. Peter Walmsley (2006) links that particular feeling to a Renaissance attitude, which Robert Burton extensively described in *The Anatomy of Melancholy* (1621). The feeling has been analysed, Walmsley indicates, in recent years in its manifestations during the Enlightenment. Knowing his friend Gray's *Elegy Written in a Country Churchyard* (1751) and other poetic creations, Walpole may have imitated the images of an inspiring, isolated context accompanied by a nostalgic mood. The few pages describing Theodore's melancholic disposition, however marginal in the plot, provide the beginning of a narrative scheme that will be absorbed and reproduced by Gothic (and also Romantic) authors following Walpole's steps. "Regardless of the tempest [announced] by a clap of thunder", Theodore goes in search of "the gloomiest shades, as best suited to the pleasing melancholy that reigned in his mind" (WO: 71). The place is surrounded by the "power of darkness". He imagines creatures living in the solitary places he crosses and thinks they might be "hermits". He even becomes frightened in thinking of the "evil spirits" that may inhabit mysterious "cavities". Theodore "indulges in his curiosity in exploring the secret recesses of this labyrinth" when he finds Isabella. He tries to help the frightened girl by hiding her in "a cavern" and "its inmost recesses" (WO: 73). He [intends] to conduct [her] "to the most private cavity of these rocks" (WO: 74). Napier (1987: 21) highlights Walpole's extremely ambiguous images and language and their latent sense of burlesque, which may be unconscious or deliberately chosen. W. Lewis (1969: iv) finds a justification for Walpole's choices: "he accepted the artificiality of the genre he had chosen as composers of grand opera and ballet accept the artificiality of their arts. If we also accept it in this spirit, we find that the style, at first apparently comic, becomes rather pleasant and even stirring". Apart from Walpole's tone, partly pathetic, and sometimes tending to the bathetic, the presence of caves, similar to grottoes, has a symbolic and cultural value, influenced by contemporary fashion and iconographies. A famous contemporary painter of Walpole, very popular in Britain during the second half of the eighteenth century, Joseph Wright of Derby painted imposing and romantic caves. His variants of an Italian marine landscape with gloomy grottoes near the sea, such as *Grotto in the Gulf of Salerno* (1774), were highly appreciated. Wright had gone to Italy to find inspiration, but he painted dramatic and spectacular caves around 1770, after Walpole had written *The Castle of Otranto*. To find caves in painting in periods preceding Walpole's romance, we have to go back to the previous century for the outstanding rendering of grottoes. The German Philipp Peter Roos moved to Italy where he was nicknamed Rosa da Tivoli, in honour of the more famous Salvator Rosa. A popular painter specialised in landscape, active in the second half of the seventeenth century, he created pastoral images of grottoes. Before him, the Flemish painter, David Teniers the Younger, painted an impressive *Landscape with Grotto and a Group of Gypsies* in the 1640s. The rocks at the entrance resemble a dark, fierce animal looming over tiny human figures. Between 1639 and 1640, Salvator Rosa completed the *Grotto con cascata* (*Grotto with Waterfall*), a perfect representation of the sublime spirit of the mysterious and the majestic in nature. The painting's dramatic rays of light, imposing ruins and melancholic atmosphere introduced sublime images with a touch of picturesque. These paintings' iconographic value was to influence eighteenth-century Gothic writers and Romantic poets and they certainly impressed Walpole, who was preoccupied with completing his majestic history of art while he completed *Otranto*.

The representations of natural grottoes, started in the seventeenth century, derived from a Renaissance iconographic and architectural trend, even though some specimens were created earlier, during the period known as Humanism (*Quattrocento* in Italian). Hazelle Jackson provides an interesting historical insight (2001: 4–6):

Renaissance architects in Italy revived the grottoes of Ancient Rome to add an air of historical authenticity to their neoclassical villas and gardens. The celebrated architect Leon Battista Alberti even gives a 'recipe' in *De Re Aedificatoria* (1485) for pouring green molten wax on to the stonework of a new grotto to simulate mossy growth. Renaissance grottoes were decorated with chips of lava rock and coloured marble, shells, coral, pebbles and *spugne*, plastered textures to resemble coral. Renaissance gardens were designed with complex iconography. Francesco Colonna's mythic romance, *The Dream of Polyphilus* (1499), which describes the hero's search for self-knowledge in an architectural classical landscape, was the theme for many allegorical gardens where a grotto with a water source was reached at the top of a terraced hillside, signifying the visitor's spiritual journey through life to knowledge. [...] By the seventeenth century, the influence of the Renaissance had spread out across Europe and reached the British Isles.

Rocks, caves and grottoes had been introduced in paintings at the end of the fifteenth century when the emphasis of representation was no longer on the sacred protagonists of the scene exclusively, but on the elements of nature. Landscapes acquired importance both in the Florentine and in the Venetian Renaissance. The most enigmatic and intriguing representation of a cave was Leonardo's metaphorical painting *Virgin of the Rocks* (1508), connoting an idea of unfathomable mystery concerning both the enigmatic protagonists of the canvas, and the landscape surrounding them, enclosed in an ideal arch of rocks, which absorbs all the viewer's attention.

Walpole inherited his father's paintings from various epochs and became a compulsive art collector himself. The catalogue (1832) of Strawberry Hill's art pieces, specifically created for an auction, only partially provides an idea of the immense cultural patrimony owned by Walpole and may in part justify how his writings, in general, and *Otranto*, in particular, with its special visual character, were influenced by the artistic masterpieces that populated his life. In his Gothic story, Walpole introduces the image of the cavern, later absorbed by the early Gothic iconography, as in the crucial scenes of Dacre's *Zofloya* taking place in a cave populated with murderous banditti. Walpole might have had many an occasion to observe romantic grottoes in his private art collections, or during his journeys. Unlike some of his imitators, and especially Radcliffe, Walpole did not seem to follow the principles that Burke had expressed in his popular essay concerning the sublimity of landscapes, and did not consider them essential in his narrative. It is true, however, that ghosts and the constant state of fear, together with disconcerting events conveying terror, can be included in the category of the sublime. Despite the scarce descriptions of landscape and nature, *Otranto*'s visual impact is astonishing in many parts of the novel due to its supernatural effects.

Besides, we should note that Walpole considers the tragedy of his characters as a prototype of the sublime, as he explains in his preface.

What characterises Walpole's novel is its cultural hybridism, founded on his Classical mould, shared by contemporary literati and intellectuals. A convinced classicist, the philosopher Henry Home, better known as Lord Kames, had addressed the preface of his *Elements of Criticism* (1761) to King George III, three years before Walpole published his literary phenomenon. After observing discrepancies in the nation's system of education, and influenced by John Locke's theories of sensory perception, also developed by David Hume, Kames proposed to enhance literary and artistic knowledge and stressed the importance of "the visual theory". In the first part of his text, Kames studies nature and human passions, whereas he delineates elements of rhetoric and literary criticism in the second part. He introduces the original notion of the ideal presence, founded on the primacy of sight and the importance of memory in the mechanism of reading. Kames argues that literature derives power from its ability to convince readers that they are present in the book world (Westover 2012: 18). Walpole absorbs this idea and the visual acquires relevance in *The Castle of Otranto* as well as in subsequent Gothic stories. A further fundamental aspect in Lord Kames' programme is the emphasis on Ancient Greece's ideals for the improvement of education, for both high and low classes: his cultural proposals were essential to understand the role that Antiquity still played during the second part of the eighteenth century. In the changing flow of history and literature, scholars in Europe and in Britain had steadily exalted the importance of Antiquity, which is recognisable among Walpole's narrative trickeries. He applied Kames' theory of visual impact, as his novel contains impressive images, concerning the dramatic phases of the story, structurally imbibed with echoes from Antiquity.

Napier considers *The Castle of Otranto* a "pleasanterie" (1987: 80). In effect, Walpole's divertissement is a sort of original, even if naive, cultural syncretism. When Matilda decides to save Theodore, disobeying her father's orders not to climb the Black Tower, she represents an example of rebellion against the patriarchal structure. Like heroines described in Boccaccio's heartbreaking love stories, or like Shakespearian young heroines, such as Hermia in *Midsummer Nights' Dream* (1595), Desdemona in *Othello* (1605), or Juliet in *Romeo and Juliet* (1594), Matilda goes against her father's will and risks her life for love's sake. Theodore views her as "an angel" or "a blessed saint" (*WO*: 69), using French Troubadours' courtly imagery to define her. Matilda is an apparition that changes Theodore's mind forever. She not only concretely saves him from certain death but also conquers his heart forever so that he "fervently entreated her permission to swear himself eternally her knight" (*WO*: 70), reproducing a medieval chivalric model. Therefore, he becomes her platonic and adoring slave of love, but their union is impossible, as Walpole's story follows the canons of medieval idealised love. Dante and Petrarch exalt the absence of the loved ones, especially after their death, as guiding spirits of their lives. The closure in Walpole's story does not follow the style of sentimental novels, but it is not completely compatible with the Gothic atmosphere either. "[Theodore] could know no happiness but in the society of one with whom he could forever indulge the melancholy that had taken possession of his soul" (*WO*: 110). Theodore gives voice to his deep sorrow, resonating with Dante's distress and anguish in losing Beatrice, and Petrarch's lifelong nostalgia for his beloved Laura. The victim of despondency, Theodore is slave to a languid feeling, assimilating him to medieval poets. Walmsley (2009) surmises that the problem of melancholy, thoroughly analysed by Burton in his encyclopaedic publication on the complexity of the feeling, continued to be part of intellectual men's cultural background in the eighteenth century. In his essay "Of the Delicacy of State and Passion", David Hume (1904: 6) speaks of "the agreeable melancholy, which, of all disposition of the mind, is the best suited to love and friendship". The early Gothic is pervaded by this sense of melancholia, sublimated in Walpole and, later, in the works by Gothic novelists, especially Radcliffe and Robinson.

The trajectory of the Gothic novel after Walpole is not linear. Walpole's work could not boast any imitators for more than a decade. Thirteen years later Reeve published *The Old English Baron* (1777), clearly influenced by Walpole. It, however, represented Reeve's re-interpretation of the Gothic in its simplified form. It was necessary to wait another ten years for the flourishing of Gothic fiction that was to become sensational at the end of the century. Despite the rigid rules envisaged by Reeve to be applied to Gothic romances, in contrast with *Otranto*'s excesses, Walpole's novel was the main source of inspiration for Gothic novelists. The supernatural, historicism, mysterious landscapes, old castles, gloomy dungeons and persecuted heroines are some of the multiple ingredients chosen by Walpole, and later used by a variety of authors in the decades after *Otranto*. If the equation Gothic fiction and Italian settings generally dominates critical interpretations, it is because Walpole's novel created a connection, introduced a special locus, an exotic place, absorbed by readers' imagination as the geography of horror. The attraction for distant places depends on cultural oppositions, and the disparaging consideration of the "other", derived from the British sense of superiority (Williams

1995: 22). Some scholars interpret "Italian" Gothic as the allegory of a sharp, one-way criticism against Catholicism, even though frightening stories are set in a variety of places, and horror can be experienced at every latitude and in quite different contexts alien to religion.

Despite receiving positive critical attention, Walpole's work was not appreciated unanimously. The usual Coleridge was dismissive of Walpole and detested his tragedy *The Mysterious Mother* for its incestuous content, even though the plot is moulded on Greek and Latin tragedies (Williams 1995), and the most horrible events are accomplished before the truth is finally discovered. Gamer (2000) considers Coleridge's and Wordsworth's systematic negative criticism of Walpole and Gothic novelists as a strategy to highlight the importance of Romanticism and does not dismiss the idea that the failure of their Gothic literary experiments may have dictated their open rejection of the Gothic genre.

One of Walpole's merits was his ability to mingle different sources and assemble multiple narrative modes. The alternating introduction of semi-farcical situations, such as the verbose servants slowing down the action with their useless blabbering, later inherited by Radcliffe and Lewis, represents a theatrical strategy and an original mixing of genres. Walpole's technique shows his need to blend tragic and comic issues. Adopting Frederic Jameson's post-modern definition of the pastiche as an ironic form of mimicry, Jesse Molesworth (2009: 405) identifies this stylistic aspect in Lewis's *The Monk*, which is deeply influenced by Walpole's work. The pastiche is a peculiar form of literature that can be adapted to Walpole's romance, Beckford's visionary creation and Lewis's strange novel. Even though Scott had considered *The Castle of Otranto* a remarkable novel, critical reception of Walpole's work was not always positive. The originality that Walpole professed may not have been entirely genuine, but he was undeniably the beginner of a new form of writing, even though his secret desire was for uniqueness was to be frustrated. As Lilley (2013: 93) puts it, Walpole's fascination is with the economy of "uniquity" and the collection of the inessential: "Walpole's famous rehabilitation of the Gothic imagines precisely such a dwelling on the commonplace of uniquity". The book that had to be unique in Walpole's mind became the primeval source of all Gothic fiction, still offering fresh perspectives and original interpretations today.

I too lament thy fate,
Fall'n by the children's hands. Th'avenging god
Dispenses justice when occasion calls.
Dreadful thy punishment.
(Euripides. *Electra*)

O Fear, I know thee by my throbbing heart
(William Collins. *Ode to Fear*)

A problematic and scandalous novel, *The Monk* (1796) took Gothic atmospheres to the extreme. It was harshly criticised and even demonised for its eroticism and violence arousing aversion in many critics and readers, but for all that, Lewis's text contains interesting and original characteristics that are worth studying. The novel is an ensemble of influences that make it a composite literary work offering multiple perspectives and interpretations. This section intends to demonstrate that among the numerous sources and themes that are instrumental in the novel's development, some hidden elements emerge, which belong to Antiquity, as the Classics, both Greek and Latin, seem to play an important role in the development of the plot. The object of opposing critical points of view, starting from its anonymous publication, the novel features multifaceted contents, liable to be variously interpreted, and disturbing images that still shock readers today. The literary universe, exploited by Lewis to write *The Monk*, is complex and invariably concealed by the writer's preoccupation with keeping readers unaware of his borrowings. His method was "assimilative and heterogeneous" (J. Watt 1999: 86) and confirms the hypothesis of multiple sources for a novel, which stages a kaleidoscope of suggestions and wide cultural substrata. Information about Lewis can be gathered among documents diligently collected by one of Lewis's mother's friends after his premature death. Margaret Baron Wilson (1839) published an apologetic biography with an extensive collection of Lewis's writings and correspondence, including unpublished works. Baron Wilson added commentaries that tended less to appreciate

Lewis's works than make the reader aware of the writer's inexperience when he became suddenly famous after publishing his first (and only) novel when still a teenager. She stressed that Lewis was an affectionate child and a man of good principles, in contrast with existing prejudices about his morality consequent on his scandalous novel.

Descending from an affluent family, young Lewis had many opportunities to improve his education. He did not actually go on a Grand Tour, but alternated between several months in foreign countries and periods at university in England. Like many of his British compatriots, he had been to France, where he had spent his summer holidays in 1791: "he was young, rich and fond of pleasures" and seemed the hedonistic doppelgänger of Raymond, an adventurous character in *The Monk*: (Louis Peck 1961: 17). While in Paris, he may have observed the degeneration of the political situation and the beginning of the Terror. As much as a number of critics consider the French period influential in the process of writing and the historian Emmet Kennedy (1989) considered Lewis's work to be a parable of the events taking place in France after 1789 (Ellis 2000: 81), Lewis's correspondence from Paris is poor of details and betrays a certain superficiality liable to exclude any political awareness or involvement on his part. Notwithstanding these limitations, some scholars agree that Lewis may have started *The Monk* in Paris. That said, recognising the sources from French works is a challenging task because the cultural ideas from France were innumerable and the country's culture had constantly attracted Britain (as we can see in the chapter about "Gothic Miscellanea"). Whereas the German literary influence was sudden and, like the poetic current of *Sturm und Drang*, had taken Britain and Europe by surprise during the second half of the eighteenth century, the impact of France was steadier and had a longer tradition in British culture. Translated editions from French contemporary and past authors were published regularly (Peter France 2005). French scholars continuingly translated from the Classics, and their French translations were "englished", as was the case of Boileau's adaptation of Longinus's text *On The Sublime*, which was to have a significant part in the literature of the long eighteenth century. In Paris, Lewis probably became familiar with plays, novels and seventeenth-century romances. Lewis's stay in Germany after his sojourn in France may have represented an important experience for his literary inspiration, a fact supported by James Watt (1999) and Maurice Lévy (1995), which cannot, however, be fully substantiated. Be that as it may, in his correspondence, Lewis very often mentions what he is writing, not what he is reading. In one letter, he laconically describes his meeting with Goethe: "Among other people to whom I have been introduced, are the sister of Schweter, the composer, and M. de Goëthe [sic], the celebrated author of Werter [sic]; so you should not be surprised if I shoot myself one of these fine mornings" (Baron Wilson I: 71–72). The wrong spelling and the silly joke betray Lewis's superficiality and his scarce knowledge of Goethe's novel, translated in English in 1779 (Appelbaum 2004). He minimised its cultural impact and he did not spell the German language correctly, which is rather bizarre, as he was supposedly studying hard at the time to become a literary translator. Lewis's third stay abroad, organised by his father to enhance his diplomatic career, was in Holland, where the young man had a difficult time socialising with people he did not like, as he confesses in his correspondence included in Baron Wilson's biography. After living in Holland in 1794 as a cultural *attaché* at the British Embassy, a post he deeply disliked, Lewis brought back to England the complete manuscript of *The Monk*, written on Dutch paper (Baron Wilson I: 120), which may prove that the novel was ready by 1794. However, Groom (2016) does not consider the "Dutch paper" as sound evidence, as it was imported to England in large quantities. The manuscript discovered in 1959 was probably used for the first edition, but was unsigned (Howard Anderson 2008) and extensively corrected by an anonymous hand (Macdonald 2000: 133, 211), a fact which still intrigues early Gothic specialists. Lévy and Peck, have assumed that *The Monk* might have been the final draft of a story Lewis had been working on ever since his return from France in 1792, an idea apparently demonstrated by Lewis's letter dated 25 March 1792, informing his mother he had started a story similar to *Otranto*. However, Lewis had been a scribbler since childhood and produced many a draft, generally incomplete. The final draft of *The Monk* may have been ready in September 1794, leading some critics to suppose that the first publication could be dated back to 1795, with a limited number of copies printed for a restricted circle of people, a hypothesis supported by both Walter Scott and Margaret Oliphant. Two copies, found in the 1960s, are marked 1795, therefore an earlier edition for *The Monk* is considered acceptable (McEvoy 2008).

Born in July 1775, the same year as Jane Austen, Lewis was twenty when he published his novel. Publishing at a young age was not so exceptional a feature, as both Gothic and Romantic authors were precocious. Lewis was to start a diplomatic and political career thanks to the role his father had played in the British Government, but his love for literature, inherited from his mother, was stronger than his taste for politics. During his studies and political training, he wrote to his mother many a time about his desire to be a full-time writer, a wish that she apparently encouraged (Byron and Punter 1999: 141). Despite his family's opulence, Lewis's letters show an obsessive pecuniary interest connected with the idea of publishing and translating, in all probability, due to the desire of supporting his mother financially after her scandalous divorce from his father. Lewis continued writing while enjoying his privileged life in England (Miles 2000: 44) until his father's death in 1812, when he abandoned writing and started travelling to and from Europe to visit his plantations in Jamaica before his sudden death at sea (Macdonald 2000). Lewis never replicated the success of *The Monk*. His subsequent literary works were based on Gothic clichés, while the tales, ballads and plays he published were mostly translations, showing that imitation seemed a stronger force than genuine inspiration (Gamer 1999a). Lewis's famous statement in a letter to his friend Scott, "A ghost or a witch is a *sine qua non* ingredient in all the dishes of which I mean to compose my hobgoblin repast" (Peck 1962: 118), highlights his indestructible Gothic mania. Byron's poetical satire aimed at mocking both Lewis and Scott, *English Bards and Scotch Reviewers* (1809), described Lewis as "Apollo's sexton", an epithet he deeply resented for its low-class connotation and funereal metaphor (Macdonald 2000: 187).

The Monk created an uproar of protests against its crude representation of violence, sexuality and incest. "Dislocation becomes as evident in the novel as to make it grotesque like *Otranto* and less credible than Ann Radcliffe's Gothic novels" (Punter 1995: 85). Its excessive graphic descriptions mixed with libertine discourse was scandalous because it addressed a wide audience, including many young women (Ellis 2000: 115). If the young clergyman Vicesimus Knox, in his *Essays Moral and Literary* published in 1778, had written that the novels of Richardson, Smollett, and Fielding had probably contributed to the "degeneracy of the age" (Gallaway 1940: 1042), he was certainly outraged when Lewis's novel appeared only two decades later. Even though the high doses of sexual desire in *The Monk* may seem a novelty, it is true that stories with erotic potential had preceded Lewis's novel, with unfortunate epilogues in Richardson, or humorously gross results in Fielding. Different forms of sexual transgressions could be found in "Tory novels of seduction", including *Clarissa*, a narrative typology that "had remained always keenly aware of the complicity of the oppressed, and deliberately complicated the categories of victim and victimiser" (Toni Bowers 2004: 157). A solution in defence of these narrating choices was to cast the responsibility onto victims, considered as sinful as the perpetrators.

Contemporary critical reviews of *The Monk* showed two trends: literary magazines of liberal or Jacobin political orientation, such as *The*

Monthly Mirror, The Analytical Review and *The Morning Chronicle* appreciated the novelty of the story and narrative contradictions were justified by the author's young age. In the *Analytical Review* dated October 1796 (Ellis 2000: 109), an anonymous critic, identified as Mary Wollstonecraft, provides a justification for Ambrosio's fall for the mysteriously captivating Matilda: "Indeed the whole temptation is so artfully contrived that a man [...] would deserve to be damned who could resist even devilish spells, conducted with such address, and assuming such heavenly forms". Readers and critics had two opposing reactions about the novel following their political orientations, one revolutionary and the other loyalist/conservative. Conservative magazines (*The British Critic, The Critical Review,* and *The European Magazine*) highlighted the scandalous side of the story by exposing the dangerous presence of the revolutionary germ. When Lewis decided to go public, the protests became innumerable due to the title M.P, written near the author's name. Once the author's identity was evident, the need to underline the work's detrimental features and Lewis's insistence on lustful details increased exponentially. In his 1797 review of *The Monk*, Coleridge could not forgive the young man for various reasons, and, in particular, the problematic episode of the Holy Scriptures. In one scene, the main character, impatient to seduce his love interest, furtively enters her room and examines what she is reading. He does not recognise the biblical text immediately because it is handwritten and censored by the girl's mother to avoid problematic passages. The anti-Catholic connotations of the novel and the description of the clergy's hypocrisy could be acceptable and welcome (Napier 1987; Rix 2014; Groom 2016). On the contrary, Lewis's description "suggesting that the Bible was unfit reading material for young girls" unchained an uproar of protests (Miles 1999: 23), even though John Locke himself had promoted a partial censorship of the sacred text in his treatise on education. It was with another contemporary critic that things went even further: James Mathias's accusations of indecency in *The Pursuits of Literature* (1798) forced Lewis to make modifications to his text. Like Coleridge, Mathias could not tolerate that the writer was a Member of Parliament and defined Lewis a pernicious example for society, comparing him to the "shameful" author of *Fanny Hill* (1749), John Cleland (Gamer 1999b: 1059). Problems did not arise with sex or religion exclusively: politics was another serious topic in that period and the case of the publisher Thomas Williams demonstrates this axiom, as he had faced legal proceedings in 1792 for publishing Thomas Paine's political work *The Age of Reason*. On the other hand, Lewis's publisher, Joseph Bell, became extremely rich by secretly selling the uncensored copies for twice their price before publishing the censored version (Groom 2016). Gamer explains that the result of Mathias's accusations was not only an expurgated version of *The Monk* in 1798 but also a permanent negative mark on Lewis's reputation, perpetuated in the next fifty years or more and worsened by the erroneous identification of the author with his negative hero (Clery 1995). From a contemporary critical perspective, Lewis's choice to mention the censored passages in the Bible could be considered less blasphemous than meta-literary. Through this intrinsic proleptic characteristic of the story, Lewis was anticipating the reactions to his novel and the consequent scandal, as he provided an extra-textual example of a perfect valid form of writing (the Biblical text), liable to be misunderstood due to an excess of moralism (Lauren Fitzgerald 2003). The initially welcome nickname "Monk Lewis" slowly but inevitably became a burden. That the shocking images in his novel had created the sediment of an unfavourable opinion was clear in the negative obituary, written in *The Tickler* in December 1818 after his death at sea, which confirmed that his literary persona was never fully accepted.

The novel was, nonetheless, creative and resourceful and, most of all, interspersed with diverse literary allusions. By way of illustration, an ingenious Renaissance text may provide an interrelation with *The Monk*. *Gargantua* (1535) tells a fantastic tale reversing medieval superstitious clichés. François Rabelais's main character, the homonymous giant Gargantua offers a convent to his friend Friar John to establish the Abbey of Thélème, ("free will" in Greek). Both girls and boys are accepted, and they spend their days studying, playing music, practising healthy activities, and celebrating the beauty of nature. "Monks" and "nuns" of this special abbey are free to leave if they want and they can even fall in love and tie the knot. A great humanist and man of science, Rabelais created his personal utopia for a better world without the obligations imposed by religion. Lewis turns Rabelais's utopian dream into a nightmare: the French writer's positive allegory is transformed into a hell. *The Monk*'s bizarre contiguity between the nunnery and the monastery does not create a harmonious union of excellent human beings, but only contributes to cruelty and horror, a ghastly experience that many saw as a form of sharp criticism of Catholic contexts. Although the violence unchained against the nuns may seem to reproduce a startling revolutionary event and dark, nocturnal images promote a state of constant fear, they recall a cultural trend that had been developed in the last two decades before Lewis's novel. During the 1770s and 1780s, Fuseli's various versions of *The Nightmare,* and its intriguing iconography, had increased the appreciation of *Schwarzkunststudien*, dark studies in the visual arts (Ellis 2000: 5). Goethe's *Werther* and German tales of mysteries had promoted the general taste for affrighting stories (Watt 1999: 71), which were popularised by imitators. Nevertheless, the creativity shown in *The Monk* was by far superior to the stylistics of popular novels. The furious mob's bloody riot in the final part of the novel was also interpreted as a metaphor for dramatic actions taking place in France, as Andrew L. Cooper notices (2001: 26):

The scene not only resonates with the Revolution, it also justifies it somewhat by portraying the target of revolt as truly corrupt and by allowing the ravages of the mob, indirectly, to bring about a happy ending for the surviving characters. Jacobin or not, Lewis infuses his work with ambivalent revolutionary tendencies that, no matter how obscure, were intolerable for anxious English critics.

Hume (1969) thought that Lewis, like Beckford before him and Mary Shelley and Maturin after him, wanted to shock his readers with graphic descriptions of murder and rape and was not interested, like Walpole or Radcliffe, in simply maintaining an atmosphere of suspense. Chaplin (2011) considers Lewis the initiator of terror narratives with his explicit descriptions of death and degradation, whereas Ian Duncan (1992) identifies analogies in extreme patriarchal attitudes in both Lewis's and Beckford's works.

Critical literature on *The Monk* has discovered themes opening the way to contrasting interpretations. Puzzling and ambiguous, either a puppet in the hands of demonic forces, or a cruel hypocrite, monk Ambrosio's pathological behaviours have been observed in psychoanalytical or Foucauldian terms (Kosofsky Sedgwick 1980; Miles 1993; Williams 1995; Doyle 2004). Peter Brooks (2004) considers Ambrosio a symbol of "desacralization" in contrast with the Enlightenment, which promoted religious tolerance, but never denied the importance of the sacred. Molesworth (2006) identifies the intermingling of both obsolete and original narrative models in anticipation of post-modernism, while Macdonald (2006) corroborates the intertextual nature of *The Monk,* connecting it with *Clarissa* (1748), and considering Ambrosio a new embodiment of Lovelace, as both characters indicate that violence is a token of their dangerous forms of love. The interrelation between Lewis and Richardson seems to substantiate the recent idea that frontiers between literary eras are becoming less definite (Wallace 2009), with influences and ideas from previous periods contributing to the diagenesis of the Gothic novels. James Grantham Turner (2005) demonstrates how unexpected libertine aspects emerge from Richardson's correspondence—his secret wish to possess a magic ring—when he comments on Denis Diderot's *Les Bijoux Indiscrets* (1748), published in the same year as *Clarissa*. Such a pseudo libertine attitude in Richardson seems to confirm how literature is a network of more or less evident interconnections. Apart from Lovelace, other villains preceded Ambrosio. The protagonist of Smollett's *Adventures of Ferdinand Count Fathom*'s (1753) is an incomparable example of human depravity for Scott, while the French Vicomte de Valmont in *Dangerous Liaisons* (*Les Liaisons Dangereuses* 1782) is callous and inhuman. De Sade's characters are horribly cruel (unbearably worse than Ambrosio) but are figurines in a grand tableau, as in *Justine, or the Misfortunes of Virtue* (1791), written in 1787 when the author was imprisoned in the Bastille (*Justine, ou le Infortunes de la Vertu*, in the original French). Ambrosio's several predecessors are cruel and/or libertine. The British monthly *Lady's Magazine*, usually read by Lewis's mother, published *The Monk and The Robbers* in instalments from August to November 1794, thus confirming the existence of various forms of libertine literature in England with different levels of scandalous content. Coincidentally, the tale in *The Lady's Magazine* was the story of a monk, Ambrose, seducing a young girl, Annette.

The double standard of moral rigour and lethal hypocrisy was present in British literature. Ambrosio's initial apparently irreproachable attitude condemning Agnes is strictly linked to Shakespeare's Angelo's hidden hypocrisy in *Measure for Measure*, as the epigraph of *The Monk*'s first chapter clearly corroborates. However, there exist more moulds behind Ambrosio's persona. Some seven years before the genesis of Ambrosio, Moore's title character of the book *Zeluco* (1789) was the epitome of all aberrations. A dialectical, but often complementary, opposite of libertine callousness, sentimentalism equally played a role in the creation of Gothic stories. Specimens of sentimentalism and so-called "benevolism" in *The Monk* seem to be inherited from Henry Mackenzie's *The Man of Feelings* (1771). The main character, Harvey, is the prototype of a "benevolist" man sacrificing himself for other people's sake. For that reason, he loses money, social recognition and love because of his unselfishness, while his immolation is useless. Similarly, some characters in *The Monk* show their good will and tender feelings, which are, however, ineffectual. In a similar way, *The Monk*'s Antonia is a person incapable of understanding the world because of her "hermeneutic inertia" (Miles 1993). Her male counterpart, and love interest, Lorenzo, is equally guilty, if not of limited understanding, at least of slowness of action. In spite of his nightmares warning him about Antonia's impending ghastly destiny, he does nothing to protect her and even accepts Elvira's absurd rejection of his courtship with unnerving indolence. He fails to activate his group of acquaintances to help Antonia recover her title and legacy in time and does not intervene to save his own sister, Agnes, apathetically accepting the news of her death without investigating the truth.

The complex literary panorama of the eighteenth century offered a vast range of sources for Lewis. A scarcely known author, William Hutchinson, published a tale similar to *The Monk* with supernatural events and a duplicitous friar (Clery 1995: 80). Even if the tale, called *The Hermitage* (1772), was not successful, young Lewis may have read the unusual novel and added it to his personal reservoir of imagination for future use. An almost imperceptible trace lies in the term "hermitage", which describes a doomful corner, however beautiful, in Ambrosio's cloister, which represents the beginning of his fall. Lewis was probably influenced by poems that described sad feelings and gloomy experiences, such as Robert Blair's *The Grave* (1743), which became part of an epigraph in *The Monk*. William Collins's *Ode to Fear* (1746), following the classical Greek structure of strophe, epode and antistrophe, represents a mixture of classical versification and themes instilled with a new form of sensibility, conveying dark evocations, essential ingredients that were eagerly absorbed by novelists for their Gothic plots. Lewis admitted being influenced by Radcliffe and Godwin. Apparently ignored by Lewis, Beckford's colourful inventions and his pastiche mode may have provided fresh ideas to Lewis. Hybridism is crucial in the development of *The Monk* and reflects the taste for assembling different narrative modes typical of *Otranto* (Clery 1995) and *Vathek*. Alternating semi-farcical situations with dramatic events is a technique inherited from Walpole and Radcliffe that Lewis verbosely exploits.

The Monk introduces a number of funny situations, clashing with the gloomy plots and subplots. One example is when Raymond's new valet, Theodore, decides to dedicate himself to the composition of ambiguously erotic odes. Another, almost grotesque, incident occurs when Agnes, dressed as the ghost of the Bleeding Nun, is forced to ring the bell of her castle after missing the meeting with Raymond for their elopement, since her fiancé has unknowingly escaped with the real ghost. A comic interlude takes place when Antonia's aunt, Leonella, flirts with a young knight mistaking him for a suitor. A ghost's apparition in Antonia's house, supposed to be ominous, unchains hilarious reactions instead. The ensuing comic effect is dissonant and incompatible with the overall upsetting context. Defined as the typical Gothic (Punter 1996; Botting 1993; Corinna Wagner 2012; Cooper 2001), and the atypical Gothic novel

(J. Watt 1999), Lewis's work flaunts an exaggerated cultural melange. The young writer's readings and his rich cultural background, which included knowledge of Greek, Latin, French and Italian Classics (and, supposedly, German), contributed to the creation of his enigmatic literary achievement. Lewis's result is full of horror and mystery featuring picaresque situations that intermingle with seemingly sentimental moments: his is a novel that creates misleading expectations of sentimentalism before developing shocking images of horror.

Lewis's novel developed in a period when writers and poets alike were trying to break with tradition and give voice to new narrative forms. However, in the changing flow of history and literature, scholars in Europe and Britain had steadily exalted the importance of Antiquity, which could be appreciated in its original forms or in translations. Multiple renderings of one Classical work were made by different scholars, and translating was popular during the eighteenth century contributing to the cultural dissemination of the Classics: "[t]he activity of translation is quite expressly the animating power in the English poetic tradition, and the decisive influence in canon-formation" (Gillespie and Hopkins 2005: 15). Literary translations were essential in the progress of culture by introducing both the known and the unknown and were instrumental in the spreading of Classical knowledge. Texts such as Johnson's *Lives of the Poets* (1781) provide evidence of the plethora of British poets' literary translations, which had a "profound influence on the embryonic English novel" (Adam Rounce 2007: 327). Both a philosophical development and a legacy of the Classics, imagination dominated the entire eighteenth century and was not an exclusive prerogative of the Romantic period. The Gothic was one of the most evident consequences of that latent passion for mystery, which was, however, imbued with Classicism.

In his preface to *The Monk* (called "Advertisement"), Lewis inserted Addison's short story of *Santon Barsisa* (sometimes attributed to Steele) among his sources. Included in *The Guardian* in 1713, it represents an "apophthegm" on human hypocrisy. Its Latin epigraph is taken from Book IV of Ovid's *Metamorphoses* featuring a sibylline sentence by the Greek goddess Athena: "it is useful to learn from our enemies as well". A holy man of moral perfection, Santon Barsisa, famous for performing prodigious miracles, requests that the Caliph's daughter, seriously ill, be brought to his cavern to cure her. In fact, the devil in person has secretly advised the old man to enjoy her beautiful body while she is unconscious. After his lustful act, the hermit kills the girl, but he is discovered and condemned to death. Barsisa asks the devil for help while climbing the gibbet. Despite his promise to save him, the devil takes his soul and lets him die. The fable represents a meditation on falsity and the pernicious influence of devilish forces, even in the best human beings. Dense with cultural elements and symbolical teachings, Barsisa's story shows the red line uniting different writers and currents throughout the eighteenth century. Following the Enlightenment canons of effective brevity, Addison's apophthegm represents an evident inspiration for *The Monk*. Lewis was particularly astute in defining his sources in a preface that also served to hide a variety of other texts inspiring his writing.

Lewis's desire to shock and frighten was partly governed by tragic Classical masterpieces that he knew from his formative years. That classical inspiration was essential for writing was reiterated by various authors and essayists of the time. The "Antiquity Muse" had been praised in William Duff's *Essay on Original Genius* (1767: 24), published in the decade of *Otranto*:

It is likewise to be observed that we regard the *Iliad* and the *Odyssey* as works of genius, not only because there appears an astonishing display of Imagination in the invention of characters and incidents in those admired productions, but also because that imagination is regulated by the nicest judgment.

Duff's hypothesis that "genius" is based on "Imagination", the great creative force behind the works of the Classics, recalls Addison's dictum and Winckelmann's works on Greek and Latin Antiquity, which had exalted their precious teachings and launched the germ of Neo-Classicism. Duff adapts to literature the German scholar's principles in *History of Ancient Art* (1764).

The Monk includes the dialectics of Antiquity and is deeply influenced by Greek Drama. If it is true that Lewis received multiple cultural influences both at home and abroad, he was not exempt from the cultural force of the Classics being part of the affluent elite. The influx of Antiquity can be uncovered in the most distressful parts of *The Monk*, in which classical learning has a preponderant weight. Ambrosio's hamartia tragically involves the beautiful and innocent Antonia and her mother Elvira; a chain of guilt is cast upon the three characters. Apart from marrying above her social level, Elvira incomprehensibly abandoned her first-born Ambrosio and turned him into an orphan, destined to years of solitude in a monastery. Williams (1995) regards this aspect as the source of Ambrosio's unconscious desire for revenge, making him a Gothic version of a tragic *Oedipus*. This is the first of the ominous mistakes that involve Elvira's responsibility for her family's destiny. She is equally guilty towards her daughter Antonia because she bases the girl's education on censorship, dooming her to a dangerous ignorance of the world's cruelty. Because of her linguistic and social dumbness, Antonia becomes insensitive to clearly uttered messages and cannot recognise dangers around her. Elvira's further mistake is breaking the idyll between Antonia and the aristocratic Lorenzo de Medina in spite of the young man's best intentions and social importance that could have protected Antonia from evil. Elvira's misunderstanding of events is even more dangerous than Antonia's cognitive "inertia" (Miles 1993) and lack of understanding. The family circle succumbs to Ambrosio destroying his own blood, a terrible predestination that the hypocrisy of his "void repentance" (Williams 1995; Napier 1987) does not preserve from the final horror.

The three characters' fate involves a sort of tragic mythology denoting a classical matrix. Juvenile inexperience is not the only factor behind the genesis of *The Monk's* horrible scenes. It is not a kind of provocative experimentation either. Tragic events transcend the novel's boundaries to hark back to the times of Greek tragedies, transposed in Lewis's horrid images, even though he does not follow Aristotelian rules as strictly as Walpole had done with *Otranto*. However, the horror of events that degenerate into a final catastrophe involving innocent victims, complies with the Aristotelian rules concerning pathos. Lewis also adheres to Seneca's dramatic criterion, which includes spirits and entities, necessary to strengthen the sense of inevitable calamity, which is out of human control. The ghosts populating Lewis's novel are the spirits of women, the Bleeding Nun and Elvira. The former belongs to the past, while the latter is still part of the present, as she appears as a character and, later, as a ghost. The spirits in Walpole's *Otranto* and Radcliffe's *Romance of the Forest* are patriarchal figures meant to re-establish a lost order, whereas the two female ghosts in Lewis have devastating effects for the young protagonists of the story. The dead Bleeding Nun almost kills Raymond when she elopes with him, replacing Agnes, and Elvira's ghost confirms her powerlessness even in the afterlife.

The Monk is shocking for its sudden changes of register when frightening occurrences follow comic moments. Brooks (2004: 255) interestingly suggests that "in *The Monk*, the forces which we deny, mock, put down, are precisely those that assert their reality and smite at us (a situation familiar to Euripides)". Euripides' influence seems to play a major role in some of the novel's most tragic circumstances. Together with Aeschylus and Sophocles, Euripides is part of the great dramatic triad of Ancient Greece. His remaining titles feature several female protagonists and their psychological torments. After Dryden's critically acclaimed adaptation of *Oedipus*, remaining in the repertory for various decades, Paulina Kewes explains that (2005: 247):

Several turn-of-the-century playwrights followed Dryden and Nathaniel Lee in rewriting Greek tragedians, mainly Euripides, as he seemed to offer what audiences particularly appreciated, *pathos* and women in distress. [...] The hierarchy of the three tragedians are revised in the Restoration. Aeschylus had been seen as the most primitive of the trio, and none of his plays had been either translated or adapted for theatrical presentations. With Aeschylus largely neglected, Sophocles was universally seen as the most refined of the three tragedians, and Euripides as the most adept at representing extremes of emotions.

Electra presents Orestes murdering his mother Clytemnestra out of revenge. His action is the consequence of inevitable vengeance for her betrayal. Even though Orestes consciously plans the murder to honour his father Agamemnon's heroic and political figure, the abomination of his act involves dire effects. Ambrosio's matricide is provoked by his delirious passion for the sister that he does not recognise as such, and the murder scene contains the perception of a tragic and ineluctable fate. However, Orestes and Ambrosio are not responsible for their crimes. Electra persuades her brother, Orestes, to kill their mother just as Matilda pertinaciously pushes Ambrosio to commit a matricide. Unlike Orestes, Ambrosio is not conscious of the true nature of his murder, which he wrongly feels is commanded by his urge to have a carnal intercourse with the one he does not know to be his kin. In the end, both characters are punished for their murders: the Erinyes pursue Orestes, whereas hideous creatures torment Ambrosio. Matricide and incest turn the characters into highly dramatic figures and are the manifestations of ill-fated predestinations. Ancestors' crimes cannot be erased and are transmitted to their scions. Elvira and her counterpart, Clytemnestra, typify the figures of guilty mothers. Like Clytemnestra, Elvira's guilt is passed down to her children. In his complexity, Ambrosio is also a Gothic version of Sophocles' *Oedipus Rex* because he is symbolically blind when he can see, and is physically blind during his unbearable torment when he finally understands the terrible truth. Ambrosio also seems a reversed version of Sophocles' tragic hero because he kills the mother in place of the father. The desire for the mother's body, which the Greek hero unconsciously feels, is not present in Ambrosio, equally unaware of the truth. The aspect that Oedipus and Ambrosio share is the lack of recognition of their kin leading to their incestuous acts. Oedipus kills the tyrant (the father) and marries the woman (the mother) to bring order to society, whereas he unconsciously unchains disorder and despair. Despite its tragic intensity, Ambrosio's act is not heroic. On the contrary, Orestes consciously kills his mother to honour and avenge his father's memory, and is ready to unchain chaos and the gods' fury. While Lewis describes every gesture of Ambrosio's murder, Euripides does not show the act directly. Clytemnestra has entered her house after a long explanatory dialogue with her daughter Electra, unmovable in her deep hatred. Orestes goes inside the house, and the audience can simply hear his mother's cries of despair while the Chorus discloses the action:

> *Chorus*   Heard you in the house her cry?
> *Clytem*   Ah me, ah me!
> *Chorus*   I too lament thy fate,
> Fall'n by the children's hands. Th'avenging god
> Dispenses justice when occasion calls
> Dreadful thy punishment; but dreadful deeds
> Unhappy, 'gainst thy husband did'st thou dare.
> Stained with their mother's recent-streaming blood,
> See, from the house they come, terrible proof
> Of ruthless slaughter. (*Electra*: 192)

Euripides' tragedy unfolds when the mother, the daughter and the son are reunited after years of separation. Ambrosio strangles his unknown mother in her house while his unknown sister is present, but sleeping. Euripides' drama stresses the fatality of sinful parents and ancestors. Clytemnestra has betrayed and killed her husband Agamemnon. Therefore, her crime is evident and punishment inevitable. Elvira, conversely, seems an innocent victim, and her sacrifice is incomprehensible. However, we may argue that her fault is of a moral nature, as all her choices have baneful consequences: she abandons Ambrosio when he is still an infant and is unconsciously the cause of his life in solitude. She dangerously promotes Antonia's existential ignorance and irresponsibly rejects Lorenzo's protection. Ambrosio acts unconsciously against the mother he does not know and destroys the sister he cannot acknowledge in time. He is a tragic hero, but is not entitled to tragic nobility because of his lustful desires and cowardice.

Further complex classical elements can be traced in *The Monk*. Euripides' prominence can be found once more in the central tale within the tale, "*un roman à tiroirs*" according to Brooks (2004), represented by Raymond's narration of his strange experience to his friend Lorenzo. After a dangerous adventure with banditti in the forest, the young man manages to escape from a risky situation and save an aristocratic woman. The Duchess misinterprets Raymond's tender interest and the occurrence resembles an amusing entr'acte in the style of Marivaux's and Beaumarchais's romantic comedies. However, the misunderstanding acquires a tragic tone when the deceived Duchess becomes a cruel antagonist, partially moulded on Euripides' enraged Phaedra in *Hippolytus*. Phaedra's story is also narrated in Ovid's *Heroides* (circa 20 BCE), a text that "combines a collection of single letters in elegiac verse imagined as written by deserted heroines of epic and tragedy with several paired letters featuring epistles of men answered by women" (Garth Tissol 2005: 204). These include Phaedra's dramatic letter to Hippolytus. In *The Monk*, the Duchess's sudden uncontrollable desire to destroy Raymond strangely resembles Euripides' Phaedra's cruel fury inasmuch as both women are ready to punish the contemptuously indifferent young men rejecting their love. Donna Rodolpha's rage suddenly replaces her loving feeling for Raymond, just as the Maenads suddenly unchain their violence against Pentheus in *The Bacchae* (405 BCE), also by Euripides. Whereas Dionysus' supernatural power guides the Bacchae, the Duchess is controlled by her desire for revenge, which will fall upon Raymond's fiancée Agnes, hence imprisoned in a convent. Whereas Raymond luckily escapes all punishment, Ambrosio seems to replace him in that he faces a destiny similar to the young hero in Euripides. A similar traumatic finale unites Hippolytus, unjustly disgraced, and Ambrosio, justly punished. While riding his chariot away from his country after his father Theseus has exiled him, wrongly believing he is guilty; a dangerous mythical creature sent by Venus and Poseidon chases Hippolytus. The monstrous creature throws him down the side of high mountains. Beaten and bruised, Hippolytus is covered in blood while suffering excruciating pain. So is Ambrosio, "thrown upon steep mountains", left to die a miserable death, "blind, maimed, helpless and despairing" (*The Monk*: 442). Hippolytus' and Ambrosio's horrid deaths are similar and the Euripidean influence plays an important role in the creation of Lewis's cruel denouement. Hippolytus' final moment is narrated by a group of men, his loyal friends and companions in his exile decreed by his jealous father, erroneously convinced his son seduced his second wife and committed incestuous adultery:

> So we made our way
> Up toward the desert region, where the bay
> Curls to a promontory near the verge

Of our Trozên, facing the southward surge
Of Saron's gulf. Just there an angry sound,
Slow-swelling, like God's thunder underground,
Broke on us, and we trembled. (*Hippolytus*: 62)

Hippolytus's companions describe frightening phenomena that disheartened them in spite of their courage. Violent natural phenomena are a reflection of the tragedy that occurs. Like Euripides, Seneca dedicates a tragedy to *Phaedra*'s story (circa 54 CE) and develops the plot following Euripides' mould, but his emphasis is on Poseidon's ravaging sea-storm, which causes Hippolytus' death. Seneca's influence in the description of Ambrosio's end is feeble, while the Greek playwright's conclusion resonates with the ending of *The Monk*. Hippolytus is approaching a solitary "desert region", analogous to the place where Ambrosio has been placed by devilish forces. The young Greek hero is riding his chariot as if he were flying, seeking to separate himself from his father and his land. The strange and upsetting "sound" announces the presence of supernatural agents ready to envelop the victim. In *The Monk*, a demon throws Ambrosio onto a stony desert where a horrendous finale takes place, whereas Hippolytus is in control of the action until his last breath:

Then straight upon the team wild terror fell.
Howbeit, the Prince, cool-eyed and knowing well
Each changing mood a horse has, gripped the reins;
Coiled them around his body; and then, as strains
A sailor backward 'gainst his oar, so swung
Back in the chariot straining. (*Hippolytus*: 62–63)

A brave hunter, Hippolytus is convinced that he can face nature's fury and disengage himself from the dramatic chains of events threatening him. After his capture by the Inquisition, Ambrosio is sure that he can overcome all incidents until a mysterious demonic being carries him away. Ambrosio shares Hippolytus's tranquillity before the tragedy. The following lines feature Hippolytus's struggle against supernatural forces:

But the young
Wild steeds bit hard the curb, and fled afar;
Nor rein nor guiling hand nor morticed car
Stayed them at all. For when he veered them round,
And aimed their flying feet to grassy ground,

In front uprose that Thing, and turned again
The four great coursers, terror-mad. But when
Their blind rage drove them toward the rocky places,
Silent, and ever nearer to the traces,
It followed, rockward, till one wheel-edge grazed,
The chariot trip't and flew, and all was mazed
In turmoil. Up went the wheel-box with a din,
Where the rock jagged, and nave and axle-pin.
(*Hippolytus*: 63)

A monstrous devilish creature has appeared in the form of a bull to punish Hippolytus for his blasphemy in the eyes of the goddess Venus. He is guilty because he refused passion and carnal desire, a major offence to the goddess of love. The young man is at the mercy of the savage creature while terror–for the frightening race–and horror–for the presence of monsters–become the scene's dominant factors. He has been actively reacting against dark entities, but he now loses control and turns into a passive victim, like Ambrosio:

And there – the long reins around him – there was he
Dragging, entangled irretrievably.
A dear head battering at the chariot side,
Sharp rocks, and ripped flesh, and a voice that cried:
Dash me not into nothing! [...]
All beside,
The steeds, the Horned Horror of the Tide,
Had vanished–who knows where?–in that wild land.
(*Hippolytus*: 64)

Hippolytus' tragic destiny is brutally accomplished. Euripides' progression of the dramatic scenes discloses desolate landscapes, anticipating the place where Ambrosio is flung to draw his last breath. The supernatural atmosphere brought about by devilish creatures confirms the analogies between the two young men's terrifying ends. Hippolytus has not committed the hideous crimes that Ambrosio has perpetrated. However, in the eyes of the divinity, his actions were sacrilegious because he did not show respect for Venus' commandments. A strange paradox characterises their different crimes, as Hippolytus is guilty for refusing love and rejecting passion, whereas Ambrosio is guilty because he has given in to an excess of blind passion that has turned him murderous.

Even though "Roman plays were more accessible, better known, and more frequently translated and adapted than Greek ones" (Kewes 2005: 241), Greek plays became widely known in the decades preceding the publication of *The Monk*. As a matter of fact, numerous tragic events in the novel betray a classic mould inherited from ancient Greek drama that Lewis probably knew through theatrical representations. "While Aristophanes was not translated completely until the nineteenth century, [...] British audiences were familiar with Greek playwrights. [...] In contrast to classical poetry and prose, which were translated for scribal and print publication, classical drama was in this period rendered in English to be performed" (Kewes: 249). The Greeks were not as well-known as the Latins, but progressively acquired importance in the eighteenth century, as Kewes further clarifies:

The tragic triumvirate of Aeschylus, Sophocles, and Euripides, on the other hand, steadily grew in stature. By the mid-1780s, their entire *oeuvre* was accessible to the English reader, and their assimilation to the corpus of translated literature had become one of the major developments of the reception of the Classics in the period. By the end of the eighteenth century, virtually all extant classical drama, with the exception of Aristophanes, was available in English in a variety of modes (literal versions, paraphrases, free imitations) and media (rhyming couplets, prose, and blank verse).

Lewis probably read the original Greek pieces and translated them as a linguistic exercise, a common practice in the didactic process of the period, but it could equally be possible that he had the chance of consulting English versions of the Greek dramatists. A theatre aficionado, as his correspondence and later literary works evince, Lewis had probably seen more than one classical tragedy, and he certainly knew Euripides and Sophocles, as their influence is pervading in *The Monk*'s characters' tragic interactions.

An amusing interlude between Raymond's adventure with the Bleeding Nun in the Black Forest and his return to Madrid further confirms the presence of Greek Antiquity. After listening to the verses composed by his servant, Theodore, Raymond makes an interesting comment about bad and good compositions and the constant risk of negative reception, potentially stigmatising any author (*The Monk*: 189). Raymond expresses an author's fears of being rejected, which David L. Macdonald has interpreted as a clear mirror of Lewis's inner incertitude apropos of his novel. As a sort of preventive exorcism, Lewis makes his character ridicule literary criticism, which has nevertheless the power to destroy any literary work, even the best ones. The servant writes a poem, "Love and Age", in imitation of the Greek Anacreon, a long-lived Greek lyric poet active between the sixth and fifth centuries BCE, popular with poets and literati through the eighteenth century:

> The night was dark; the wind blew cold;
> Anacreon, grown morose and old,
> Sat by his fire, and fed the cheerful flame:
> Sudden the Cottage-door expands,
> And lo! Before him Cupid stands,
> Casts round a friendly glance, and greets him by his name.

> 'What is it Thou?' the startled Sire
> In sullen tone exclaimed, while ire
> With crimson flushed his pale and wrinkled cheek:
> 'Wouldst Thou again with amorous rage
> Inflame my bosom? Steeled by age,
> Vain boy, to pierce my breast thine arrows are too weak.
> (*The Monk*: 195)

The story apparently describes a skirmish between Anacreon and Cupid. The former is reluctant, but the latter threatens the old poet with his arrows of love. The old man is not willing to resume his lyric poetry. He would like to get rid of the young, impertinent divinity, as he still remembers the pain he suffered because of the horrible pangs of unrequited love. Slowly, baby Cupid turns into a handsome young man and, once he strikes the poet with his dart, the snow starts melting and beautiful landscapes replace the aridity of winter. If carefully analysed, the poem reveals a series of double meanings strongly connected to homoerotic sensuality, especially evident in the thirteenth stanza, when we discover that Cupid is sitting on the poet's lap, reviving him. While reiterating classical influences inscribed in the novel, the choice of Anacreon conveys further libertine ideals that add to the scandalous atmosphere of *The Monk*'s plots and subplots.

The novel not only reveals elements of Greek poetry and drama but also contains several Latin Classical echoes. Among the different sources that Lewis absorbed, Latin Antiquity had no small part in the genesis of *The Monk*. Before the start of the story, Lewis inserts two Latin passages: the former is taken from Horace and the latter is a poem to introduce the story. The first quotation is an aphorism from one of Horace's epigraphs:

"Somnia, terrores magicos, miracula, fagas, nocturnos lemures, portentaque" (*The Monk*: 1). The words warn the reader and evoke "nightmares, strange events, supernatural creatures, magic and terror" that might be found in the text. The rhetorical convention of inserting Latin sentences as a preface to literary works was fashionable amongst British scholars of various epochs. Walpole had used an ironic epigraph (however misquoted) from Horace to present *The Castle of Otranto*. Apart from imitating Walpole, Lewis's choice of Horace was justified by the author's fame, as he was "much admired in the eighteenth century, and extremely influential in the English satirical tradition" (McEvoy 2008: 443). The second quotation is a poem written by Lewis in imitation of Horace's style (*The Monk*: 3) to present himself apologetically. Lewis offers the stanzas to the book and its destiny, a dedication in vogue at the time of Horace, Virgil, Ovid, and other important Latin poets. Short compositions of this kind expressed both a desire for a good reception and an apology for the possible flaws in the work. The focus is first on the effects of the book, and then Lewis formulates two hypotheses concerning the future of his novel, one negative and one positive. Finally, the author introduces his persona physically and emotionally. The conclusion is a request of forgiveness in consideration of his young age. Choosing Horace may not have been coincidental for Lewis, as the Latin poet was an important cultural reference, appreciated for his lyrical poems and stylistic elegance, while his self-descriptions, which influenced the development of autobiographies and memoirs, abounded with irony and good humour. Horace shared biographical aspects with Lewis, as the Latin poet was a man of many means thanks to his father, a public officer when Caesar ruled Rome. Horace was a contemporary of Virgil and occasionally met the younger Ovid. Mentioning Horace is therefore an astute strategy that Lewis uses to be included in the firmament of more mature and renowned writers. If Horace is important in Lewis, other Classical influences are more pervasive and need to be investigated.

With the aim of establishing the roots of the Gothic, Williams (1995: 52) has identified traces of Romantic and Gothic sensibilities in previous literary periods and convincingly states that Pope had described gloomy landscapes and dark situations that were more suitable for Gothic settings than for an Augustan poet. Echoing Ovid and inspired by Eloisa's real correspondence, Pope's *Eloisa to Abelard* (1688), which had also influenced Walpole, features a heroine who appears "inconsistent and irrational [...] hysterical, subject to fantasies of an almost psychotic intensity". Pope borrowed the Ovidian melancholy and adapted it to a sad protagonist, condemned to live inside the walls of a convent and manifesting an irrational disposition. Pope's synthesis of Eloisa's altered psychological state materialises in Lewis's main character, Ambrosio. Lewis's cultural background allowed him to understand the Classics in the original Latin, but he may have used Ovid's popular English versions. References to Ovid in *The Monk* are not as explicit as in Pope's *Eloisa* or Richardson's *Clarissa*. Richardson compares his characters to gods, goddesses, and mythological entities from *The Metamorphoses*, even though the author had no sufficient knowledge of the Classics to join modern experience to ancient stories. Douglas Murray (1991: 116) demonstrates the importance of the Latin poet in *Clarissa* and notes that Richardson acquired familiarity with the Classics despite his poor education:

> Though his schooling ended in his tenth year, and he had less Latin and Greek than Shakespeare, he developed a high degree of cultural literacy from reading, printing, theatre-going, and conversation. [...] When in *Clarissa* Richardson represented sexual struggles between the powerful and the powerless, he borrowed and adapted characters, situations, and meaning from the culturally approved treatments of the theme: the numerous Greek and Roman accounts of a god raping, or attempting to rape a mortal.

Murray also highlights that even *Pamela* (1740) contains a strong influence from Ovid and considers Richardson's young protagonist as a metaphor of Psyche, the human loved by Cupid, turned into a "godhead herself" (Murray: 117). Pamela's social ascension is comparable to a mythological apotheosis and her case of "hypergamy" or, more commonly, marrying up, provoked serious debate due to the representation of a maidservant's successful social climbing. Moreover, scholars and critics reputed *Pamela* scandalous for its multiple sexual allusions, which Richardson included to represent a moral lesson. Lewis inserts mythological contexts in more subtle ways than Richardson. Several mythological connotations in *The Monk* refer to the character of Ambrosio that Matilda considers "endowed with every virtue", a real "divinity" (*The Monk*: 56). Although the term "divinity" conveys an idea of religiosity, the deeper sense shifts towards the connotation of a pagan cult. Matilda later calls Ambrosio her "idol" (61), while Ambrosio regards Antonia as graceful as "Venus" herself and as desirable as a "nymph", imitating one of Radcliffe's clichés in defining her main characters. Like an Olympian god, he intends to seduce the mythological creature. While not easily detectable, Classical presence is ubiquitous in *The Monk*. Several events disclose an Ovidian mould and they all concern Ambrosio.

The first one takes place when Ambrosio is alone in his cell and starts admiring the beautiful image of a Madonna, seemingly looking at him with an ambiguous smile. The moment of adoration is religious, but turns into a pagan form of exaltation through a process, which becomes instrumental to Ambrosio's sexual exaltation. The definition of *"ékphrasis"*, given by Philip Hardie (2002: 193), incorporates a double structure involving what he calls "absent presence". The first level creates the illusion of presence, thanks to the power of the visual arts, while the second level tests the power of the writer, creating the illusion of an illusion. Philosopher Massimo Fusillo (2012: 34–39) carries out an interesting analysis and defines *"ékphrasis* as a verbal description of a visual representation". Fusillo investigates the literary device by analysing the *ékphrasis* of Achilles's shield in Homer's *Iliad,* whereas Hardie examines the same *trope* in the tales of Narcissus and Pygmalion in *The Metamorphoses*. Apart from the potential criticism of the Catholic Church and the superficial adoration of images that some scholars supposedly consider as one of Lewis's basic themes, the episode acquires classical connotations. Ambrosio expresses, in fact, the desire for the painting to become real; thus, he becomes similar to the pagan Pygmalion, as he has fallen in love with an art piece. Dryden's translation of *The Metamorphoses* (henceforth *Met* in quotations, with volume and page, taken from Ovid's version by Dryden) highlights the mesmerising appearance of the statue that Pygmalion has created: the sculptor "admires", "adores" and "desires" the wonderful work of art made of cold marble. His masterpiece becomes "his idol", whose face is virginal and pure. "Had she mov'd", she would have been universally considered a "living Maid". Pygmalion's artwork is so perfect that it seems to be alive and its beauty is not vulgar but conveys "Modesty" instead, as if it seemed "asham'd to move". The statue embodies a perfection that does not reflect reality and is a token of unparalleled purity, incompatible with real life women that Pygmalion seems to abhor for their intrinsically sinful nature (*Met* II: 17). Ambrosio's painting is a similar form of perfection comparable to Pygmalion's statue. The harmonious image coincidentally describes and envisions the attractiveness of the mysterious novice Rosario, later transformed into the sensual Matilda. Rosario/Matilda is a sort of first corporeal manifestation of the painting for her astounding perfection, the whiteness of her body and her apparent purity, all features recalling Pygmalion's white marble statue, described in the lines above. Innocent Antonia is a further physical manifestation of Ambrosio's painting. Her grace seems to be divine and mythical, but it is her innocent appearance that mostly attracts the monk. The modesty conveyed by both the image and the statue, incompatible with Matilda, recalls Antonia's main attributes of timidity and propriety. Even more extraordinary, the monk obtains what he was secretly asking for, while praying in front of the painting, namely a person in flesh and blood resembling the mythical image. The context is similar to the coming to life of Pygmalion's masterpiece. The result of Ambrosio's rapture in front of the Renaissance picture is the sudden appearance of a real human being, incarnated in the fake novice Rosario, Matilda's alias. The tempting portrait seems to materialise out of the frame to assume the form of a perturbingly beautiful woman, who is at first presented as an adolescent boy, whose face cannot be distinguished until a later unexpected revelation. Intriguingly, Lewis reproduces and adapts Pygmalion's story, narrated in the tenth book of Ovid's poem, by adding a deeper level of gender incertitude. Lewis inlays the episode in a context of ambiguous personation. Ironically, the mysterious, young novice Rosario enters the monk's cell seconds after Ambrosio has implored God to transform the comely image on the canvas into a real creature. Rosario's persona is initially perceived as masculine, and his status does not change for some time. He becomes Ambrosio's faithful protégé, and his companion of studies. Later the novice Rosario turns out to be the stunning Matilda. Her sensuality is dangerously seductive, as she is a miraculously perfect copy of the sacred painting. Several critics have underlined the ambiguity intrinsic in the character of Rosario/Matilda, and William Brewer (2001), among others, assumes that Matilda's indefinite essence is connected with gender uncertainty and transvestism. Like mythological Pygmalion, Ambrosio is disgusted and offended by women's licentiousness. Living in total solitude like Ambrosio, Pygmalion is a misanthrope, who has lost his faith in humankind. He is also a misogynist, who rejects the company of women, as he judges them lecherous creatures:

> Pygmalion, loathing their lascivious life,
> Abhorr'd all womankind, but most a wife;
> So single chose to live, and shunn'd to wed,
> Well pleased to want a consort of his bed;
> Yet fearing idleness, the nurse of ill,
> In sculpture exercised his happy skill,
> And carved in ivory such a maid, so fair,
> As nature could not with his art compare,
> Were she to work; but in her own defence,

Must take her pattern here, and copy hence. (*Met* II: 17)

Ambrosio inherits Pygmalion's misogyny, which manifests on several occasions. The first time readers see Ambrosio he is distant from the congregation, reciting his powerful sermon from his pulpit in the Capuchin Church. His words have a mesmerising effect on his audience. Ambrosio is proudly conscious of his beautiful voice and wonderful appearance. Once alone in his cell, he admires the imaginary woman in the painting, but despises all other women: "What charms me, when ideal and considered as a superior Being, would disgust me, become a Woman and tainted with all the failings of Mortality" (*The Monk*: 41). Ambrosio expresses the same sense of "loathing" that was uttered by Pygmalion. After rejecting the company of women, Pygmalion dedicates himself to art and sculpture and lives in a sort of monastic seclusion. He creates a statue of such ethereal and superior beauty that he falls in love with it. While embracing its ivory-white, perfect body, kissing its lips and touching its sensuous breast and limbs, he prays to the Goddess Venus for a miracle. He would like the statue to become a real woman. Most of all, he would like the statue to love him:

> Pleased with his Idol, he commends, admires,
> Adores, and last, the Thing adored desires:
> A very Virgin in her face was seen,
> And had She moved, a living Maid had been:
> One would have thought she could have stirr'd, but strove
> With Modesty, and was ashamed to move:
> Art hid with art, so well perform'd the cheat,
> It caught the carver with his own deceit. (*Met* II: 17)

The passage presents some interesting points. Pygmalion is Ambrosio's antecedent, as he lives the secluded life of a hermit and rejects the outside world. Art preserves his purity and does not allow vice to be part of his life. In the same way, Ambrosio primarily dedicates himself to religion and to intellectual activities in the monastery. The difference lies in the fact that Ambrosio has not painted the image he loves, but has received it as a mysterious gift. The statue that Pygmalion creates is characterised by two special aspects: one is supreme beauty, and the other is modesty. Beautiful Matilda and sweet Antonia share these characteristics. It is as if Pygmalion's ideal statue, which turns human, becomes Ambrosio's beautiful painting, later embodied in two equally marvellous creatures. The next lines in Dryden's translation show the wonder the sculptor feels vis-à-vis his masterpiece:

> He knows 'tis madness, yet he must adore,
> And still the more he knows it, loves the more.
> The flesh, or what so seems, he touches soft;
> Fired with this thought, at once he strain'd the breast
> And on the lips a loving kiss impress'd. (*Met* II: 18)

Once the statue becomes human, she reciprocates her creator's love. Pygmalion's story is one of the few with a positive conclusion in Ovid's *Metamorphoses* since the couple has no apparent obstacles to surmount. Considering the figure of Matilda in *The Monk,* we can observe that she is the only character left untouched by the story's problematic events. In the end, she completely disappears, and most critics see her disappearance as a confirmation of her infernal nature. However, she may be a figment of Ambrosio's imagination, intent on fantasising in front of the mysterious painting until his lustful rage explodes and affects young and naïve Antonia. Similarly, Robert Kiely (1972) posits that the dangers in Radcliffe's *Mysteries of Udolpho* do not exist, but are simply within the mind of the protagonist, Emily. In a similar way, Ambrosio seems to live in a different dimension when he is by himself. He loves the image in the painting. He would like to see it come to life and he asks God to satisfy his desire. In this first Ovidian moment, Ambrosio uses words that are almost identical to those uttered by Pygmalion, when he asks the divinity to give life to his statue:

He fixed his eyes upon a picture of the Virgin, which was suspended opposite to him: This for two years had been the Object of his increasing wonder and adoration. He paused, and gazed upon it with delight. "What beauty is in the countenance! [...] How graceful is the Turn of that head! What sweetness, yet what majesty in her divine eyes! How softly her cheek reclines upon her hand! Can the Rose vie with the blush of that cheek? Can the Lily rival the whiteness of the hand? Oh! If such a creature existed, and existed but for me! Were I permitted to twine round my fingers those golden ringlets, and press with my lips the treasures of that snowy bosom!" (*The Monk*: 40–41)

Whereas the religious Ambrosio implores his Christian God to satisfy his pagan adoration of an idol, the pagan Pygmalion addresses his religious prayer to the goddess of love:

Pygmalion offering first approach'd the shrine,
And then with prayers implored the power divine:
Almighty gods, if all we mortals want,
If all we can require, be yours to grant,
Make this fair statue mine, he would have said,
But changed the words for shame, and only pray'd,
"Give me the likeness of my ivory maid." (*Met* II: 18)

The analogy between the respective invocations of Pygmalion and Ambrosio is remarkable, and Lewis arguably had Ovid in mind when he was writing Ambrosio's adoration of the work of art. However, *The Monk* is drastically ambivalent in its inclusion of Matilda's disturbing double-faced character. Dryden's rendering of Pygmalion's statue becoming alive can be applied to the mysterious painting in the monk's cell embodied by Matilda. A Spanish-speaking audience may not grasp the duality Rosario-Matilda (male-female), linguistically acceptable by an English-speaking readership, but incomprehensible for Hispanics, as both names generally refer to female characters. It is not possible to say whether Lewis made this choice by mistake, or on purpose. More likely, he confused the Italian Rosario, masculine, with Spanish Rosario, which is feminine instead. Matilda, however, represents a disturbing ambiguity for her satanic traits: she is a dangerous charmer seducing Ambrosio's virtue. Later, Ambrosio is stupefied when he catches a glimpse of Matilda's ivory hand. Here, Lewis reiterates the impressive similarity with Ovid's tale, in which Pygmalion adores the whiteness of his ivory statue: "his heart throbbed with desire, while his hand was pressed gently by Matilda's ivory fingers" (*The Monk:* 62). A similar detail occurs when Lorenzo notices a beautiful girl representing Saint Clare during the procession's sacred representation. Surrounded by "silver clouds", "dazzling light", and with a luminous "wreath of diamonds" on her head, the nun Virginia de Villa-Franca enchanted the audience, but Lorenzo "considered her only as a fine Statue" (348), reiterating the comparison/contrast between the women in the narration and mythological beings and /or works of art.

After Ambrosio has rejected her, Matilda threatens to commit suicide. It is on that occasion that she uncovers her breast, and "[t]he Moon-beams darting full upon it, enabled the Monk to observe its dazzling whiteness" (65). Matilda's body seems to retain the beautiful ivory whiteness that Ambrosio had observed in the painting, which also corresponds to the colour of Pygmalion's statue. Ambrosio's slow discovery of Matilda's body is a complex process. First, he sees Matilda's hand, and then her breast, but he cannot yet see her face. During the night, "[t]he image of his favourite Madona [sic]" appears in his sleep, and the analogy to Pygmalion's experience becomes more relevant. "[Ambrosio] pressed his lips to hers, and found them warm: The animated form started from the Canvas, embraced him affectionately, and his senses were unable to support delight so exquisite" (67). In the following days, Ambrosio discovers Matilda's "coral lips" and "a Chin in whose dimples seemed to lurk a thousand Cupids". Playing the harp, she uncovers an arm, "the delicacy of whose skin might have contended with snow in whiteness" (78). Then the revelation is complete when Matilda's cowl falls back, and Ambrosio can admire her face: "Her features became visible to the Monk's inquiring eye. What was his amazement at beholding the exact resemblance of his admired Madona?" (81). Later in the story, Ambrosio notices Antonia, and the whiteness of her perfect body recalls a Classical statue of Venus. Matilda and Antonia represent the agathokakological metamorphoses of the work of art into human beings, embodying the dichotomy between good and evil. Ambrosio's story is Ovid's Pygmalion's myth revisited, with a dangerous change.

The second Ovidian moment in *The Monk*, which is one of the novel's crucial occurrences, takes place in the beautiful garden of the convent, called the "hermitage". Tranquil nature, perfumed flowers and crystalline water may represent the exaltation of aesthetics, or a medieval philosophical symbolism: the garden is at the centre of beauty and knowledge. The bucolic scene features echoes of *Vathek*'s sensual experiences and Radcliffe's alluring descriptions of a gorgeous nature in *The Romance of the Forest* and *The Mysteries of Udolpho*. However, the garden in Ambrosio's cloister becomes a place of dangerous sensuality, which is not only a reminder of the biblical Garden of Eden but also a reference to a problematic idyll in *The Metamorphoses* concerning the ancient myth of Hermaphroditus. Salmacis, a solitary nymph, collects flowers near a small pond, surrounded by trees and soft meadows, when Hermaphroditus, Venus and Mercury's beautiful adolescent son, approaches the bucolic scene:

> A river here he view'd, so lovely bright,
> It show'd the bottom in a fairer light,
> Nor kept a sand concealed from human sight:
> The stream produced nor slimy ooze, nor weeds,
> Nor miry rushes, nor the spiky reeds,
> But dealt enriching moisture all around,
> The fruitful banks with cheerful verdure crown'd,

And kept the spring eternal on the ground.
A nymph presides, not practiced in the chase,
Nor skilful at the bow, nor at the race; [...]
Now in the limpid stream she views her face,
And dress'd her image in the floating glass:
On beds of leaves she now reposed her limbs,
Now gather'd flowers that grew about her streams.
(*Met* I: 114–115)

A pleasant place surrounded by nature, Ovid's beautiful *locus amoenus* reveals the quintessence of beauty and peace in a sublime landscape, perfectly rendered by Dryden's translation. However, it is the oxymoron of a terrifying tranquillity, which announces terrible events. The young man's appearance provokes an uncontrollable desire in the nymph Salmacis, a latent agent of destruction. Like Salmacis, the apparently weak and delicate Matilda has collected flowers for Ambrosio (*The Monk*: 43). Matilda is going to seduce the solitary monk, and entangle him in her mysterious schemes. Salmacis and Matilda are aggressive female agents, like the Naiads seducing Hylas in Beckford's tale (see: "Hedonism, Anxiety and Horror: Lucretius and the Classics in *Vathek*"). Nostalgic, lonely and striving for the unknown, Ambrosio goes to the beautiful cloister garden of the monastery, which offers a rare picturesque image of nature in the novel:

The choicest flowers adorned it in the height of luxuriance, and though artfully arranged, seemed only planted by the hand of Nature: fountains, springing from basons of white Marble, cooled the air with perpetual showers; and the walls were entirely covered by Jessamin, vines, and Honey-suckles. The hour now added to the Beauty of the scene [...] the waters of the fountains sparkled in the silver beam: a gentle breeze breathed the fragrance of the Orange-blossoms along the Alleys. (*The Monk*: 50)

"Gardens presented a particularly rich *topos* of 'associative aggregates', of connotative figures that might induce a visual train in the viewer. But there was always, as in Gothic writing, latent danger" (Miles 1993: 59). Commenting on the *Bower of Bliss* in his *Observations on the Faerie Queene of Spenser* (1754), Thomas Warton, had noted that "Sir Guyon's temptation consists in great measure in the gratification of sense afforded by a delicious garden" (Miles: 61). A series of authors in the early and mid-eighteenth century had highlighted that nature had a strong and risky connection with desire. Like Warton, the theologian (and scientist) Joseph Priestley had warned in his didactic writings that vigilance in descriptions of nature was essential, as the garden could turn into a perverse pastoral. Ambrosio enters the peaceful place, surrounded by a serene atmosphere, in the same way that Hermaphroditus plunges into the pond. Both scenes highlight the sweetness of nature and the extraordinary peace enveloping the enchanted place. However, the calm atmosphere is deceptive. Ambrosio finds the novice Rosario, and discovers her feminine, sensuous aspect, made to tempt him. Like Hermaphroditus, he is frightened by Matilda's love that he initially rejects: "recovering from his confusion, the Monk quitted the garden, and sped with precipitation towards the Abbey" (*The Monk*: 59). His escape from the woman is similar to Hermaphroditus' reaction when Salmacis introduces herself to the astonished legendary adolescent and praises his beauty. He is surprised, flushing at the unwanted compliments. When the nymph tries to embrace him, he firmly rejects her:

> Now gather'd flowers that grew about her streams,
> And then by chance was gathering, as she stood
> To view the boy, and long'd for what she view'd.
> Fain would she meet the youth with hasty feet,
> She fain would meet him, but refused to meet
> Before her looks were set with nicest care,
> And well deserved to be reputed fair.
> "Bright youth," she cries, "whom all thy features prove
> A god, and, if a god, the god of love;
> But if a mortal, bless'd thy nurse's breast,
> Bless'd are thy parents, and thy sisters bless'd:
> But O! How bless'd, how more than bless'd thy bride!
> Allied in bliss, if any yet allied.
> If so, let mine the stolen enjoyments be;
> If not, behold a willing bride in me."
> The boy knew not of love, and, touch'd with shame,
> He strove, and blush'd, but still the blush became;
> [...] He, innocently coy,
> Replies, "O leave me to myself alone,
> You rude incivil nymph, or I'll be gone." (*Met* I: 115)

Salmacis is as astute as Matilda the very moment she tries to seduce Ambrosio. Whereas Matilda uses her arts strategically, the nymph is yearning to have her passion fulfilled while admiring the handsome divinity, and she is impatient with desire. Hermaphroditus' latent sexual anxiety proves justified, but his lingering in the place is incomprehensible. The aggressive nymph approaches the young divinity and beguiles him before suddenly clasping him. While terror paralyses the divine adolescent, the water creature is determined to turn her embrace eternal by asking the gods for a never-ending union of their bodies. The two creatures mysteriously become one being, a new form of divinity uniting their masculine and feminine essences. Ovid explains that one may say the creature is both or neither of them:

> "O may the gods thus keep us ever join'd!
> O may we never, never part again!"
> So pray'd the nymph, nor did she pray in vain:
> For now she finds him, as his lips she press'd.
> Grow nearer still, nearer to her breast,
> Till, piercing each the other's flesh, they run
> Together, and incorporate in one:
> Last, in one face are both their faces join'd,
> As when the stock and grafted twig combined
> Shoot up the same, and wear a common rind. (*Met* I: 116)

The gods' decision to unite Hermaphroditus with Salmacis is inexplicable and unmotivated, just like Matilda's obsessive presence that forcibly attaches Ambrosio to her devilish intentions. From a philosophical point of view, the joining of the two creatures can be interpreted as an ideal Platonic union. However, the gods literally interpret the nymph's supplication for eternal love. They satisfy the creature's plea in unexpected and ambiguous ways, misinterpreting her lustful desire and playing with the literal meaning of her prayer. Interestingly, we can also observe a mysterious change in both characters in *The Monk*, as they undergo a process of "feminization" (Ambrosio) and "masculinization" (Matilda), which has been highlighted by a number of scholars, amongst whom Williams (1995) and Brewer (2001) are notable for their analyses. Matilda becomes strong-willed, and her strategy obliges the young man to discover physical joy provoking a metamorphosis, turning him into a dependent and weak being. The fact that Hermaphroditus and Salmacis become a single being is obscure and creates a linkage to the characters' relationship in *The Monk*. In effect, Ambrosio and Matilda are often together after she reveals her identity to the monk, as if they had metamorphosed into a single entity. When other characters appear on the scene, Matilda vanishes or at least becomes invisible. The monk Ambrosio and the novice Rosario/Matilda seem to represent but one person. A possible explanation of Matilda's unfathomable indefiniteness could be that she only exists in Ambrosio's mind. A potential clue is provided by the fact that the monk is in a "delirium" (*The Monk*: 41) after he has observed the voluptuous painting for some time, and Rosario/Matilda strangely appears at his cell door impersonating the Madonna. Some scenes increase the mystery surrounding Matilda's actual presence or absence. After Ambrosio has committed a hideous crime in the dungeons of the monastery, Don Ramirez and the archers arrive in the crypt and look for "the Fugitive's retreat" (393), even though he was not alone on the scene, as Matilda had been helping him all along. Once authorities discover the crime, the Capuchins as well as "all Madrid" talk about "the Perpetrator", but no mention is made about Matilda. When the trial (420) of the Inquisition begins, "He was conducted to a spacious Hall" (422), but again there is no mention of Rosario/Matilda as if she had completely dissolved. Matilda seems to become real only within Ambrosio's mind when we follow the scene through his point of view. No one else seems to acknowledge her presence in the story, as she is invisible when other characters/narrators describe contexts, in which she is supposed to be. Matilda permanently disappears when Ambrosio is on the brink of disaster. Although she may embody a rich and spoiled girl, saved by her powerful family, no justification is given for her constant invisibility when face to face with other characters and her disappearance remains shrouded in mystery.

In the fourth book of *The Metamorphoses*, the tragic story of unfortunate Byblis, in love with her twin brother, Caunus, could be a further instance of an Ovidian myth partially absorbed in *The Monk*–which had influenced Mary Robinson's *Vancenza* (1792). Byblis' suicide, caused by her incestuous desire and disgusted Caunus' rejection, is not, however, compatible with Antonia's ethical figure or Ambrosio's cowardice, which makes him seek self-preservation despite his crimes. The real third Ovidian moment in *The Monk* contains a strong analogy with another story, which is of a general nature and involves sexual abuse and rape. Several episodes in *The Metamorphoses* introduce themes of gods and men desirous of possessing the women or men they are in love with and are ready to use violence to achieve their goals. The fierce actions of gods and humans, generally provoking extreme suffering, are reiterated throughout the narration. Critical analyses of *The Metamorphoses* and/or ancient mythology highlight the danger of intrinsic violence, frequently present in the relationships between the sexes, either divine or human (L.C. Curran 1978; Susan Deacy and Karen Pierce 2002). In her analysis of

Greek myths, Mary Lefkowitz (1994: 21) challenges scholarly opinions and unconvincingly asserts that acts of gods' seduction have a different connotation, as it is not possible to talk of rape in modern terms:

Even though the encounters between gods and mortal women are almost always of short duration, they have lasting consequences not only for the females involved but also for civilization generally, since the children born from such unions are invariably remarkable, famous for their strength or intelligence, or both. Whether we moderns choose to approve of it or not, most women in archaic Greek epic, perhaps because they believe that the gods exist and do not question the historicity of their mythology, tend to cooperate in their seduction.

Whereas the stories of Io and Danaë seem to corroborate the idea of compliance with Gods' fancies, it would be enough to analyse the tragic episode of Apollo and Daphne, its intrinsic violence and, most of all, the female rejection of the act to demonstrate the opposite. The Latin Ovid absorbs many Greek myths and includes stories of blood and horror that not only concern gods but also mortals. Many of the tragic acts in *The Metamorphoses* have gloomy consequences, and Lewis appears to imitate the Ovidian stance, which includes gratuitous violence in the tragic progress of humankind. The horrible climatic moment of the rape in *The Monk*, partially reproducing Lovelace's rape in *Clarissa* and confirming the intertextuality between the two novels (Macdonald 2006: 159), recalls the violence against and the indifference towards the woman, considered as a victim and an object. In mythological narratives, Jupiter appears to be justified in his actions because he is the most important divinity but, despite their secondary role in the pantheon, other gods and goddesses follow their desires and carry out forbidden acts. Jupiter's brother and god of the underworld, Pluto suddenly experiences a violent passion as soon as he sees the young Proserpina, and presently kidnaps her. The moment before the abduction is suffused with delicate joy. The atmosphere is in profound contrast with the god's furious desire, similar to Ambrosio's frenzy:

> Fresh fragrant breezes fan the verdant bowers,
> And the moist ground smiles with enamell'd flowers:
> The cheerful birds their airy carole sing,
> And the whole year is one eternal spring.
> Here while young Proserpine, among the maids,
> Diverts herself in these delicious shades;

While, like a child, with busy speed and care,
She gathers lilies here, and violets there;
While first to fill her little lap she strives,
Hell's grisly monarch at the shade arrives;
Sees her sporting on the flowery green,
And loves the blooming maid as soon as seen.
His urgent flame impatient of delay,
Swift as his thought he seizes the beauteous prey,
And bore her in his sooty car away.   (*Met* I: 150–151)

Pluto's kin (a very important detail, considering that Antonia is Ambrosio's relative), Proserpina is carried to Hades, the reign of darkness, to become his wife. The young woman invokes the help of her distant mother, the goddess Ceres, initially unable to hear her. Proserpina's mother tries to stop Pluto but is powerless, just like Elvira is incapable of action. Proserpina is childish and innocent, and Antonia seems her perfect copy. The analogy with Proserpina's story is remarkably precise. After administering "a juice [which] brings the exact image of Death" (*The Monk*: 329), Ambrosio leads Antonia to the subterranean dungeon to keep her forever with him in a place that is similar to Pluto's dark hell of the mythological tradition:

The depths profound through yielding waves he cleaves,
And to hell's centre a free passage leaves;
Down sinks his chariot, and his realms of night
The god soon reaches with a rapid flight. (*Met* I: 151)

Antonia is not only similar to Proserpina, but her sad story also recalls Creusa, the girl that Apollo seizes while she is collecting flowers. The god rapes Creusa in a dark deserted cave where nobody can see or hear her. As Murray (1991: 117) explains, "Many rape myths involve trickery and disguises", just like the magic potion used by Ambrosio to trick Antonia and bring about her doom. Ovid's victims of rape are abandoned to a cruel destiny, and only a metamorphosis can alleviate the pain. In the same way as Tereus, in the fourth book of *The Metamorphoses*, decides to cut out Philomela's tongue after raping her, to ensure that nobody can discover his violation of his sister-in-law, Ambrosio would like to silence Antonia so that she cannot reveal his abominable crime. Gods' and men's carnal desire and violence are reproduced in egotistical Ambrosio, continuously exalted by Matilda's apparent adoration.

106

Further stylistic analyses between Ovid's original version and Dryden's rendering may contribute to a more thorough understanding of Lewis's narrative techniques and his borrowings either from the original Classical texts or from the "englished" versions. Such studies could explain how various sources may have linguistically influenced Lewis. If, on the one hand, he might have read the original versions of the Classics by virtue of his education, on the other hand, he may have chosen to use translations for an inspiring thesaurus. Ovid was a popular poet starting from the sixteenth century and was still in vogue in the eighteenth century. His works were regularly rendered in English, starting from the Renaissance onwards. "Many of the best post-Restoration englishings of Ovid are collaborative in character and many reflect the dominant influence of John Dryden, whose own translations of Ovid were often ranked amongst his finest achievements" (Tissol 2005: 204). In his *Arts of Logick and Rhetorick*, the versatile historian, editor and poet John Oldmixon (1728: 291) claimed, "Dryden seems to have entered as far into the Genius of the Poet as any of his Translators". Sir Samuel Garth's collective translation of *The Metamorphoses,* published in 1717, was a successful collaborative effort that united the versions of many poets and included the verses translated by the late Dryden, used throughout the eighteenth century, which became a precious source for poetry and literature.

Together with influences of the Greeks tragedians, the Latin classical matrix played an important role in the creation of a novel inspired by miscellaneous cultural influences. Several scholars interpret Lewis's tendency to punish his characters in psychoanalytical terms. Ambrosio's violent rejection of post-coital connections with his female lovers seems an indicator of latent homosexuality. However, the motivation for a number of crude descriptions in the story are related to Ovid and other classical sources, detectable in the various plots and subplots of Lewis's novel. *The Monk* contains the different voices of past and contemporary authors. Its eclectic style generates contradictory elements, in which opposing narrative aspects co-exist. Lewis's strange novel is a rich cultural token, summarising different forms of literature, and is worth analysing by virtue of the wide range of hypotheses it can offer. The Ambrosio-Antonia plot shifts towards the libertine style, then changes to echo Euripides' tragedies and Ovid's *Metamorphoses* and finally dissolves into a Dantesque Inferno, as we explain in the chapter dedicated to Dante, Boccaccio and Ariosto. Lewis was able to take Burke's dictum to its extreme consequences (1757: 334):

Now, as words affect, not by any original power, but by representation, it might be supposed, that their influence over the passions should be but light; yet it is quite otherwise; for we find by experience, that eloquence and poetry are as capable, nay indeed much more capable, of making deep and lively impressions than any other arts, and even than nature itself in very many cases.

The explanation for tragic behaviours lies in the classical pattern of Greek tragedies' violent denouements, and Ovidian narrations of tragic love. *The Monk*'s apparent incongruousness, linked to dreadful events from the Classical world, betrays the author's anxiety to show his encyclopaedic cultural knowledge. The halo of mystery does not only envelop the different plots within the novel. A greater mystery is contained in Lewis's manuscript of *The Monk*, which was the only novel he wrote during his literary career. A different hand from Lewis's made many corrections in the manuscript, and no page contains the author's signature. A possible hypothesis is that a co-author, perhaps a more adult one, could have helped Lewis in writing, editing and correcting the novel. Lewis was precocious in his love for literature, but the creation and completion of such a complex work as *The Monk* at the age of twenty may create doubts. Somebody in his entourage could have taken part in the construction of the work, especially considering the amount of time that would have been necessary to write it while studying at university, living abroad, learning languages, translating, starting his political career, and being a socialite. Baron Wilson's (I: 278–281) biography may offer some useful insight into the matter. Lewis's private correspondence includes one curious letter to his mother. In it, Lewis has a strange reaction to the possibility that his mother, a great lover of literature and an amateur authoress, may publish her writings. The letter clearly demonstrates how Lewis was not keen on the idea, as he vehemently (and rudely) prohibits his parent from publishing any works whatsoever. Although Lewis's reaction seems dictated by a fear of moral judgment concerning his mother's scandals, in reality, his deeper obsession is the thought that his mother might be considered the writer of *The Monk*, which is an odd argument for such a letter. On 18 March 1804, Lewis wrote (italics and spelling are reproduced as in the original): "I never before heard of *your* being *accused* of having written '*The Monk*'. This goes nearer to put me out of humour with the book than all the fury of the 'Pursuits of Literature &c'. What the world knows I care not, provided *I* do not know it". Finally, he formally asks his mother to avoid publishing:

But surely it is not worth while to take the trouble of composing a work, when 'to avoid the dangers of authorship your only safety, perhaps, would be in the want of genius in its composition'. You will equally avoid those dangers by *not* publishing your work, and, at the same time have the advantage of keeping your want of genius a secret. *Au reste,* I should much doubt there being a single soul at present existing who thinks '*The Monk*' was written by any body but myself.

In the letter, Lewis uses the very same misogynist arguments in Mathias's *Pursuits of Literature* (1794) and Polwhele's *The Unsex'd Females* (1798) to discourage his mother from publishing. Then Lewis inexplicably expresses a poor consideration of his mother's literary efforts, which is rather offensive, as if Lewis was having a childish tantrum. The third notable aspect of the letter is that Lewis mentions the fact that nobody would believe he was not the author of *The Monk*, an ambiguous statement that cannot, however, be clarified because of the missing letters of Lewis's mother. The hypothesis of a heavy intervention by Lewis's mother on *The Monk* may not be excluded, as the novel displays adult and libertine perspectives. A constant need for money may have pushed Lewis and his mother—in a precarious economic situation after her elopement—to come to a solution in order to obtain financial advantages from publishing. Howard Anderson (2008), the creator of "the most authoritative scholarly edition of the work", admits that some of the changes between the manuscript and the first edition are "rare and problematic" (Rudolph Glitz 2013: 24). In his note on the text, generally reproduced in most editions of *The Monk,* Anderson (2008: xxxii) also contemplates the possibility of modifications made by a compositor. Doubts have not been cleared, and some mystery about the corrections in *The Monk*'s manuscript persists, as these changes do not apparently correspond to editing activities. His mother may have been involved in the process of writing, but publishing in her name would have been out of the question since the former Mrs. Lewis still carried the stigma of her scandal, and Lewis might have been selfish enough to avoid sharing his literary glory.

Despite the mystery behind its composition, Lewis's novel is not only a Gothic story but also a cultural enterprise. The classical influence in Lewis is a constant presence not only in *The Monk* but also in his adolescent literary experiments as well as in his more mature works. In her biography, Baron Wilson includes some of Lewis's juvenile experiments, such as *The Effusions of Sensibility* (II: 242), and a number of miscellaneous poems, which show his eclectic knowledge. One of Lewis's most moving poetic compositions is an ode dedicated to *Danaë* (Baron Wilson II: 302), written in imitation of the Greek poet Simonides, active between the sixth and the fifth centuries BCE. The beautiful Danaë, once seduced by the "mighty Jove" in the form of golden rain, must face the dangers of the night alone at sea with her infant child. The poem is a strange and moving anticipation of Lewis's tragic destiny, which proclaims his constant love for Antiquity, much more deeply rooted than previously argued.

A young female, of a slender form, came forth. Her light brown
hair floated in the hazy breeze of the twilight. A troop of young
maidens attended her on tip-toe.
(William Beckford. *Vathek*)

William Beckford's *Vathek* introduces a series of unsolved problems.
Complications concern the chronology of the publication together with
the linguistic dualism of the novel, first appeared in Samuel Henley's 1786
anonymous English translation, followed by Beckford's supposedly
previous French version in 1787 (Boyd Alexander 1962; Roger Lonsdale
2008). Beckford rejected the help of his tutor, John Lettice, considering
him inadequate for the task. He employed Henley instead, who also
compiled a series of extensive and cultivated annotations, highly
appreciated by reviewers and scholars for their superior intellectual level
(André Parreaux 1960b). Beckford later reduced the long notes and
adapted them to the reading public for the 1816 edition. He monitored
the English translation and made various changes. In publishing the
translation without the writer's permission, Henley supposedly forced
Beckford to accelerate the publication of the French version, probably
completed by 1782 when he was only twenty-two years of age. Different
editions of the novel, both in English and French, appeared between the
1790s and the first decades of the following century. These later editions
contained several revisions that were evident compared to the initial texts
(Kenneth Wayne Graham 1975). The difficulty of determining the exact
date of writing and the actual language of the first edition was increased
by a series of undated and unsigned manuscripts with numerous
variations. The reason why Beckford decided to write *Vathek* in French is
unclear. Beckford's young age and lack of linguistic expertise necessary to
complete a complex tale may be a possible explanation for not writing in
English, while his long stays in Switzerland and France had provided him
with a variety of linguistic models that he could copy. Beckford was
essentially bilingual after his various journeys to Gallophone countries

(Norton 2000b). Graham's studies aim at demonstrating the authority of the English version, considered prior to the French one by a restricted number of scholars. Beckford's linguistic choice may originate from the high stylistic level reached by French translators in the domain of Oriental tales. He likely found it easier to imitate their style, leaving to his translator the task of elaborating an adequate English version. A baffling aspect is that Beckford spent months, even years, revising and modifying both versions personally after he had entrusted other people with the translation of his work into English and the correction of the French text. In Adam Roberts and Eric Robertson's opinion (1996: 199): "[t]he textual status of *Vathek* is interestingly unsettled. It straddles English and French, and although Beckford initially crafted the work in French, which suggests that the English version [...] is a 'translation' with all the associations that word carries with it, the situation is not as simple as it might appear", as the novel did not follow the traditional trajectory of a text that is published and then translated. The translation becomes a sort of hermeneutic endeavour involving the reader.

A problematic event could be a further reason for publishing in French. A notorious predicament that Beckford faced prior to the publication of the text was a sexual scandal that threatened to see him stand trial, as we more extensively explain in the chapter about "Innocence in danger". For that reason, it may be likely that Beckford tried to keep public attention away from his name; writing the work in French (and anonymously translating it later into English) would make the connection between the author and the book more difficult to detect. The sources of the novel represent an additional aspect that has required extensive research. Studies on *Vathek* focus on the imitation of Eastern narratives, which are undoubtedly relevant in one of the most bizarre texts in English literature, but the classical side of the work has generally failed to arouse much interest. Although Beckford's contemporary critiques tended to appreciate *Vathek* and connect it with great authors of the past, such as Dante, Ariosto and Milton, deeper analogies have not been comprehensively examined, since the construction of an Oriental mytheme seemed to permeate the story entirely. Although Guy Chapman (1952) and other scholars observe that Beckford's novel did not receive any critical attention, Lonsdale (2008) highlights that the reception was almost unanimously favourable in consideration of the positive commentaries published in *A New Review* (1786), *The Critical Review* (1786), and *The Monthly Review* (1787). The only contrasting opinion, voiced by *The English Review* in September 1786, expressed doubts about the work's ambiguous moral meaning.

The genre of the novel could not be pinpointed with certainty from the very beginning. Numerous scholars (Miles 1993; Kilgour 1995; Gamer 2000; Napier 1987; Lévy 1995) do not consider *Vathek* a Gothic novel, while others (Ellis 2000) dedicate but a few lines to Beckford's work. Notwithstanding its nebulous literary status, Clery (1995: 90) maintains that the novel's "acceptance was made easier by the addition of scholarly notes, written by Henley and edited by Beckford, which were praised for their erudition and cited at length in reviews" in a historical period when terms such as "caliph" or "genie" were not yet common in the English language. Some notations in *Vathek* contain a detailed explanation of the political value of the word "caliph", whereas other translator's notes include the term "genius", and all its variants in Latin and Greek. Saglia (2002), Ros Ballaster (2005a, 2005b) and Laurent Châtel (2013) see Beckford's work as belonging to the rich phenomenon of the Oriental Renaissance in Europe in the eighteenth century. In particular, Saglia includes *Vathek* in the Romantic critical discourse, while Châtel considers it a handicap for Beckford's text to be included in the Gothic. A perverse Arabian fantasy in the words by Brian Stableford (2009: 39), the novel is considered a queer tale orientalising the East in Ahmed Alali's analysis (2014: 81). John Garrett (1992) asserts that Beckford's novel is not "a simple veneer" but a deeply specialised text centred on themes from the East, despite the interference of a Christian perspective in the finale. However, sublime and picturesque aspects in the work, added to the gloomy conclusion of the story, have allowed critics to include the text in the Gothic current. Frederick S. Frank (2005) and Ian Duncan (1992) consider Beckford's novel a Gothic romance. Sandro Jung (2011) demonstrates that its architectural variety is a pre-configuration of the Gothic that would be absorbed by subsequent Gothic authors. The supernatural and magic arts in *Vathek* seem to confirm the intrinsic Gothic nature of the story, even though Beckford's introduction of bizarre situations and grotesque adventures generates doubts about its true essence. This section shows Beckford's eclecticism and the importance of works of Antiquity in the creation of the story. It demonstrates that its Oriental mould is only one of the novel's many facets.

Beckford wrote some narrative experiments before turning seventeen. His heterogeneous writings highlight his taste for hyperbolic narrations. *The Biographical Memoirs of Extraordinary Painters* (1780), published when he was twenty, is a surreal text apparently written as a parody of Walpole's *Anecdotes of Painting in England,* a sui generis encyclopaedia of art history (James Folsom 1964) that Beckford satirised for its biographical method of interpretation. One common factor uniting

Walpole and Beckford was their wide artistic knowledge that both writers nonchalantly showed off and had acquired from a young age at home by virtue of their respective art collections. While Walpole's family had become real aristocrats and his bourgeois origin had been long forgotten, Beckford and Lewis, irrespective of their wealth, were considered parvenus and were never able to obtain a peerage. The status of *nouveau riche*, together with his dubious reputation, accompanied Beckford throughout his life. His petitions for peerage were rejected, and the discovery of his forbidden homoerotic liaison certainly alienated him from British society, both in England and abroad, for the rest of his life (Parreaux 1960b; Ellis 2000). Walpole's, Lewis's and Beckford's high social status, financial advantages and political careers may have given them a detached sense of superiority, even though a mark of infamy was latently hanging over Beckford and Lewis due to the former's sexual scandals and the latter's problematic publication of *The Monk* (universally considered obscene). Walpole, Beckford and Lewis belonged to extraordinarily rich families, and their resources were virtually unlimited, although Walpole and Beckford squandered many financial resources by turning their architectonic dreams into eccentric abodes. Beckford imitated Walpole by modifying Fonthill Abbey, the mansion built by his father. Whereas Walpole's Strawberry Hill has resisted the passing of time, Beckford's residence crumbled to pieces just a few years after he had sold it for an impressive sum in 1823, following a series of structural problems. Fonthill was a more extreme exaggeration of an expensive Gothic reverie than Strawberry Hill, but very little remains of it. Because of Beckford's immense fortune, even more substantial than Walpole's and Lewis's, Alexander (1962) reports that Lord Byron nicknamed him "England's wealthiest son". Observing their experiences, both literary and political, we may consider Beckford as Walpole's ideal heir and Lewis's symbolic predecessor, even though they did not seem to acknowledge each other in their writings or correspondence. Lewis Melville (1920: 299) cites a piece of Beckford's conversation concerning the apparent mutual antipathy between Walpole and himself: "Mischief-making people annoyed [Walpole] by saying that I intended to buy up all his nic-nackery when he was dead. Some things I might have wished to possess—a good deal I would not have taken as a gift. The place was a miserable child's box—a species of gothic mousetrap—a reflection of Walpole's littleness. [...] My having his playthings he could not tolerate, even in idea, so he bequeathed them beyond my reach".

Despite their apparent reciprocal indifference, Walpole, Beckford and Lewis form a very interesting triad in the history of literature during the second half of the eighteenth century. They created strange literary divertissements contributing to the development of the Gothic. Beckford's creativity was the result of various cultural influences, extensive reading, frequent travelling and an unlimited imagination. He also had some special private tutors. Artists such as de Louthenbourg and the Russian expatriate painter, Alexander Cozens, promoted young Beckford's artistic interests and encouraged him to use his imagination. A painter of ruins and dramatic landscapes and a master of theatrical effects for the stage, de Louthenbourg organised the celebrations for Beckford's coming of age as well as the Christmas house party that he still remembered in his mature years (Lonsdale 2008: xii). Beckford described the effects of the artist's *mise-en-scène* as a wonderful work of illusion, beyond space and time, "the realisation of romance in its most extravagant intensity". The rich scenery that pervaded the atmosphere of Beckford's estate provided the twenty-one-year-old with ideas for the composition of his novel *Vathek,* probably started after the remarkable event. Beckford variously described the strong impressions he gained from de Louthenbourg's spectacle and admitted on more than one occasion that the highly emotional event influenced him deeply: "I composed *Vathek* immediately upon my return to town thoroughly imbued with all that passed at Fonthill during this voluptuous festival" (John Walter Oliver 1932: 91). Parreaux (1960b: 205) mentions a further memory: "I wrote V[athek] upon my return at the close of this romantic *villeggiatura*".

The phrase "romantic villeggiatura" contains important elements. Reflecting the semantic changes the word was undergoing, Beckford used the term "romantic" in an original way to define beautiful fairy tale atmospheres that he enjoyed in a natural setting surrounded by nature and beauty, and delights in recollecting the joyous experience repeatedly. He professes a Wordsworthian creed more than two decades before the romantic poet proclaimed the idea. Even though De Louthenbourg's show may have included artificial details, what strikes Beckford's imagination is nature's delicate array. The second term underlines Beckford's wide cultural refinement. The use of a specific Italian term, such as "*villeggiatura*" (family summer holiday), not only denotes Beckford's knowledge of the language but is also a clue about the linguistic and cultural corpus Beckford had acquired during his stays in Italy, especially in Venice, where the playwright Carlo Goldoni was a relevant cultural figure. A genuine connoisseur of European literature and a great admirer of Molière, Goldoni modernised Italian theatre by transforming the *Commedia dell'Arte* (based on regional masked characters, use of Italian dialects and improvisation) into comedies promoting realism and a novel vision of society. Goldoni's plays feature funnily corrupted aristocrats, self-aggrandising middle classes and wise plebeians, the only ones able to provide successful conclusions to problematic plots. The trilogy of the *Villeggiatura*, describing bourgeois families before, during and after the summer holidays, was one of Goldoni's most famous theatrical works. Beckford's use of the word not only reveals his knowledge of the Italian playwright's works, probably discovered during his many stays in Venice, but also highlights the special magic atmosphere conveyed by the term.

In all probability, the Oriental mania in literature and the arts, which had started at the end of the seventeenth century and developed in various European countries, profoundly charmed young Beckford. Precious handicrafts and literary works coming from different Asian countries attracted major interest. Philosophers Montesquieu and Voltaire adopted the style of the Oriental tale in some of their works for political reasons. Translated by John Ozell (1722), Montesquieu's *Persian Letters* (*Les Lettres Persanes*, 1721) used exoticism to ridicule French society through the eyes of naive Persian visitors in Paris. In reality, Montesquieu's ideas were not original, as he borrowed from the Genoese Giovanni Paolo Marana, author of the *Letters Written by a Turkish Spy* (*L'esploratore turco* 1684), translated into French in 1686 and rendered in English by William Bradshaw (1687). According to Ballaster (2005a: 41–45), Marana was the first to start the Oriental tale in Europe, featuring "one of the most familiar 'Oriental' voices for readers in eighteenth century prose, [...] the male 'reverse' or pseudo-traveller, a fictional correspondent who travels from East to West and writes of his experiences". Marana's popular stories and his deistic approach were also appreciated by Daniel Defoe, who wrote the *Continuation of Letters written by a Turkish Spy at Paris* (1718), extending the time of the story until 1693. Like Montesquieu, Voltaire made his characters move in distant Eastern lands so that he could create stories that were kinds of parables used to criticise contemporary France. Interestingly, the Genoese writer Giovanni Ambrogio Marini published a story, *Il Calloandro Fedele* (*Faithful Calloandro*), under a pseudonym in 1640. The protagonist is the son of an Emperor in a distant Eastern country and he has to experience multiple adventures before finding his love. The story, which is characterized by the style of an Oriental novella, is considered the first novel in the Italian language.

Among the writers that marked Beckford's work, an author had a meaningful impact on his Eastern themes as well as magical atmospheres. Beckford probably discovered an Italian playwright during his frequent journeys around the Continent and his many stays in Venice, even though that particular author has not been mentioned in relation to his work so far. Carlo Gozzi was a fierce cultural antagonist of the playwrights Carlo Goldoni and Pietro Chiari, who had been dominating the theatrical scene in Venice for some decades of the eighteenth century. Gozzi, who had noble origins, harshly criticized their works and accused them of having denaturalized Italy's theatrical tradition, the former for writing comedies depicting lower classes and the latter for his exaggerated sentimentalism. Gozzi was a Venetian-born intellectual, who progressively started writing plays for the theatre in order to restore the tradition that he felt contemporary playwrights unjustly neglected. The dispute between Gozzi and Goldoni continued for some time in Venice and further enflamed the interest of the audiences, divided in two opposite parties, until the latter decided to abandon Venice and work for the French monarchs.

Gozzi's comedies, which were not initially written for publication, had a peculiar structure. The story of the *Love of the Three Oranges* (1761) is an interesting example of Gozzi's strange stylistic choice, as the first act is more similar to a novel than a play. It consisted of a long speech providing stage directions for actors and actresses, who were supposed to improvise. These instructions stood for the ancient *canovaccio* (a sort of a rough scenario). Players developed the *canovaccio* by extemporising the dialogues on stage during their performance, a technique dating back to the Renaissance. The operation Gozzi intended to carry out was to preserve the *Commedia dell'Arte* dramatic tradition—a kind of drama, which the Webster dictionary defines as "Italian comedy of the 16th to the 18th centuries improvised from standardized situations and stock characters". Gozzi also wanted to preserve the role of masked characters, or *maschere*, that were representative of different regions, with their typical dialects and social behaviours. Moreover, they featured a range of moral attitudes, either positive or negative, expressed with a comical intent. In spite of his strong conservatism, Gozzi was also extremely innovative because he enriched his stories with cultural novelties. One is the introduction of folk stories in his plots that he took from ancient legends and from the collection of fairy tales written by Giambattista Basile, *The Tale of Tales* (1634–36). Written in the Neapolitan dialect, Basile's stories of *Lu Cunto de li Cunti* in the original Southern dialect were considered a minor form of literature until systematic translations into Italian and various languages together with critical studies revealed their value. The collection includes early versions of *Cinderella, Rapunzel,* and *Sleeping Beauty*, later used by French and German writers, such as Charles Perrault, and the Brothers Grimm. Therefore, Gozzi's plays introduced a different and fantastic dimension juxtaposed to the comedic. The second innovation was the insertion of the Oriental setting in imitation of *Les Mille et un Jour* (1710–1712), by the Orientalist François Pétis de la Croix, a European version of the *Arabian Nights*. The most famous of Gozzi's theatrical fables inspired by de la Croix is *Turandot*, adapted for the theatre in 1762. The play was so successful that it was not only repeated for many years but also interested Goethe and Schiller, who both created adaptations of the work. Whereas Gozzi's star was slowly forgotten in favour of Goldoni, starting from the nineteenth century on, the success of *Turandot* continued independently of its author. Many versions and remakes were made, one of the most famous being Giacomo Puccini's opera in three acts, which was produced in 1926 for the first time. Turandot is an Oriental princess, whose incredible beauty blends with a terrible cruelty. Also *La Donna Serpente* (1762), or *The Snake Woman*, was inspired by de la Croix. Gozzi set the fable in the land of distant Caucasia where King Farruscad and the fairy Cherestani have to face many ordeals for their love. *La Donna Serpente* was adapted by Richard Wagner in his first complete opera that he entitled *Die Feen* (*The Fairies*), written in 1833. While adding "a more Orpheus-like rescue scene", Wagner found "value in Gozzi's handling of the prince's final trial, with its attention to fearful feelings mingled with sexual desire" (Katherine Syer 2014: 38). The third new feature in Gozzi's plays was the invention of extremely elaborated sceneries, continually changing in order to impress the public with a wide assortment of special effects, which were meant to frighten and to attract with beautiful Eastern settings and sublime storms, accompanied by lightning and thunder. The Galli Bibiena family from Arezzo, in Tuscany, but active in Bologna, had started and spread the tradition of extreme scenic backgrounds and infinite perspectives for the Italian theatre with the use of *trompe l'oeil* and special effects in the seventeenth century, which were largely used in the eighteenth century. They were the forerunners of the Baroque apparatus and the taste for theatrical illusions, which developed in the following centuries. A further ingredient added by Gozzi was magic, constantly intermingling with reality. The effect of Gozzi's theatrical syncretism was quite similar to a form of *pastiche,* altogether amusing, ironic, exotic and tragic. Moreover, Gozzi could boast a series of cultural references to authors that he particularly cherished, such as the usual Ariosto, whose inventiveness he exploited for his dramatic material. Despite the success of the performances for decades to come, Gozzi's collection of *Theatrical Fables* (1772) were progressively shunned by Italian critics in favour of Goldoni, which determined the neglect of his creations, whose mingling of *genres* and contexts was considered a mark of low quality. Goldoni is reputed one the best playwrights and has been compared to the Latin Terence (Alberto Beniscelli 1997), whereas studies on Gozzi are generally scarce. Gozzi's rich sceneries and the strange characters he could admire on the Venetian stage arguably inspired young Beckford, and the Venetian playwright's syncretism was a further cultural ingredient in Beckford's fusion of styles and sources.

Ballaster (2005a: 77–78) cites parts of Ahmad Gunny's *Images of Islam in Eighteenth Century Writings* (1996) to explain how scholars of Eastern studies developed the Oriental fashion in Europe: "Scholarship in Middle Eastern languages, literatures, and theology, after the brief flowering of English scholarship under Edward Pococke in the 1670s, was also largely mediated in Britain through France". Barthélemy d'Herbelot created the monumental *Bibliothèque Orientale* (1697), based on the bibliographical dictionary of the Ottoman historian Haji Khalīfa. D'Herbelot contributed to the dissemination of Eastern culture in Europe and the introduction of new words into the English language. Another great Orientalist, Antoine Galland, acquired knowledge of Arabic, Persian and Turkish and collected manuscripts to add to the Bibliothèque du Roi. The Dutch scholar Adrien Reland explained Shi'ite Islam in *The Mahometan Religion* (1712), a key text in the Protestant rehabilitation of Islam, also used to discredit Catholicism. The early eighteenth-century Orientalist Simon Ockley published *The History of the Saracens* (1718). Robert Mack (2005) argues that Eastern literature inspired British authors, such as Addison and Johnson. Along with his apophthegm entitled *Santon Barsisa*, Addison published the allegorical tale *The Vision of Mirzah*, in *The Spectator* in 1711, while Johnson's *Rasselas* (1759) was an example of Orientalism used for didactic and moralising purposes. James Ridley's *Tales of the Genii* (1764) probably influenced Coleridge's *Kubla Kahn* (1816). In his discussion on *The Arabian Nights*, Mack (470, 472) explains that:

The publication of the French Orientalist Antoine Galland's translation of *Alf Layla wa Layla* as *Les Mille et une Nuits* in twelve volumes from 1704 to 1717 represented the earliest appearance in Western Europe of the collection of stories commonly known as the *Arabian Nights Entertainments* or (rather more accurately) *The Thousand and One Nights*. Galland's approximately forty-eight individual narratives were drawn from more than one cycle in the Arab collection, and it is important to stress that even today there is not–nor could there ever be–a text of the *Nights* that could claim to be truly definitive or even complete. [...] The nature and appeal of the book lies as much in its ability to transform itself according to the needs and desires of its individual audiences, be they readers or listeners, as in its unique synthesis of the eternal and the ephemeral, the magical and the mundane.

Galland had created a "free adaptation" that he had "deliberately pruned" so as to avoid accusations of lewdness, and his version "was to remain the sole English version of the *Nights* until the nineteenth century". In agreement with Ballaster (2005a, 2005b), Mack's hypothesis is that *The Arabian Nights* would probably form "a subtext in Gothic-influenced novels", whereas Lonsdale holds the collection of tales relevant in the creation of *Vathek*. Besides *The Arabian Nights*, several texts on Eastern culture were available, both in English and in French, when Beckford started writing his novel, and he could choose among historical essays, exotic fantasies or satirical tales. Coincidentally, one of Beckford's ancestors had created an interesting Western example of literature imitating Eastern sources. Anthony Hamilton, an Irishman of Scottish descent living on the Continent and occasionally writing literary texts in French, had created "far-fetched and ludicrous" parodies of Oriental tales in a "witty, ironic tone", inventing Dinarzade, Scheherazade's fake sister. Used for private entertainment, Hamilton's tales were published posthumously (Lonsdale 2008: vii). Ballaster (2005a: 3) highlights that: "Hamilton's Dinarzade speaks up directly against the despotic, paranoid, and self-obsessed Sultan Schariar, using her tale to undermine the myth of his potency, which her sister's deferential stories seek to enhance".

Although it was not a pioneering tale in the Oriental fashion, *Vathek* mixed a remarkable amount of existing materials that conveyed a special touch of exoticism. Beckford tried to reproduce the mutable prerogatives of Middle Eastern tales, adding his original style for a unique result. *Vathek* represents the only serious work produced by Beckford, as his "other fictional endeavours are satirical and, more important, are satires of 'polite' eighteenth-century fiction" in a sort of *"reduction ad absurdum* of the artificialities"* of contemporary authors (Folsom 1964: 55). The novel was not, however, a simple parody. Beckford and Henley not only illustrated the meaning of new and foreign words in the novel but also provided an illuminating bibliography containing the names of influential authors in their glosses. They were George Sale's translation of the Koran (1764 edition), Alexander Guiga's translation of Elias Habeshi's *Present State of the Ottoman Empire* (1784), and John Richardson's *A Dissertation on the Languages, Literature, and Manners of the Eastern Nations* (1777). If, on the one hand, Beckford's and Henley's long explanations show the exquisite intellectualism the novel is based on, conveying a certain level of self-conceit, on the other hand, they reveal a remarkable number of cultural sources that partially explain the epistemological development of the story.

Peter Knox-Shaw (1995) spotlights *Vathek's* cultural complexity and underlines the importance of William Jones's *The Seven Fountains* (1770) for its connections with Beckford's tale. The elegant poem, based on one of the stories in the *Arabian Nights* collection, mixed the Oriental atmosphere with classical tones from Antiquity. The young protagonist in the allegorical poem explores the mysteries hidden behind a series of doors when he lands on a magic island, after navigating a distant sea. Apparently, "pleasure", "mirth" and "beauty" dominate everything until the protagonist finds a gloomy cavern after entering the seventh door. The old man walking with the protagonist warns him against the alluring aspects of physical enjoyment and suggests following the paths of wisdom, instead. The poem ends with enigmatic lines:

> The youth o'er walks of jasper takes his flight
> And bounds and blazes in eternal light"
> (*The Seven Fountains*: 250)

The Seven Fountains' mystical experience, interspersed with a strange dreamlike atmosphere, could represent a voyage to the afterlife. The apotheosis is heavenly, as all elements are inundated with light, just as Dante is surrounded by the strongest divine brilliance in the final, glorious part of his journey, *Paradise*, at the end of a supernatural experience in the *Divine Comedy*. The imagery connected to Jones's description of the fountains can be found at the beginning of *Vathek* when the protagonist, taken by an infinite thirst, drinks from his many springs. However, Beckford soon abandons the aesthetic representation of the fountains in favour of other concepts. The only connection between Jones and Beckford lies in their extreme aesthetic taste, the love for Oriental mysteries and, most importantly, their latent classical atmospheres.

Beckford's education was brilliant and he became widely learned in many subjects. The story of Mozart giving him music lessons while in England surrounded young Beckford with a positive halo, even though the anecdote might not have been true (Norton 1999a). As the adolescent Beckford had decided to teach himself Arabic, he translated some parts of the *Arabian Nights* between 1780 and 1783 that he intended to publish in 1787. Inexplicably, he did not persist after *Vathek* and only decided to print a tale called *Al Raoui* in 1799, published anonymously since the novella featured homoerotic content that could potentially increase the damage to the author's reputation, already badly shattered by previous scandals (Lonsdale 2008). Even though Mack (2005) states that Beckford was competent in Arabic, Robert Irwin (2010) is more sceptical and postulates that Beckford's knowledge seems to have come through the works of Galland and other Orientalists. After years of immersion in an imaginary Middle Eastern world, Beckford abandoned his projects on Oriental translations and production altogether. His further endeavours resulted in the publication of four episodes of *Vathek*, sometimes attached to the main novel in certain editions. His interest in Eastern literature turned out to be only one of many layers of knowledge he attained from his unusual education, deeply rooted in the Classics. Beckford did not continue with his adolescent and post-adolescent Oriental flair, arguably because his erratic tastes constantly drove him to find new literary stimuli.

Beyond the Oriental facade, it is possible to discover the existence of multiple cultural layers beneath the excessive aestheticism of Beckford's novel. The Gothic in *Vathek* seems to find confirmation in Dani Cavallaro's (2002) definition of the Gothic as a locus of torment or Williams's (1995) description of the genre as a desire to escape. In Jung's opinion (2011: 302), "Beckford's attempt to construct a multigeneric tale of Gothic didacticism [through] physically manifested architectural forms [move the novel] towards a generic identity created by a repertoire". The novel's "repertoire" is "integrated" into Gothic stories, "therefore theorising and regularising the emerging Gothic *genre*". *Vathek* is picturesque and ironic, romantic and adventurous, philosophical and frightful. An intellectual exercise in Orientalism with recurrent classical elements, the novel reveals Beckford's knowledge of languages, literatures, and cultures and foregrounds his predilection for fairy tale atmospheres he amalgamated with a Western knowledge based on Classical Antiquity. The novel is a puzzling narrative for its peculiar way of moving in one direction before suddenly changing and going against the reader's expectations, a technique obsessively repeated, and epitomised in the colourful episode of the pageant shockingly ending with a mass killing. Despite the scene's gory effect, the tone changes again and becomes grotesque losing all pathos. With the exception of the solemn portrayal of the Palace of Eblis, the extreme and sudden changes in plot and tone were deprecated by critics and readers alike for their "mockery, coarseness and flippancy" (Folsom 1964: 56). Beckford shifts his narrative technique unexpectedly to shock his readers, as if he rejected being confined to a specific narrative genre.

The classical world by Latin and Greek authors significantly dominates the novel, creating a further layer of possible interpretations beyond canonical analyses. Even though Beckford made extensive use of the grotesque in his works, his private correspondence and diaries introduce a different mode of writing, full of sensibility and romantic impressions. Alexander (1962: 74) includes a suggestive passage describing the remains of the dying winter in the house garden, which recalls Virgil's scenes in the *Georgics* when the snow melts before the arrival of spring:

Last night I stole from the Saloon and, led by a glimpse of moonshine between the arcades of the Egyptian Hall, went out at the Southern Portal. The dissolution of the snow next the pavement had left round it a narrow circle of verdure beyond which all was white. A grey mist had risen from the waters and, spreading over the lawn, seemed to enclose the peaceful Palace on every side. Thro' the medium of these vapours the moon cast a dim bluish light just sufficient to discover the surrounding woods, changed into groves of coral. I was so charmed with the novelty of the prospect that, setting the cold at defiance, I walked to and fro on the platform for several minutes, fancying the fictions of Romances realised, and almost imagining myself surrounded by some wondrous misty barrier.

Beckford's power of imagination and taste for the mysterious create a special atmosphere. A restricted space is more than enough for the adolescent writer to imagine strange stories developing behind the "grey mist" slowly surrounding the objects. A passage in *Vathek* seems to create a line of connection with descriptions of nature anticipating Radcliffe's sensibility:

At the distance of a few miles from Samarah stood a high mountain, whose sides were swarded with wild thyme and basil, and its summit, overspread with so delightful a plain that it might have been taken for the Paradise destined for the faithful. Upon it grew a hundred thickets of eglantine and other fragrant shrubs, a hundred arbours of roses, entwined with jessamine and honey-suckle, as many clumps of orange-trees, cedar, and citron, whose branches, interwoven with the palm, the pomegranate, and the vine, presented every luxury that could regale the eye or the taste. The ground was strewed with violets, hare-bells, and pansies: in the midst of which numerous tufts of jonquils, hyacinths, and carnations perfumed the air. Four fountains, no less clear than deep, and so abundant as to slake the thirst of ten armies, seemed purposely placed here, to make the scene more resemble the Garden of Eden watered by four sacred rivers. Here the nightingale sang the birth of the rose. (*Vathek*: 13)

The narrative method and the themes provide ample material for discussion. The introduction of luxuriant nature in a prose description was a novelty at the time of the publication of Beckford's novel, whereas poetry had already introduced important natural settings. The Graveyard Poets and James Thomson's *The Seasons* (1747) had featured images of nature starting in the 1740s. Jung (2010: 23–24) highlights the importance of Thomson's visual impact, highly praised by his contemporaries. Jung further explains that "[t]he poetry of Thomas Gray, Edward Young, James Macpherson, and Robert Burns, among many others, was frequently interpreted visually, and it is the visual or painterly adaptation of these poems that frequently enhanced, sustained, and prolonged their, and their authors', reputation in the nineteenth century". It is difficult to infer whether Beckford's aesthetic taste or other motivations determined his description of landscapes in a great variety of passages. What is certain is his introduction of landscapes in a prose narrative. The most beautiful landscape scene in *Vathek* occurs when a sensual seduction takes place, and Beckford seems to adopt Payne-Knight's libertine viewpoint that we delineated in the second chapter. The motivations for Beckford's aesthetic attention to nature are not clear. However, two aspects can be extrapolated from his narratives of nature: first, they make Beckford a precursor of Radcliffe's romantic exaltation of natural settings and, second, the passages describing nature clearly appeal to the senses and appear to follow Lucretius' doctrine of the exaltation of the physical world. This aspect leads us to interpret Beckford's initial introduction of Vathek's court as a place of delights. Descriptions of charming landscapes are common throughout the text before the final turn of events, when dark atmospheres dramatically replace the inaugural beauty of the first and central pages:

The evening was serene, the air refreshing, the sky clear, and the flowers exhaled their fragrance. The beams of the declining sun, whose mild splendour reposed on the summit of the mountain, shed a glow of ruddy light over its green declivity, and the white flocks sporting upon it. No sounds were heard. (*Vathek*: 25)

The scene offers an image of bucolic calmness by the use of positive words ("serene" "declining sun" "green declivity"), and pastoral peace is represented by the "flocks sporting" on the green hill. However, if one eye perceives the classical image inherited from Virgil, the other faces the horrible, lurking danger of a menacing "dreadful chasm". Beckford did not seem to be involved in the contemporary discourse on the sublime and the picturesque, and his frequent landscape descriptions do not entirely conform to Burke's sublime ideals or Gilpin's picturesque precepts. Nevertheless, Beckford's constant quest for the beautiful and his love for charming settings, invented more than a decade before *The Lyrical Ballads* (1798), betray a precocious romantic sensibility, although an insinuating irony frequently interrupts or precedes his charming scenes of nature. The description of a terrible storm, for example, is first introduced by semi-satirical commentaries that make the situation humorous, in spite of its growing horror:

The females and eunuchs uttered shrill wailings at the sight of the precipices below them, and the dreary prospects that opened, in the vast gorges of the mountains. Before they could reach the ascent of the steepest rock, night overtook them, and a boisterous tempest arose, which, having rent the awnings of the palanquins and cages, exposed to the raw gusts the poor ladies within, who had never before felt so piercing a cold. The dark clouds that overcast the face of the sky deepened the horrors of this disastrous night, insomuch that nothing could be heard distinctly. (*Vathek*: 45)

The words chosen by Beckford create a bleak atmosphere anticipating Gothic settings that were to become dominant in the following decades.

Like Lewis, Beckford did not go on a single Grand Tour. Instead, he went on many journeys to the Continent and lived in different countries for large periods; he resided in Switzerland, Italy, France, Spain, and Portugal. In 1778, Beckford's intransigent mother interrupted his stay abroad after he had manifested mildly scandalous behaviours in Italy. As if following the script of some comedy of errors or a libertine eighteenth-century play, Beckford had fallen for a young Venetian man who reciprocated his affection (Alexander 1962; Parreaux 1960b). In addition, the young aristocrat's sisters fell in love with the charming young Englishman and were desperate for his attention, which made them commit several faux pas. To celebrate his adventures and his (male) object of desire, Beckford wrote a dramatic composition most likely dedicated to his crush. Beckford imitates Theocritus's ode in honour of *Hylas* to create this fantasy. Dryden had partially translated the Greek poet's *Idylls* and included them in his popular *Miscellanies* (1685). Penelope Wilson (2005: 184) explains, "Thomas Creech's complete translation appeared in 1684.

[...] It was nearly eighty years before the next full scale version appeared, by Francis Fawkes (1767), with another by Richard Polwhele following in 1786". Polwhele's version received positive attention in the *Monthly Review* in 1788, but it was probably behindhand to influence Beckford. The text by Fawkes adhered more closely to the original Theocritus and did not contain the sensual paraphrases used by Dryden. Beckford probably knew both versions by Creech and Fawkes (together with the one by Dryden). As we have seen in other chapters, translations from classical authors were not only addressed to private readers but also (and mostly) to tutors and learners for didactic reasons. Even though the Latin Propertius, contemporary of Emperor Augustus, synthetically mentioned the unfortunate Hylas in his *Elegies* (I, 20: 53), Theocritus's version is more likely to have inspired Beckford. The Hylas that Theocritus had portrayed was the mythical figure of a young man, a squire to the legendary Hercules. The dramatic development of his story shows some analogies with the Ovidian tale of Hermaphroditus and Salmacis in *The Metamorphoses*. Gone to a spring to find water, Hylas is captured by the Naiads and hidden in the pond. After his disappearance, Hercules desperately looks for him in vain. Beckford's adaptation of Hylas's story shows his remarkable narrative skill in the description of the young man observing the world from underneath the water:

He perceives the features of the Naïads, flushed with desire. Fain would he fly from their importunities. [...] In the midst of his afflictions, the well-known voice of Hercules descended faintly through the waters. Thrice did the lovely captive reply; and thrice did the unavailing sound rise bubbling from below. The malicious Naïads sported with his perplexity, and as he sat dejected on a mossy fragment, danced wantonly around. And now the moon, rising to illuminate that world to which he never could return, [...] darted her lustre on the humid realms below. Shadows without number, reflected from the impending vegetation, glanced on the playful group and chequered their lucid forms. But Cynthia, disgusted by their wantonness, soon lost herself in clouds. Hylas now mourned in darkness. (Alexander 1962: 68)

This short passage offers rich poetic images and shows Beckford's narrative expertise at a young age. Never published, the story probably had a very strong emotional impact on Beckford. The text is a wonderful specimen of diversified narrative technique for the characters' different perceptions moving, as if in a filmic shooting, from Hylas under the water to Hercules's desperate vision of the empty meadow nearby, then to the dancing Naiads' indifferent glance. The description of the scene moves vertically to the sky where the moon, Cynthia, seems to be observing the dramatic development from far above. Finally, the point of observation suddenly descends and is again with Hylas, surrounded by darkness, forever a captive in that dark, liquid prison. Equally striking is the young man's despair and his frustrating attempt to emit sounds that are lost in the watery element, whereas the images of Hercules, whom he can see but cannot reach, are clear but dramatically unattainable. The eighteen-year-old Beckford shows exquisite classical knowledge. He masterfully expresses his anxiety for an impossible love by imitating an example of Greek Antiquity to describe his anguish for an incurable heartbreak, a theme he later inserted in *Vathek*. Beckford also evinces stylistic elegance blended with an impressive descriptive ability, which both reveal his many readings. The nocturnal vision of despair, in partial imitation of graveyard poetry, is imbued with classical imagery. Hercules, Diana, and the Naiads are famous characters, whereas Hylas belongs to a relatively lesser-known myth, which demonstrates the high intellectual level of the young Beckford and the impact of Greek and Latin culture in his works.

Beckford's extensive knowledge can be traced in *Vathek* as well. Beneath its exotic exaggerations, we can detect multiple elements, however fragmentary; of classical literature and many a passage betray the mould of Antiquity under the Oriental surface. Vathek decides to seduce a beautiful adolescent girl, Nouronihar, notwithstanding her young age and formal pre-engagement to her pubescent cousin, Gulchenrouz. The blooming and innocent girl "loved her cousin, more than her own beautiful eyes" (*Vathek*: 65). The poetic simile is taken from a popular poem by Catullus on the "Death of Lesbia's Sparrow", a metaphorical prolepsis for the young boy's destiny, "[t]han her very eyes, oh! Dearer to her far" (Catullus: 29). "Catullus was by reputation the best known of the Latin love poets other than Ovid, but despite his popularity, and the existence of a handful of well-known earlier renderings by Ben Jonson, Thomas Campion, and Richard Crashaw, translations appeared in this period only of a select few poems, and rarely more than one at a time" (Wilson 2005: 186). Beckford was aware of Catullus' powerful connotation of love, and he chose this fragment to highlight the presence of love for the first time in the story. Nouronihar's "languishing looks" of her dark eyes (*Vathek*: 148) can be found in the beautiful and attractive *"negri occhi, anzi due chari soli"*, Angelica's deep black eyes, as luminous as shining stars in Ludovico Ariosto's *Orlando Furioso* (Canto VII, Stanza xii, 2–3). The music that is constantly playing in Vathek's *Temple of Melody*, recalls the atmosphere in Ovid's collection of erotic elegies, *Amores*, in which eunuchs are to protect women from the poet's attempts to seduce them. Coincidentally, eunuchs are remarkably important in *Vathek*, as they must protect the women of the *seraglio* and the emir's daughter, Nouronihar, although they awkwardly fail. Classical references to Ovid's works are numerous due to the immense popularity of the poet. The theme of the metamorphosis does not appear in *Vathek* unless we consider the fatal psychological change that the characters undergo when they are doomed in hell and transfigured into desperate, indistinguishable beings. In her analysis of Ovidian contexts that we discovered in Lewis, Corinna Wagner (2012: 19) concludes that:

Ovid's poem is filled with erotic, violent and even lurid stories evoked with consummate sophistication. [...] Ovid's moral sense does not direct the reader; indeed he often seems remarkably indifferent to responsibilities and judgement; didacticism is utterly alien to him. However, through his profoundly ironical fatalism, he frequently appears to be enjoying unmasking divine cruelty, caprices, and revenges, and he engages mordantly with human capacities for wickedness, for rape, incest, murder.

What Wagner defines as typical Ovidian features—eroticism, irony, divine revenge and cruelty—are widespread in *Vathek*. If Ovid dominates several parts in *The Monk*, certain Ovidian contexts may be equally applied to Beckford, in particular his irony in describing the "caprices" and "cruelty" of his characters. A reference to Ovid, albeit unhappily satirical, lies in the image of the tragic Philomela, transformed into a nightingale, whose melodious voice is compared to the eunuch Bababalouk's shrieks, creating a grotesque contrast with the classical source. Other themes in *Vathek* are admittedly taken from various authors such as Homer, Plutarch, Pliny and Lucian. In some cases, the sources are mentioned in the novel's explanatory notes, filled with cultivated allusions reinforcing the impression of the author's classical polish. Beckford creates descriptions of rituals for the dead imitated from Homer and Lucian, or natural elements and customs inherited from Pliny. When Vathek's disorderly imperial procession ravages the beautiful flowers of some holy men, "the bees [...] thinking it their duty to revenge the insult offered to their masters, the santons, assembled so zealously to do it with good effect" (*Vathek*: 101). Beckford creates a mini-epos featuring the courageous tiny creatures, a classical allusion to Virgil's fourth book of the *Georgics* that contain the exaltation of a tranquil life in the country and an epic description of hard-working bees. Virgil's text also includes entomological observations of bees and a scientific description of honey's medical properties. The *Georgics'* epos of the tiny creatures is a philosophical meditation on the contrasting microscopic and macroscopic dimensions of the universe, which also offers a metaphor of human activities and political organisations (Alex Hardie 2020). In *Vathek*, the bees represent a form of nature's ironic justice against the macroscopic iniquities of humankind.

While several hints of classical sources resonate in *Vathek*, Lucretius' influence seems to play a major role in the novel. *On the Nature of Things*, dating back to the first century BCE, is Lucretius' only remaining work. The poet was a mysterious figure of Latin literature, and his vast, complex masterpiece would influence the most important authors of Roman Antiquity, including Horace, Virgil, and Ovid, not to mention his impact on the Renaissance and the Enlightenment (Valentina Prosperi 2007). Notwithstanding the complexity of his axioms, Lucretius was incredibly pervasive and became a tributary model for the works of the time, even though it is not easy to find clear references to his name. Eric Baker (2007: 274–275) explains that, "to characterise Lucretius' impact on the age of the Enlightenment is a daunting task. Virtually every major figure of the period was in some way influenced by Lucretius, and many of the engagements represent a complex, often polemically charged dialogue with previous interpretations". Baker identifies three major currents of thought in the eighteenth century, a clear consequence of Lucretian ideas: the exaltation of science, the promotion of deism, and the faith in progress. Lucretius' encyclopaedic text influences Beckford even though he does not directly mention or quote the Latin poet. This strange absence in the cultivated notes may be somehow due to the questionable ideas expressed by the mysterious Latin author. Lucretius represents the satisfaction of the senses, a leitmotiv in *Vathek*. Although *Vathek* is a highly inventive tale, it includes a variety of classical references underneath a finely constructed Eastern surface, and Lucretius seems to be prevalent as a source of inspiration.

Edward Ernest Sikes (1936) opines that it has always been difficult to say whether Lucretius was a poet describing philosophical theories, or a philosopher using elegant forms of poetry to convey his ideas. "Didactic" has become the most common adjective to interpret his works (Paul Davis 2005). His life was an enigma. Cicero's correspondence provides Interesting details about him, while some scholars even presume that Cicero was the editor of his book, called *De Rerum Natura* in the original Latin version. The great Latin orator and senator may have published the masterpiece after Lucretius' premature death, perhaps by suicide. Despite

Cicero's apparent respect for Lucretius, this hypothesis seems to be antithetical to his Stoic attitude, which was in contrast to Lucretius' Epicurean doctrine. Strange stories circulated regarding Lucretius' life, and his figure was surrounded by a halo of mystery that was never dissipated due to the lack of documentation of his life, perhaps due to *damnatio memoriae*, a peculiar Roman strategy that effected the elimination of historical or social memory of a political enemy or a public figure potentially pernicious to the institutions. The atheism that Lucretius expressed in his work probably sounded inauspicious for the Stoic Latin intelligentsia and the Roman political establishment. Lucretius lived in a turbulent political period, during which the most frightful event was the assassination of Julius Caesar in 44 BCE after a series of devastating wars. The poet was progressively forgotten after his death, and his manuscripts were lost, maybe not coincidentally.

A researcher of ancient texts, the Italian humanist Poggio Bracciolini found a manuscript of *De Rerum Natura* in 1417. This discovery allowed scholars to study the poet's philosophical theories directly from the source rather than from secondary testimonies. Lucretius' axioms led to extreme cultural changes from the Renaissance onwards. However, translations of Lucretius' opus were not as common as other more popular and easier-to-understand Classical authors' works. The Elizabethan Edmund Spenser, who used Lucretius' invocation to Venus in the *Fairie Queene* (1590), translated some passages of the Lucretian masterpiece. Lucretius frequently repeats the prayer to the goddess, whereas Spenser introduces the supplication in the tenth stanza of Book IV of his masterpiece. One century later, Dryden translated some passages that he adapted for his collection of miscellanies called *Sylvae,* published in 1685, a reminiscence of Statius's poetical masterpiece. Neither Spenser nor Dryden translated the poet's work in its entirety. John Evelyn was the first to translate the first two books of the *Nature of Things* in the seventeenth century. Thomas Creech published his complete translation of Lucretius in heroic couplets anonymously in 1682, featuring the symbolic title of *Daphnis*. Creech's second edition was issued the following year with the original title and the translator's name. Creech's translation, which went through eight editions between its first printing in 1682 and 1793, would remain the standard complete English translation of the didactic poem. In addition to Creech's poetical version, Dryden's partial translation, while deemed particularly licentious, was equally popular. Davis (2005: 185) explains, "The reputation of Lucretius flowered as never before in English culture during this period, in tandem with that of the philosopher Epicurus, whose atomistic cosmology and rationalist ethics the *De Rerum*

Natura was written to inculcate". A prose translation was published in 1743, complete with the Latin text. The anonymous translator mentions previous translations, and the text resonates with the language used during the second part of the eighteenth century, later absorbed by Gothic writers.

The complexity of the Latin masterpiece introduced uncertainties about its actual meaning. His theories derive their intricacy from the underlying contradictions of some ambiguous precepts that led scholars to the definition of an obscure Lucretian philosophy. The poet's ideas, based on Epicureanism, contextually developed a latent paradox, which can be explained as a co-existing anti-Lucretian ideology, founded on scepticism and pessimism. An example of a contradictory statement occurs when Lucretius describes the Olympian gods' peaceful and eternal life in Book III, after stating that nothing exists beyond physical matter, namely seeds, which he also calls atoms, an idea that he adapts from Anaxagoras's principles. Paul Hammond (2001: 158) writes that it was easy "to find Lucretius taken to exemplify the ultimate threat to Christian orthodoxy, or to consider Epicureanism synonymous of libertinism", as he was reputed to be the epitome of unbelief. He changed the mechanical atomistic theory by adding the notion of "swerve" (the Latin *clinamen*), a soft movement allowing atoms to change their direction. Thanks to the notion of swerve, he could therefore deny determinism and introduce the idea of free will, a positive element, whose counterpart is the blind cruelty of nature that can violently strike humankind at any moment. Stephen Greenblatt (2011) highlights how the revolutionary idea of swerve in Lucretius had a remarkable influence on the Quattrocento and the Renaissance.

The Nature of Things comprises six books that develop three major themes. The first theme contains observations of physics, based on atomism and Epicurus' teachings. The second theme features the anthropological theorisation of the characteristics of humanity and the last theme concerns distressing manifestations of nature, and the puzzling essence of the universe. The poet starts by showing categories and oppositions such as being and nothingness; matter and void; body, mind, and soul; time, space and infinity. He then describes and explains all forms of physical phenomena. Hammond (2001) highlights that Dryden was frequently associated with the Latin poet, as he was one of the most attentive British scholars of Epicurean philosophy. Lucretius extensively analysed Epicurus' doctrine in his masterpiece in order to demonstrate that it was the best philosophical way to improve human existence and the life of all creatures on earth. However, Epicurean lines of reasoning were often misinterpreted due to the focus on the term "pleasure", present in both Epicurean and Lucretian argumentations with relative frequency. Hammond also remarks that Dryden was interested in distinguishing the genuine Epicurean philosophy from its distorted libertine version during the Restoration, by stressing that Epicurus' exaltation of pleasure in fact referred to the tranquillity of the mind, a concept reiterated in every book of *The Nature of Things* (henceforth *LN* in citations). Peace of mind and tranquillity in the Epicurean sense are brought about by the absence of pain and fear, two feelings that unjustly dominate the lives of human beings and turn them into unhappy creatures. Epicureanism is, in reality, a doctrine that sets moral serenity as its aim. The peacefulness that it targets is different from the purely hedonistic philosophical thoughts of late seventeenth- and eighteenth-century libertine ideals, less involved with peace of mind and soul than with carnal desire and fulfilment. Despite the intrinsic differences between Epicureanism and the various currents of thoughts that originated from it, especially libertine philosophy, Epicurean and Lucretian teachings seemed to be an invitation to indulge in the senses. A further problem was connected with the negation of any metaphysical creative principle behind the existence of things: "Nature was not form'd by Powers Divine" (*LN*, 1: Book II, 203), a statement which is often interpreted as a declaration of atheism. The third book starts with a dedication to the great Epicurus. Lucretius wonders when the Greek philosopher first realised that Nature was not created by a divine entity. Following the Epicurean teachings, he intends to make superstition and the fear of death disappear and adds that all elements in the world are made of atoms alternating with the void. Like the body, mind and soul are made of similar parts called atoms, or seeds, what Aristotle had categorised as *homoeomery*. The poet's analysis continues: "but say, that common Seeds of many Things in various Order join'd, are mix'd in every Thing, and lie conceal'd" (*LN*, 1: II, 204). Therefore, according to Lucretius the death of one's body is inevitably followed by the death of one's soul.

The Latin author's influence is pervasive and has been unexpectedly found in Romantic authors. Willard Spiegelman (1985) and Martin Priestman (2007) have studied the relationship between Wordsworth and Lucretius. Commenting on the discovery of a manuscript at the end of the 1990s containing Wordsworth's translation of Latin works, Gillespie (2011: 111–112) suggests the Romantic poet's interaction with classical authors is now considered much more complex than was previously believed. Evidently, Wordsworth wanted to create general oblivion on his knowledge of the Classics to highlight the myth of his primeval and innate inspiration:

The shadowy status of this translation in the Wordsworth corpus raises questions about the reception of both Juvenal and Wordsworth. [...] If today we call Wordsworth a 'Romantic', a member of a school we oppose to that of his 'neoclassical' predecessors, one reason is that, perhaps partly following his own lead, we have been willing to play down his links to classical Greek and Roman poets (the latter being the stronger). No effort was needed to overlook his work on Juvenal: its demotion in his lifetime and its obscurity ever since is an orientation of the record, which in later life he himself wished when he asked for the manuscripts to be destroyed. The connections between the Classics and the romantic poets run deep despite all attempts, by Wordsworth, in particular, to erase them.

Spiegelman (1985: 27) claims, "a comparative analysis between two authors can either be based on tropes or topics: the first a rhetorical and formal, the second a thematic and ideological way of establishing connections among writers". The quest for Lucretian influences in Beckford may be based on both stylistic and thematic aspects of their works, and on their philosophical affinities, if any, in order to find what Spiegelman calls a "meeting-place" between two writers. Norton and other scholars agree that Beckford started learning the Classics when he was still very young. In all probability, he had read either the Lucretian original or its translations. His fluency in ancient languages would help him to understand the difficult Lucretian masterpiece. A series of allusions in *Vathek* substantiate the Latin poet's influence. One of the majestic palaces built for Vathek should give joy to the eyes, but it does not exclusively contain exquisite works of art. One part of the marvellous construction "exhibited in their several classes the various gifts that Heaven had bestowed on our globe" (*Vathek*: 2). Beckford uses the term "naturalist" to describe this section of the palace, which reproduces all aspects of nature. It is a reference to the Greek Hesiod and, most of all, to the Roman Lucretius, who were the two authors depicting the works of nature in their astounding totality. Theirs was a didactic celebration of the world's mysteries and marvels. The introductory sentence in *Vathek* is particularly interesting, as it shows a connection with the atheistic creed in Lucretius by mingling it with eighteenth-century libertinism:

Being much addicted to women and the pleasures of the table, he sought by his affability, to produce agreeable companions; and he succeeded the better, as his generosity was unbounded and his indulgence unrestrained: for he did not think [...] that it was necessary to make a hell of this world to enjoy paradise in the next. (*Vathek*: 2)

Beckford presents some ambiguous statements that Graham (1975) finds extremely ironic in tone. In reality, they are contradictory and hermeneutically unclear, but show a connection with the Lucretian doctrine and make readers realise from the very beginning of the story that the caliph is intent on satisfying his senses hedonistically, interpreting Lucretius through the lenses of libertinism *a la mode* in that period. Being the only instruments that all creatures have to understand the world, the senses are the most important factors: "And what can be more sure than are our Senses to us, by which we fully know Falsehood from Truth?" (*LN* 1: I, 59). These words are a strong assertion of the phenomenological value of sensory experience and indicate his desire to employ the senses as the only source of truth in the physical world. Interestingly, Vathek orders the construction of palaces dedicated to the five senses and uses them to enjoy life and acquire unlimited knowledge. By showing "affability", Vathek is following an Epicurean rule, suggesting harmony in human relationships to improve both personal and general conditions. The caliph and his actions initially seem to be linked to positivity. However, the admirable quality conveyed by his "generosity" is accompanied by the ambiguous presence of "indulgence", connected with tolerance but also selfishness. Finally, the short passage culminates with the Manichean dichotomy between "paradise" and "hell". The two terms introduce a pessimistic feeling and a sharp contrast, as they are the only two possible alternatives in caliph Vathek's existence, the extremes dominating his sumptuous life and miserable destiny. Lucretius explains that the constant fear of death and the afterlife mar our lives. He writes that we should create a better world by using the means at our disposal to enjoy life to the fullest since we only have one. He also thinks that certain categories of men do not comply with the Epicurean suggestions of inner tranquillity and become violent and disruptive, desirous of ruining theirs and other people's lives. Vathek's wants to avoid hell and create paradise on earth. However, the character's ambiguity becomes immediately evident when we discover a few pages later that Vathek is, in fact, making a hell of this world for everyone surrounding him. He has a boundless thirst for power; therefore, he represents the Lucretian negative version of a human being. *Vathek's* initial short passage appears to reproduce the caliph's future dramatic parable in a nutshell. The third book of *Nature* describes the excesses of cruel men, which may be easily adapted to Vathek:

Covetousness and the blind Desire of Honours, which compel unhappy Men to exceed the Bounds of Right, and urge on the Partners and Assistants of their Crimes to strive Day and Night with the utmost Pains, to arrive at the Height of Wealth. These Plagues of Life are chiefly nourished by the Fear of Death; for Infamy, and Contempt, and sharp Want, seem far removed from a sweet and pure State of Life, and, as it were, hover about the Gates of Death; and therefore whilst Men, possessed by a false Fear, labour to avoid, and stand at the remotest distance from them, they add to their Heaps by Civil War, and, insatiable as they are, double their Riches, heaping one Murder upon another. They laugh with cruel Delight at the sad Funeral of a Brother, and hate and fear the Entertainments of their nearest Relations. (*LN* 1: III, 207)

This is one of gloomiest and most pessimistic descriptions in the poem. It deeply contrasts the idealised image of an Epicurean state of *ataraxia* that aims to remain distant from every form of suffering, either physical or moral. The passage features one of the dark visualisations in Lucretius' work, betraying his pessimism about the painful essence of human existence. Not all men are ready to follow the dictum of a serene life because they feel envy and "covetousness". Vathek belongs to that category of men "at the height of wealth, laugh[ing] with cruel delight", indifferent to the suffering of the less fortunate. The Latin poet claims that the fear of death transforms men into frightened creatures, whereas greed turns others into murderers and tormentors. Lucretius considers these unhappy men "insatiable". "Insatiable" is the term Beckford often uses to define Vathek and his actions that turn him into a "tormentor". Whether he feels infinite thirst, or extreme hunger, excessive lust, the desire for power or wisdom, the caliph is "insatiable" in a way that recalls Lucretius' "unhappy Men". This problematic dissatisfaction is part of many individuals in a dangerous way: "And then to be always obliging an ungrateful Mind, to be ever pouring Favours upon it, and never satisfy it, which the Seasons of the Year, as they turn about, are always doing; they produce their fruits, and the whole variety of their Delights, and yet we are never filled with the Blessings of Life" (*LN* 2: IV, 280). This pessimistic idea is repeated by Robinson's character St Clair in *Hubert de Sevrac* (1796), as we see in the chapter dedicated to that novel. The impossibility for the human race to reach full enjoyment is one of the limits of existence. Similarly, this constant lack of satisfaction and multiple forms of anxiety doom Vathek's life despite his unlimited riches and power. Like the cruel men in *The Nature of Things*, Vathek is convinced of his immortality. He is sure that he will be able to avoid what Lucretius calls "the Gates of Death". However, Vathek's urge to have infinite riches, knowledge and control leads him to the mysterious and fatal "gates of Eblis", a metaphor for hell and death. Lucretius expresses a philosophical pessimism concerning mankind (the world of men around him), which is mirrored in Vathek's complex character. Whether consciously or unconsciously, Beckford follows the Latin poet's dichotomy in alternating positive beginnings and negative conclusions. He conveys this oscillation between two contrasting poles by means of a narrative strategy of unexpected contrasts. This strategy is not only what Graham defines as "irony" and does not represent a writing mode tending to bathos either. Beckford's stylistic technique reflects what he calls "the ominous preliminary of a "sink[ing] with terror" that awaits the characters at the end of the story (*Vathek*: 111). Before his fall, the caliph starts his life surrounded by pleasant diversions that cannot, however, satisfy his anxious desire for more. On the other hand, Lucretius explains that humankind's physicality guides people to start their search for peace, which is bodily, mental and emotional and represents the absence of pain:

Because the Spirits or Particles of Matter that maintain the Course, must be got together from all parts of the Body, and stirr'd thro' every Limb, and fitly united, that they may readily follow the eager Desire of the Mind. You see then, the Beginning of Motion rises in the Heart, proceeds then by means of the Will, and is thence diffused thro' every Limb, over the whole Body. (*LN* 1: II, 121)

However, Beckford's protagonist caricatures the Lucretian ideals and becomes the slave of his inclinations. The paradise he enjoys on earth turns into a hell for him and everyone else. Vathek's desire for absolute power and boundless indulgence culminates in the labyrinthine Hall of the daemonic Eblis, a gloomy maze of eternal despair, where suffering never stops. The mysterious deities governing the magic place are indifferent to hardships falling on humankind. When Eblis appears, Vathek and Nouronihar observe that "his person was that of a young man" and that he spoke "with a voice more mild than might be imagined" (*Vathek*: 111). Even if a "veil of melancholy" covers his eyes, the devilish divinity is calm and indifferent to Vathek and Nouronihar, and to the rest of humanity as well, recalling Lucretius' distant and disdainful divinities living peacefully in an unfathomable region:

The Deity of the Gods, their calm Abode appears, which neither Winds disturb, nor Clouds o'erflow with Showers, nor the white-falling snow, congealed by sharpest Frost, does spoil; but the unclouded Air surrounds them always, and smiles on them fully with diffused Light. Nature in every thing supplies their Wants; nothing at any Time destroys their Peace. (*LN* 1: III, 203)

A further analogy between indifferent divinities in Lucretius and Beckford lies in their extreme verticality. Lucretius' superior entities live on a distant space above the world, far away from human beings. The maze-like abode of Eblis, distant and untraceable, lies in a mysterious abyss. Beckford's deities hide in an immense chasm that Garrett (1992) interprets as an infinitude of tribulation. To follow the divinity, the caliph and the other characters experience what Jung (2011: 304) calls "a narrative of sublime fall". From the very first lines of the novel and despite its pompous beginning, recalling *The Arabian Nights* and other exotic narratives, Beckford's text is intertwined with hedonistic ideals:

[Vathek] surpassed in magnificence all his predecessors. The palace of Alkoremi, which his father, Motassem, had erected on the hill of Pied Horses, and which commanded the whole city of Samarah, was, in his idea far too scanty: he added therefore, five wings, or rather other palaces, which he destined for the particular gratifications of each of the senses. (*Vathek*: 2)

The passage introduces the protagonist's hedonistic penchant for pure enjoyment to satisfy his senses. He can indulge in beautiful forms, sweet perfumes, harmonious music, soft textures and luxurious meals in every moment, and his contentment knows no limits amid "substantial pleasures" (*Vathek*: 14). Interestingly, the satisfaction of each and every sense is essential for Lucretius, interested as he is in advocating mankind's physical life. However, the bizarre caliph becomes a parody of the poet's teachings and eventually embodies the negative stereotype associated with the followers of Epicurus, the paradigm of superficial enjoyment abhorred by the philosopher's detractors. More than on empty gratification, the message concentrates on the scientific physicality of the senses:

So plain it is that so*me*thing is continually flowing off from All Bodies, and is scattered all about; there is no Intermission; the Seeds never cease to flow, because we continue to feel, to see, to smell, and hear. Besides, since any Figure we feel with our Hands in the Dark, we know to be the same we before saw by Day, and in the clearest Light, the Touch and Sight must need be moved by the same cause. (*LN* 2: IV, 25)

Exaggerating the Lucretian creed, Vathek's life is a carrousel of unrestrained Epicureanism and explicit eroticism. He seems a sincere adept of Lucretian teachings, which imply the development of pacific behaviour in order to let Venus, the goddess of love and divine beauty, rule over his life: "Notwithstanding the sensuality in which Vathek indulged, he experienced no abatement in the love of his people, who thought that a sovereign giving himself up to pleasure, was able to govern, as one who declared himself an enemy to it" (*Vathek*: 3). The passage shows the exaltation of the protagonist's sensuality, the atmosphere of an ancient fairy tale, and the importance of physical satisfaction, but the sentence ends with a flat statement introducing irony and questioning previous utterances. Ironically, Vathek's subjects have changed their opinion and a feeling of resignation has replaced their initial exaltation for the young ruler. Once more, Beckford starts his sentence by introducing an optimistic context, which is inevitably turned into a pessimistic or malicious conclusion, namely a caustic amplification of the dichotomy of contradictory precepts in *The Nature of Things*.

Lucretius and Beckford share other similarities. Learning plays an important role in both their works: "The Caliph [...] had studied so much for his amusement in the life-time of his father, as to acquire a great deal of knowledge, though not a sufficiency to satisfy himself; for he wished to know every thing". In his mother's words, Vathek is also "certainly possessed of every important science" (*Vathek*: 3, 9). Vathek's boundless desire for knowledge and power has been interpreted as a Faustian characteristic and the monstrous Giaour, mysteriously appearing and disappearing, would represent Mephistopheles tempting a weak man in order to obtain his soul. However, the constant ironic stance and the comic situations experienced by the main character make it difficult to compare *Vathek* and *Faust* (that Goethe published eight years after *Vathek*). Graham (1972: 244) provides the following explanation for Vathek's ambiguity, leading to an unresolved dichotomy:

Beckford's *Vathek* arose from this period of aesthetic unease. It reflects this period [...] by combining an optimistic view of man's capabilities with a pessimistic sense of man's anti-heroic ludicrousness. The obvious manifestation of Beckford's merging of an earlier and later concept of man is in his transformation of his central character from a romantic Faust-figure into a kind of Don Quixote.

In Book III, the Lain author describes the "divine pleasure" he feels in the pursuit of the Epicurean philosophy and infinite learning. The poet experiences a strange feeling, linked to amazement and exalted sensation, through the prodigious improvement of his knowledge. However, the ultimate wisdom that he needs is to improve the life of human beings, whereas Beckford's caliph is egoistically interested in himself and his personal satisfaction. Incapable of translating the mysterious changing words on the golden sabre that the hideous Giaour has given him, Vathek falls into a state of despair, which has a strange physical consequence:

Agitated with so much anxiety, Vathek entirely lost all firmness; a fever seized him, and his appetite failed. Instead of being one of the greatest eaters, he became as distinguished for drinking. So insatiable was the thirst which tormented him, that his mouth, like a funnel, was always open to receive the various liquors that might be poured into it, and especially cold water, which calmed him more than any other. (*Vathek*: 12)

One of the most evident effects of Vathek's anxiety and frustration is his "insatiable thirst", which is not only physical but also represents a reiterated metaphor of his "voraciousness", his "insatiable curiosity" and his frustrated desires. The perennially unsatisfied caliph and his inexhaustible longing for what he cannot obtain seem to forerun French literary trends. Half a century later, Beckford's story influenced the French symbolists. One of Charles Baudelaire's poems in *Flowers of Evil* (*Les Fleurs du Mal* 1857) is entitled "Sed non satiata", or "unsatisfied thirst". It describes the poet's anguish and sense of oppression because his lover, ostensibly taking him to God, leads him to a devilish place instead, reproducing Vathek's trajectory. Parreaux (1960b) posits that Beckford's novel played an important role in French literature for its evocative force. The knowledge that Vathek desires is part of the "power of darkness". He passes from one craving to the other, taken by the *sitis* that Lucretius illustrates, the "thirst" that human beings feel for their objects of desire. He asserts that "[T]he Pleasure we covet eagerly exceeds every thing we enjoyed before, as long as it is absent; but when we have it in our possession, we long passionately for another, and the same Thirst of Life hangs upon us, still gaping for more" (*LN* 1: III, 287). This passage seems to paraphrase and herald the caliph's story. *Vathek* offers more analogies associated with the angst described in *The Nature of Things*. A remarkable form of linguistic anxiety unites Beckford and Lucretius. On more than one occasion, Lucretius admits that the theme he has absorbed from Epicurus is complex, but it is difficult for him to find the correct words in Latin. Latin is for him too simple a language to express the Greek philosopher's difficult ideas: "I know it is hard to express in Latin verse the dark and mythic Notions of the Greek (for I have Things to say [that] require new Words) because the Tongue is poor, the Subject new" (*LN* 1: I, 17). The Latin author's awareness about his pioneering work makes him reason on the distinction and relationship between signifier and signified and in meta-literary terms. He has to borrow some words from the elegant Greek and adapt them to his philosophical speech in Latin, or use similes, metaphors and euphemisms to convey difficult concepts. The differences of men and women and their positions in the varied geographies of the world have created different sounds, words and idioms to express similar concepts in different languages:

And then, what is there so very wonderful in This, that Men, to whom Nature has given a Voice and a Tongue, should, according to the various knowledge they had conceived of the great Variety of Things, distinguish each of them by a proper Name; when mute Cattle, and the several Kinds of wild Beasts, express their Passions by different Voices and Sounds, when their Fear, their Grief, or their Joys are strong upon them? (*LN* 2: V, 201)

Lucretius reveals a metalinguistic sensibility as well as a meta-literary conscience when he emphasises that his poetical effort is a landmark in literature and philosophy. On the other hand, Vathek's linguistic musing becomes evident when he tries to guess the meaning of the mysterious words carved on the Giaour's sabre. No one can decipher their significance and this failure enrages the caliph. Roberts and Robertson (1996) interpret the Babel-like tower built by Vathek as a metaphor for the confusion of languages and, consequently, of meanings that prevents all characters from fully understanding each other. The incapability of mutual understanding and the powerlessness at deciphering the messages from superior entities become a central problem. Carathis' inaccurate reading of the stars, Nouronihar's ephemeral communication with the "dives", the incomprehensible divinities in the grotto, Vathek's misinterpretation of the Giaour, together with the changing words of the sabre and the strange words on the portal of Hell in Eblis are significant metalinguistic specimens of misunderstanding, misinterpretation, and epistemological unintelligibility, provoking anxiety in every single character. The caliph's inability to decipher meanings or his tendency to misunderstand messages are akin to the elusive character of interpretation and the risk of an impossible disambiguation of real significance, a problem conjectured by Umberto Eco (2001; 2004) in his studies on the problematic but indispensable nature of translation and its diachronic and/or synchronic difficulties. The virtual impossibility of transposing one language into another, anxiously felt by Lucretius and, in a different way, by Vathek, can be found in Eco's and other linguists' texts. The anonymous translator of the prose version writes about the difficulties in translating *The Nature of Things* in his Preface:

The Matter of this Poem must be confessed to be rugged, subtle, and stubborn; and every Composition of this Kind is like a Landscape, where craggy Mountains and broken Walls are intermixed with fair Meadows and smooth Streams. Our language [...] runs into Froth and Bubbles, is copious in Complement, and in Love Expressions, but very narrow and barren in Terms of Art, and Phrases suited to Philosophy; and those technical Words we have, more coarsely and cloudily in Verse. For these Reasons the Poetical Translation of Lucretius is often more perplexed and harsh than the Original. (*LN*: v)

Similarly, the anonymous translator underlines that his predecessors, Evelyn and Creech, encountered many difficulties in their translations and maybe only Dryden was able to acquire the Lucretian spirit and adequately translate it. Lucretius passes on his metalinguistic awareness to future generations concerning the mysteries of his masterpiece. Strangely aware of imprecise or contradictory interpretations, Vathek offers a reward to the translator of the mysterious message on the sabre, which he received as a gift. He sceptically promises to punish anyone improvising or pretending and confirms that: "I have skill enough to distinguish whether one translates or invents" (*Vathek*: 9). When an old, wise man finally manages to unveil the inscription, Vathek understands that the words on the sabre magically change, and their significance is consequently altered. He angrily dismisses the old man: "but it was not long before Vathek discovered abundant reason to regret his precipitation; for, though he could not decipher the characters himself, yet, by constantly poring upon them, he plainly perceived that they everyday changed; and, unfortunately, no other candidate offered to explain them" (14). This scene not only conveys one of the many comic effects but also offers a metalinguistic observation on the innumerable variety of lexicons. The mutating message on the golden sabre is an illustration of the myriad languages and the difficulty of knowing and understanding them. The task of translating is an art that is not easy to perform. On the other hand, Vathek is incapable of translating into words his rage for being the dupe of the monstrous Giaour. Roberts and Robertson (1996) regard the mutating and incomprehensible words on the sabre as emblematic of *Vathek's* "textual uncertainty", reflected in the character's permanent anxiety. The constant mutating of words may also represent the difficulty of interpretation of the novel, which offers a multiplicity of meanings. In a different context, Vathek is again furious at not being able to obtain a special "key" that the Giaour had promised him: "No language could express his rage and despair. He execrated the perfidy of the Indian; loaded him with the most infamous invectives; and stamped with his foot, as resolving to be heard" (27). Vathek cannot come to terms with multilingualism and the mystery hidden in an unknown speech. On the other hand, the great Latin poet is afraid that his language will not be up to the hauteur of the Greek language. Lucretius and Beckford share the same modern sensibility towards languages and seem to foretell the problem of sense and the reliability of translation, systematically tackled by linguists, semioticians and pragmatists.

Vathek's linguistic frustrations are not his only setbacks. Despite his immense power, the caliph faces some insurmountable limitations, which he tries to erase to no avail. Finding obstacles on his way, Vathek imitates the tyrannical attitude of his ruthless mother, Carathis, the quintessence of cruelty. One significant example of her malice occurs when she prepares for Vathek's expedition:

> During these preparations, Carathis, who never lost sight of her great object, which was to obtain favour with the power of darkness, made select parties of the fairest and most delicate ladies of the city: but in the midst of their gaiety, she contrived to introduce vipers amongst them, and to break pots of scorpions under the table. They all bit to wonder, and Carathis would have left her friends to die, were it not that, to fill up the time, she now and then amused herself in curing their wounds, with an excellent anodyne of her own invention: for the good Princess abhorred being indolent. (*Vathek*: 38)

The surreal passage illustrates the woman's wickedness, described in a light style interspersed with irony, tending to the grotesque. Indifferent to suffering or pain, Carathis (that some contemporaries identified as a parody of Beckford's mother) embodies the arch-villain of the story. However, the hideous human sacrifices she is ready to perform to obtain the Giaour's favour are inexorably useless; whether fifty innocent children, her zealous subjects, or whoever may be in her way to power, she is ready to complete the ghastliest actions in view of her conquest of supreme magic. However, her blind devotion to the dark forces proves to be delusional, as she is ferocious, but hermeneutically inadequate. She represents a further embodiment of *Nature*'s negative exemplifications of hard-hearted humankind.

Beckford introduces high doses of sensuality in his novel, which he clearly inherits from the Latin poet. It is in Book IV that Lucretius explicitly describes the *blanda voluptas*, or sexual pleasure, "the genial Feat of Love" in Dryden's version. Translators had constantly avoided Book IV for its straightforward descriptions of sexual intercourse. Dryden was the only one to transpose the graphic passage literally. The anonymous translator of the prose version naively admits that he can translate no further and prefers to insert Dryden's explicit rendering to complete the scandalous final part of Book IV. Lucretius illustrates the union of the bodies without using understatements, whereas *Vathek* only contains sexual innuendoes. He also provides a suggestion concerning the nourishment necessary to honour the carnal acts ruled by Venus, rendered with a certain degree of prudishness by the translator: "And the food we live upon is of no small importance; for the Seed increases through the limbs by some Meats, and it becomes watery and feeble by others" (*LN* 2: IV, 105). It might not be a coincidence that one of Vathek's palaces dedicated to the five senses in the hill of Pied Horses contains "tables continually covered with the most exquisite dainties, which were supplied both by night and by day, according to their constant consumption; whilst the most delicious wines and the choicest cordials flowed forth from a hundred fountains that were never exhausted" (*Vathek*: 2–3). The great variety of food is a stimulus for Vathek's sensuality. The passage not only describes abundance but also underlines Beckford's elegant prose, where the alliteration of the letter 'f' represents a rhetorical device meant to reproduce the eternal flowing of the delicious libation.

When the caliph embarks on his journey in search of the mysterious Hall of Eblis, he parts with his mother, but a new feminine figure enters the scene. The celestially beautiful Nouronihar conquers the caliph's heart. Although she is betrothed to the equally dazzling pre-adolescent Gulchenrouz, Vathek decides to seduce her even though the beautiful boy stands between them, embodying an ambivalent presence for his feminine traits and mysterious nature that exacerbate Vathek's feelings. Readers did not generally appreciate this latent sensuality and when Beckford's authorship of *Vathek* was clear, negative commentaries submerged the book and its author. Hester Lynch-Piozzi made some remarks in 1791 about "Mr. Beckford's *favourite propensity,* [which] is all along visible I think; particularly in the luscious Descriptions given of Gulchenrouz" (Lonsdale 2008: xxi). Even though there is no explicit sexual interaction between the caliph and other male characters, moralistic readers' morbid attention was always concentrated on that latent homoerotic aspect connected with the author's sexuality. Even if Gulchenrouz does not interact with the Caliph, his languid ingenuity creates a sexual tension that Beckford frequently emphasises. A passage in the fourth book about love makes a peculiar distinction between different forms of passion. Cupid's arrows can create multiform desires, either gynephilic, for a beautiful maid, or androphilic/ephebophilic, for a young man or a pubescent boy:

So he that is struck with the darts of *Venus* (whether some beauteous Boy, with Female Charms, the Arrow casts; or some more beauteous Maid, that shoots out Love from every Pore) tends to the Part that gave the Stroke; he is in Raptures to enjoy, to inject and to consummate; for the hot Desire to the Act foreshows the mighty Pleasure that attends it. (*LN* 2: IV, 89)

Although Beckford stresses Vathek's love for the beautiful sultan's daughter, he ambiguously stresses the boy's superior beauty. Once Vathek meets the two young people, he becomes obsessed with lust and exemplifies Lucretian ideas on physical passion. Lucretius does not only write about physical love and passion but also includes tragic descriptions in his narrations. He conveys one of the most vivid images when he explores the meaning of the sacred in a moving passage that warns against superstition and cruel rituals. He adds that Agamemnon's intention to sacrifice his daughter Iphigenia to propitiate the gods before leaving for Troy is horrendous and unnatural:

But in these things I fear you will suspect you are learning impious Rudiments of Reason, and entering in a Road of Wickedness. So far from this, reflect what sad flagitious Deeds Religion has produced; by her inspired the Grecian Chief, the First of Men at *Aulis, Diana's* altar shamefully defiled with Iphigenia's Blood; her Virgin Hair a Fillet bound, which hung in equal length on either side her Face [sic]; she saw her Father, cover'd with Sorrow, stand before the Altar; for pity to his Grief the butchering Priests concealed the Knife; the City at the sight o'erflowed with tears; the Virgin, dumb with Fear, fell low upon her knees on the hard

Earth; in vain the wretched Princess in Distress pleaded that the first gave the honoured Name of Father to the King's but hurried off, and dragged by wicked Hands, she trembling stood before the Altar: Alas! Not as a Virgin, the solemn Forms being duly done, is drawn with pleasing Force to Hymen's noble Rites, but a chaste Maid, just ripe for nuptial Joy, falls a sad Victim by a Father's Hand, only to beg a kind propitious gale for Grecian Ships: such scenes of Villainy Religion could inspire! (*LN* 1: I, 13)

Through his passionate harangue, the poet intends to convince his readers of the rightness of his thought and denounce the excesses dictated by irrational belief. Cruel sacrifices are performed in Beckford's novel as well. Most victims in *Vathek* are young, and even though their destruction is often narrated in an apparently superficial tone, the innermost cruelty and injustice of these actions are dramatically evident. Carathis and Vathek exhibit a distorted form of religiosity that turns into superstition, similar to the one abhorred by Lucretius and described in the passage above. Vathek's gloomy ending serves as the metaphor of an Epicurean ideal gone wrong. What the poet writes in his fifth book is intriguing because it coincidentally anticipates the characters' epilogue in *Vathek*: "But Men strive to be renowned and powerful, that their Fortune may stand firm upon a lasting Foundation, and the Wealthy cannot fail to live at ease. All absurd! For those who labour to reach the highest Honours, make a very unhappy Journey in the End: Envy, like a Thunderbolt, strikes them from the Pinnacle of their Glory, and tumbles them down with Scorn into an Abyss of Misery" (*LN* 2: V, 205). The "Abyss of Misery", rendered with a splendid alliteration in Latin as "Tartara taetra" (the gloomy Tartarus), is represented by the Hall of Eblis, where "the ruins of an immense palace" with "gloomy watch-towers [...] of an architecture unknown inspired emotions of terror". The mystery of Eblis will forever enclose Vathek. The following words in *Nature* create images that match Vathek's everlasting anguish:

One, tired at home, leaves his noble Seat, and goes often abroad but returns suddenly again; for he finds no Relief by shifting his Place. Another hurries and drives full-speed to his Country-house, as it was all o' fire, and he came to extinguish it; he no sooner sets his foot within the doors, but presently begins to yawn, or falls heavily to sleep, and strives to forget himself, or else posts as hard back, and returns to Town again. Thus he tries all ways to fly himself, but that Self it is, as it must be, out of his power to escape; he sticks close to him against his will, and sorely torments him. The restless Fool does not know the Cause of his Disease, if he thoroughly did, Every one would give up all other Pursuits, and apply chiefly to search into the Nature of Things. (*LN* 1: III, 287)

The only way out of these existential conundrums lies in the will to study the physical world and discover the real essence of existence, an impossible task for Vathek, a constant prey to his unrelenting proclivities. *The Nature of Things* provides further topics that are omnipresent in *Vathek*. The descriptions of the ruins at the entrance of Eblis or the destruction of Carathis' high tower allude to the fifth book, showing the inevitable laws of nature against men's creations. Nature's extreme violence equals its unparalleled beauty. One of the images conveying nature's major impact includes the representation of a terrible sea storm at the beginning of Book II. Almost entirely dedicated to the most intense phenomena, Book VI conveys dramatic portrayals of Nature's disruptive character. Troubling atmospheric events also take place in *Vathek,* and their effects are both devastating and ominous. A formidable storm breaks out when Carathis starts her last journey towards Eblis, and dramatic atmospheric effects accompany the characters during their fatal journey. Vathek's earthly power can do nothing against the destroying forces of nature. Intriguingly, both Beckford and Lucretius depict a particularly lugubrious environment, instilling deep pessimism and foreshadowing the mournful ending of Lewis's *The Monk.* A horrid finale awaits some characters to conclude their sad parable. Once the illusion of power has been destroyed, Vathek and his companions are taken by a terrible inner pain in "their hearts" that "took fire", a fire that will burn in perpetuity. The intriguing equivalent in Lucretius is the account of the plague in Athens, which describes similar effects:

The Head was first attack'd with furious Heats, and then the Eyes turn'd bloodshot and inflamed; the Jaws within sweated with black bloods; the Throat (the Passage of the Voice) was stopt by Ulcers; the Tongue (the Interpretation of the Mind) o'erflowed with Gore, and faulter'd with the Disease, felt rough, and scarce could move (*LN* 2: VI, 321).

Lucretius describes all the terrible consequences of the disease. The interior damage finally flows to the victim's heart before provoking a horrible death. The strong image of the heart as the centre of physical (Lucretius) and moral (Beckford) contamination further confirms the deep connection between the two authors and the undeniable, unrelenting influence the Latin author had on Beckford.

Vathek's excesses might recall not only Eastern despotic rulers but also Roman emperors' follies, such as those of Caligula and Nero, revived by Beckford's contemporary Edward Gibbon, whose six-volume *History of the Decline and Fall of the Roman Empire* was published between the 1770s and the 1780s, creating a remarkable impact on contemporary readers. It may be plausible to think that Beckford, an attentive student, had reversed much of his knowledge in *Vathek,* a text that is comparable to a literary blend of composite styles. A highly inventive classical text, written around 60 CE and profoundly critical of the corrupted society of the time, Petronius's *Satyricon* features the shamefully rich Trimalchio, indulging in every pleasure. A negative character embodying the decadence of the times, Trimalchio shares several traits with *Vathek*'s extravagant and bizarre caliph and could be considered his double in his unlimited hedonistic pursuit. Active in the first century CE and a person of rare elegance, the Latin author Petronius Arbiter Elegantiarum was a contemporary of Emperor Nero. According to Tacitus's testimony in his *Annals* (circa 110 CE), Petronius, a lover of riches and luxury, leading a profligate life, described the decadence of Rome in his celebrated *Satyricon*, a semi-fantastic ironic story full of graphic allusions to real people. The protagonist is in love with his young servant, a handsome sixteen-year-old boy, an object of sexual desire for both men and women. Narrated in the form of a novel, *Satyricon*'s entire text was never recuperated in its entirety. An example of "late arrival" in England's cultural panorama, Petronius was first "englished" in 1659 (Gillespie 2005: 132). William Burnaby's translation in 1694 "prioritises the virtue of liveliness over that of accuracy. There is an attractive inventiveness in the way in which Burnaby plays off one linguistic register against another. His control of long sentences is real and for the most part assured, though with a winning air of improvisation" (Glynn Pursglove and Karina Williamson 2005: 303). This form of literary originality is also noticeable in Beckford's unusual novel. Other translations of *The Satyricon* in the eighteenth century were expurgated because of the constant risk of obscenity: some translators applied "the traditional fig-leaves" to the obscene parts of the text, as Pursglove and Williamson humorously explain. Notwithstanding its scandalous nature, the text offered a valuable analysis of the customs of the times, especially of the lower classes, generally ignored in literary works when Petronius was active. It is plausible that Burnaby's style of translation, with his frequent changes of "linguistic register", may have been contributory to the narrative development of *Vathek*. One of the possible meanings of Petronius's text

147

is that opulence and wealth cannot save Trimalchio. Like Trimalchio, Vathek is doomed to a harrowing end.

Beckford's sources, ideas and images make it difficult to decipher his novel in a satisfactory way, as its dimension is complex and its real meaning obscure. Even though its Oriental façade seems majestic, it is but a theatrical curtain that progressively reveals different cultural universes. Whereas the French Enlightenment leaves some traces, and Dante's *Inferno* moulds parts of Beckford's finale, as we will see in other chapters, the Gothic dominates the plot on various occasions, releasing strange fears, running deeper than in previous Gothic novels by Walpole, Reeve, or Lee. Beckford constructs a strange narrative performance that is at the same time poetic and dramatic, based on extreme visual effects. The text's classical stance and Lucretius' concepts permeate several pages despite the text's apparent exoticism, hiding a subtly moral message. Misunderstanding the dangers of excess and greed, Vathek cannot use his unlimited riches to save himself from his horrible doom in a Gothic hell. The destiny of Vathek in Beckford's novel becomes the perfect representation of Lucretius' tormentous "Abyss of Misery".

The innumerable roseate tints which the parting sunbeams reflected on the rocks above, and the fine vermil glow diffused over the romantic scene beneath, softly fading from the eye, as the nightshades fell, excited sensations of a sweet and tranquil nature.
(Ann Radcliffe. *A Sicilian Romance*)

Featuring an adventurous and passionate story, *The Romance of the Forest* (1791) is not generally considered Radcliffe's most important novel, as *The Mysteries of Udolpho* (1794) is almost unanimously reputed to be her masterpiece, though it frequently shares this tribute with *The Italian* (1797). Despite its apparent secondary role, *The Romance of the Forest* was universally acclaimed and made the author famous, as various critics have convincingly demonstrated (Deborah Rogers 1994; Lévy 1995; Clery 1995; Norton 1999b; Gamer 2000; Chloe Chard 2009). Her third novel allowed Radcliffe to abandon literary anonymity and become one of the most important writers at the end of the eighteenth century, influencing generations of Gothic writers and Romantic poets, including Coleridge, Wordsworth, Byron, Shelley and Keats. Her fame was obscured after a number of dismissive opinions that had a durable negative effect. Wordsworth abundantly used images taken from Radcliffe's works but did not admit to borrowing from the authoress he had harshly, though indirectly, criticised in his "Preface to *The Lyrical Ballads*" (1798). The prologue to the poetic collection was not only the manifesto of Romanticism but also a strong statement to demonstrate the superiority of the author's works to eclipse his popular rival. Coleridge had mixed feelings about Radcliffe's literary creations, a fact that did not prevent him from using and adapting images from her *repertoire*. Byron was also ambiguous in his critical judgment concerning Radcliffe, although his ambivalence did not prevent him from copying themes and images from her novels. In his exhaustive biography, *The Mistress of Udolpho* (1999), Norton claims that the characterisation of Schedoni, one of Radcliffe's most powerful characters, musing on his crimes, clearly influenced Byron. On his part, the poet conceded the impression Radcliffe's description of Venice had on him when creating *Childe Herold's Pilgrimage* (1812), while critics almost unanimously remarked that *Lara* (1814) was close to plagiarism (Rogers 1996). Scott, whose *Waverley* novels imitated the atmospheres of her works, recognised Radcliffe as the "Mighty Enchantress" in his *Life of the Novelists* (1826). However, he also expressed unfavourable opinions, which, in certain circumstances, seemed to be a strategy to discredit contemporary female writers with subtlety when critically analysing their works, intent as he was on constructing his literary identity and "romancing the past" (Lowell T. Frye 1996). Scott's ambiguously laudatory and, at the same time, disparaging analysis considered Radcliffe's poetic quality to be the result of an exuberant imagination with a talent for the romantic and the mysterious. However, his definition of her typical readers was not particularly commendatory when he specified that only "the lonely invalid and neglected votary of celibacy" could appreciate her works. Scott's critique was not without contradictions, marked as it was by a strange form of alternating judgment, oscillating between appreciation and dismissal. Scott unflatteringly concludes, with a sort of litotical discourse, "Mrs. Radcliffe rather walks in fairy land than in the region of realities, and she has neither displayed the command of the human passions, nor the insight into the human heart, nor the observation of life and manners, which recommend other authors in the same line. But she has taken the lead in a line of composition" (Scott 1826: 100). Like Wordsworth heralding his poetry, Scott preserves his own profile as a novelist and is fundamentally pitiless at Radcliffe's expenses.

Gamer (2000), along with Baldick and Mighall (2000), conjectures that Wordsworth played a major role in destroying Radcliffe and the early Gothic. An unrelenting detractor of Radcliffe, Jane Austen was even more lethal than any vehement critic. *Northanger Abbey* (1817) was the ultimate parody of Radcliffe, while *Emma* (1815) connects *The Romance of the Forest* with a character of poor discernment: "[Emma] was not struck by anything remarkably clever in Miss Smith's conversation [...] Harriet certainly was not clever [...] Harriet had no penetration". When Harriet confesses that she read *The Romance of the Forest,* her stupidity is universally acknowledged (*Emma*: 32–37). The consequent demolition of Radcliffe's reputation is complete. Shelley, Mary Shelley and John Keats were sincere in their admiration for Radcliffe and outspoken in admitting her great influence on their works. The epithet "Mother Radcliffe" in Keats's private correspondence to George and Georgiana Keats celebrates her influence on the creation of some of his poems (Beatrice Battaglia 2008: 7). Thomas De Quincey dubbed her "the Great Enchantress" in *Confessions of an English Opium-Eater* (1821). Positive critical opinions on Radcliffe's novels were general but not unanimous. One of the most aggressive critiques was expressed by Polwhele in his 1798 poem *The Unsex'd Females*. The conservative intellectual and well-known translator of Greek authors attacked the most popular women writers of the day, including Radcliffe, throwing a lasting shadow on their works. Nancy Armstrong (1987) reveals that the Anglo-Irish novelist and writer of children's books, Maria Edgeworth, authored a text about proper activities for women with unflattering observations, indirectly aimed at Radcliffe, implying that her novels dangerously distracted young women from their duties. Anna Seward's caustic judgement concerning *The Plays of Passion*, written by Joanna Baillie, but wrongly attributed to Radcliffe on their publication, were detrimental. Additional negative commentaries by Seward demonstrate she had a blunt conception of Radcliffe's works. Such a severe judgement probably disappointed Radcliffe, considering she had honoured Seward by citing some of her verses in her novels (Rogers 1996: 41, 48). Unpromising reviews and more or less understated negative opinions contributed to the decline of Radcliffe's literary reputation in the decades to come. Margaret Oliphant was one of the few scholars, together with Cristina Rossetti, to express a positive opinion about the writer in the nineteenth century. Julia Kavanagh's (1862) was peremptory in denigrating Radcliffe. She wrote brutally unflattering commentaries, reflecting Victorian detrimental opinions on Radcliffe. Confirming Kavanagh's opinion, an American critic, Bridget MacCarthy, delineated a scathing profile of Radcliffe in the 1940s, acidly describing her as a hopeless illiterate, incapable of arousing the least interest in the public. Unfavourable critical opinions dimmed Radcliffe's fame starting from the first decades of the nineteenth century and continuing into the twentieth century. Rogers (1994) suggests that the oblivion and the indifference, ignited by Wordsworth's criticism, Polwhele's attacks, Austen's caustic irony and further fault-finding commentaries, persisted for quite a long time, with the exception of three favourable biographies published by women scholars (Clara McIntyre 1920; Alida Wieten 1926; Aline Grant 1951). *The Gothic Flame* (1966) by Varma was the turning point in Radcliffe's re-evaluation (Rogers 2007: 46).

Radcliffe has been frequently included in the category of female Gothic writers (Miles 1993; Castle 1995, among various others). Traceable in some of the first reviewers and critics of her novels, this idea was adopted by Scott himself as a latent confirmation of the superiority of male writing with a derogatory nuance. As we saw in previous chapters, a distinction was sometimes identified between male and female writers. Pioneering feminist studies identify women's works as distinguishable from male writers' (Ellen Moers 1976; Juliann Fleenor 1983; Jane Spenser 1989), a perspective supported by several critics. Deborah Ross (1991) recognises the importance of these studies, but avoids using the phrase "female Gothic". This rigid definition does not include the variety of works by male and female writers of the last decades of the eighteenth century and beginning of the nineteenth century. Gendered authorship became fluid in a period in which women used male pseudonyms (or anonymity) to avoid criticism against their sex, and on the other hand, some male authors pretended to be women in order to be successful writers of sentimental or horror fiction. The male Gothic is usually circumscribed to Walpole's, Lewis's and Beckford's works, which are rather unique per se and difficult to be categorised or gendered, apart from their tendency to make up negative finales for some characters. In fact, Radcliffe's writing is complex and moulded by the influence of multiple sources, mostly Classical and Renaissance, seldom acknowledged and frequently overlooked, although they are not casual but deeply rooted and consciously used.

Tracing Radcliffe's profile is rather complicated because of the lack of biographical material. She penned five books in less than eight years. All her novels became literary and financial bestsellers in Britain and across the Continent, and were frequently translated and widely read (Rogers 1996). Although Radcliffe, born Ward in 1764, the year of *Otranto*'s publication, into a lower middle-class Unitarian family of haberdashers (Thomas Noon Talfourd 1826; Rogers 1996), she had important relatives and ancestors on both parents' sides. She lived for some years with her uncle Thomas Bentley, a writer himself and the owner, together with Josiah Wedgwood, of the renowned Wedgwood china factory. An enlightened intellectual, Bentley was interested in art, philosophy, literature and politics, inviting academics, politicians, philosophers, architects, painters, musicians and writers to his house. This childhood experience enhanced Radcliffe's diverse cultural interests, promoted her avid readings and magnified her desire for knowledge. She published her first novel, *The Castles of Athlon and Dunbayne*, in 1789, followed by *A Sicilian Romance* in 1790. After *The Romance of the Forest*, her fame extended rapidly when reviews praised her literary genius. *The English Review* (1792) exalted the novel as an example of first-class writing. Lévy

(1995) affirms that it was Radcliffe's third novel that accelerated the Gothic, after two decades of sporadic creativity in the genre following Walpole's example. When she published *The Mysteries of Udolpho* in 1794, she was acclaimed as a great writer and became one of the best-paid novelists of her generation. Norton (1999b) assumes fame and money went hand in hand with an excessive scrutiny that disturbed the socially reluctant writer. Her last novel, *The Italian* (1797), published during her lifetime, was an enormous success, even though critical opinions were mixed (Rogers 1994). In spite of her growing fame, she stopped writing altogether. Anna Laetitia Barbauld was certain that Radcliffe could but write about hell, having gone too far with her horror stories (Norton 1999b: 136). Radcliffe apparently rejected any comparison between her works and *The Monk*, considered a direct consequence of her Gothic endeavours. After the expression "Radcliffe school" was coined at the end of the 1790s, she could not sustain the analogy between her creations and lower quality Gothic romances and *Schauerromane* (horrid novels influenced by German examples). In all probability, she did not accept being included in the literary hoi polloi imitating her style without reproducing her romantic touch. Published after her death, *Gaston De Blondeville* (1826) was her sixth novel, but it did not replicate her previous literary successes. Radcliffe's essay *On the Supernatural,* defining the differences between terror and horror in literature, was also published posthumously in the *New Monthly Magazine* in 1826 as a cultural meditation on narrative techniques (Gamer 2000). When Radcliffe died on 7 February 1823, she had not published anything for almost thirty years, and unless she had published anonymously, an assertion that we might hypothesise but we cannot demonstrate, her original Gothic and Romantic inspiration had apparently vanished. *Gaston de Blondeville* and her essay "On the Supernatural" both seem, if not antithetical, at least inexplicably discordant compared with her previous works. The mystifying change of style in her posthumous novel, written in an unusual language (Samuel Baker 2014; Clery 1995), might lead to the conclusion that she wanted to experiment with different forms of narration, provided she actually wrote it. Her apocryphal essay on the supernatural conveys many doubts about its genuine authorship. It might easily have been written by her husband in an effort to follow cultural stereotypes, orientate opinions on his wife's works and exploit her literary fame for financial reasons.

A further inexplicable mystery surrounding Radcliffe is the quasi-complete elimination of her writings and manuscripts after her death. Rogers, Norton, Miles and other scholars have scrutinised existing documents to counter-balance the lack of information; nevertheless, many points remain obscure. Obsessively edited by Radcliffe's husband, Talfourd's (1826) biographical portrayal cannot give an exhaustive image of the writer, and questions still remain unanswered. In his biography, Norton (1999b) embraces the idea that her husband may have masterminded her life in solitude and provoked her lasting depression. After his wife's death, he hurriedly married their governess and moved to France. He left his second wife a remarkable legacy of £ 80,000 when he died, only a few years after Ann. These events have generated speculation about possible wrongdoing. A casual finding in 2014 seems to confirm that things were difficult in Radcliffe's household. The British *Guardian* (Thursday 30 January 2014, 16.15 GMT) reported "a chance discovery in an archive of an extraordinarily rare letter by the queen of Gothic fiction" addressed to her mother-in-law, which seems to prove that family relationships were tense. Before this discovery, only two manuscripts existed in Ann Radcliffe's hand. Greg Buzwell, a curator at the British Library in London, came across the document inside a volume of miscellaneous letters. The date only mentions the day and the month, "but Buzwell suspects it was written in 1797", the year *The Italian* was published, and ironically argues that the story of Ellena de Rosalba and Marchesa de Vivaldi, the cruel mother-in-law in the novel, may have been inspired by her situation in real life. We might infer that the "Queen of Gothic fiction" lived a mysterious life dense with suspense. Radcliffe's novels have been analysed to find clues about her personality and detect biographical elements in an effort to understand the enigma of her secluded existence. Some scholars speculate that the intricacies and sense of anguish in her novels may represent the sign of an unsatisfactory life (Pierre Arnaud 1976) and critical literature on Radcliffe has sometimes adopted a psychoanalytical interpretation (Williams 1995; Rogers 2007; Miles 1993). Her plots have been interpreted as the symptom of possible painful personal experiences and/or hidden confessions (Lévy 1995; Norton 1999b). Duncan (1992) perceives a dualism within Radcliffe's Gothic that he defines as simultaneously alien and domestic, while Napier (1987) argues that Radcliffe's obsessive urge to stabilise her stories creates a tonal imbalance reflecting deeper issues. Other scholars, including Clery (2008), Chard (2009) and Alison Milbank (2014), have opted for textual and literary analyses of Radcliffe's works, which have uncovered a number of problems.

The first problem concerning Radcliffe's works implies her political perspective. Trying to determine whether Radcliffe's works were conservative or revolutionary has created two conflicting opinions about the true nature of her political views. Writers' different nuances of politicisation, either conscious or unconscious, were considered inevitable after the dramatic facts of the French Revolution (Paulson 1981; Punter 1996). Even though Radcliffe did not share Wollstonecraft's, Robinson's and other writers' political engagement in favour of the Revolution, she expressed understated political opinions according to Johnson (1995), a hypothesis dismissed by Chard (2009), while J. Watt (1999) asserts that she used aesthetics to avoid political discourse. In partial contradiction to Bakhtin's theories of dialogism and *heteroglossia*, conveying the interrelation between authors and their contemporary influences, either cultural or political, Howard (1994) believes that Radcliffe's novels were not openly subversive. Butler (1981) considers Radcliffe a sentimentalist but also a revolutionary, as her protagonists see the world through women's eyes, while living in a period when any potential form of subversion was constantly detected and rejected after the French Revolution. Feminist critics have the tendency to see Radcliffe's revolutionary message in favour of her own sex. Literary female experiences show a schizophrenia provoked by unbreakable patriarchal paradigms, which Moers (1976) and Fleenor (1983) consider particularly evident in the Gothic and in Radcliffe. Clery (1999b) asserts that Radcliffe was moderately liberal and the figures of her usually beautiful and reactive female protagonists seem to embody her latent radicalism. Adeline, Emilie and Ellena are perhaps the best examples for demonstrating the existence of the dialectics of freedom that is inherent to her novels. Radcliffe could not and would not be utterly radical because she obsessively conformed to the rules of propriety imposed on women due to her upbringing. Her female characters are compliant with social requests at the conclusion of their adventures. Radcliffe's writing is an epistemological compromise of the positivity of rationalism, the languor of sentimentalism and the extremes of Gothic fiction united to the writer's passionate expressions of Romanticism. Mary Poovey (1979) assumes that Radcliffe investigates the paradoxical role that sensibility plays in providing women power and an arena for action.

The second dichotomy in Radcliffe concerns the definition of her stories, wavering between the romance and the novel. Critics' inclination for genre codification to distinguish the novel from romance denotes a need for ordering, which recognises the novel as an expression (generally masculine) of pure realism, and romance as a description of female reactions to harsh patriarchy. Dieter Schulz observes (1973: 77) that "English and American criticism in fiction has traditionally distinguished between two chief modes of prose narrative, the realistic novel, and the non-realistic, poetic, and mythic romance". In her 1991 study on romance and realism, Ross rejects the traditional division between romance and the novel in female writing, as neither definition embraces multiple narrative nuances. According to Scott, the term romance justified the strangeness of Radcliffe's stories and, at the same time, excluded her from elite novelists of the calibre of Defoe, Richardson, Fielding, Smollett, Sterne and Scott himself. Summers (1969: 30) thought that her stories magically offered three different kinds of Gothic romance: the "historical", the "sentimental" and the "horror Gothic", a distinction that he did not clarify. Kilgour (1995) argues that the Gothic is a blended form of novel and romance, reinterpreting an idea expressed in the 1960s by Northrop Frye, who saw the novel as a "realistic displacement of romance" (Spenser 1989: 181). Like Baron Wilson (1839) in Lewis's biography, Talfourd (1826) included a brief survey on romance, explaining how Radcliffe had been able to create a new and stately literary form. One century before, Dryden had considered romance as a "fib", probably a reaction to contemporary romance novels of the French *Préciosité*. Traditionally, romance was not accepted as a literary form, and its re-introduction with Walpole's *The Castle of Otranto* had been considered a literary caprice, even though Hurd (1762) had given new dignity to the genre in his famous essay. Radcliffe certainly added an unusual and personal style to the romance, influencing a cohort of writers. Like Walpole, Reeve and Lee before them, Radcliffe, Lewis, Robinson and Mary Anne Radcliffe use the term romance, either in the title or as a subtitle, whereas Beckford entirely ignored it, even though his story may represent a romance. The early Gothic writers' intention is to communicate that the reader is entering a different narratological dimension. However, unlike Walpole, neither Radcliffe, nor Reeve nor Lewis use the term "Gothic" in their titles, even though the word can be frequently found in their narrations, albeit in relation to general architectural connotations.

A further interpretative problem in Radcliffe is linked to the so-called explained supernatural. Summers (1969) had defined this specific narrative choice as "anagnoristical elucidations" and, unlike the majority of critics, he seemed to enjoy this particular technique, whereas Coleridge, Scott, Barbauld and many others, were disappointed with her strategy of rationalising prodigious events. Radcliffe's obsession with providing explanations for the mysteries in her novels has been frequently seen as a stylistic fault. Norton (1999b) interprets it as a consequence of her religious background, while Clery (1995, 1998b) considers it an acceptance of the literary rules of balance and measure, and theorises that Radcliffe did not have real freedom of narrative choice, as a woman writer: Radcliffe may have let her readers fly in the realms of imagination on the condition that they came back to earth at the conclusion of her stories. However, some scholars are of a different opinion. *The Romance of the Forest* shows darker aspects that cannot be clarified even with the conclusive rationalisation of events. One element that remains unexplained is the physicality of Adeline's nightmares, connecting her with the netherworld: what Adeline experiences in her dreams is the image of a shocking crime with dire consequences. Moreover, the fairy-tale aspect and the mysterious situations of the novel are not accounted for. *The Italian* contains a similar situation, and Chaplin (2004: 137) reckons that "the marriage of Ellena and Vivaldi is celebrated in the mode of a fairy-tale. The novel's closure, instead of distancing the text from romance, reaffirms its status and thus commits itself to a sexually and textually anarchic mode of writing". Similarly, Groom (2017) identifies an atmosphere of suspended supernatural that is never exhaustively unveiled in the novel. Castle (1995: 83) focuses on the strange preternatural finale of *The Mysteries of Udolpho*, whose "mood of hypnotic, sweetish melancholy carries over into the last sentence of the novel. [...] Enchantments, shades, haunts, sacred spots, the revivification (through memory) of a dead father, a perpetually mourning reader: the scene is tremulous with hidden presences [...] home itself has become uncanny, a realm of *apophrades*". Doody (1977: 563) finds that "in *A Sicilian Romance* there is a variety of impressively intense dream-like sensations", while Lévy speculates that the supernatural is only partially explained and mystery subsists in the majority of Radcliffe's novels. It may seem that Radcliffe's narratives timidly but steadily tend towards genuine supernaturalism. After detecting incongruences in preternatural occurrences in *The Mysteries of Udolpho*, David Sander (2011) concludes that Radcliffe attempts to domesticate the supernatural, but her inadequate clarifications are incomplete glosses. It might seem that these observations on Radcliffe's treatment of the supernatural are evidence of the novelist's desire to experiment with multiple narrative possibilities while letting mysteries linger even after the narration ends. Other narrative aspects that convey further layers of ambiguity in her narrations also confirm Radcliffe's complexity.

Some stylistic aspects, such as the use of epigraphs and quotations, play an essential role in Radcliffe, who was desirous of literary fame. Citations of the Ancients were a must in eighteenth-century mainstream literature. The use of Latin (and, more rarely, Greek) epigraphs from Horace, Ovid, Juvenal, Statius and other classical authors can frequently be found in Richard Steele, Joseph Addison, Samuel Johnson, and the great majority of eighteenth-century male authors. Gender conventions or socio-cultural obligations might have motivated Radcliffe's exclusion of classical epigraphs in the original language. A female writer could receive universal recognition insofar as she did not trespass into intellectual male territory. Using epigraphs from Latin or Greek authors, either in their original language or in English, might not have been appreciated by a male audience or could have provoked mockery in case of misquotes. Citing the Classics implied using their original language, an enterprise that only scholars felt rightly entitled to and from which Radcliffe probably felt inevitably excluded. Popular in male poetry and prose, and used by Walpole and Lewis to introduce their Gothic tales, Horace was out of the question for a woman writer due to his ironic and even libertine connotations. Quoting from the elegant and daringly erotic Ovid was equally risky, as his influence could potentially be hazardous even for a man. Lucretius could have been misinterpreted and was too difficult an author to quote. A further reason for avoiding classical passages in Latin could represent a form of delicacy intended for her female readership, whose cultural knowledge was not homogenous, although at least half of Radcliffe's readers were men and the conviction that women were her exclusive public is the fruit of a long-established prejudice (Clery 1995: 98). Radcliffe probably wanted to avoid pomposity or bluestocking intellectualism. However, explicit references to the Classics or the mention of great authors from Antiquity such as Homer and Virgil are frequent in her texts. Their presence is not fortuitous and conveys significant meanings in the development of plots. Although she excluded the fashionable convention of Latin and Greek quotations from her epigraphs, she made two exceptions to this rule. First, Chapter XIII in Volume III of *The Mysteries of Udolpho* features a passage from Pope's translation of *the Iliad* that describes a horrible tempest. The epigraph may be read as an understated analogy of Emily's ordeals with the Homeric heroes' sufferings. Second, Chapter XVIII in *The Romance of the Forest* inserts a line by Joseph Trapp dedicated to Virgil's tomb that highlights Radcliffe's affinity with the Latin poet.

Radcliffe used multiple sources to show her respect for both ancient and contemporary works. *The Romance of the Forest* marks the beginning of the insertion of epigraphs conveying special messages, intended to connect with the deep meaning of the story. This device seems to perform two functions: one is suggestive, and the other is cultural. The epigraph usually creates some expectations and clues about the chapter, even though there is not always a strict correspondence between the short introductory passage and the development of the story; the epigraph has more of an evocative function that implies an imaginative response in the reader. The second function symbolises Radcliffe's homage to the author of the selected passage. In this way, Radcliffe's text becomes an ideal anthology of literary figures both past and present that she delights in including in her novels. Radcliffe's originality resided in her encyclopaedic mentions of authors, reinforcing cultural dissemination meant to reach larger audiences. Radcliffe shows appreciation for eighteenth-century writers. She frequently quotes Thompson's *The Seasons* (1730) and *The Castle of Indolence* (1748), poems exalting "the works of nature in imitation of the *Georgics* with panegyrics of country life, interspersed with tones of proud admiration for technological advancement, inherited from Newton" (James Sambrook 1972: xiii). Both poems imitated the Virgilian style with their didactic qualities describing the phases of agriculture and the inspiring cycles of the seasons. *The Seasons* exalted the changes of nature, also described by Oliver Goldsmith's *The Traveller* (1765) and Adam Smith's *The Wealth of Nations* (1776). Generally praised, Thompson was also the object of pungent criticism for his sentimental tones (Sebastian Mitchell 2013: 11). A contemporary of the Graveyard Poets, he did not share their taste for melancholic nocturnal scenes, but opted for the exaltation of nature in its manifold aspects. Another source for Radcliffe's epigraphs was Cowper's *The Task* (1785). Here, the poet sympathises "with the simple and humble of the earth" (Butler 1991: 36), in the manner of Gray's *Elegy written in a Country Churchyard* (1751). Radcliffe chose Beattie's meditations on nature from *The Minstrel* (1774), written in imitation of Spenserian stanzas. Radcliffe also cited the graveyard poets, especially Collins and Gray, whose gloomy visions provided her with atmospheres exalting obscurity and conveying a deep sense of mystery, complementary to the eminence of light in Neoclassicism and the Enlightenment. All these authors shared the representation of nature as a common denominator.

While some scholars have looked for German influences in Radcliffe's works, the possibility is remote, as she never cites German authors, in either her epigraphs or her stories. Contradicting her previous statements on Radcliffe as an original genius, Joyce Tompkins added an unconvincing appendix to the second edition of *The Popular Novel in Britain* (1969) to show a supposed analogy between Radcliffe and Schiller with no convincing evidence. In Summers' opinion (1969), the British public felt that German authors were unpatriotic, blasphemous and even unhealthy. Norton (1999b) reverses the myth of the German influence, supported by Ellis (2000) and others, by claiming that it was Radcliffe's style to influence the translators of German authors into English, and not the other way round.

Radcliffe showed reverence for Walpole, an important source of her inspiration. Even though he did not specifically mention Radcliffe's name, Walpole admitted knowing about the Gothic development in novels in one of the several letters written to Lady Ossory, dated 1794: "I have read some of the descriptive verbose tales, of which Your Ladyship says I was the patriarch by several mothers. All I can say for myself, is that I do not think my concubines have produced issue more natural for excluding the aid of anything marvellous" (Rogers 1996: 38)—a commentary which reveals a light-hearted reaction to Gothic mania and the development of popular novels. Radcliffe's final novel during her lifetime, *The Italian*, and her last work to feature epigraphs, introduces a few lines from Walpole's tragedy, *The Mysterious Mother* (1768), in an attempt to convey darker and more tragic atmospheres, distantly referring to the gloomy finale in *The Monk*. Radcliffe introduces some essential changes in *The Italian*. While she includes the common symbol of a cruel male protagonist, embodied by Schedoni, Radcliffe also includes the figure of the ruthless matriarch incarnated by the Marchesa de Vivaldi, an even more dangerous character than her male equivalents, thus overturning the idea of the Gothic as the locus for patriarchal menace. Radcliffe also reverses the characters of Walpole's Matilda and Lewis's Antonia by changing their negative destinies and creating a successful heroine enjoying a positive, independent life after overcoming negative contingencies. Radcliffe shares Walpole's fascination for Shakespeare, which is consistent in her works, as several of her epigraphs are dedicated to the great bard, with a preference for *Hamlet* (Milbank 2008) and *Macbeth* (Johnson 1995). She also introduces citations from a vast gallery of plays (*Julius Caesar; A Midsummer's Night Dream; Romeo and Juliet; Titus Andronicus; King John; Richard II; Anthony and Cleopatra; Twelfth Night; As You Like It; Measure for Measure; The Tempest*). The extracts from her travel journals further confirm her adoration for the Elizabethan playwright, reflected in every sound of nature and its extreme manifestations (Talfourd 1826: 80). The selection of texts chosen for the introduction of chapters in *The Romance of the Forest* and *The Mysteries of Udolpho* includes a plethora of authors and styles. On the other hand, Radcliffe takes her selection of epigraphs in *The Italian* exclusively from Walpole and Shakespeare, with the exception of two unidentified short poems that it may be interesting to investigate.

The atmosphere of speculative musing in some of Radcliffe's pages recalls her Uncle Bentley's philosophical passion and the teachings of philosophers, especially from the eighteenth century. Radcliffe's main characters are often the mouthpieces for theories concerning social, cultural and metaphysical aspects. They meditate on the value of art, literature and the power of the universe, the intermediary between a spiritual superior entity and human creatures. Johnson (1995) considers Radcliffe's attention to social interactions a form of bland Rousseauism, more evident in the final part of *The Romance of the Forest*. Rousseau's romantic ideals become evident in his later works, especially *Julie, or The New Heloise* (1761), an epistolary novel featuring a Petrarchan-Neoplatonic message of love, in which the protagonist is torn between two women's affection in the same way as Adeline feels a strong affection for two trustworthy young men.

Poetry, literature and philosophy are not, however, the only intricacies in the cultural catalogues of Radcliffe's novels. Music is another important aspect in Radcliffe's plots for its connection with strong emotional moments. Characters in Radcliffe's novels have a special relationship with music that both soothes the spirit and announces events of great importance (Frits Noske 1981). Despite moralists' warnings against the negative influence of Italian opera, Handel, Radcliffe's favourite, treated music as an emotional reflection in his compositions, which dominated the musical scene in England and Europe until the end of the century. Shearer West (2014) reveals that Dennis's frequent attacks against Handel were part of a tradition started by Ben Jonson's warning apropos of the dangerous challenge of Italianate masques. In spite of Dennis's ideas, expressed in his *Essay on the Operas after the Italian Manner* (1706), this kind of musical and theatrical works continued to be extremely popular in the eighteenth century. West explains that (295):

Dennis argued that the pernicious consequence of Italian opera was that poetry (and, by a circuitous connection, liberty) had effectively been driven out of the country. Dennis claimed that the Italian opera was 'a mere sensual Delight, utterly incapable of informing the Understanding, or reforming the Will, and for that very reason utterly unfit to be made a public Diversion'. Xenophobic disdain for the spectacle of opera was reformulated in various ways throughout the century.

Notwithstanding Dennis's remonstrations against Italian opera, melodrama and Italianate masques, the love for these forms of artistic creations continued attracting vast audiences throughout the century.

One of the many aspects defining Radcliffe, landscape becomes a more important narrative figure in her novels than in her contemporaries' works. She enriched landscapes with a special dimension that did not exist before. The inclusion of nature, however, seems to be in contrast with historical reality because "by 1800 England was one of the least wooded of all north European nations" (Denis Cosgrove and Stephen Daniels 2000: 43). The question is to understand why Radcliffe had a penchant for presenting luxuriant vegetation. The explanation may reside in her desire to reproduce *loci*, compatible with the sublime, the picturesque and the classical, and to mirror the luxuriant forests of her beloved painters in her prose writing. *The Romance of the Forest* may seem the least Burkean of her novels, the atmospheres being generally picturesque or romantic but rarely horrific. The beautiful forest where Adeline hides with her companions is mysterious and changeable, and seems to convey metaphorical meanings. Some events taking place in the forest and the abbey within it communicate suspense, while the natural setting surrounding the ruins is majestic and protective. The horrors that can be found in some grim settings in *The Italian* and *The Mysteries of Udolpho* are almost absent in *The Romance of the Forest*, even though the mysterious ruins of the abbey and the scenes from Adeline's nightmares resonate with Burke's description of the sublime as the consequence of extreme emotional states. Radcliffe conveys sublimity without excess in *The Romance of the Forest*, harmoniously blending it with classical influences and romantic contexts. The most difficult moments in the story suggest more fear and suspense than terror, even though the danger for the characters is concrete. It is true that tones are softer than in the typical Gothic visualisations of other writers' violent and dangerous plots. The episode describing some gentlemen, incarcerated for debts inside a pre-revolutionary Bastille does not convey the dark oppression that could be found in the real-life violence of the revolutionary attacks on the established power. Adeline's terrifying nightmares, however, are the objective correlative of an appalling crime that she can unveil at the very end of the story.

The Picturesque, The Sublime, Terror and Horror are included in *The Romance of the Forest* with a balanced distribution of narrative elements. The image of a deer browsing in the garden around the cloister is picturesque, while the descriptions of the forest's mystery is sublime. The abbey's labyrinths inspire feelings of terror, whereas the discovery of a skeleton and the intelligence of a murder convey a sense of horror. Basing his theory on clichés, Joseph Wiesenfarth (1988) reputes Radcliffe's search for sublimity an excess of confusion, whereas David Morris (1985) implausibly states that the sublime can surround women, but not vice versa, as it represents a penetrating masculine force. Morris's generalisation cannot be easily adapted to Radcliffe since her sublime scenes occur in moments of high tension, equally felt by both male and female characters. Therefore, the sublime acquires a universal status with no distinction of gender. *The Romance of the Forest* incorporates both the sublime, theorised by Burke, as well as the picturesque, idealised by Gilpin, and, in describing the mysterious forest, the gloomy ruins and the strange messages of Adeline's nightmares, Radcliffe exploits the different nuances connected with wonder, astonishment and fear. On the other hand, the second part of the novel features several picturesque images in Savoy, an emblem of soothing tranquillity announcing positive adventures. The novel is a clever compromise of two dominant cultural elements. As John Whale (2010: 176) specifies:

The Picturesque has often been considered as a safe middle ground, a compromise category, happily mediating the dangerous Burkean opposites of the Sublime and the Beautiful. It has been thought of as offering a particularly English aesthetic of landscape and even as playing a formative role in the construction of a particular kind of Englishness.

Radcliffe is perhaps the only author using both aesthetic categories within a single work. Stephen Copley and Peter Garside (2010: 3) affirm that the "Picturesque is a difficult category to define. Offered by its original proponents as a third category to set against Burke's 'Sublime' and 'Beautiful', it also plays an important part, directly or by default, in the definition of the 'Gothic' and the 'Romantic'. [...] The Picturesque has [acquired] ideological implications in more recent critiques". Punter (2010) asserts that a precise idea of what the picturesque is can be found in Pope's lines on *Windsor Forest* (1713), thus confirming the pre-existence of these categories decades before the Gothic and the Romantic.

Unlike Walpole, Robinson, Beckford and Lewis, Radcliffe apparently left Britain only once to visit Germany, and it is not clear how she could extensively describe landscapes she had never seen. Natalie Schroeder (1980) mentions Louis Ramond de Carbonnière as a possible influence thanks to his *Observations Made in the Pyrenees, To Be Useful in Observations of the Alps*. De Carbonnière published the text in 1789, two years before *The Romance of the Forest*. Pam Perkins (2006) maintains that Radcliffe did not need to travel, having read a lot of travel writing, and includes Moore's novel *Zeluco* (1789) among her potential influences for *A Sicilian Romance* and *The Italian*. *Zeluco*'s main character is a cruel, profligate man of Sicilian origins. His cold-hearted and remorseless disposition may have provided the mould for the callous characters of Montoni in *Udolpho* and Schedoni in *The Italian*. The novel contains abundant descriptions of Sicily and Italy, denoting Moore's greater ability in travel writing than in delineating plausible plots. In all probability, Radcliffe was also familiar with Brydone's and Swinburne's accounts of their journeys to Southern Italy (see the first two chapters), even though her evocative imagination, extensive reading and artistic knowledge all contributed to her original descriptive narrations. While Walpole, Reeve, Lewis and, under certain aspects, Beckford limited the description of places to the essential without providing details, which could make the settings identifiable, Radcliffe deliberately created word-paintings to match the canvasses of her favourite painters, Rosa and Claude. In addition to the sublime and the picturesque, the following passage in *The Mysteries of Udolpho*, inspired by Virgil, seems to arise from a real autobiographical travel experience for its profusion of details:

The Cottage was nearly embowered in the woods, which were chiefly of chestnut, intermixed with some cypress, larch and sycamore. Beneath the dark and spreading branches, appeared, to the North, and to the East, the woody Apennines, rising in majestic amphitheatre, now black with pines, as she had been accustomed to see them, but their loftiest summits crowned with ancient forests of chestnut, oak, and oriental plane, now animated with the rich tints of autumn, and which swept downward to the valley uninterruptedly, except where some bold rocky promontory looked out from among the foliage, and caught the passing gleam. Vineyards stretched along the feet of the mountains, where the elegant villas of the Tuscan nobility frequently adorned the scene, and overlooked slopes clothed with groves of olive, mulberry, orange and lemon. The plain, to which these declined, was coloured with the riches of cultivation, whose mingled hues were mellowed into harmony by an Italian sun. (*The Mysteries of Udolpho*: 389)

In danger of being captured and killed by Montoni, Emily escapes through an unknown territory that introduces a major sublime context. The serene beauty of the scene discloses a picturesque setting that provides a momentary pause in the dramatic series of events. The bucolic aspect, represented by the vineyards, the olive trees and the cultivations, is Radcliffe's special value. The beautiful landscape, partly created through human labour, as in Virgil's *Georgics*, is an intermezzo of peace in the middle of horror. Idyllic images create an atmosphere imbued with Classicism, "Emily had been taught to venerate Florence as the seat of literature and the fine arts; but that its taste for classic story should descend to the peasants of the country, occasioned her both surprise and admiration" (397). "The Arcadian air of the girls next attracted her attention" (427), then she admired "the pastoral valleys of the Apennines" and "the pastoral margin" of the Arno with "vineyards" and "olive trees" (433). Radcliffe frequently exalts bucolic scenes of a classical Arcadia as if honouring Virgil's clichés. However, the speed with which the characters pass from one place to the other in the different regions of Italy seems to betray Radcliffe's unawareness of realistic distances, perhaps revealing a theoretical knowledge of the land acquired through literature and the visual arts, and not through real journeys. Unquestionably, Radcliffe did not need to travel to describe breath-taking geographies, and, with the exception of her first and last novels, respectively set in Scotland and in England, she meticulously described French and Italian sublime atmospheres in her four central novels. *The Romance of The Forest* develops in France and the Alps of Savoy, which at the time were part of Italy. Radcliffe generally favoured Italian locations, originally introduced by Walpole. The historical events taking place in France and the dramatic Italian political situation may have occasioned her choice. Her cultural knowledge, both literary and artistic, was probably instrumental in the creation of her settings. Endowed with a special talent for suspense, Radcliffe's original descriptions changed the convention of Augustan fancy, turning it into Romantic imagination filled with Gothic atmospheres and classical echoes, which all satisfied the readers' desire for escapism and mystery.

A number of scholars judge that Radcliffe could not possess sufficient cultural knowledge and, being a woman, she could know very little of the Classics, a gentleman's cultural prerogative. With the exclusion of rare exceptions, young women did not have access to higher education, which was the monopoly of men, as cultural knowledge was viewed as incompatible with propriety and modesty (Mary Poovey 1985; Sarah Annes Brown 2012). However, many women possessed high levels of education together with a sound knowledge of Antiquity. Translations helped women without a classical education to discover the Classics and widen their cultural horizons. The copiousness of classical works and their frequent translations had an important didactic and cultural role. This idea can be applicable to Radcliffe's case as well, as she could enjoy the enriching effects of the Classics through literary translations, and compensate for a probable lack of a systematic education. Radcliffe was more intellectually prepared compared to what critics deemed during the nineteenth and early twentieth century. She acquired genuine literary knowledge, which included Classical, Medieval, and Renaissance masterpieces and references to ancient authors in her four central novels are not accidental. Several women were part of the cultural elite in that period. Elisabeth Montague, Hannah More, and Hester Lynch Piozzi not only gravitated around scholars and artists such as Samuel Johnson, Joshua Reynolds, David Garrick and many others but also formed their own intellectual circles. The bluestocking and late Augustan Elisabeth Carter, a brilliant translator of Epictetus, expressed enthusiastic opinions of Radcliffe's novels, especially *A Sicilian Romance* and *The Mysteries of Udolpho*, as her biographer Montague Pennington (1807: 300) confirmed:

But of all authors of this class, Mrs. Carter thought most highly of Mrs Radcliffe, and was most delighted with the perusal of her Romances. The good tendency of all her works, the virtues of her principal characters, supported on the solid foundation of religion, the elegance of her style, and her accurate, as well as vivid, delineations of the beauties of nature, appeared to her such as to raise Mrs. Radcliffe to a degree of eminence far superior to any writer of *romance* of the present day.

Carter's positive opinion was, however, a rare accolade coming from a female scholar, as women belonging to the contemporary intelligentsia generally expressed vitriolic comments on Radcliffe, probably caused by her immense success, unquestionably superior to other women's literary efforts. Classical studies were generally a male cultural convention, necessary for future activities, either political, legal, economic, or academic, and the stereotype of women's inescapable ignorance was difficult to overcome. Growing up surrounded by cultural events at her uncle's home, Radcliffe became an avid reader and art lover, even though it is not possible to know what kind of education she received. Scott recognised that Radcliffe could brilliantly follow classical rules, as in a perturbing scene, taken from *The Italian*, showing highly dramatic qualities, perfectly blended with the sense of horror of an impending crime. The following passage features *The Italian*'s actual villain, Marchesa De Vivaldi, who, intent on punishing Ellena for loving her son, is for the first time struck by a pang of guilt for her own unlimited cruelty. Hints of Aeschylus's idea of an inevitable divine punishment and Seneca's horror of an unnatural crime dominates the following passage:

"Avoid violence, if that be possible" she added, immediately comprehending him, "but let her die quickly! The punishment is due to the crime". The Marchesa happened, as she said this, to cast her eyes upon the inscription over a Confessional, where appeared, in black letters, these awful words, *"God hears thee!"* It appeared an awful warning; her countenance changed; it had struck upon her heart. Schedoni was too much engaged by his own thoughts to observe or understand her silence. (*The Italian*: 176)

A general conviction that "the tragedians of Ancient Greece were the privileged intimates of fear" forged some literary creations of the period. That exaltation of fear, deeply rooted in Antiquity models, was traceable in Radcliffe's romances (Clery 1995: 48). Detecting the sources of Radcliffe's knowledge of the Classics is a difficult task but investigations into a cultural issue that has frequently been overlooked in the history of literature can provide answers. The centrality of literary translations, especially from Latin and Greek, became essential for the propagation of culture and the determination of literary canons. The proven availability of authors in translations gave access to classical knowledge, as Hopkins (2005) demonstrates in his observations on Dryden's translations of the Ancients. The epic (Robin Sowerby 2005), the ancient pastoral (Penelope Wilson 2005) and complex poets, such as Ovid and Horace (Garth Tissol 2005), could be enjoyed by large number of people thanks to literary translations, which allowed the discovery of masterpieces from Antiquity and their poetical, intellectual and philosophical messages. However, the myth of cultural elitism was difficult to overcome. Classical scholar Richard Bentley did not welcome translations of the Classics, while literary historian, poet and, ironically, translator (and Joseph Warton's brother), Thomas Warton avowed that: "public taste was vitiated by translations" (Gillespie 2011: 99). Despite existing prejudices, translations from the Classics were of crucial importance during the late seventeenth century and the entirety of the eighteenth, as an effect of the cultural impact brought about by Dryden's *Aeneid* (1697) together with Pope's *Iliad* (1720) and *Odyssey* (1725). Translations of major classic authors were astonishingly numerous, and a constellation of works from antiquity were "englished". "The scale and centrality of translations from ancient Latin and Greek works in the literature of the Anglophone world over the centuries" is of essential importance in the understanding of literary reception and literary production. "In every phase of English literature, and for that matter many phases of other western literatures too, much of the innovative impulse comes directly or indirectly through translation from ancient Greek and Roman texts, and in some eras their impact is fundamental" (Gillespie 2011: 2). One of the most revered poets of Antiquity, Virgil was translated various times during the century. A relatively popular version of the *Aeneid* was written by Christopher Pitt in 1740 while the *Eclogues* and *Georgics* were rendered into English by

Joseph Warton and collected in a single edition in 1753 (John Thackeray 1992). The vast range of versions of Virgil's works is remarkable, as Wilson highlights (2005: 183):

There had been six complete translations of Virgil's *Eclogues* before 1660, and Virgil's exalted standing ensured that the years 1660-1790 saw many more, both in verse and in prose, often primarily intended for use in schools. [...] Two prose translations of the 1740s are worthy of note: James Hamilton's was intended to raise a subscription to advance the arts of Scottish agriculture, and in that of John Martyn, Professor of Botany at Cambridge, the notes focus particularly on the accuracy of Virgil's botanical details.

The complete *Georgics* were rendered by Dryden in 1697 and "remained standard until the twentieth century, [while] the 1780s saw a spate of [Virgil's] new renderings by James Tyler, William Greene, and William Graham" (Davis 2005: 191). The availability of Virgilian examples was extended and suitable for both erudite and less educated readers. In all likelihood, such an extraordinary amount of Virgilian material had an impact on Radcliffe, whose works frequently echo the Latin poet. When writing the *Georgics,* Virgil was inspired by the philosopher Theophrastus' *Enquiry into Plants* (*Historia Plantarum*), composed between the fourth and the third centuries BCE. Another source for Virgil was Greek Hesiod's *Works and Days* (700 BCE). The following extract, taken from Virgil's second book of the *Georgics,* translated by William Sotheby (henceforth GEs, book, lines, pages), is one of the many examples of botanical descriptions that became very popular in a period when interest in botany and agricultural improvements started being relevant:

> First, trees diversely rise: here native woods
> O'rspread at will wide plains and mazy floods;
> There the tall poplar tow'rs, the broom extends,
> O'er her dark bed the pliant osier bends,
> And azure willows waving with the gale
> Turn their hoar leaf, that silvers o'er the vale.
> Some high in air from scatter'd seeds arise;
> Hence the tall chestnut spreads her stately size,
> Huge æsculus o'ershadowing all the grove,
> And oaks that spoke to Greece the will of Jove,
> Here self-form'd forests gather round the root,
> Thus branching elms and clustering cherries shoot,

And e'en the tender bay's Parnassian bloom
Springs up beneath its mother leafy gloom.
Thus varying nature first the desert crown'd,
And shrub, and grove, and forest rose around. (*GEs*: II, 11–
26, 92–93)

During the first decades of the eighteenth century, Sotheby published
The Georgics with Dryden's *Aeneid* and Wrangham's *Eclogues* in a
complete collection of Virgil's works. The following is Dryden's creative
rendering of the same lines in the 1697 edition (printed in London for
Jacob Tonson), still popular in the nineteenth century and characterised
by several poetic licences. It presents a free translation, reflecting the
original with some differences. The number of lines in the Latin version of
the *Georgics* by Dryden (Henceforth *GEd*) does not strictly correspond to
the number of Virgilian lines (9–21). While Virgil starts with the "osier"
and the "broom", then mentions the "poplar", Dryden chooses to change
the order of trees, therefore the "poplar" comes after the "osiers" and the
"willows":

Some Trees their birth to bounteous Nature owe:
For some without the pains of Planting grow.
With Osiers thus the Banks of Brooks abound,
Sprung from the wat'ry Genius of the Ground:
From the same Principles grey Willows come;
Herculean Poplar, and the tender Broom.
But some from Seeds inclos'd in Earth arise:
For thus the mastful Chestnut mates the Skies.
Hence rise the branching Beech and vocal Oke,
Where Jove of old Oraculously spoke.
Some from the Root a rising Wood disclose;
Thus Elms, and thus the salvage Cherry grows.
Thus the green Bays, that binds the Poet's Brows
Shoots and is shelter'd by the Mother's Boughs.
These ways of Planting, Nature did ordain,
For Trees and Shrubs, and all the Sylvan Reign.
(*GEd*: II, 13–27, 71–72)

The colour of the willow is "grey" in Dryden, while it is "azure" in
Sotheby. In the Latin text, Virgil had defined it as *glauca*, a colour that is a
mixture of azure and green. Sotheby's translation renders Virgil's scientific
knowledge and poetic sensibility, whereas Dryden tends towards

musicality and a picturesque rendering. Starting from a general vision of the "woods", he perceives the "plains" and "mazy floods". Virgil describes the varieties of trees and their qualities, the "tall poplar", the "azure willow", the stately-sized "chestnut", the sacred "huge æsculus", the "oaks", the "the branching elm", the "clustering cherries", and the "green bay", also known as the laurel. Dryden is more concentrated on rhythm and rhymes and his poetic choices prevail compared to the original Virgilian text.

Like in other passages of the *Georgics*, the prevalence of the colour green dominates the scene. The "seeds", previously depicted by Lucretius as the essence of existence, become the positive roots of life in Virgil. Trees can grow spontaneously or be the result of men's hard work. A superabundance of green dominates the images: "shrub", "grove", and "forests" fill the earth with their beauty. Interestingly, one entry in Radcliffe's diary, written in 1802, and included in Talfourd's memoir, is fascinating and revealing. She was impressed when she visited Blenheim Castle, but her descriptions often concern the surrounding gardens (italics are added for emphasis):

This walk continues on the brow, for about half a mile, very sweetly, and leads to a sloping lawn shaded with the *noblest trees* in the garden. More struck with this spot than with any, except about the large lake. First, two *poplars* of most astonishing height [...]. At their feet, the light *green spray foliage* of these deciduous *cypresses* had a most charming effect. Near the poplars, a lofty *plane* but inferior in height. Near this, a surprising Portugal *laurel* swept the ground, and spread to a vast circumference; a very extraordinary tree for size. (Talfourd 1826: 61)

Virgilian echoes dominate Radcliffe's text. Virgil shows great attention to the different families and kinds of trees. Likewise, Radcliffe describes several trees in her private diary with a sort of intellectual propensity for botany in a period when she has apparently stopped writing novels. However, her words sound like a literary exercise. Her reiterated interest in trees, which was evident in *The Romance of the Forest*, *The Mystery of Udolpho* and *The Italian*, denotes a love of nature as well as a botanical knowledge, imitated from Virgil, an author that she frequently emulated in her bucolic scenes. The words in her diary may represent a form of literary self-fashioning, as Radcliffe never stops imagining aesthetic and cultural effects on her readership even when she writes for herself. The passage shows editorial awareness, as she was probably conscious that her diaries would be published someday, whether during her lifetime or afterwards. A further hypothesis is that she might have created passages to insert in a novel she perhaps had the intention to write. Her biographer explains that she had developed a keen interest in botany:

There was scarcely a tree of importance, with the peculiar form of which she was not familiar, and the varieties of whose aspects in light and shade she could not picture in words. With reference to their age and to the analogy she fancied the lines of monarchs, with which they might be coeval; she described the trees separately as Plantagenet oaks, Tudor beeches, or Stuart elms. (Talfourd 1826: 97)

Like Virgil, Radcliffe acknowledges that nature is a sacred place: memories of an ancient past linger among trees and flowers in a beautiful landscape. It is not only the incessant toil of nature, continuously producing wonders but also its magic link to historical figures who lived in the previous centuries to attract her attention. The passages in Radcliffe's diary reflect the *Georgics*: she proceeds to describe the trees, beginning her list with the "poplar", the first tree that Virgil had described in his botanical enumeration. The way she describes the "noblest trees" clearly denotes an admiration for the majestic in nature, connected with the beautiful descriptions in the *Georgics*, a work that Addison had qualified as one of the most complete pieces of all Antiquity. Radcliffe describes "the cypresses", also mentioned by Virgil in Sotheby's translation: "the cypresses of the Idæan height" (*GEs*: 97). Dryden added his poetic genius to Virgil's poetry, and his translation results in a gloomy, quasi-Gothic image of the "fun'ral Cypress rising like a Shroud" (*GEd*: 74), reflecting the mournful connotation of the "Cypress" in Latin-Italian culture, a melancholy myth narrated by Ovid, and whose sombre nature has its northern equivalent in the yew tree. Book I and Book II of *The Georgics* contain various sections dedicated to descriptions of magnificent trees, reproduced in Thomson's *The Seasons*–all powerful inspirations for Radcliffe's romantic passages.

Unlike Lucretius, Radcliffe's ideal mentor, Virgil, exalts the immanent presence of the divine in nature, the agent responsible for its beauty. Virgil's *Georgics* represents a masterpiece not only for its use of the language but also for its themes, which were uncommon even during his lifetime. The poet unites beautiful verses to useful observations and reveals the secrets of agriculture and the dignity of hard work. His text was always popular, but became especially important in the eighteenth century when agriculture and landscaping were the results of technical efforts meant to improve the land in a period when the country was starting to change because of the development of the Industrial Revolution. Virgil's major interest in nature, and his description of different samples of flora, found fertile ground in Britain where, according to Mavis Batey (2005), botany was becoming an important science, and varieties of trees and flowers were used to change the landscape as a probable reaction to the growing negative effects of the process of industrialisation. In one of her picturesque anachronisms, Radcliffe describes St. Aubert and his neighbour intent on making complex botanical experiments in *The Mysteries of Udolpho* (1794), even though botany was only known in monasteries and some universities when the novel's action takes place in 1584. Anna Seward, Erasmus Darwin (Charles Darwin's grandfather) and Sir Brooke Boothby had created the *Lichfield Botanical Society* in the 1770s, a pioneering example of studies in botany that reflected the growing interest in the subject after Carl Linneus had invented a system to describe plants in the mid-eighteenth century.

Pastoral and bucolic aspects are a prelude to the sublime in Radcliffe's novels and their source is inevitably Virgilian. Radcliffe was not, however, an exception in the cult of Virgil. The letters and anecdotes that Johnson published, impersonating Mr Dubious in *The Adventurer,* were an intellectual strategy to divulge cultural knowledge and spread the rudiments of Latin classical authors. Number ninety-two of the magazine was published on 22 September 1753 and contained an article on Virgil: "Criticism on *The Pastorals* by Virgil". It highlighted the best qualities of the Virgilian text without hiding its problematic aspects. An inevitable couplet from Horace unsurprisingly precedes it. Horace's lines are an aphorism on the important role of a literary critic:

> Bold be the critick, zealous to his trust
> Like the firm judge, inexorably just.

The reason for systematically evaluating ancient authors and writing critical essays unveiled Johnson's intention to disseminate his laudable culture and intervene in the dispute between the Ancients and the Moderns. Started in France at the end of the seventeenth century to determine whether the true value of literary creation was in the ancient models or contemporary creations, the diatribe had spread to Britain. In replying to the fictitious Adventurer, Mr Dubious (Johnson) promotes a balanced judgement and recognises his interlocutor's merits as a literary critic by virtue of "a just distribution of praise amongst the Ancients and the Moderns: a sober deference to reputation long established, without a blind adoration of Antiquity; and a willingness to favour later performances, without a light or puerile fondness for novelty" (*The Adventurer* 1753: 68). Johnson creates a textual analysis of the Virgilian *Eclogues* (38 BCE), also known as *The Bucolics*, or *Pastorals*, and quotes from Horace to inaugurate his review: "Horace justly declares, that the rural muses have appropriated to [Virgil] their elegance and sweetness" (*The Adventurer*: 69). Johnson examines the ten *Eclogues* and carries out a stylistic observation, introducing his personal comments on Virgil's verses, shown in their original language, and in Joseph Warton's elegant translation. Written by men and (mostly) addressed to men, these scholarly articles could provide cultural information for a less educated public. Johnson enthusiastically appreciates the first and tenth Eclogues for combining "all the images of rural pleasures [and] the idea of rural tranquillity" (*The Adventurer:* 75). He specifies that the third Eclogue "is filled with images at once splendid and pleasing". Johnson does not fully appreciate the second Eclogue for reasons that strangely sound more Romantic than Augustan: "I know not that it contains one affecting sentiment or pleasing description, or one passage that strikes the imagination or awakens the passions" (*The Adventurer*: 72), as if Virgil was not complying with sublime ideals in certain parts of his poem. The new discourse on the sublime had been going on for some decades after it had been (re)introduced by Addison and Dennis (via Boileau) when Johnson was writing his analysis in 1753. Moreover, he had probably had the opportunity of perusing Graveyard poems that were published in those years.

It is perhaps not far-fetched to think that Radcliffe had a knowledge of Johnson's commentary and was able to balance the apparent lack of evocative power in the second Eclogue with her narrative inventions a few decades later. Johnson's erudite commentaries, together with the growing number of translated versions of Virgil's masterpieces turned the Latin poet's works into essential instruments for a refined education, an example to be read, commented, imitated and, of course, translated, translation being the most popular tool in language teaching and learning at the time. Although the taxonomy of literary translations is not complete yet, the figures are remarkable, as, "between 1550 and 1800, Virgil collects 103 entries, 95 of which are in verse. The most substantial are half a dozen complete *Works* and the same number of separate *Aeneid*, followed by nine or ten complete translations apiece of the *Georgics* and *Eclogues*. Most of the remainder are selections of one or more Books of the *Aeneid*" (Gillespie 2011: 11). Of all the ancient poets, both Greek and Latin, extolling Nature, Virgil exalted its beneficial and transcendent aspects, his spirituality being a prelude to the Christian age according to

Dante and Scholastic commentators. Younger than Lucretius, Virgil was one of the few poets who alluded to his predecessor and developed his intuitions about natural life. His bucolic images appear to have influenced many an author and moulded Radcliffe's various descriptions of nature. In particular, *The Romance of the Forest* (henceforth *RF* in quotes) features interesting passages dedicated to a delicate nature, which becomes essential for both characters and the plot. The following extract shows Adeline discovering an ample landscape for the first time:

They entered upon a land confined by high banks and overarched by trees, on whose branches appeared the first green buds of spring glittering with dews. The fresh breeze of the morning animated the spirit of Adeline, whose mind was delicately sensible to the beauties of nature. As she viewed the flowery luxuriance of the turf, and the tender green of the trees, or caught between the opening banks, a glimpse of the varied landscape, rich with wood, and fading into blue and distant mountains, her heart expanded in momentary joy. With Adeline the charms of external nature were heightened by those of novelty: she had seldom seen the grandeur of an extensive prospect, or the magnificence of a wide horizon, and not often the picturesque beauties of more confined scenery. (*RF*: 9)

The distant mountains are geographically vague: they do not correspond to Savoy, where Adeline will later escape with a servant after crossing forests and navigating a river in the second part of the novel. Radcliffe might refer to the mountains in Auvergne, separated from the Alps by the river Rhone. The relatively precise descriptions of certain geographies in *The Romance of the Forest* may derive from travel books, but a careful analysis of existing maps could have intensified them. Cartography was one of the many scientific fields improved during the Enlightenment. While working for De L'Isle family, publishers of geographical maps since the seventeenth century, the cartographer Philippe Buache de La Neuville had published a physical map of France in 1770 that had become popular at home and abroad. Radcliffe presumably consulted physical maps of France, as *The Romance of the Forest, The Mysteries of Udolpho* and *The Italian* contain broad geographical details.

Saved from certain death by Pierre de la Motte and his family, Adeline has joined their escape from Paris. Trying to get as far away from the capital as possible, they travel for days until they find a place that seems to emanate a magic quality, a mysterious forest. Its green leaves are fresh and brilliant because of the spring dew. The analogy with Virgilian scenes is once more astonishing, especially considering that the Latin poet exalts the power of spring with remarkable frequency. The entries dedicated to spring in the *Georgics* are the highest in number, compared with autumn and summer. Virgil mentions winter many times because the season is in contrast with the arrival of spring, renovating the apparently dead land after the reign of frostiness. The following examples from Book I and Book II of the *Georgics* from both Sotheby's and Dryden's translations can help us better understand the intellectual and emotional analogies between Virgil and Radcliffe. The first two are from Sotheby's translation, whereas the others are taken from Dryden's:

> When first young Zephyr melts the mountain snow,
> And Spring unbinds the mellow'd mould below
> Press the deep plough, and urge the groaning team
> Where the worn shares 'mid opening furrow gleam.
> (*GEs*: I, 51–54, 63)

> The blade dares boldly rise new suns beneath,
> The tender vine puts forth his flexile wreath,
> And, freed from southern blast and northern shower,
> Spreads without fear, each bud, and leaf, and flower.
> Yes! Lovely Spring! When rose the world to birth,
> Thy genial radiance dawn'd upon the earth,
> Beneath thy balmy air creation grew,
> And no bleak gale on infant nature blew. (*GEs*: II, 383–390, 110)

> While yet the Spring is young, while Earth unbinds
> Her frozen Bosom to the Western Winds;
> While Mountain Snows dissolve against the Sun,
> And Streams, yet new, from Precipices run. (*GEd*: I, 64–67, 51)

> When Winter's rage abates, when cheerful Hours
> Awake the Spring, and Spring awakes the Flow'rs,
> On the green Turf thy careless Limbs display,
> And celebrate the mighty Mother's day.
> For then the Hills with pleasing Shades are crown'd
> And Sleeps are sweeter on the Silken Ground.
> (*GEd*: I, 463–467, 63)

> The Spring adorns the Woods, renews the Leaves;

The Womb of Earth the genial Seed receives. (*GEd*: II, 438–439, 84)

Scholars have detected the proximity between Virgil's pastoral descriptions and Radcliffe's exaltation of idyllic contexts but have not yet deeply analysed it. The tepid recognition of her classical influences are probably due to prejudices concerning her non-systematic education. However, some crucial elements show how deep Radcliffe's classical knowledge was. Virgil's sensibility and his delicate poetic masterpieces seem to suit Radcliffe's narrative style perfectly. The Latin poet was universally acknowledged as one of the greatest geniuses of Antiquity, and his works were not at risk of moral censorship, as Virgil was not considered sensual, indecent or offensive, unlike Lucretius, Horace, Ovid and others. The description of Dido and Aeneas's passionate meeting in a cave during a sudden storm in the *Aeneid* is one of the sensual exceptions in Virgil. Their passion is unchained when the characters are alone and surrounded by a sublime landscape ravaged by a violent storm, a metaphor of their tragic love. Radcliffe's literary spirit resonates with the more idealised *Georgics* and *Eclogues* than the epic *Aeneid*. However, not all of Virgil's descriptions are idyllic. The following extract belongs to Book I of the *Georgics*. Virgil replaces his usual pastoral atmospheres to convey terror and describe a sudden and frightful storm:

> Oft have I seen a sudden Storm arise,
> From all the warring Winds that sweep the Skies:
> The heavy Harvest from the Root is torn,
> And whirl'd aloft the lighter Stubble born;
> With such a force the flying rack is driv'n;
> And such a winter wears the face of Heav'n:
> And oft whole sheets descend of sluicy Rain,
> Suck'd by the spongy Clouds from off the Main:
> The lofty Skies at once come pouring down,
> The promis'd Crop and golden Labours drown.
> The Dykes are fill'd, and with a roaring sound
> The rising Rivers float the nether ground;
> And Rocks the bellowing Voice of boiling Seas rebound.
> The Father of the Gods his Glory shrowds,
> Involv'd in Tempests, and a Night of Clouds.
> And from the middle Darkness flashing out,
> By fits he deals his fiery Bolts about.
> Earth feels the Motions of her angry God,

Her Entrails tremble, and her Mountains nod;
And flying Beasts in Forests seek abode:
Deep horrour seizes ev'ry Humane Breast,
Their Pride is humbled, and their Fear confess'd:
While he from high his rowling Thunder throws,
And fires the Mountains with repeated blows:
The Rocks are from their old Foundations rent.
(*GEd*: I, 431–455, 62–63)

This passage from 1697 version of Dryden's *Georgics* exhibits nature's strength and the horror provoked by the fury of natural elements. The poetic force of the passage can help us understand why Dryden's version remained unparalleled for almost two centuries. The visual scene is dense with dreadful terror in the face of Nature's horrible fury. Interestingly, Dryden's lexicon of horror was later exploited in many Gothic narratives. Graveyards poets, Gothic authors and even the Romantics absorbed expressions such as the "lofty Skies", the "roaring sound", the "Night of Clouds". Radcliffe herself may have described Virgil's nightmarish scene, which "seizes" men's souls with "Deep horror". The image of the "warring Winds" is particularly important, as *The Romance of the Forest* almost literally reproduces it. The terrible moment when the cruel Montalt meets the fugitive de la Motte in the forest abbey occurs during a terrible storm, a harbinger of dreadful events. The tempest's disquieting sounds nearly cover their voices:

It happened one stormy night. [....] The storm was now loud, and the hollow blasts, which rushed among the trees, prevented his distinguishing any other sound. [...] A loud gust of wind, that burst along the passage [...] overpowered his voice and that of the Marquis. [...] The rising tempest again drowned the sound of their voices. [...] Nothing was to be seen through the darkness of the night—nothing heard but the howling of the storm. (*RF*: 85–86)

De la Motte is flustered following the "impression of horror" (90) that he suffers during the terrible encounter in the middle of the furious blast. The forest that had hitherto been a soothing and picturesque refuge turns into a place of horror, ravaged by the violence of air and water elements. The fury of the elements is physical because nature has become destructive, but also metaphorical because evil enters the place when Montalt appears. A careful and direct reading of Radcliffe highlights how the distinction of horror and terror is implausible and the essay, published after her death theorising such a void separation, was probably penned by her husband in order to avoid the image and the prejudice of Radcliffe as the dark queen of Gothic horrors.

The function of Virgil's *Georgics* is not exclusively didascalic. Nor is it only an encyclopaedic appreciation of the gifts provided by agriculture through men's hard work. Adeline in *The Romance of the Forest* and Emily in *The Mysteries of Udolpho* meet farmers and peasants content with their toil or celebrating the end of labour at sunset. Radcliffe's choice may be directed by Virgil's influence and have philosophical roots as well. Fiona Price (2006: 4) explains that in *An Inquiry concerning the Principles of Morals* (1751) "Hume argues that, in the case of pastoral poetry, 'images of a tender and gentle tranquillity' should be communicated to the reader and to replace these with 'the idea of toil, labour and danger suffered by a fisherman' is an error". Harshly criticised by Robinson, as we see in the chapter dedicated to *Hubert de Sevrac*, Hume's precept, which might sound problematic today, is instead an ideal representation, meant to hide suffering from reality. Hume's doctrine is an echo of Virgil's ideas: the Latin poet describes the farmers' hard work as a source of joy originated by a simple but happy life in the midst of nature. One of the leitmotivs of the novel, inherited from the Virgilian contrast between the corrupting urban life and the spiritual life in the countryside, is found at the very beginning of *The Romance of the Forest*. If de la Motte has fallen into vice and has become a worse man, it is because he has succumbed to several temptations in the corrupted city. However, even though he is a dishonoured man, he lets nature enter his soul as he resides in the forest, and briefly becomes a different person while admiring the beauty surrounding him (*RF*: 23):

In the mean time he spent the anxious interval of Peter's absence in examining the ruin, and walking over the environs; they were sweetly romantic, and the luxuriant woods, with which they abounded, seemed to sequester this spot from the rest of the world. Frequently a natural vista would yield a view of the country, terminated by hills, which retiring in distance, faded into the blue horizon. A stream, various and musical in its course, wound at the foot of the lawn, on which stood the abbey; here it silently glided beneath the shades, feeding the flowers that bloomed on its banks, and diffusing dewy freshness around; there it spread in broad expanse to-day, reflecting the sylvan scene, and the wild deer that tasted its waves.

The enchanting effect of nature is powerful and can alter a person of vacillating morals such as de la Motte. The bucolic surrounding conveys moments of serenity for the anguished character, momentarily oblivious of the evils haunting his mind. Radcliffe borrows from the Virgilian lines to complete her appeasing description of the landscape. Unlike de la Motte, Monsieur La Luc, living in the mountains and leading a peaceful, uneventful life, is the quintessential pastoral ideal of an honest man, revering nature. Life in the city and the apparent progress of mankind are a source of anguish for Virgil, pessimistically aware of the world moving towards annihilation because of people's inexhaustible desire for power and their blind need for war. Before Virgil, Lucretius had expressed the same idea in *The Nature of Things*, but his conclusions were more negative and hopeless than Virgil's, who insists that Divinity is a source of harmony helping to preserve the earth and her inhabitants, a consideration which resonates with Radcliffe's sensibility and is frequently repeated in her novels.

The dichotomy of urban vivacity versus rural life also characterises *The Mysteries of Udolpho*: the lavish and sumptuous attractions of a city like Venice hide hypocrisy and crime. Shameful vices are embodied in the cruel character, Montoni, whereas the simple life of Emily's father, St. Aubert, is a model of ethical conduct, respectful of both humanity and nature. The bucolic atmosphere of St Aubert's garden near the Pyrenees resembles a Virgilian pastoral, as it represents the ideal locus of nature's purity exalted by the Latin poet and deeply admired by Radcliffe. The quintessence of nature is in its immense variety and breath-taking beauty represented in *The Mysteries of Udolpho* (5): "these tremendous precipices were contrasted by the soft green of the pastures and woods that hung upon their skirts; among whose flocks, and herds, and simple cottages, the eye, after having scaled the cliffs above, delighted to repose". A very important aspect in the *Georgics* is the narrating voice, who represents a character that suffers for the loss of his property after the unjust confiscations of his beloved land–a topic recreated in Radcliffe, revealing a further analogy with Virgil's ideas. The unjustified and undeserved loss of property oppresses Radcliffe's main characters. The concepts of loss, exile and nostalgia, also included in *The Bucolics* (Eclogue X), abound in Radcliffe's novels, in which characters, forced to abandon their places of origin, express their chagrin while observing their lost source of joy and repeating Virgil's original lament, here rendered by Wrangham's translation:

We leave our country's bounds,
Our much-lov'd plains;

We from our country fly, unhappy swains.
(*Eclogues* I, 3–5)

Madame de la Motte and Adeline express a similar sentiment while leaving the place of their lost happiness, a feeling that Emily voices in *The Mysteries of Udolpho* and Ellena pronounces in *The Italian*. Elvira's husband, Gonzalvo, conveys the same nostalgic sentiment (probably derived from Radcliffe) in *The Monk*, when the couple is forced to escape from Spain after their thwarted marriage. The peregrinations of the upright person, unjustly tormented, is exemplified by Adeline, initially exiled from Paris and then from the protective forest. Equally desperate, Monsieur de la Motte has to abandon his aristocratic and luxurious life in the capital due to the mistakes he made. Interestingly, Book II of the *Georgics* mentions the escape of an impure man, tormented by secret demons. This concept is full of anguish, and recognisable in Lucretius' description of men unable to enjoy life. Like his predecessor, albeit more rarely, Virgil offers images of terror when he describes ghosts infesting the earth after unnatural crimes have been committed. The next passage, taken from Dryden's 1697 translation, powerfully demonstrates the sense of horror that nature transmits when it announces gloomy events:

> Earth, Air, and Seas, with prodigies were sign'd [...]
> Pale spectres in the close of night were seen
> And voices heard of more than mortal men
> In silent groves. (*GEd*: I, 634; 641–644, 624)

Virgil describes nightmarish natural events foreshadowing a tragedy. Supernatural manifestations, whether they are visions or reality, are both terrifying and threatening in that they testify to a monstrous crime, the assassination of Caesar. In a similar manner, *The Romance of the Forest* presents mysterious phenomena as an omen of crimes that were committed inside the abandoned abbey, surrounded by Virgilian "silent groves", and are to be revealed in a supernatural way to the company of fugitives visiting it. The spectres in Virgil are the prolepsis of revelation. The ghosts that Adeline sees in her dreams perform an identical chthonic role, as they connect the young woman with the underworld. In this case, they represent analepses, helping her unveil past mysteries concerning the tragic destiny of her family. Now hidden in the impenetrable vegetation, de la Motte explores the labyrinthine ruins of the abbey inside the forest:

[De la Motte] was proceeding when he was interrupted by an uncommon noise which passed along the hall. They were all silent – it was the silence of terror. [...] Across the hall, the greater part of which was concealed in shadow, the feeble ray spread a tremulous gleam, exhibiting the chasm in the roof, while many nameless objects were seen imperfectly through the dusk [...]. If spirits were ever permitted to revisit the earth, this seemed the hour and the place most suitable for their appearance. [Adeline] was interrupted by a return of the noise. (*RF*: 18–19)

Virgil's "voices" are transformed into the mysterious "noise" pervading the ruins of the abbey. The Virgilian "spectres in the close of night" become the tormented spirit of Adeline's murdered father, appearing at night to reveal the truth. Radcliffe's sensibility is in unison with Virgil's: they both love serene landscapes but also feature frightening scenes of horror. It might be interesting to observe that classicists tend to call the Latin poet Vergil, with a spelling that reflects his original name (Publio Vergilius Maro). Fervent admirers of the poet, who considered him a mentor, a pure soul (*anima candida*) and a magician determined the change in the spelling. The approximate analogy between *virga*–magic wand–and the poet's name was at the basis of the vowel change, which purists tend to consider imprecise. The vision of Virgil as a necromancer, able to predict the destinies of future generations has remained along the centuries (Anna MacVay 1948: 233). One thousand and three hundred years after his death, Dante reiterates the idea in his *Comedy*, in which Virgil represents his guide across the horrors of hell and purgatory. Like Homer in his epic poems, Virgil had his hero explore the underworld and vaticinate the destiny of his progenies. For this reason, his poetry acquires a special aura of mystery, which coheres with Radcliffe's eerie stories.

The Romance of the Forest is interspersed with Virgilian influences even though Radcliffe introduces other classical authors, who become dominant in one of the most alluring and, at the same time, problematic episodes of the story. In fact, one of Radcliffe's narrative climaxes corresponds to a complex classical moment in *The Romance of the Forest* when Adeline's story takes a strange turn. Kidnapped from the abbey in the middle of the wood by means of a cruel stratagem, she is carried to a mysterious mansion and taken into a majestic room, "splendidly illuminated" with "a silver lamp of Etruscan form". The lamp "diffused a blaze of light that, reflected from large pier glasses, completely illuminated the saloon" (*RF*: 156). The excessive luminosity of the scene is in contrast with the dark ruins where she was hiding in the previous days. The dialectical paradox between darkness and light, which was mentioned in the previous chapters, is a popular contrast with the French philosophers of the Enlightenment and a recurrent theme throughout the eighteenth century. In this context, however, light is not synonymous with knowledge but with danger. The obscurity of the forest was protective, and the dark ruins unveiled important secrets. Adeline is now a captive in a place inundated with excessive light, and luxuriantly enriched with precious decorations, beautiful paintings, silk sofas, classical statues, and sensual frescoes covering the walls. The bizarre building "seemed the works of enchantment and rather resembled the palace of a fairy than any human conformation" (*RF*: 156). Adeline has entered a fairy-tale land. The enchantment is in part due to representations of Armida's story, the sensual sorceress in Torquato Tasso's *Jerusalem Delivered* (1581), which decorate some walls. Surrounded by artificial light, Adeline had to abandon her Virgilian idyll in the middle of the magical forest against her will, and is now held captive, immersed in an atmosphere of exaggerated luxury and eroticism. It is not a coincidence that Virgilian contexts are not in a passage, which is more relevant for the presence of other classical poets populating the scene. Other intriguing paintings inspired by Ovid are on the walls, probably erotic representations from *The Metamorphoses*.

Generally painted during the Renaissance and the Baroque period, Ovidian stories showed an exuberance of harmonious bodies, sensually embracing each other. Using Shakespeare's definition of Ovid as "the most capricious [lascivious] poet" in *As You Like It*, and Byron's description of the poet as "a rake" in *Don Juan*, Chloe Chard (2009) dismisses the ancient author as a "Latin poet with a reputation for profligacy" in her introduction to Radcliffe's novel without mentioning *The Metamorphoses*, by far his most important work. A contemporary of Horace and Virgil, Ovid was a great elegist. The insertion of Ovidian scenes, which will eventually influence *The Monk,* conveys an idea of sensuality as well as of lurking danger, primarily for female characters, with rare exceptions (e.g. Hermaphroditus). Radcliffe introduces an erudite connection between Ovid and Pierre de la Motte, as both end their lives in exile for a fault they committed. Here, the enigmas of history are juxtaposed with concealed insinuations in fiction. In light of Radcliffe's knowledge, much wider than many have thought possible, the link is certainly not a coincidence. The author of the *Art of Love* and *Love Affairs,* Ovid's fame rests on his masterpiece *The Metamorphoses*, a mythological and symbolic cosmogony followed by the history of humans and their fateful encounters with divinities. Stories of tragic loves and cruel seductions follow one after the other. Ovid's stories on the walls of Montalt's rich abode are a clear signal that the place is dedicated to seduction and is intrinsically dangerous. In her description of Adeline's gilded prison, Radcliffe's usual verbosity is blocked, and instead of describing the scenes from Ovid, she focuses her attention on marble sculptures.

The busts reproduce the effigies of Horace, Ovid, Anacreon, Tibullus and Petronius Arbiter. These authors from Antiquity, both Roman and Greek, have a special connection with the world of the senses, confirming the latent idea of excess, sensuality and erotica. Horace was the poet for all seasons in the Augustans' ideal poetic pantheon, summarising classical measure, stylistic elegance, philosophical attitude and wide knowledge. Acclaimed as the first autobiographer, the study of his works were the incentive for the great amount of biographies, autobiographies and memoirs that constellated the eighteenth and the nineteenth centuries. His motto "carpe diem" was interpreted as a libertine ideal (Richard Tarrant 2007). Tibullus, who died one year after Virgil at a relatively young age, was an elegiac poet. Horace describes his qualities ("Pow'r of words, and ready eloquence") and his physical aspect ("The Gods to thee a Beautiful Form assign'd") in an elegy in his honour (Tibullus 1720: xlix). Ovid dedicated an ode to him recalling his erotic adventures and unfortunate loves:

> Thus Venus often takes delight
> Ill-suited vot'ries to unite. (Tibullus 1720: xliii)

A Mr Dart, probably a pseudonym, translated Tibullus's elegies and love poems, and published them in 1720 in an edition containing biographical details. Radcliffe's unusual inclusion of Tibullus connotes explicit physical love and sensuality, permeating the atmosphere of Montalt's "saloon". The only Greek poet of the group, Anacreon, was famous for his explicit love poems and bacchanalian lyrics, whose poetic rhythm was based on the long and short sounds of ancient Greek vowels. Lorenzo da Ponte used Anacreon's verses for *Leporello's Aria* in Mozart's *Don Giovanni* (1787), the cruel seducer, punished in the end. Although Mozart's work represents an opera buffa (with a tragic end for the negative character), Anacreon is included by Radcliffe to add a further connotation of sensuality, which also inspired Lewis in his poetic intermezzo in *The Monk* dedicated to the Greek poet. The last statue described by Radcliffe portrays the mysterious Petronius Arbiter (mentioned in chapter about *Vathek*), author of the *Satyricon,* who devoted his short life to luxury and pleasure. He may represent Montalt's ultimate embodiment, an intellectual allusion anticipating the man's destiny, an understated prolepsis, intelligible to cultivated readers. The introduction of a gallery of poets, known for their sensual verses, is unusual in Radcliffe and her vibrant description remains unique in her novels, revealing an intense emotional context apparently imbued with aestheticism, in reality intertwined with upsetting danger.

The unusual focus on a different kind of Antiquity, one expressly linked to sensuality, is Radcliffe's conscious demonstration of her classical knowledge. A superabundance of erotic tinge surrounds Adeline, who faces a distressing threat but remains strangely calm. Tragic Ovidian passions or Anacreontic erotica cannot taint her Virgilian idyllic personality. The presence of classical poets in Montalt's "saloon", used for cajolery, is an exaltation of the eroticism linked to his ambiguous character. A refined aesthete, Montalt is a dangerous seducer, but his cruelty has not yet been revealed. His love for Adeline is like a fire that consumes him from the very first moment he meets the young woman's eyes. Like Montalt, Louis and Theodore, two sincere young male characters in the story, are mesmerised by Adeline and feel the same passion, mediated by their honesty and sense of chivalry. It is like the flame that Virgil repeatedly describes in Book III of the *Georgics*, as the natural process in nature, and that Lucretius graphically depicts with all its physical effects, as it is possible to see in the chapter dedicated to *Vathek*.

Montalt's love is under the sign of libertinism and dishonesty, whereas Louis's affection and Theodore's love are synonyms of innocent and uninterested adoration. The sacrifices and risks Theodore faces for Adeline's sake highlight his generous heart and honest feelings. On the contrary, Montalt's apparently simple personality hides a dangerous mask, and a Machiavellian self soon replaces his artificial persona. Once Montalt discovers Adeline's hidden identity, he turns into an unscrupulous murderer. The metamorphosis, generally involving the victims of the seduction in Ovid, is in this case reversed. It is the potential seducer himself who changes, whereas the potential victim, Adeline, is not contaminated or changed, as she manages to avoid danger. Adeline acquires the status of a superior being, a sort of goddess, an idea confirmed by her comparison to a mythological being and a beautiful nymph. The motif of sylvan nymphs, ethereal creatures moving in the most beautiful spots of nature, is often present in Virgil's *Georgics* and *Eclogues*. Coincidentally, the narrator constantly highlights Adeline's beauty, "Her figure [was] of the middling size, and turned to the most exquisite proportion; her hair was dark auburn, her eyes blue, and whether they sparkled with intelligence, or melted with tenderness, they were equally attractive: her form had the airy lightness of a nymph, and, when she smiled, her countenance might have been drawn for the younger sister of Hebe" (29). Her likeness to the nymphs living in the forests and the goddess Hebe, one of Aphrodite's sisters and the symbol of eternal youth, endows Adeline with a status of mythological superiority. Lewis's handsome Ambrosio is himself compared to a pagan god and is therefore Adeline's mirror image, but a diabolical one.

Radcliffe's choice of classical details is not casual but systematic. By using classical comparisons and contexts, she not only wants to be creative but also aims at giving her writings literary *gravitas*. Matthew Wickman (2005) posits that the dichotomy between horror and terror was a direct inheritance from Antiquity and, in particular, from Virgil. Radcliffe took both categories to perfection, consciously imitating and developing classical canons. Reversing Durant's opinion that "Mrs. Radcliffe made her heroines discover a nightmare beneath the pastoral", we might claim that the pastoral and the idyllic help her female characters to overcome the Gothic ordeals they face. It is possible to infer from the patterns presented in this chapter that Virgil and classical authors had an important function in *The Romance of the Forest*, a function that we can also recognise in *The Mysteries of Udolpho* and *The Italian*. Radcliffe's appreciation of nature, a feature inherited by the Romantics, has a Virgilian matrix. Radcliffe's journeys into the mysteries of ancient buildings and the beauty of nature seem to create a contrast with an undefined, lurking oppression. The political revolutions taking place between the 1770s and the 1790s shockingly changed the common perspective on power. Yet Radcliffe does not seem to acknowledge the existence of political or social unrest. When her stories introduce conflicts, they concern a distant past, historically unidentifiable, as in *The Castles of Athlin and Dunbayne* or in *The Mysteries of Udolpho* despite their apparently clear chronology. The former introduces the struggle between ancient Scottish clans, whereas the latter mentions Renaissance *condottieri*, who turn out to be more similar to *banditti* than honourable knights. A possible hypothesis is that Radcliffe was not interested in politics. Her plots underline the importance of individual struggles and the single character's capacity to face unpredictable circumstances. Her anachronisms are not due to a lack of historical knowledge but represent her refusal to describe contemporary events. Her stories mix imprecisions with moral fables and fairy tales, wherein innocent and good-hearted dramatic personae must fight against forms of evil agency, unjustly intruding in their lives. Johnson (1995) supposes that anachronism is a device to mask Radcliffe's real social criticism of contemporary Britain. In reality, her genuine interest lies elsewhere. Her plots, especially the ones in her four central novels, reveal a form of latent rejection, not systematically organised, against what was threatening nature. What Radcliffe repeatedly introduces are primordial natural settings with no trace of industrial revolution, even though the author seemed to possess a proto-awareness of environmental problems. She is strangely silent about the social transformations brought about by the industrial revolution or the abrupt political changes produced by the French Revolution. Yet she probably had the chance to learn how the new techniques of manufacturing were changing thanks to her connection to the Bentley & Wedgewood factories. She used her majestic word-painting to keep reality away.

Her novels demonstrate that she had a profound cultural awareness she was anxious to transmit. Radcliffe was endowed with narrative sophistication, and *The Romance of the Forest* seems to confirm this hypothesis because of the technical perfection of its plot (Miles 1995). The novel's Gothic themes are interspersed with important Virgilian evocations and chivalric atmospheres. They reveal Radcliffe's meta-literary consciousness, which is expressed in a few lines at the beginning of a dramatic action, which takes place in the banditti's cottage. The ambiguous de la Motte, thinks that "the savage manners of the inhabitants [of the house], seemed to him like a romance of imagination. [...] He ruminated on the late scene, and it appeared like a vision, of one of those improbable fictions that sometimes are exhibited to a *romance*: he could reduce it to no principle of probability or render it comprehensible by any endeavour to analyse it" (*RF*: 7-8). These examples of post-modern, meta-literary irony transform Radcliffe into an exquisitely complicated and imaginative author.

The epigraph in *The Romance of Forest* introducing Joseph Trapp's poem and dedicated to the great Latin poet, adored by Radcliffe, often accompanied a nostalgic painting by Wright of Derby, showing the ruins of Virgil's Tomb in Naples. Trapp's lines seem to convey the deepest sense of Radcliffe's works:

> T'was such a scene as gave a kind relief
> To memory, in sweet pensive grief.
> (*RF*: 271)

It is near here, in this magic and mysterious site in Naples, that Radcliffe will set the intriguing story of Ellena de Rosalba in *The Italian* (1997).

A thousand visages
Then marked I, which the keen and eager cold
Had shaped into a doggish grin; whence creeps
A shivering Horror o'er me.
(Dante, *Inferno*: Canto XXXII, Dante Gabriel Rossetti tr.)

Deeply they plunged beneath the deadly shade
Of mental Night, that her broad wing display'd
Throu' many a dark age o'er the slumber'ng Soul
(Dante, *Paradiso*: Canto VII, Henry Boyd tr.)

A suddain Horror seiz'd his giddy Head,
And his ears tinckled, and his Colour fled
Nature was in alarm; some Danger nigh
Seem'd threaten'd, though unseen to mortal Eye
(Dryden, "Theodore and Honoria from Boccace",
Fables Ancient and Modern)

He, wearied and confused with wandering wide,
Perceived the place was by enchantment wrought
(Ariosto, *Orlando Furioso* Canto XXII, xvi, W. S. Rose tr.)

The early Gothic contributed to new forms of narration that were the
result of the cultural crossover of several literary influences from different
authors and epochs. This far, we have seen how Antiquity and Classics
played a remarkable role. This section looks at Beckford's, Lewis's, and
Radcliffe's texts as examples of works rich in cultural substrata combining
multiple sources from other literary eras. Critical literature on the Gothic
has been haunted by two questions that have posed a series of
interpretative problems. One enigma behind the genesis of the Gothic
novel is the impossibility of determining how such a strange form of

writing could develop at the end of a century apparently dominated by the development of science and the predominance of rationalism. The other doubt concerns the halo of mystery surrounding the actual sources that might have had a substantial part in forming the Gothic.

As far as the first problem is concerned, scholars have investigated the dialectical contrast between the intellectual brilliance of the Enlightenment and latent forms of pervasive darkness. They have drawn attention to the co-existence of problematic shadows during the age of "light", which exalted reason, science and tolerance. These shadows included the attraction of superstition and magic. After presenting Denis Diderot's rational entry on "Magic'" in the *Encyclopédie, ou Dictionnaire Raisonné,* meant to disabuse humanity of the dangers of superstition, Lizanne Henderson (2016) reports that during the eighteenth and nineteenth centuries there were not always clear-cut distinctions between magic, the occult, demonological theory and science. The combination of astrology and medicine, for instance, continued to play a role in some medical procedures, whereas scientific techniques were employed by some in hopes of finding proof of the spirit world, or explanations of second-sight and paranormal phenomena. John Fleming's study (2013) examines even more extreme topics, as he concentrates on the dark side of the Enlightenment and on the strange personalities that populated that epoch, such as Count Alessandro di Cagliostro, Giuseppe Balsamo's pseudonym, who was involved in a series of mysterious events. His strange story and the dichotomy of his persona, never satisfactorily clarified, became legendary and attracted the interest of the masses as well as of powerful people including bishops, politicians, aristocrats and monarchs. Goethe was so intrigued with his adventurous life that he decided to investigate Cagliostro's story at his place of origin in Sicily during his Grand Tour in Italy in the 1780s. Having grown up in dire poverty, Balsamo, alias Cagliostro, escaped from the monastery where his relatives had sent him. Fleming recounts that he exploited his rudiments of chemistry and pharmacy to become a healer. He was also interested in alchemy, occult science and magic rites. These rites were perfected during his numerous journeys across Europe, from Russia to Portugal, Poland and Malta, via Great Britain, Switzerland and France, where he resided for longer periods. He created freemason lodges in Europe attracting large numbers of adepts. Wealthy members of one of the German secret societies, probably the Illuminati, were thought to bankroll him for political purposes. An adventurer, a forger and a swindler, eager to exploit his wife's good looks in exchange for economic and social advantages, he was accused of being involved in the so-called "Affair of the Diamond

Necklace", which indirectly inspired *The Romance of the Forest*. Later, the Roman Inquisition sentenced him to life imprisonment in the Castle of San Leo, near Rimini.

The Victorian historian Thomas Carlyle could not conceive how the Count's contemporaries might have been so gullible, especially considering his unattractive appearance, lack of education and the improbability of his pretensions. Some of his contemporaries hated Cagliostro. Giacomo Casanova and many of his compatriots absolutely abhorred him. Notwithstanding his suspicious activities, Cagliostro enjoyed immense popularity. Mozart even created the character of Sarastro in *The Magic Flute* (1791) with Cagliostro in mind. Giovanni Barbieri (1791), who had access to Inquisition documents, published the records of his interrogations, tortures and trial. Barbieri's records and Cagliostro's memoirs were immediately translated into English in the very same year. Before falling from grace, Cagliostro had become friends with de Louthenbourg (Beckford's master of ceremonies). He met the popular painter during his stays in London and in Switzerland. Alexander (1962) affirms that the young Beckford might have met the pseudo necromancer and taken part in some of his Masonic rites, at the invitation of de Louthenbourg. Coincidentally, traces of mysterious rituals can be identified in Beckford's works and *Vathek*. The dark ambiguities underlying the apparently luminous cultural mainstream of the eighteenth century might be at the origin of the love for unusual and strange characters and situations that brought about the development of the early Gothic literary phenomenon.

The second problem comprised within the Gothic concerns the identification of its sources. Influences of the distant past did not play a secondary role in the development of novels that were a congeries of multiple ideas. That works from past centuries and from other countries continued to be relevant at the end of the eighteenth century and well into the nineteenth might be clearly supported by the ongoing publication of Classical, Medieval and Renaissance masterpieces and their translations. Gillespie and Hopkins (2005) underline the importance of literary translations in the development of British literature. Their systematic research on translations of past authors have cast an interesting light on potential sources and literary connections that may have been overlooked. One of Shelley's friends, the poet, essayist, and critic Leigh Hunt is an example of the continuing interest for works of the Italian past. He published a collection of selected poetic extracts well into the mid-nineteenth century, named *Stories from the Italian Poets* in 1846. The literary miscellany included Dante, Ariosto and Tasso, but the inclusion of both Luigi Pulci and Matteo Maria Boiardo was less common a choice and demonstrated Britain's rich cultural level as well as an unfaltering love for Italian literature. In 1830, two decades before Hunt's poetic collection, the British Museum librarian Antonio Panizzi, an Italian expat, published a series of volumes devoted to the rich analysis of the "Romantic narrative poetry of Italians", including critical commentaries and long passages of the same authors chosen by Hunt, plus commentaries on Petrarch and Boccaccio. The term "Romantic" conveyed different meanings from those connected with the same word today. Including poets from the Middle Ages, such as Dante, Petrarch and Boccaccio, or poets from the Renaissance, such as Pulci, Boiardo, Ariosto, and Tasso, under a general "Romantic" category was acceptable and welcome, a fact that confirms the fluid vision of literary history at the time.

The distinction between literary eras was yet to be demarcated, as the periodisation of literary currents was introduced at the end of the nineteenth century. Butler (1981: 122) acutely observes that the clear-cut distinction between the Middle Ages and the Renaissance that we use today was not common in past centuries, and figures such as Dante, Boccaccio, Petrarch, Shakespeare, Ariosto, Tasso and Milton were seen as a cultural expression of an indefinite past under the global sign of Romanticism. The literary distinctions created at the end of the nineteenth century are rethought today, as the borders between literary currents are becoming blurred and less clear once more (Wallace 2009). William Galperin and Susan Wolfson (1997) provocatively labels the time span between 1750 and 1850 as the "Romantic dominion", starting with the melancholic voices of the Graveyard poets and extending into the mid-Victorian era. A considerable number of past authors, namely what we now call Medieval and Renaissance, supplied ideas for the Gothic and influenced *The Castle of Otranto*, *Vathek*, *The Monk*, *The Romance of the Forest* and other Gothic novels to a greater or lesser extent.

Critical literature has tried to identify possible models for early Gothic novels, but it has not dedicated much attention to Medieval inspiration or Renaissance contents. These are of crucial importance to several parts of the texts analysed here, which demonstrate that Italian *Trecento*, Humanism and the Renaissance continued to play a very important role in poetry and literature at the end of the eighteenth century. Dante, together with Boccaccio and Ariosto, are significant sources and influences for the early Gothic. Despite his intrinsic difficulty and the lack of a complete translation before the nineteenth century, Dante had represented a steady influence throughout the centuries since Chaucer's translations of some fundamental passages:

It may be a matter of some surprise for those who have not had their attention called to the fact, to learn how far back the influence of Dante on English literature extends. Chaucer translated and imitated a number of passages in the *Divine Comedy*; there is frequent mention of the great Florentine by the poets of the sixteenth century; while Milton's debt to his predecessor in the religious epic has already been pointed out. (Oscar Kuhns 1899: 176)

This revealing remark by Kuhns is only half the story. Mainstream Augustan literati as well as Pre-Romantic poets and Gothic writers promoted the interest in the medieval poet in the eighteenth century (Richard Bates 2005: 395). A poet, historian, prose-writer, philosopher and politician living between the thirteenth and the fourteenth centuries, Dante is reputed to be the greatest poet of Italian literature. The renowned Florentine's studies covered many important subjects: he was a linguist *ante litteram*, and his works were foundational in promoting the Italian vernacular over Latin. Dante developed *volgare,* the medieval antecedent of the Italian language, from the Florentine speech by carrying out a philological inclusion of terms belonging to other regional speeches of the peninsula, in addition to borrowing from Latin, Greek, medieval French and other languages. His masterpiece is the *Divine Comedy,* or *Divina Commedia,* completed in 1320, an allegorical epic narrative, in *terza rima* stanzaic form, of the poet's supernatural journey in the three loci of the Christian after-world, *Hell, Purgatory* and *Paradise.* Authors of following epochs appreciated and reproduced some of Dante's bloodcurdling descriptions of the netherworld and, as Diego Saglia (2006) has demonstrated, Dante provided an immense range of images for both the Gothic novel and Romanticism. A number of his characterisations of the infernal world were absorbed and interiorised by the early Gothic novelists, who reproduced them in their fearsome stories. Like Horace, Dante was one of the most renowned poets in Britain during the long eighteenth century. Even though a complete version of the *Divine Comedy* was not carried out until the beginning of the nineteenth century, its complex symbolism and allegorical constructions were part of a shared cultural universe. In a section of the *Encyclopaedia of Literary Translation*, Edoardo Crisafulli (2001: 340) traces an illuminating account of Dante's *Divine Comedy* translations:

A multitude of translators and poets, from Chaucer to Seamus Heaney, have tried their hand at rendering single episodes or entire canticles of the *Comedy* (e.g. Count Ugolino, *Inferno* XXXII–XXXIII), which have always aroused interest in the English literary tradition. William De Sua demonstrated there was a great number of rewritings of Dante's poem into English, perhaps more than into any other language, and Dante is, together with Horace, the most widely translated poet [...] The British Henry Boyd's (1802) is the first complete translation of the *Comedy*. His version (in pentameters arranged in six-line stanzas rhyming aabccb) is clearly a part of the 18th century modernising and naturalising tradition of translating (as in Dryden and Pope): Boyd takes great liberties in rewriting the original and makes no effort to reproduce Dante's tercets. However, his imagination has a Romantic vein, since he grasps the significance of the redemption of man in the *Comedy* and stresses Dante's sublime genius (critics in the late 18th and early 19th century found in Dante elements of a Barbaric age such as 'terror', 'pathos' and 'sublimity'). Boyd's free version was based on Dante's literary borrowings in Shakespeare, Spenser, Milton, Dryden, and Pope.

Crisafulli's compendium of the multiple renderings in English confirm the high literary status enjoyed by the illustrious Florentine and, notwithstanding the lack of a standard Italian version of the poem before the early twentieth century and its intrinsic difficulty, Dante's gloomy descriptions in the *Divine Comedy* were popular throughout the centuries. Interestingly, an Italian version of the *Inferno* was published in Paris in 1787 (printed by Hubert-Martin Cazin), which demonstrates the continuous popularity of the *Comedy*'s Italian version and the cultural knowledge of Italian in Europe during the eighteenth century. Meanwhile, translations continued to attract many readers. In 1783, Count Antoine de Rivarol had completed a prose version of the *Inferno* in French, which deeply inspired René de Chateaubriand's *Le Génie du Christianisme* (1802). Different schools of thought have developed contrasting hypotheses concerning the proper translation of Dante's verses in the *Comedy*, a poem that embraces the Pythagorean formula of the number three as a symbol of perfection. The three canticles are formed by thirty-three cantos, with the exception of the first canticle that contains thirty-four, so that the final number of cantos is one hundred, a further addition to the text's numerological symmetry. Every canto contains thirty-tree tercets, called *terza rima*. The difficulty in translating involves different challenges including diachronic and synchronic renderings of a literary work into a different language without losing its linguistic, cultural and epistemological value. Technically speaking, the English translations of Dante's poetic work have been divided into three categories assigned by one of the most eminent American scholars of Dante, Oliver Wendell Holmes, as Joseph Chesley Matthews (1957) indicates in his essay. Crisafulli helpfully clarifies (2001: 340):

From Oliver Wendell Holmes comes the idea of the three main types of verse form: mimetic (*terza rima* in English); analogical (a form, such as blank verse, having the same cultural significance in the target tradition as the original had in the source tradition); the organic (a form, such as free verse, that has little or no relationship with the original one). From Holmes also: the distinction between different large-scale policies: (a) exoticizing (e.g. retaining a *terza rima* and source language syntax) vs. naturalizing (e.g. blank verse and target language syntax) (b) historicizing (e.g. use of archaisms) vs. modernizing (e.g. use of modern English). From Lawrence Venuti the seminal notion of transparency (the dominant canon in the English tradition of translating), i.e. a policy domesticating the foreign elements and achieving easy readability and fluency, as opposed to a foreignizing policy (synonymous with Holmes's exoticizing policy).

The choice of the poetical form and the language of translation, Crisafulli explains, determine remarkable differences in the final output, which may or may not thoroughly reflect the original version. The canonical Italian version of the *Divina Commedia* was established in 1921, and has since been replaced by Italian scholar Giulio Petrocchi's 1960 adaptation. The gnoseological complexity of Dante's poem, the difficulty of categorising it and the existence of diversiform versions of the *Commedia* did not generally facilitate the task of translators. In particular, earlier translators of the *Comedy* were forced to work on more than one original text. In Britain, the country where the dissemination of culture through periodicals and the printing press was higher than in other European nations, literary translations were instrumental in the propagation of knowledge for all social categories (Gillespie and Hopkins 2005). Early Gothic novels by most established authors equally show the importance of Dante. Following Saglia's (2006) convincing argument that "Gothic overtones were found in the most popular narratives of the *Inferno*", the aim of this chapter is to demonstrate how Dante's *Inferno* and *The Divine Comedy*, together with elements from the medieval Boccaccio and the Italian Renaissance, were part of early Gothic narratives. While Walpole had inserted only imperceptible elements from Dante in *The Castle of Otranto*, Beckford and the other authors absorbed more influences from Italian Middle Ages and Renaissance models. Both *Vathek* and *The Monk* are interesting examples of how Dante's replicas permeated late eighteenth-century literature. Beckford's and Lewis's mastery of both Italian language and literature was frequently mentioned in their correspondence and memoirs. It is not a coincidence that one distinctive and very interesting element in Beckford and Lewis is the pervading presence of Dante at the grim conclusions of their stories. The two authors epitomise the most fortunate readers of Dante, as they could enjoy the Tuscan poet directly or through the elegant versions of eminent English poets, or even French translators, insomuch as they were fluent in all three languages. It is unlikely that Beckford and Lewis read Boyd's complete translation before composing their novels, as it was published after their first editions of *Vathek* and *The Monk*. Boyd's *Inferno* had, nevertheless, been available starting from 1785, and this rendering may have had some relevance thanks to its chronological proximity. Moreover, the two novelists had probably read the Dantesque cantos in translations by Chaucer, Milton and Pope, or by Walpole's friend and graveyard poet Gray. In all probability, they also read the poem, or at least some of its best-known parts, in Italian thanks to their proven fluency in the language. Sincere admirers of the Italian language, both Beckford and Lewis could read and understand Dante's *Comedy* in its original version, like Walpole, Gray and several British intellectuals of the time.

Dantesque influences materialise in the last parts of *Vathek*, conveying gloomy and infernal atmospheres. Although Beckford's reviewers have connected the text to great authors of the past, these analogies have not received much attention. While the genre of *Vathek* cannot be determined with certainty, some scholars identify sublime and picturesque aspects in the story that, when added to its gloomy conclusion, allow them to place the novel in the Gothic current. The supernatural and magical contexts adorning the novel seem to convey a further confirmation of the intrinsic Gothic nature of the story, in spite of its bizarre situations and grotesque adventures. Jung (2011) convincingly inscribes *Vathek* and its architectures in the gestalt of the early Gothic that was to influence novelists during the following decades before the turn of the century. A thorough analysis of the final part of the novel, where the presence of Dante is dominant, clearly reveals its Gothic essence.

Three versions of the Comedy are referenced for this chapter, two in poetry and one in prose. One poetic version reflects the division of the cantos into tercets (three-line stanzas, or *terza rima*) and is a modern rendering taken from the Princeton website dedicated to Dante, which includes his complete works with an extensive bibliography. The second reference is a poetic version in six-line stanzas by Henry Boyd, who completed the *Inferno* in 1785 and translated the whole *Commedia* in English for the first time in 1802. The prose version by Charles Eliot Norton (1892) is linguistically compatible with the prose used by Lewis and Beckford in their novels, even though it belongs to a later date.

After a tourbillon of fantastic events, comic episodes, and tumultuous adventures, the pacing of *Vathek*'s narrative becomes slower and the atmosphere darker. The protagonists' parable culminates in the subterranean palace of Eblis that the caliph, his lover and his mother have incessantly been in search of, thinking that it was the supreme locus of knowledge and power. Beckford's narrative style changes profoundly upon their arrival at Eblis: the Eastern lustre and Lucretian hedonism are abandoned in exchange for a dark and anguishing desolation. The pages are pervaded with Dantesque imagery and its mutable contexts are mostly borrowed from the *Inferno*. Once at the gates of the strange palace of Eblis, whose architecture has never been seen before, the caliph and his companions can observe "the colossal forms of four creatures, composed of the leopard and the griffin, and though but of stone, inspired emotions of terror" (*Vathek*: 107). The creatures of stone at the entrance represent animals that have their flesh and blood doubles in Dante's *Comedy*, wherein an oppressive dark forest entangles the poet. The forest is an allegorical symbol of strong emotional trauma, which has inspired writers and painters in the centuries to come. In the gloomy landscape, Dante encounters three heinous animals, which are fierce and menacing and intend to freeze the poet's attempts to save himself. The poet is trying to escape from the dangerous wood and climb a steep mountain to overcome his plight. Charles Eliot Norton's 1892 prose translation describes the scene from the first canto as follows (hence, the quotations from Norton's prose and Boyd's poetic translations include the canto and the page, or the lines from the Princeton website): "And lo! Almost at the beginning of the steep a she-leopard, light and very nimble, which was covered with a spotted coat. And she did not move from before my face, nay, rather hindered so my road that to return I oftentimes had turned" (*Inferno*: I, 2). After the paralysing effect of the mysterious leopard, the poet meets a menacing lion and a covetous she-wolf, all fierce creatures threatening the protagonist in mysterious ways. In an agony of indecision and fear, Dante almost succumbs to horror. The symbolic animals in the first Canto are the alliterative "lonza", "leone", and "lupa", respectively translated as "leopard", "lion" and "she-wolf" in both Norton and the Princeton version, whereas Boyd chooses "panther" to describe the "lonza". The significance of the horrendous creatures is rather obscure.

The beasts have been variously deciphered as potential embodiments of the emperor, the pope, or the Florentine government that exiled Dante away from Florence and Tuscany. Philosophical, religious, political and metaphorical explanations have been added without ultimately unravelling the actual message hidden behind the allegorical creatures, as Dante's meaning is intentionally enigmatic. Although less profound and much more limited in scope, Beckford's *Vathek* is equally ambiguous. It is, therefore, not possible to determine a single interpretation for the variety of bizarre creatures and puzzling events of the story. The novel becomes even more abstruse in the finale. Beckford introduces the images of animals at the portal of hell to describe the entrance to Eblis and he does so by combining Dante's complex symbols in the First and Third Cantos. The mouth of the Inferno is Vathek's final destination, not the beginning as in Dante's mythical adventure. Interestingly, wild creatures are positioned at the gate of Hell in both Dante and Beckford. The stone animals that the caliph finds are at the portal, which is inscribed with carved words that constantly mutate, reiterating the linguistic obsession and recalling the strange inscriptions on the Giaour's magic sabre, forever metamorphosing. When entering hell, Dante sees "words of colour obscure [...] at the top of a gate", and these words are "dire" to him (*Inferno*: I, 11, Norton). Dante has to face a hideous and gloomy place to reach his final bliss. On the contrary, Vathek starts his journey in a sublime condition only to end up in a place of fear and terror. Dante and Vathek share the same curiosity, the thirst for knowledge and the desire to enter the unknown, but their state of mind is dissimilar and their destinies incompatible.

An interesting feature in the novel is the description of extreme verticality that seems to convey deeper meanings. The characters in *Vathek* move both upwards and downwards. The upward movement takes place in the high tower belonging to Vathek's mother, Carathis, who had it built to carry out her mysterious dark magic. What is more, she performs her magical rites and bloody sacrifices upon the highest part of it. The downward movement is first found in the description of the chasm where the Giaour, the monstrous creature haunting the caliph, disappears to carry out macabre rituals. The most extraordinary example of downward movement into the abyss is, however, represented by the Hall of Eblis. The corridors are labyrinthine and dangerously "steep". All vertical movements are part of a Dantesque phenomenology, as they mirror Dante's progression along the arduous and horrid recesses of the Inferno with extreme difficulty. The entrance to Eblis creates a specular reflection of Dante entering Hell. In the very beginning, the poet finds darkness and walks on almost perpendicular paths. Later, he can observe devilish creatures, punishing sinners doomed to eternal sufferings. Dante's guide is the great Latin poet Virgil, whereas the ambiguous and obscene Giaour, Vathek's nemesis and the devil's emissary, leads the caliph and his group. Other equally disgusting creatures perambulate in the mysterious subterranean citadel of Eblis and the reiteration of an ever-descending vertical movement towards the chasm is accentuated by a number of synonyms (some are repeated many times): "ascendancy", "chasm" (alternatively "black", "dreadful", and "accursed"), "gulph", "precipice", "mysterious recesses", "valleys of darkness", "the centre of the earth", and "gorges". The hypothesis here contrasts Garrett's (1992: 25) interpretation of "Vathek's horizontal perspective". Dante's downward movement throughout the *Inferno* is described in the first part of his story, whereas Vathek's progress takes him downwards at the very end of his strange adventure. After the momentary ascension in his mother's majestic tower, almost touching the sky, the caliph constantly moves downwards and becomes itinerant, thinking, like Dante, that he has lost his way. When he finally finds the opaque labyrinth of Eblis, he descends into its entrails to find "the region of wonders", wrongly convinced he will obtain "all kinds of delights" (*Vathek*: 36). The dark subterranean region contains boundless misery instead. In a reversed state of mind, a frightened and desperate Dante cautiously moves along the circles of Hell, towards the centre of the earth and Satan's kingdom. Dante's senses are awake while his wise companion, Virgil, a beacon of probity and rectitude, constantly warns the poet against the dangers lurking in the devil's hideous realm. Virgil awakens Dante's empathy. On the contrary, the Giaour definitely silences Vathek's conscience and nourishes his greed inside the dark labyrinths of Eblis.

Virgil accompanies Dante as far as Purgatory, and then leaves him with the idealised love of his youth who passed away while still in her prime. The virtuous Beatrice has to drive the poet to the highest empyrean spheres. Vathek's first meeting with Nouronihar, the adolescent girl who unconsciously seduces him, somehow recalls the medieval idealisation of the angel-like woman, a trend started by troubadours and adapted by Guido Guinizzelli, Guido Cavalcanti and Dante himself to their poetic school, called the *Dolce Stil Novo* or "sweet new style", the poetic manner of late medieval poets exalting the purifying raison d'être of the beloved woman. The first meeting between the caliph and the sultan's daughter is peculiar. Ballaster (2005a: 367) interestingly highlights that the description of Vathek's first meeting is told in "the third person personal narration", i.e. from the protagonist's inner perspective, while Beckford generally adopts a "detached and cynical irony" to narrate the entire story. Hence, the meeting acquires special connotations that make the main character's experience similar to a medieval encounter with an idealised woman. The perfume and the beauty of girl and her maids inebriate the caliph, who thinks that they are not creatures of this world but mythological "Peries come down from the spheres", the legendary creatures whose name means "the beautiful race of creatures which constitutes the link between angels and men" (*Vathek*: 146). Nouronihar's introduction is comparable to the angelical woman's healing appearance in the poems of the *Dolce Stil Novo*. The idealised woman's ethereal beauty provokes a languid torment in the medieval poets' senses because she unites goodness and sensibility and has the power to better the man she loves. Even the hedonistic caliph seems to change because of this fatal tryst, perchance, a new phase interrupting his trajectory of debauchery and indifference. However, instead of instilling him with peace, the beautiful girl becomes an agent of evil. Spellbound by Vathek's negative influence, she becomes as evil as he is, turning avid and insatiable. Unlike Dante and Beatrice, the caliph and his lover cannot find happiness. Nouronihar is diametrically opposed to Dante's Beatrice. Her negativity is reiterated at the gloomy portal of the infernal palace when the magic stone figures reveal to Vathek that "in favour of [his] companion [...] Eblis pemitteth that the portal of this palace shall be opened" (*Vathek*: 108), whereas Beatrice obtains the opening of paradise doors for Dante by virtue of her goodness. The epiphany of the ethereal beauty's cruel essence occurs at Eblis.

The common attribute uniting Dante and Vathek is their sinful state at the commencement of their strange adventures. Dante obtains his long searched-for purification. Inversely, the caliph becomes more sinful and his crimes accumulate, making his redemption impossible. Their guides are antithetical; Virgil represents moral strength and superior knowledge, whereas the Giaour has many cryptic meanings all connected with wrongdoing and misdeeds. Beautiful and ethereal women accompany Dante and Vathek during the final part of their peregrinations. The women's alliances with the two heroes take different directions, as Beatrice leads Dante through the heavenly kingdom towards apotheosis and forgiveness, while Nouronihar is responsible for Vathek's ultimate fall and perpetual despair. Beatrice's name is symbolic of the beatitude she concedes: she is now a celestial creature helping Dante reach the highest part of heaven and admire the elevation of all creatures divine. She also sustains the poet, as he is purified of his earthly sins. Nouronihar's superior beauty and sweetness do not help Vathek since his darkest sins and shameful greed inexorably spoil and contaminate her. As a result, she must share his eternal suffering and dramatic downfall, in a place that resembles Dante's *Inferno*, eternally excluded from happiness. Conversely, after his tragic suffering, Dante finally finds a way out of obscurity and enjoys the vision of the firmament (here in Norton's rendering in prose):

A place is there below, stretching as far from Beelzebub as his tomb extends, which not by sight is known, but by the sound of a rivulet that there descends along the hollow of a rock that it has gnawed with its course that winds and little falls. My Leader and I entered through that hidden way, to return to the bright world. And without care to have any repose, we mounted up, he first and I second, till through a round opening I saw of those beauteous things which heaven bears, and thence we came forth to see again the stars. (*Inferno*: XXXIV, 193)

Dante abandons the lower world and his movement is upward and out of the recesses of the earth. He arrives at a place where he can finally admire a marvellous starry sky: "E quindi uscimmo a riveder le stelle" (Canto XXXIV, Line 139), "thence we came forth to see again the stars", is the well-known last line of the *Inferno*, blending deep joy at the conclusion of the infernal nightmare and admiration for the celestial vault's evocative beauty. Interestingly, the term "stelle", "stars", is at the very end of all three major sections (*Inferno*, *Purgatorio* and *Paradiso*). The sense of relief and the image of the scintillating night are also found in *Vathek*, but the context is unlike Dante's, as the protagonists do not leave the place of doom. They are moving towards the fatal entrance, instead:

The rock yawned, and disclosed within it a staircase of polished marble, that seemed to approach the abyss. Upon each stair were planted two large torches, like those Nouronihar had seen in her vision: the camphorated vapour of which ascended and gathered itself into a cloud under the hollow of the vault. This appearance, instead of terrifying, gave new courage to the daughter of Fakreddin. Scarcely deigning to bid adieu to the moon and the firmament; she abandoned without hesitation, the pure atmosphere, to plunge into these infernal exhalations. (*Vathek*: 108)

Deeply absorbed by Vathek's greed, the once pure Nouronihar becomes her lover's impatient guide and she voluntarily enters the evil palace, leading the group. Vathek's entrance into the mysterious subterranean vault in the finale is in contrast to Dante's newly-found freedom after his escape from the dark abyss of horror. The poet breathes the pure air and admires the stars in a limpid sky, whereas, in a perfect specular but antithetical instance, Beckford's characters abandon the marvels of the "firmament" and enclose themselves in the dark devilish place, overwhelmed by "infernal exhalations". Beckford demonstrates he not only had the *Divine Comedy* in mind but also intended to create a reversed story, interspersed with Bakhtinian carnivalesque interludes, wherein the progress of corrupt individuals culminates in a Dantesque hell of dark despair. A further reversed echo resounds a few paragraphs later when Vathek and Nouronihar look at each other, but they can only see reciprocal hate. On the contrary, in every canto, when climbing the spheres of paradise, Dante and Beatrice look into each other's eyes filled with and surrounded by rivers of refulgent light. Another symmetrical opposition can be observed when the caliph and his lover have similar feelings to Dante and Beatrice before being engulfed by the abyss of darkness: "As they descended, by the effulgence of the torches, they gazed on each other with mutual admiration; and both appeared so resplendent, that they already esteemed themselves spiritual intelligences" (*Vathek*: 108). The tragic illusion for Vathek and Nouronihar is the thought of having reached the status of heavenly creatures, as they consider themselves "spiritual intelligences". Interestingly, both the apparent state of ecstasy that the caliph and his companion feel when "gazing on each other" and the great luminosity ("resplendent", "effulgence") that surrounds them before they succumb to doom reflect the tropes of radiance and glorification in *Paradise*. In Dante, Beatrice's effulgent aura and the Empyrean's utmost luminosity determine Dante's transfiguration, i.e. his change from a physical being into a sort of intellectual entity, an aspect that has been analysed by Juan Varela-Portas Orduña (2019) and other famed scholars. It is also oddly similar to the last time Dante looks at Beatrice in the splendour of the Empyrean, in Canto XXXI in Boyd's 1802 poetic version:

> [Beatrice], crown'd with glory, sate above;
> Yet, wing'd with ev'ry glance, the shaft of Love
> Still reached my heart across the boundless Sky.
> (*Paradise*: XXXI, 347)

Beatrice's brilliance gives the poet sheer delight and promises a future of happiness in the afterlife. The refulgence surrounding Dante and the divine creatures in heaven has a tenebrous parallel in *Vathek*'s finale. Beckford's ingemination of Dante's images progresses and the following passage is an evident symmetric repetition of Dante's lines in Canto III of the *Inferno*:

In the midst of this immense hall a vast multitude was incessantly passing; who severally kept their right hands on their hearts; without once regarding any thing around them. They had all, the livid paleness of death. Their eyes, deep sunk in their sockets, resembled those phosphoric meteors that glimmer by night, in places of interment. Some stalked slowly on; absorbed in profound reverie: some shrieking with agony, ran furiously about like tigers, wounded with poisoned arrows; whilst others, grinding their teeth in rage, foamed along more frantic than the wildest maniac. They all avoided each other, and, though surrounded by a multitude that no one could number, each wandered at random, unheedful of the rest, as if alone on a desert where no foot had trodden (*Vathek*: 109–110).

This scene of the "immense multitude" of sinners condemned to eternal suffering is among the most impressive and best known of Dante's *Inferno* and was famously re-elaborated by T. S. Eliot, among others. The punishment inflicted on the damned is the same for everyone in *Vathek*, whereas Dante is much more articulate in his descriptions of chastisement. Beckford vividly renders the sense of deep anguish and tremendous agony. It is possible to argue that Dante's words in the third Canto, corresponding to lines 24–32 and 56–61 in the original three-verse stanzas, represent a clear source for Beckford. Here follows a passage from Norton's prose translation:

Here sighs, laments and deep wailings were resounding through the starless air; wherefore at first I wept thereat. Strange tongues, horrible cries, words of woe, accents of anger, voices high and hoarse, and sounds of hands with them, were making a tumult which whirls forever in that air dark without change, like the sand when the whirlwind breathes [...] And I, who was going, saw a banner, that whirling ran so swiftly that it seemed to me to scorn all repose, and behind it came so long a train of folk, that I could never have believed death had undone so many. (*Inferno*: III, 11–13)

Although Beckford does not seem to have adopted Dante's triadic division of the *Comedy*, his novel *Vathek* may be ideally divided into three parts. Randall Craig (1984) identified a classical structure and a division into three phases, reproducing the scheme of *agon* (conflict), *pathos* (death-struggle) and *anagnorisis* (final discovery), partially influenced by Frye, who highlighted the structure of a threefold classical division in his critical studies of poetic mythology. Despite Craig's interesting motivations, the three-phase classical development would be more suitable to describe the narrative structure in Radcliffe' novels or in *The Monk*. In effect, life in Samarah is a form of paradise with all its extraordinary beauties, in which Carathis' immense tower may lead to the Empyrean, a context that does not seem to be compatible with *agon,* or conflict. The difficult central journey to the lake, where Nouronihar and Gulchenrouz have taken refuge, is symbolic of purgatory, an idea that is confirmed by the hero's feeling of deep suffering when he is convinced he has forever lost his beautiful princess. Images of Hell prevail in the final part in the Palace of Fire belonging to a mysterious demon, further contradicting Craig's theory. The variety of echoes reminiscent of Dante in the closing pages of the story casts a different light on Beckford's chameleonic narration, resulting in an inverted and grotesque *Divine Comedy*. In the light of multiple corroborations, it is difficult to consider Beckford's novel as an Oriental tale exclusively. Rather, it is a philosophical exercise and a show of knowledge that the young author was eager to transmit. Vathek and his beautiful companion's tragic destiny becomes a distorted version of Dante and Beatrice's story. When the doomed couple arrive at the mysterious palace, they find an iconographic terrifying ensemble that appears to reflect Piranesi's imposing architectural structures:

A death-like stillness reigned over the mountain and through the air. The moon dilated on a vast platform, the shades of the lofty columns which reached from the terrace almost to the clouds. [...] On the right rose the watch-towers, ranged before the ruins of an immense palace, whose walls were embossed with various figures. [...] The rock yawned, and disclosed within it a staircase of polished marble, that seemed to approach the abyss. (*Vathek*: 107–108)

In the end, when fatal punishment strikes the protagonists, "[t]heir hearts took fire and they, at once, lost the most precious gift of heaven: - HOPE. These unhappy beings recoiled with looks of the most furious distraction [...] all testified their horror" (*Vathek*: 119). Intriguingly, Dante sees and hears similar words at the gate of Hell in the third Canto of the *Inferno* (Norton's version): "Through me is the way to the woeful city; through me is the way to eternal woe; through me is the way among the lost people. [...] Leave every hope, ye who enter!" (*Inferno*: III, 20). These fateful words become the décor of Beckford's gloomy final image, confirming the hypothesis that his novel constitutes an inverted *Comedy*, merging mediaeval Dante and classical Lucretius. Saglia (2006: 65) observes that "the diffusion of Italian materials in late Gothic or Gothic-inflected narratives" is substantiated by the literary and poetic production at the turn of the century and later on:

[Authors] turned to Dante and Boccaccio for their powerful Gothic-style combinations of pathetic plots of hopeless love and disturbing tales of persecution and agony. Through their stereotypical situations and characters, these poems provided finely tuned descriptions of somatic and psychic states, especially the deformation of sensory perception, as well as sensitive and sympathetic portrayals of profoundly distressed human beings.

Saglia offers some striking examples and clarifies that Count Ugolino's atrocious sequence in Dante's *Inferno* had a strong visual and emotional impact, confirmed by the plethora of imitations it inspired. Romantic poets of the calibre of Byron and Shelley "were deeply fascinated by Dante" (Saglia 2006: 66) and, as many before them, were puzzled by the story of Count Ugolino's, a medieval nobleman of the Ghibelline faction living in thirteenth-century Pisa. Accused of treason after ambiguous alliances with the Guelph side, he was imprisoned in a tower and left to starve with his sons and nephews. Legends were born from the horror of their captivity, vividly narrated in Dante's *Comedy*.

Like *Vathek*, *The Monk* includes a stratification of sources. Despite the connection with classical elements, Lewis's narrative exaggerations frequently tend to cast a shadow on its cultural essence. Apparently, the novel followed the literary fashion of the time, but the creativity and literary technique shown in *The Monk* were by far superior to the poor stylistics of popular novels. Lewis's borrowings from Dante are not as extensive as Beckford's are, but two episodes in *The Monk* are significant for their analogies with events in the *Inferno*. Agnes's subplot presents an important correlation with Ugolino's horror-inspiring story. An aristocratic girl, Lorenzo's sister and Raymond's fiancée, she has been forced to live in a convent because of her deceased parents' decision and Donna Rodolpha's furious jealousy caused by her unrequited love for Raymond. After the abbot Ambrosio has discovered a secret letter unveiling her pregnancy and intention to elope with her fiancé, he orders the ruthless Abbess to imprison Agnes in a dark cell with her newborn infant in the nearby convent. She is left to starve with her child in the same way as

Ugolino is, walled up and forced to see his offspring die. Even if Agnes is saved in the end, she is no longer the person she was before, transfigured by the deadly experience. Similarly, Ugolino's blood-soaked destiny is appalling. The count is locked in a dark tower and left starving with his heirs. His torment becomes unbearable when he has to witness the children's agony. When Agnes wakes up from an artificially induced torpor to find herself in a dark dungeon, she moves tentatively around in the obscurity until she touches a slimy object:

I was opprest by a noisome suffocating smell; and perceiving that the grated door was unfastened, I thought that I might possibly effect my escape: As I raised myself with this design, my hand rested upon something soft: I grasped it, and advanced it towards the light. Almighty God! What was my disgust, my consternation. In spite of its putridity and the worms which preyed upon it, I perceived a corrupted human head. (*The Monk*: 403)

When Dante reaches the lower parts of Hell (*Inferno*: XXXIII), he casts a glimpse at Ugolino and sees the damned count grabbing the skull of the man who was his enemy. The poet conveys an atrocious doubt about the image: "From that savage repast the sinner raised his mouth, wiping it with the hair of the head that he had spoiled behind" (*Inferno*: XXXIII, 181). Although Agnes and Ugolino have different modes of introducing themselves and their stories are antipodal, it is nevertheless quite interesting to highlight the horrid detail of a skull that is near the narrator of the gory event. Later, Agnes's extreme pathos in describing the unbearable pain of witnessing her beloved child's starve to death is remarkably similar to Ugolino's powerless despair rendered in Norton's translation:

After we had come to the fourth day, Gaddo threw himself stretched out at my feet, saying, "My father, why dost thou not help me?" here he dies: and, even as thou seest me, I saw the three fall one by one between the fifth day and the sixth; then I betook me, already blind, to groping over each, and two days I called them after they were dead (*Inferno*: XXXIII, 184).

The passage in Lewis's novel—a clear echo of the episode of Ugolino—is equally dramatic when Agnes describes the loss of her infant child:

I witnessed [the child's] death with agonies, which beggar all description. But my grief was unavailing. My Infant was no more; nor could all my sighs impart to its little tender frame the breath of a moment. [...] I placed it on my Bosom, its soft arm folded round my neck, and its pale cold cheek resting upon mine. Thus did its lifeless limbs repose, while I covered it with kisses, talked to it, wept, and moaned over it without remission, day or night. (*The Monk*: 412)

The Dantesque mould is evident in the dramatic scene of a powerless parent losing their child, immersed in despair for the painful vision. Lewis imitated images from Dante, and like Beckford, used them especially in the concluding part of his novel with an eschatological intention. The hideous creature haunting Ambrosio in the final pages embodies the devil, who throws the sinful monk in the desert, where the wretched man finds horrid monsters similar to infernal creatures. Whereas *Vathek*'s Hell is based on dark images contrasting the previous colourful narrations of the caliph's adventures, the last two chapters of *The Monk* are marked by a crescendo of horrible visions, contrasting the original peace of the monastery. The final images of Ambrosio alone in the middle of a desert bear remarkable resemblance to scenes from Dante's *Inferno,* and are anticipatory of Coleridge's *The Rime of the Ancient Mariner* (1798):

The Sun now rose above the horizon; its scorching beams darted full upon the head of the expiring Sinner. Myriads of insects were called forth by the warmth; they drank the blood which trickled from Ambrosio's wounds; He had no power to drive them from him, and they fastened upon his sores, darted their stings into his body, covered him with their multitudes, and inflicted on him tortures the most exquisite and insupportable. (*The Monk*: 442)

Some scholars see the final scene as a reversal of the *Book of Genesis* considering that Ambrosio's agony lasts seven days, but a more striking resemblance with Lewis's description is in Dante's *Divine Comedy* (Princeton version):

> Beyond all doubt that this was the dreary guild
> Repellent both to God and His enemies-
> Hapless ones never alive, their bare skin galled
> By wasps and flies, blood trickling down the face,
> Mingling with tears for harvest underfoot
> By writhing maggots. (*Inferno*: III, lines 53–57)

In the scene, Dante crosses the abandoned space before Limbo and Inferno when he sees the souls of the Uncommitted, cowardly people incapable of acting. They are forever stung by horribly voracious insects for the law of *contrappasso,* a symbolic poetic justice imposing different punishments, distributed according to various forms of sins. The pain provoked by the insects is an allegory of the sting of conscience that pusillanimous people did not follow in life. The horrible punishment for Ambrosio seems to declare his lack of moral strength in life and his sinful cowardice. Ambrosio's excruciating pain and his forced silence are in contrast with the beautiful sound of his voice and the sweet rhetoric of his words pronounced during his sermon in the novel's opening. The great medieval poet's influence, which is evident in both Lewis and Beckford, is once more highlighted by Saglia (2006, 75), who convincingly argues, "[t]he eighteenth century has been recognised as the beginning of a systematic re-evaluation of Dante", who early Gothic writers were eager to imitate. Saglia remarks that Italian literature of the Trecento provided unusual stories that were the object of "assiduous and analytical studies" in Britain between the end of the eighteenth and the beginning of the nineteenth century. An interesting argument, modifying the perspective of the traditional clichés about Italy, negatively judged and obscurely represented in the Gothic, is that disparaging images of the country were paradoxically provided by its own literary sources and by Dante and Boccaccio, in particular (Saglia 2006, 74). Lewis's remarkable syncretism, his classical studies and the fact that in 1792 he was already speaking of the romance he was writing, in the manner of *The Castle of Otranto,* are elements that support the theory that a wider number of sources influenced *The Monk.* Lewis's novel contains rich cultural substrata, in which medieval literary inspiration is as strong as Classical influences. The development of images from Dante is undeniable and the *Comedy* inspired Beckford's and Lewis's dramatic finales, respectively. Dante will provide Mary Shelley with interesting material for her Frankenstein (1818). The early Gothic, which was to become a durable genre in literary tradition, absorbed the Dantesque factor, together with influences from authors of Italian Trecento.

One of the so-called three crowns of Florence, together with Dante and Petrarch, as per Lorenzo Bruni's and other fifteenth-century humanists' definition, Boccaccio's influence can be detected in Lewis, even though his novel is basically tragic, whereas the stories in the *Decameron* (1351) have a happy or a morally positive ending. The collection of the one-hundred novellas narrated in ten days also contains salacious stories of libertine monks or fake priests enjoying promiscuity hidden inside monasteries, an element that provoked the Church's formal ban and saw the masterpiece prohibited for centuries. Day one and day three of the collection present short stories, in which the clergy is described as corrupt and lubricous. The first novella of the third day introduces Masetto, a handsome young man who, pretending to be deaf and mute, can live happily in a convent, working as a gardener, eating abundantly and enjoying secret meetings with the nuns. There is a moment at the inception of Ambrosio's tale that recalls the light-hearted atmosphere of Boccaccio's first novellas. However, Boccaccio introduces rare tragic traits in some of his stories and the general pleasing narrative is lost in the tales belonging to the fourth day, dedicated to unfortunate and tragic love stories, dissonant with the rest of the *Decameron*. The fourth day introduces reflections about the meaning of life and the tales' gory details contain disturbing scenes and anticipate themes of horror more suitable for the early Gothic genre. The fourth day's first story offers the cruellest example of unrestrained patriarchal power. Enraged by her secret love story, Ghismonda's jealous father forces his daughter to drink from a cup containing her lover's heart that she fills with poison to end her wretched life. Translated as "Sigismonda and Guiscardo", the tragic tale is one of the stories selected, adapted and translated by Dryden for his collection of *Fables Ancient and Modern* (1700), comprising stories by Homer, Ovid, Boccaccio, and Chaucer. Mary Wollstonecraft's *Maria, or The Wrongs of Woman's* (1792: 85–86) young character, unjustly confined to an asylum, has received some books that "come from a wretch like her. [...] She took up a book on the powers of the human mind; but, her attention strayed from cold arguments on the nature of what she felt, while she was feeling, and she snapt the chain of the theory to read Dryden's Guiscard and Sigismonda [sic]". This is a clear evidence of what Gillespie (2005, 2011) describes as the unconscious reception of works through translation and their incorrect attribution. In spite of her wide culture, Wollstonecraft thinks that the tale is Dryden's genuine creation, and does not seem to acknowledge that Boccaccio authored the original story of Ghismonda ("Sigismonda" in Dryden). Another tragic character, Lisabetta of Messina, is the victim of her ruthless brothers, who kill her kind and honest lover because of his inferior social status. The supernatural, otherwise uncommon in *The Decameron*, is included in the story when the dead fiancé appears in the girl's dreams and reveals where his body is buried, a situation analogous to an episode in Radcliffe's *The Romance of the Forest*. Unlike the characters in *The Monk*, who do not possess the cognitive readiness to understand the supernatural messages they receive, Lisabetta follows her dead lover's instructions in her dream. Lisabetta's heart-breaking story was frequently translated and adapted, an incontrovertible sign of Boccaccio's influence on the Augustans as well as Gothic writers and Romantic poets. Keats dedicated a poem to Lisabetta da Messina, calling her "Isabella", inspired by a lecture on Boccaccio by William Hazlitt. William Holman Hunt reproduces her timeless iconography in his Pre-Raphaelite painting, *Isabella and the Pot of Basil* (1868), dedicated to her moving story.

Another rare supernatural event in Boccaccio can be found in one of the novellas dealing with happy endings in love, narrated during the fifth day. A woman covered in blood is running at great speed in the middle of a forest near Ravenna, where the young aristocratic character, the heart-broken Nastagio degli Onesti, has taken refuge after the woman he adores has pitilessly rejected him. Having wasted his fortune in sumptuous gifts, extravagant banquets and rich offers for the cruel woman, Nastagio has decided to live in solitude and muse on his unfortunate condition in the middle of nature. While he is lost in his thoughts, a fierce knight chases the frightened woman. The scene is repeated until the young man manages to discover that the characters are in reality ghosts eternally playing their tragic roles. Dryden translated the novella of Nastagio and inserted it in his collection of *Tales*. Yet Dryden is not a simple translator, as he borrows from both Dante and Boccaccio and creates a strange narrative mélange in "Theodore and Honoria from Boccace", partly a reproduction of Nastagio's story and partly a real story from Dante's life. In Dryden's version, the famous Florentine poet Cavalcanti embodies the anonymous knight's ghost. The setting of the story, Ravenna and its surroundings, is the place where Dante completed the *Divine Comedy* and spent his last years as an exile before his death. Cavalcanti, one of his best friends, had died in his prime because of some mysterious fever when on exile for political reasons. As in many other cases, Dryden changes the characters' names and adds grisly details to the narration. Nastagio, called Theodore in Dryden's version, is frightened and believes that the two figures in the forest may represent a danger when he realises that the running woman and the knight, Cavalcanti, who pursues and kills her time and again, are both erring spirits. The gory murder is to be eternally repeated. Dryden, who uses words more suitable for a tale of terror in the Gothic style, translates the context preceding the terrifying tableau in verses anticipating Romantic tones:

> While list'ning to the murm'ring Leaves he stood,
> More than a Mile immers'd within the Wood,

At once the Wind was laid: the whisp'ring sound
Was dumb; a rising Earthquake rock'd the ground:
With deeper Brown the grove was overspread:
A suddain Horror seiz'd his giddy Head,
And his ears tinckled, and his Colour fled
Nature was in alarm; some Danger nigh
Seem'd threaten'd, though unseen to mortal Eye:
Unus'd to fear, he summon'd all his Soul
And stood collected in himself, and whole;
Not long: for soon a Whirlwind rose around,
And from afar he heard a screaming sound,
As of a Dame distress'd, who cry'd for Aid,
And fill'd with loud Laments the secret Shade.
(*Fables Ancient and Modern*: 260–261)

The woman is eternally doomed to run and re-enact the scene of her tragic end in atonement for her cruelty in life–Sandro Botticelli reproduced the terrifying scenes of Nastagio's tale tale in a series of paintings in the fifteenth century. She had rejected Cavalcanti's love and had rejoiced when he had died. Even though Boccaccio's conclusion is happy, since Nastagio (alias Theodore) will use the frightening episode to convince the disdainful woman he loves to abandon her haughtiness and accept his courtship, the tale has a striking resemblance with Lewis's episode of the *Bleeding Nun*, perpetually doomed to rehash her tragic fate. Lewis asserts in his prologue that he had borrowed the story from some unidentified Germanic legend. It is possible to argue that he is consciously misleading readers and provides one source in order to hide the others. Lewis wants readers to accept his incomplete truth by apparently unveiling all his sources at the opening of his novel, but *The Monk*'s influences are much more numerous than what Lewis claims. Paraphrasing Napier's metaphor of false unveiling and real veiling, and applying it to Lewis's narrative, we can argue that he keeps his real sources hidden while feigning to reveal them.

Academic analyses have tended to overlook the prolonged contact Lewis had with Classic, Medieval and Renaissance literature. Confirming what could be defined as the Italian factor in the early Gothic of the authors analysed in this book, Lewis's epigraph of Chapter II in Volume I of *The Monk* presents Tasso's verses exalting the joys of Love, taken from the pastoral poem *Aminta* (1573). Lewis was an admirer of the works of both Ariosto and Tasso. Early Gothic writers choose these authors' courteous atmospheres to introduce idyllic scenes, as in *The Monk*, or to present libertine contexts, as in Radcliffe's *The Romance of the Forest*. In some letters written to his mother included in Baron Wilson's biography (1836: I, 122, 295), Lewis mentions that his sister is learning Italian and hopes she will progress quickly to read Ariosto, like him. In another letter, he specifically emphasises that he spent his time reading Ariosto while travelling. Apart from Greek, Latin and French, Lewis knew Italian and translated from it, as some of his later works demonstrate. He probably knew Italian better than he knew Spanish: Don Christoval exclaims "Diavolo!" (31), an interjection of surprise at the entrance of Lorenzo's sister Agnes. Other linguistic imprecisions are the use of the word "Segnor" instead of the Spanish "Señor", perhaps due to a wrong process of transliteration. Elvira's sister Leonella uses an Italian expression, "caro sposo" (311), to describe her "dear husband". Although Lewis only went to Italy after his father's death in 1812, when he abandoned writing to travel to the Continent, he already had a remarkable cultural knowledge of the country, its language and its literature.

The medieval spirit of Boccaccio and Dante is relevant in Lewis's novel. Despite his appreciation of Tasso and Ariosto, he does not seem to have inserted their themes and atmospheres in *The Monk*, with a couple of exceptions. On the other hand, Beckford and Radcliffe absorb elements from Ariosto. A significant figure of the Italian Renaissance appreciated across Europe, Ariosto lived at the turn of the century between the Quattrocento and the Renaissance. He published three revised editions of his masterpiece *Orlando Furioso* between 1516 and 1532, adapting his work to the needs brought about by the emerging printing press and the revolutionary birth of books. It is a chivalric romance developed from the medieval popular literary cycles about heroic Orlando, which he enriched with fantastic episodes of *King Arthur* sagas. His work was to influence a great number of authors during the Renaissance and afterwards. Tasso's *Jerusalem Delivered* (1581) had to be a religious epic set during the first Crusade. Although it reflected the anguish and gloom provoked by the Counterreformation of the Roman Church, the chivalric text contains many amorous interludes in the manner of Ariosto, whereas battles and sieges are influenced by Homer's and Virgil's epic narrations. The text ideally concludes the Renaissance period and anticipates Baroque themes. Pulci and Boiardo, the first to write comic and romantic variations of *Chansons de Geste*, were men of the fifteenth century, a period that coincided with the flourishing of *Signorie,* local governments headed by neo-aristocratic mercantile families, replacing democratic governments of previous medieval city-states while sustaining the development of humanism and the arts. Active some years before Ariosto, both Pulci and

Boiardo had developed poetic episodes based on the legend of Charlemagne and his paladins. Pulci created a mock-heroic epic, *Morgante,* whose main character is a giant in the service of the French king. Boiardo exploited Charlemagne's war against the Saracens, though he highlighted the romantic side of the story, focussing on Orlando and introducing Angelica as the beautiful and sensual heroine (in contrast with traditional medieval female representations), with whom every Paladin (and Saracen, too) falls in love. A poem of great erudition, in which even minor events betray intertextual affiliations with the Classics and especially with Homer, Virgil and Ovid (Paola Boccassini 1997), *Orlando Innamorato* turns the heroic paladin into an unhappy lover. Ariosto composes the *Orlando Furioso* to continue the story of Boiardo's unfinished masterpiece.

While Dante's renditions dominate the last part of *Vathek*, the inclusion of Ariosto's and other Renaissance poets' imagery is evident throughout Beckford's story. Ariosto's chivalric narration, mixing the supernatural and romance, featured some elements of the Oriental tale. The main female character, Angelica, is an exotic beauty from the distant Cathay, the land of Eastern mystery, and her seductive modes entangle the Paladins, who become oblivious to their duties, in the same way that the beautiful Nouronihar attracts Vathek and makes him heedless and dreamlike. Nouronihar's "beautiful eyes", "languishing looks" and "fair complexion" (*Vathek*: 65) are the tokens of temptation. Nouronihar shares Angelica's traits, as she is beautiful, capricious and rebellious and, like Galland's Scheherazade, she is the indulged daughter of a powerful man. (Ballaster 2005b). Vathek is seduced in the middle of nature, like Orlando, Rinaldo and other knights. In spite of his temples of the senses, offering him infinite delight, the moment a beautiful and mysterious landscape surrounds him, the caliph becomes the victim of love for the first time. Pulci, Boiardo, Ariosto and, to some extent, Tasso offer Beckford rich material, including mysterious landscapes, spells, supernatural creatures and witchcraft. Alcina, Morgana, Melissa, Armida are examples of the witches that populate the works of Renaissance poets; but some of them are the bearers of cruel and dangerous magic, like Vathek's mother, Carathis. Pulci's philosophical demon, Astaroth, presumably Marsilio Ficino's alter ego, introduces the logic of Neoplatonist freedom, somehow connected with Lucretian atheism, which is latent in Vathek. A protégé at the Medici court and a friend of Lorenzo de' Medici, the Magnificent, Ficino was a humanist, and a Neo-platonic philosopher interested in astrology and magic, and his figure was influential during the Renaissance. *Vathek* offers analogies with other magical characters in Italian

Renaissance works, including Ariosto's inept wizard, Atlante, who recalls the failures committed by Beckford's characters, such as the emir and the eunuchs. Beckford inherits multiple features from the Italian authors: Pulci's comic effects, Boiardo's sensuality, Ariosto's magic and Tasso's sense of inevitable pessimism. *Vathek*'s Ariostean suggestions are sometimes found in the learned footnotes to the novel: "the talismans", "the simurgh", "the magical tablets" and "the fountain of Merlin" are devices recalling Ariosto's resourceful universe.

If on the one hand, Dante and Boccaccio do not seem to play essential parts in Radcliffe, Ariosto and Tasso are relevant in her novels. The influence of their epic poems are particularly important in *The Romance of the Forest*, in which Ariosto's romantic character, Angelica, moulds the main character's fashioning. Kenneth Sills (1905) demonstrated that ever since their appearance the Renaissance poets' works had been frequently imitated and not only on Italian soil, as "the romantic epics of Ariosto and Tasso had lent themselves easily to imitation" in France and Britain from the sixteenth well into the eighteenth century. That Ariosto and Tasso played a role in the creation of Radcliffe's works seems indisputable. Both are mentioned with relative frequency: the name of Tasso is pronounced in *A Sicilian Romance* and *The Italian*, and Ariosto enchants all classes of people in *The Mysteries of Udolpho*. Frequent episodes of love at first sight, copying *Orlando Furioso,* occur in *The Romance of the Forest.* When men fall in love with Adeline, but receive her cold response, her persona is transformed into an ideal Angelica's doppelgänger. Moreover, both Ariosto's *Orlando Furioso* (1532) and Tasso's *Gerusalemme Liberata* (1575) attach great importance to scenes in forests, and nature is the dominant factor in many of the adventures they narrate, which is similar to what happens in Radcliffe. When her biographer, Talfourd, describes the high praises Radcliffe received from her contemporaries, he reveals that even a severe critic such as Mathias acclaimed her as "the mighty magician, bred and nourished by the Florentine muses in their sacred, solitary caverns" (Talfourd 1826: 12). Librarian to the king and author of *The Pursuits of Literature,* Mathias was hostile to the majority of women writers, but he admittedly admired Radcliffe's genius, even though he was equally extremely cautious about the potential danger of women's literary efforts. In his preface, dated November 1798, to *The Shade of Alexander Pope on the Banks of the Thames* (1799: 51), he concluded, "the poetry of Mrs. Charlotte Smith and the sombrous fancy of Mrs. Radcliffe cannot be mentioned without admiration". He compared Radcliffe to one of the damsels, "Damigella Trivulzia", chanted by Ariosto in the final canto of his *Orlando Furioso.*

Radcliffe had demonstrated that she not only knew the Classics but that she had also read the geniuses of Italian literature. She had access to multiple translations of the Italian authors that were available throughout the century (Bates 2005). Translations of Ariosto and Tasso were relatively easy to find. John Hoole translated *Jerusalem Delivered* in 1763. He published *Orlando Furioso* in 1783, in an adorned edition of five volumes with illustrations by Francesco Bertolazzi and Angelica Kaufmann. *The English Review* published a positive analysis of Hoole's translation in July 1783, and the critic (who seems to favour Tasso), evokes Ariosto's characteristics and claims, "[his] merits, it must be allowed, are very uncommon and great; but perhaps, he was too little directed by cultivation and art. He owes everything to nature" (*The English Review* 1783: 171). This is an interesting analogy between Ariosto and Radcliffe. Some operas by Handel that Radcliffe particularly enjoyed were based on stories from Ariosto and Tasso and their remarkable descriptions. *Orlando Furioso* is one of the foundational works of Western literature, and its complicated and powerful evocations have influenced a large number of works through the present day. Echoes of this Renaissance masterpiece can be found in Edmund Spenser's *Fairie Queene* (1596), William Shakespeare's *Much Ado About Nothing* (1598), Miguel de Cervantes's *Don Quixote* (1615) and Scott's *Rob Roy* (1817). Ariosto's introduction of a magic ring, which gives invisibility and power to those who wear it, and the series of epic battles, was diversely absorbed and used during the eighteenth century. One of the most important example is Diderot's *Bijoux Indiscrets*. Allusions to Orlando Furioso's magic ring, wars of wizards and mythical winged creatures are even found in twentieth-century novels, such as J. R. R. Tolkien's *The Lord of the Rings* (1956) and J. K. Rowling's *Harry Potter* saga (1997–2007). The proliferation of successive literary translations may have caused the original texts to disappear from cultural memory, and sources may become almost imperceptible, but their effects are incontrovertible. The pages of Radcliffe's novels reveal analogies with famous authors, even though sources from the Renaissance have rarely been analysed in their entirety. The protagonists in Radcliffe's romances, either males or females, are generally fond of literature: they read the Classics and essential writers of previous epochs. An example is Emily's love interest, Valancourt, wandering on a solitary journey through the Pyrenees, browsing texts of Classic and Renaissance authors, a fact that strikes Emily's father positively: "St. Aubert was somewhat surprised to find in his room volumes by Homer, Horace and Petrarch; but the name Valancourt, written in them, told him to whom they belonged" (*Udolpho*: 36). The choice of Homer, Horace and Petrarch may not be casual, as is often the case in Radcliffe. Homer, the great epic poet, whose life was surrounded by innumerable legends, roved towns and villages reciting his poems, the milestones of Western culture. In this context, he may serve as a symbol of Emily's and Valancourt's itinerant adventures and their separation for some years to come, recalling the tribulations of epic heroes and heroines. As seen before, Horace is representative of the poetic measure, but he is strictly limited to men's reading. Horace may be a symbol of the latent epicurean side tending towards the carpe diem ideal of enjoying every single moment, which Valancourt seems to appreciate. The Italian pre-Humanist Petrarch, the "third crown" of Florence, a great Latin scholar and late medieval poet, was famous for his neo-platonic love sonnets and odes collected in the complex *Song Book* (*Canzoniere* 1374). Composed progressively over the course of many years in vernacular Italian, as a divertissement, Petrarch poetic songs became the basis for the development of modern Italian together with Boccaccio's *Decameron* and Dante's *Comedy*. Petrarch's presence among the books of Emily's suitor denotes the idealised and intellectual love that Valancourt experiences. In the second part of *The Romance of the Forest*, when Adeline is safe in Savoy, she discovers her new friend Clara's love of nature and cultural accomplishments:

Born amid scenes of grandeur and sublimity, she had quickly imbibed a taste for their charms, which taste was heightened by the influence of a warm imagination. To view the sun rising above the Alps, tinging their snowy heads with light, and suddenly darting his rays over the whole face of nature—to see the fiery splendour of the clouds reflected in the lake below, and the roseate tints first steal upon the rocks above—were among the earliest pleasures of which Clara was susceptible. From being delighted with the observance of nature, [Clara] grew pleased with seeing her finely imitated, and soon displayed a taste for poetry and painting. When she was about sixteen, she often selected from her father's library those of the Italian poets most celebrated for picturesque beauty and would spend the first hours of morning in reading them under the shade of the acacias that bordered the lake. (*RF*: 248–249)

The first part of *The Romance of The Forest* is set within an intricate, beautiful forest, apparently enchanted. Time has outwardly stopped, and the place is not only a Virgilian idyll but also a place recalling Ariosto's magic atmospheres. Stanzas XII and XIII of *Orlando*'s First Canto illustrate a natural environment inspiring the beautiful protagonist with thoughts of love. Pursued by one of her many suitors and Orlando's cousin, Rinaldo, Angelica finds refuge in the middle of a wood. Protected by the shadowy branches, Angelica encounters another knight, who is equally enamoured of her, ready to sacrifice his life for her sake. However, the beautiful damsel does not give her heart to any of her suitors. The next extracts are taken from two translations of Orlando *Furioso* (John Hoole's 1783 version does not signal stanzas, preferring a fluid narration in verses that mainly follows Ariosto's number of lines):

> This was the Paladin for valour known,
> Lord of Mount Alban, and Duke Amon's son,
> Rinaldo nam'd, who late when fortune crost
> The Christian arms, his steed Bayardo lost.
> Soon as his eyes beheld th' approaching fair
> Full well he knew that soft enchanting air;
> Full well he knew that face that caus'd his smart.
> And held in love's strong net his manly heart.
> Meantime th' affrighted Damsel threw the reins
> Loose on her courser's neck, and scour'd the plains;
> Through open paths she fled, or tangled shade,
> Nor rough, nor bushy paths her course delay'd;
> But pale and trembling, stuck with deep dismay
> She let her flying palfrey choose the way.
> Now here, now there, amidst the savage wood
> She wander'd till she saw a running flood;
> (*Orlando Furioso* 1783: lines 87–102)

Highly appreciated by contemporaries and resonating with Radcliffe's language, Hoole's version describes Angelica's flight. Ariosto resumes the story where Boiardo had left it, when the beautiful Angelica is Orlando's prisoner. To avoid resentment among his paladins, Charlemagne decides to keep the young woman separated from the rest of the army, but she manages to escape, chased by Orlando and other knights. Seen by heroic Rinaldo, also in love with her, she rides her horse in frantic search of a refuge. The forest she reaches, as with most wild places in Ariosto, is full of enchantment like Angelica herself, a charmer stealing all the men's hearts. The next stanzas, dated 1855, belong to William Stuart Rose's rendering and reflect *Orlando*'s structure more closely. Both Hoole and Rose capture Angelica's elusive beauty that Radcliffe elegantly transposes to Adeline:

XII   This was that Paladin, good Aymon's seed,
Who Mount Albano had in his command;
And late Bayardo lost, his gallant steed,
Escaped by strange adventure from his hand.
As soon as seen, the maid who rode at speed
The warrior knew, and, while yet distant, scanned
The angelic features and the gentle air
Which long had held him fast in Cupid's snare.
XIII   The affrighted damsel turns her palfrey round,
And shakes the floating bridle in the wind;
Nor in her panic seeks to choose her ground,
Nor open grove prefers to thicket blind.
But reckless, pale and trembling, and astound,
Leaves to her horse the devious way to find.
He up and down the forest bore the dame,
Till to a sylvan river's bank he came. (*Orlando Furioso*
1858 I: 3)

Ariosto's favourite settings, forests are the magic places where love explodes and incredible adventures take place. Many scenes in the epic poem, centred on Angelica, develop within luxuriant woods or bewitched groves. Angelica's presence is in harmony with the surrounding nature, which seems to highlight her beauty and enchantment and the fascination of the woodland is exalted by her presence when she wanders or rides within it. Similar to a superior being or a mythological nymph, she transmits her magnetism to the surrounding world. The young woman's inescapable attraction pitilessly strikes every man she meets. Like Angelica, Adeline is a fugitive and her charms capture everyone with her beauty. The abbey where Adeline and the others take refuge is surrounded by a forest that transmits a supernatural impression much like the woods in Ariosto. "The abbey is protected by a supernatural power, and none of the country people dare approach it" (*RF*: 69). It is inside the apparently "magic" forest that the young soldier Theodore meets Adeline for the first time and falls in love with her. The fugitive Parisian gentleman, his upright son Louis, and the cruel Montalt fall for Adeline in proximity to nature, as she is Angelica's alter ego, subjugating every male character with her beauty. According to Cynthia Griffin Wolff (1979), situations of desire (and therefore of sexual danger) exist only in particular inner spaces. However, Adeline's constant potential for seduction and the consistent danger of violation exist whenever she is with dangerous people, either inside a majestic abode and outside, surrounded by luxuriant nature. "Radcliffe keeps returning to the both seductive and invigorating appeal of Adeline's distress [...] Obviously, Adeline's glowing charm solicits not reason, not sexually neutral humanity of sexually nonspecific onlookers, but heterosexual manhood in particular: Adeline's body arouses various degrees and a mixture of tenderness and desire in the gentlemen bending over her" (Johnson 1995: 74). In the following passage, her beauty suddenly captivates the fugitive de la Motte (*RF*: 5–7):

Her features were bathed in tears, and she seemed to suffer the utmost distress. [...] He now seized the trembling hand of the girl, who shrunk aghast with terror, and hurried her towards de la Motte, whom surprise still kept silent. She sunk at his feet, and with supplicating eyes that streamed with tears, implored him to have pity on her. Notwithstanding his present agitation, he found it impossible to contemplate the beauty and distress of the object before him with indifference. Her youth, her apparent innocence, the artless energy of her manner forcibly assailed his heart. [...] De la Motte raised the lovely girl from the floor. [...] Her features, which were delicately beautiful, had gained from distress an expression of captivating sweetness. A habit of grey camlet, with short slashed sleeves, shewed, but did not adorn her figure: it was thrown open at the bosom, upon which her hair had fallen in disorder. He determined to protect her.

Unfeeling and harsh de la Motte suddenly softens when faced with Adeline's superior beauty. Depicted as a cynic, tempted by intrigue and vice, he now succumbs to Adeline's charms and forgets the danger of being arrested. It is as if time has stopped and the usually indifferent de la Motte is captured by the girl's beauty that Radcliffe describes from a special narrative perspective, a particular point of view, generally defined as a male gaze in critical terms. Adeline's first appearance in the novel and her irresistible appeal has an immediate impact on the other characters. Even the cruel banditti cannot resist her, and do not carry out their criminal plan against her. Her aspect intensifies the sweetness of her character and the aesthetic relevance of her persona–an apparently unconscious tempter, nonetheless able to manoeuvre her power. The amoral Pierre de la Motte instantly becomes a paladin for the girl, and his son Louis, equally enthralled by her, turns into her faithful champion. After the enraged Marquis de Montalt discovers that the Parisian aristocrat is hiding on his property, he suddenly forgets his recriminations because he sees Adeline and is instantly enamoured of her. One of his soldiers, Theodore, swears to be her protector after falling in love at first sight. Even the good reverend La Luc, old and weak, finds the strength to accompany her on a long journey in search of Theodore. Adeline's seductive qualities are confirmed near the end of the story as well:

> When she appeared before the tribunal, Adeline's emotion surpassed all the arts of disguise [...] She attracted the universal pity and admiration of the assembly. [...] She immediately threw herself at the feet of the monarch in behalf of Theodore and de la Motte. [...] The monarch would have granted his pardon to a pleader less irresistible than Adeline. [...] The passion which Louis had so long owned for Adeline was raised almost to adoration. (*RF*: 351–354)

An equally sensual heroine, Angelica, conquers every heart but in the end prefers the knight Medoro, though inferior in rank, to other paladins, princes and kings who have tried to seduce her. Adeline's situation reflects Angelica's, as she chooses Theodore, whose name bears a noncasual resemblance to Medoro: "Her affection for Theodore had induced Adeline to reject several suitors which her goodness, beauty and wealth, had already attracted, and whom, though infinitely his superiors in point of fortune, were many of them inferior to him in family, and all of them in merit" (*RF*: 356). However, Adeline is not only beautiful but is also astute enough to reject Montalt's dangerous love diplomatically when he kidnaps her. "Montalt's household is a sex palace where, with genteel erotica, aphrodisiac collations of confections, ices, and liquors, and a bevy of depraved demoiselles, he urges Adeline to succumb to his passion. All men in the novel act according the suggestions of their feelings" (Johnson 1995: 45). What Radcliffe calls "Montalt's saloon", apart from being the erotic locus of classical references we have discovered before, is full of "enchantment" and seems to be the work of fairies. Adeline can feel a persistent form of magic, never rationalised or negated. The magic performed by the wizard Atlante in *Orlando Furioso* and the witchery used by the sorceress Armida in *Jerusalem Delivered,* are at work within the mysterious mansion where Adeline is held prisoner. Montalt's house of seduction is under the sign of Classicism, for its multiple references to Latin and Greek authors, but it also contains Ariosto's Renaissance enchantment. Adeline tries to escape the consequences of her irresistible charm to no avail, as Montalt's blind desire is on the brink of ruining her. However, she uses her intelligence and magniloquent abilities and, helped by the courageous Theodore, can successfully escape danger.

In the following lines of *Orlando Furioso's* Canto I (Stanzas XLIX–L), Angelica casually meets Sacripant, one of the many unfortunate noblemen in love with her; in spite of her disdain and her technique at keeping all suitors at a distance, she egoistically accepts his protection, as we can observe in W.S. Rose's version:

> With deep attention, while the warrior weeps,
> She marks the fashion of the grief and tears
> And words of him, whose passion never sleeps;
> Nor this the first confession which she hears.
> But with his plaint her heart no measure keeps,
> Cold as the column which the builder rears.
> Like haughty maid, who holds herself above
> The world, and deems none worthy of her love.
> But her from harm amid those woods to keep
> The damsel weened she might his guidance need;

Angelica invokes Sacripant and exploits his love to her sole advantage. Adeline uses similar survival strategies to protect herself from the Marquis and other dangers: "A little reflection showed Adeline the danger of exasperating his pride, by an avowal of the contempt which his pretended offer of marriage excited; and she thought it not improper, upon an occasion in which the honour and peace of her life was concerned, to yield somewhat to the policy of dissimulation. She saw that her only chance of escaping his designs depended upon delaying them" (*RF*: 159). A strange mixture of innocence and cunning, Adeline uses Angelica's stratagems to avoid tragic consequences, and their analogies, both physical and psychological, are significant. Angelica moves alone within the dangerous context of the war between Charlemagne and the Moorish army. Her extraordinary beauty puts her at even greater danger, but she manages to escape from the most horrible situations, deeply aware of her beauty that she uses to her advantage. Young and inexperienced Adeline moves in a male-dominated world with self-assurance and, like Angelica, promptly reacts to dangerous predicaments. *The Romance of the Forest* offers double or even triple parallel readings of its plot. The story of Adeline is a Gothic narrative among picturesque landscapes and sublime ruins. It is a classical narration with Virgilian bucolic and pastoral moments alternating with potentially tragic situations. It is a timid and lyrical representation of the chivalric adventure of an extraordinary girl of supreme beauty. Adeline is assertive and, like Angelica, chooses the man she desires rather than the one that convention would impose on her. Paladin Rinaldo's unconventional statement, rejecting the unjust differences between a woman and a man in social conventions (Canto IV, stanza LXVI, 62, Rose's version), innovatively promotes gender equality centuries before feminism:

> Say why shall woman–merit scathe or blame,
> Though lovers, one or more, she may caress;
> While man to sin with whom he will is free,
> And meets with praise, not mere impunity?

Ariosto promotes an ideal of equality between men and women and exalts the figure of an independent woman such as Angelica, whom Radcliffe seems to reproduce in Adeline. Angelica represents beauty, strength, independence and the freedom of choosing the man she loves. Rinaldo's proto-feminist speech reveals *Orlando Furioso*'s thoroughgoing ideal of equality of gender, clearly absorbed and implicitly advocated in *The Romance of the Forest* and Radcliffe's other novels, ultimately based on a form of eudemonic ethics.

A diversified hymn to intertextuality, early Gothic novels assimilate models and echoes from masterpieces of different epochs and languages. As Shelley, inspired by Dante and Milton, rightly observed, past literary works are an inextinguishable source of inspiration, an idea that early Gothic writers perfectly anticipated.

> A great poem is a fountain forever overflowing with the
> waters of wisdom and delight.
> (Percy B. Shelley. *A Defense of Poetry*)

It seems an unaccountable pleasure which the spectators of a
well-written tragedy receive from sorrow, terror, anxiety, and
other passions that are in themselves disagreeable and uneasy.
The more they are touched and affected, the more are they
delighted with the spectacle.
(David Hume. *Essays Moral, Political and Literary*)

One of the most striking aspects of early Gothic narratives is the technical
originality that makes them different from previous literary works. Once
Walpole's early Gothic progeny became effective, remarkable narrative
differences emerged. *Vathek*'s carnivalesque situations, Radcliffe's
mixture of different cultural ingredients and *The Monk*'s eclectic style
generated original and diversified forms of horror, involving also their
cohort of imitators. Unlike Beckford's *Vathek* and Radcliffe's novels that
had preceded it, the iconography of *The Monk* concentrated more on
characters and interiors than on landscapes, with the exception of the
scenes when the title character, Ambrosio, unveils his ominous secrets
and faces his destiny. Groom (2016) partially contradicts Kilgour's (1995)
definition of the story, and considers *The Monk* a failed *Bildungsroman*, in
which coming of age does not improve the characters. Au contraire, all
occurrences seem to contribute to a progressive worsening of both
characters and actions. The story's various plots share a common tragic
theme of failure contradicting their apparently positive incipits, and *The
Monk* could be interpreted as a representation of the inadequate power
of adults, victims of inevitable fate, frequently manoeuvred by
supernatural events. Characters are not allowed to act or, if they act, they
commit mistakes, or carry out actions that will have gloomy
consequences. Ambrosio as well as the other male protagonists, Lorenzo
and Raymond, make decisions that are either futile or excessive. Raymond
and Lorenzo cannot save the women they love, and Ambrosio destroys
the one he venerates.

The imprecise geography of early Gothic novels is a further interesting feature. Walpole had been the master of imprecision with *Otranto*, in which the only geographic characteristic is the name of the setting. Similarly, Punter and Byron (2009) highlight the "poor mapping" of Lewis's story, which is virtually inexistent. The supposed Spanish setting is an indefinite territory, as Lewis does not provide any details about architectures or landscapes. *The Monk*'s undefined geographies of Madrid, or the Black Forest, do not convey any panoramic view beyond the characters' actions, and not a single scenery is provided, the only exceptions being the cloister garden in the monastery or the arid desert in the finale. Beckford's places are midway between dream and reality and his geographies are amply described, even though they cannot be identified or mapped, while Radcliffe dedicates pages to landscapes minutiae and provides geographical details, but she adds a dreamlike atmosphere to both her gothic and romantic settings.

Whereas Gothic writers describe vague locations, adding to the overall sense of mystery, they tend to be more pragmatic in narratological techniques. The diversification of narrative points of view is, in fact, quite interesting in the early Gothic. *Vathek*'s protagonists are outlined from the perspective of an external narrator, and their feelings are not generally communicated to the reader, except when the caliph falls in love, or when the characters acquire conscience of their tragic destiny before falling into a hopeless oblivion. Their actions are panoramic and it is not possible to understand their inward motives. Like Beckford and other Gothic authors of the first generation, Lewis generally uses the third person narrative in *The Monk*, with one exception, represented by Raymond, who narrates his Black Forest adventures in the first person. Lewis's narrative experiment is not new: while conversing with Madame de la Motte, Adeline tells her tragic story in the first person in *The Romance of the Forest*, whereas the whole novel is narrated in the third person. Sophia Lee's *The Recess* (1783) offered another peculiar narrative strategy, wherein the author experimented with a first person narration with a limited point of view to convey a deep sense of anguish and claustrophobia. *The Monk*'s narrative system is quite complex, as the text introduces different levels of third-person narrations, both omniscient and non-omniscient, while some characters' viewpoints are dangerously limited.

In spite of his obscure origins and "the mystery behind his birth" (*The Monk* 17), Ambrosio, whose austerity is highly commended and revered, becomes the Abbot of the Capuchin Monastery and his sermons attract ecstatic congregations. The novel starts during one of his famous speeches when other important characters, such as Antonia and Lorenzo, instrumental to the plot, meet for the first time. The reader is inside the church of the Capuchins among the congregation and, sharing their point of view, progressively moves within some characters. The narration focuses on two women: the ridiculously vain Leonella and her shy niece Antonia. Then, the reader can observe the events through the perspective of Don Christoval and his friend, Lorenzo de Medina, who both become interested in the girl's harmonious silhouette. At this stage, the point of view is from within the male characters, who earnestly observe Antonia and are delighted by her figure, full of "delicacy and elegance", but also frustrated because of her veiled face. The perspective then moves to Antonia's point of view when the girl is strangely impressed by Ambrosio's grandiloquent speech and sweet voice. At the end of the church scene, when Ambrosio has enraptured the congregation with the powerful words of his sermon, the reader is once more with Lorenzo, following his thoughts, deeply concentrated on Antonia. Left alone and surrounded by darkness, Lorenzo falls into a deep slumber while sitting in the empty nave. He has a strange dream concerning Antonia's horrible fate, which is one of the various examples of prolepsis in the novel, thoroughly analysed by Fitzgerald (2003). The horrible dream lingers in his mind, and he is anxious to have a second rendezvous with Antonia. While Lorenzo tries to meet his sister Agnes after waking up from his disturbing nightmare, the narration moves to the other characters and the point of view is from within Antonia and her aunt Leonella, who attentively watch a gypsy on their way home. Antonia's perspective becomes relevant, as we observe the scene through her eyes: she listens to the gypsy's song and its omen, but without grasping its deeper meaning. Antonia's cognitive misunderstanding of the exterior world anticipates the danger lurking about her. The third-person narration, told through Antonia's point of view, is non-omniscient and reflects the character's scarce cognition of the events.

A further example of limited perspective inside a single character takes place when Lorenzo's friend, Raymond experiences an ambush at a squalid inn in the Black Forest. The reader is empathically petrified when the banditti are about to kill him in a most violent way while suspense is stressed by a first-person narration, conveying a sense of terror. Some characters remain unfathomable all along just like the two-faced novice Rosario, whose thoughts are completely unknown whenever the character is present on the scene, thus increasing his fluid ambiguity and reinforcing the halo of secrecy around him: "A sort of mystery enveloped this Youth [...] no one had ever seen his face" (*The Monk*: 41–42). In fact,

Rosario/Matilda never reveals his/her thoughts, exacerbating the character's disconcerting mystery. The only one interacting with Rosario, Ambrosio is, however, incapable of understanding the novice, who turns out to be Matilda, a dangerously fascinating young woman, whose essence remains an enigma, which can never be fully fathomed. Rosario/Matilda's opinions are never disclosed and the reader only knows the character through Ambrosio's eyes and opinions.

Lewis introduces parallel plots and subplots—a strategy exploited by Godwin in *Caleb Williams* (1794), used by Charlotte Dacre (*Zofloya* 1806) and Mary Anne Radcliffe (*Manfroné* 1809) and perfected by Maturin in *Melmoth the Wanderer* (1820)—to make his story less linear and more ambiguous. The text-within-a-text, providing a complication of past events that have to be deciphered, is an original narrative methodology. It is skilfully used in Mary Anne Radcliffe's *Manfroné* (1809) and absorbed by Victorian novelists to increase ambiguity. Examples are provided by Emily Brontë's *Wuthering Heights* (1848), Anne Brontë's *The Tenant of Wildfell Hall* (1848) and Robert L. Stevenson's *The Strange Case of Dr. Jekyll and Mr. Hyde* (1886). According to Brooks (2004: 254), Lewis created stories-within-the-story to convey deeper concepts and introduce the supernatural. The legends of "The Bleeding Nun" and "The Erring Jew" are two horrifying episodes, inserted as contrasting inlays in secondary plots. These mysterious characters are not real people, but embody supernatural entities, whose introduction is a technical device with "a functional role" to justify the supernatural element that is about to enter Ambrosio's plot. Lewis's micro-stories deviate from the principal text. However, they also reflect the main plots' future events (Ambrosio/Matilda; Lorenzo/Antonia; Ambrosio/Antonia) as a sort of *composition en abîme*, a representation of which can be found in Jan van Eyck's *The Arnolfini Portrait* (1434): the two main figures are reflected within the convex mirror hanging behind, in which a third figure, possibly the painter, is distinguishable (Erika Langmuir 1996: 44). For these anomalous interludes and other peculiarities, Lewis's novel poses a series of problems of interpretation for the difficult meanings of events liable to be read in multiple ways.

Radcliffe's moments of bathos, which cause a fall in the narrative tension when mystery is rationalised, are opposed to Lewis's pathos, caused by his terrifying contents. Radcliffe's apparent soothing conclusions are replaced by an intensely dramatic closure in Lewis, whose novel is seen as the satanic reverse of *The Mysteries of Udolpho,* forcing Radcliffe to create an adequate response, a sort of correlate antithesis to *The Monk*, through the publication of *The Italian* (1797). Early Gothic characters are difficult to grasp for their indefiniteness. In Radcliffe's novels, their psychology is not effectively unveiled, as the main narrative perspective is generally limited to the heroine's non-omniscient viewpoint. There are, however, some exceptions. In order to increase the level of suspense, Radcliffe makes the readers observe some scenes through other characters' perspective. In *The Romance of the* Forest, she exploits the fugitive's vision when he is terrified, expecting a criminal ambush. Louis, de la Motte's son, witnesses his father's unusual and secretive behaviour, and Madame de la Motte spies on the encounter between a ruthless character, Montalt, and her husband. Before Adeline's point of view becomes dominant in the story, Radcliffe moves the narrative perspective from one character to the other in order to increase the tension. A thriller-like situation, with a restricted point of view, takes place when the fugitive Monsieur starts his solitary exploration of the abbey before being joined by the other terror-stricken characters. Interestingly, the perspective becomes panoramic and exterior to the characters, in general, when they meet for the first time. Thus, the author can communicate the physical impressions they have of each other, especially when describing Adeline's beauty. Like Johnson (1995), Chard (2009: xvii) argues that "the reader is implicitly invited to scrutinise [Adeline] through the eyes of a male spectator" and also that "Adeline's traits and appearance [serve] to display her body to particular advantage for the pleasure of the spectator, since they allow the usual requirements of decorum to be cast aside". The heroine's story in *Clermont* is a specular reproduction of Radcliffe's usual plots. Mysteriously forced to abandon her home and her father, Madeline has to overcome obstacles and dangers and her situation is precarious because of a limited knowledge of events, a strategy increasing the level of fear and suspense until the very last pages. Aside from Manfred's furious musing and Theodore's melancholy in *The Castle of Otranto*, interior life is not clearly delineated in Walpole's characters, still derived from eighteenth-century narrative mechanisms. On the contrary, imagination and inventiveness are Beckford's, Radcliffe's, Lewis's and other Gothic authors' common denominators, even though these writers provide ambiguous clues about the true essence of their dramatis personae.

Analysing *The Romance of the Forest*, Johnson (1995) observes that Adeline becomes stronger and undergoes a process of "masculinisation", the opposite of what happens to Ambrosio in *The Monk,* because of his latent change towards a sort of psychological feminisation. However, Adeline's increasing strength cannot be compared to Lewis's duplicitous Matilda, who seems to acquire more and more power right through the story. Notwithstanding her young age and the difficulties she faces, Adeline preserves her integrity and remains in control of every situation vis-à-vis other characters. Jung (2011) notes that Radcliffe and Lewis develop themes and situations that Beckford's *Vathek* had introduced, albeit in nucleus. While similarities between Walpole and Radcliffe exist, it is difficult to say whether Beckford influenced Radcliffe, even though her unconventional predecessor's elegant landscape descriptions and images of terror may have represented a useful source of inspiration. Lewis absorbs various ideas and devices from Walpole, Beckford, and Radcliffe, taking them to the extreme consequences in order to create what his forerunners might have only vaguely conceived.

Notwithstanding the dogmas of New Criticism, scholars of the early Gothic have frequently been tempted to look into writers' biographies to understand their works and vice versa. Radcliffe's novels have been examined in search of biographical evidence to compensate for the scarcity of information about her life. As much as Beckford, and for that matter also Walpole and Lewis, wrote a profusion of letters and memoirs, their novels have been inspected with care to retrieve personal details. Contrastingly, Russ Gill (2003) proposes a reverse operation, starting from David Hume's description of the mind as a theatre. Here "perception is inseparable from the activity that records it", a result of Hume's empiricism, derived from a series of Lucretian arguments concerning the acquisition of knowledge through the senses. Comparing this notion to Jacques Derrida's ideas on experience, Gill proposes to use *Vathek* not as a hidden biography, but as a text that has moulded Beckford and his life, as if the fictional caliph's unchained hedonism was to influence the author's existential choices and attitudes—a hypothesis which Gothic scholars have not generally embraced.

Lewis not only uses narrative techniques, such as the story-within-the-story, flashbacks and anticipations but also introduces various characters that outnumber the protagonists in other Gothic stories, a characteristic shared by Robinson's Gothic. Beckford's and Radcliffe's itinerant protagonists do not share the characters' claustrophobic internment in *The Monk*. Lewis's mother suffered from a particular idiosyncrasy that may have provided inspiration for certain parts of her son's novel (Groom 2016: xii). Macdonald (2000: 7) reveals that in her letters of apology to her husband after she had eloped with another man, Lewis's mother confessed that she lived in constant fear of being buried alive, an obsession that probably had an impact on the description of Raymond's fiancée's ghastly destiny, secretly kept in captivity in the dungeons of a convent. Antonia, Lorenzo's love interest, is a young girl of inferior rank and scarce economic means. She does not have freedom of movement and is constantly chaperoned when she dares to leave her house. In a similar way, Ambrosio is destined to live within the walls of his monastery. The only itinerant character in *The Monk*, Raymond, experiences some adventures that are dramatic and infernal. Even though in the first part of Beckford's novel, the caliph Vathek has not started his adventurous journey, he can move freely around his fabulous palaces and indulge in different pleasures. In *The Romance of the Forest,* Adeline, like other Radcliffe's female characters, is itinerant throughout the story. In spite of being a young girl of no means, Adeline moves with relative freedom and travels to various places. *The Monk, The Romance of the Forest* and *Hubert de Sevrac* feature a cottage infested with banditti. Painted by seventeenth-century Salvator Rosa, banditti involve a socio-historical dichotomy, as they can be either "rogues" or members of "a new movement" to revise "an unjust culture" (John Whatley 2003: 4–6). In a period of tormented political and social changes, characterised by the birth of mysterious cults dedicated to science, discoveries and the "immortalist thinking", banditti could be the embodiment of inexplicable mysteries. Lethal in Lewis, Robinson and Dacre, but compassionate in Radcliffe, these figures acquire a legendary and mythical halo in Gothic and Romantic narrations.

Despite their predilection for supernatural occurrences, early Gothic novelists absorbed the importance of science, which was one of the main traits of the Enlightenment. Johann Lavater's discoveries in physiognomy in the second half of the eighteenth century had cogent cultural repercussions. Corinna Wagner (2012: 87) notices that:

Science (like art, like politics) is always in danger of enforcing and promoting pre-existing biases whilst veiling such biases in disinterestedness, neutrality and nature. [...] eighteenth-century attitudes about sexed bodies are particularly and purposefully exaggerated in *The Monk:* when Ambrosio drugs and rapes the young Antonia, he blames her—and more to the point, her appearance—for her own shameful 'dishonour'. Ambrosio's charge is a vivid articulation of his society's gendered attitudes.

Apart from Ambrosio's misogynistic stance and gender prejudices, which pervade several pages in *The Monk,* the novel highlights how contemporary scientific discoveries emerge in the early Gothic discourse. The physical aspect in individuals brings about serious consequences in their lives. Physiognomy and phrenology were the results of Locke's challenge to Descartes's dualism. Locke's definition of consciousness as a physical element had replaced the French philosopher's rigid division of body and soul. This intuition had inspired scientists and philosophers alike to decipher the unseen that was supposedly hidden within the body. New scientific discoveries concerning the relationship between human behaviour and physical aspect introduced ontological doubts, and scientists wondered whether good and evil were in the forms of beauty and ugliness respectively. *The Monk* features a further allusion to contemporary sciences. The novel introduces a dialectic comparison between the images of Antonia and Matilda, both representatives of an ethereal beauty to which corresponds an angelic, but almost dumb, character in the former, and a devastating devilish nature in the latter. Hume (1741: 234) deems that "beauty is no quality in things themselves: it exists merely in the mind contemplating them; and each mind perceives a different beauty". Ambrosio uses a pseudo-scientific and subjective form of physiognomy that he believes to be universal in contradiction to Hume's statement. He reveals his own deviated ego when he imputes his crimes to Antonia's beauty.

Another quandary, the opposition between the physical world and the supernatural, poses a further series of problems in early Gothic writing. While supernatural events in *Otranto* are determined by adverse fate, unchained by Manfred's usurpation, Radcliffe's and Lewis's forms of the uncanny have unclear and complex roots. Radcliffe's protagonists face the supernatural, but are never overwhelmed by its enigmatic force, which manifests in different ways. Emily, Adeline, Ellena and Julia are reactive young women. Lewis's characters, especially the male protagonists, Raymond and Ambrosio, experience, and passively accept, supernatural occurrences, which accompany real life events. Haggerty (1989: 4) considers that Lewis was particularly good at manipulating Gothic effects in a much less refined way compared to Radcliffe. However, if on the one hand, he was able to present the readers with repugnant situations, on the other hand, he did not want to be convincing. He actually created what Haggerty calls "a new rationale for fictive expression". Unlike Radcliffe, he concentrated on the physicality of situations and introduced the supernatural without the Radcliffean ambiguity, just for the taste of sensationalism, which made him write excessive tableaus, which influenced Dacre's literary excesses. Lewis's truculent scenes of crude realism are more effective and credible than any of Radcliffe's sublime descriptions. The most clear-cut difference that distinguishes Radcliffe and other Gothic authors such as Reeve, Harley, Smith, Roche, Robinson, Lathom and Mary Anne Radcliffe from Walpole, Lee, Beckford, Lewis and

Dacre (and also Mary Shelley and Maturin for that matter) is the choice of an apparently positive and reassuring end. Bizarre events in Beckford may be considered supernatural manifestations, even though it is not always clear if they are expressions of pure divertissement, complex metaphors, or ominous incidents. Whereas Radcliffe's indefinite supernatural effects are unsuccessfully objectivised and never completely clarified, Harley, Roche, Lathom, Robinson and Mary Ann Radcliffe opt for contexts of suspense with only scarce hints of a latent supernatural, which never turns evident.

That Gothic fiction belonging to the last decades of the eighteenth century created forms of exalted appreciation for the genre cannot be disputed. The strange attraction that readers felt for Gothic stories could even become problematic, as in the case of a self-defined mystic and seer, Joanna Southcott. Southcott's autograph manuscript, written in 1803, was not a traditional critical analysis of Radcliffe's *Romance of the Forest*. In fact, it was a mystical reading of the novel. The Spirit of God supposedly dictated this appraisal to Southcott, who emphatically averred that *The Romance of the Forest* was an allegorical prophecy. She had detected obscure messages in Radcliffe's novel, which she considered "the channel for God's prophecies", in which Adeline is a religious emissary of God and her major antagonist, Montalt, is the embodiment of Satan (Norton 1999: 90–91). Although Southcott's interpretation may seem unusual, or even absurd, it was not a rarity at the time. Richard Maxwell (2003: 449) notes that her strange personality, together with her bizarre theories, had a strong impact on a number of people, who became the followers of her "millennial prophecies". When Charles Dickens wrote *A Tale of Two Cities* (1859: 5) to create a lively as well as gloomy, description of the last decades of the eighteenth century, which launched the seeds for the imminent revolutions, he introduced a variety of essential themes (including young Joanna Southcott), systematising the chiaroscuro spirit of the period:

It was the best of times, it was the worst of times, it was the age of wisdom, it was the age of foolishness, it was the epoch of belief, it was the epoch of incredulity, it was the season of Light, it was the season of Darkness, it was the spring of hope, it was the winter of despair, we had everything before us, we had nothing before us, we were all going direct to Heaven, we were all going direct the other way. [...] It was the year of Our Lord one thousand seven hundred and seventy-five. Spiritual revelations were conceded in England at that favoured period, as at this. Mrs. Southcott had recently attained her five-and-twentieth blessed birthday, of whom a prophetic private in the Life Guards had heralded the sublime appearance.

Despite the author's ironic tone in mentioning Southcott, the presence of the woman at the beginning of the text has a sinister value. The revolutionary events in France, especially the Terror, had fuelled great anxieties about the future that betrayed a revived sense of "millennialism", whose manifestation "was the belief that ancient prophecies were now being fulfilled" (Norton 1999: 91). The unusual narration in *The Romance of the Forest* evidently seems to convey subterranean meanings, apt to be interpreted as mystical messages by impressionable minds. However, it is not clear if Radcliffe was conscious of the strange and arcane lure of her novel. Even if she might have gone further on the path of mystery, she decided to abstain from entering further into the realms of the uncanny. Some scholars interpret Adeline's story from a Foucauldian perspective involving anticipation and deferral, essential concepts of the Gothic genre. Michel Foucault includes the tales of terror in his literary analysis and speculates that the transformation in the use of language takes place at the end of the eighteenth century when "something more obscure and paradoxical" happens (1977: 60–61, 65):

These languages which are constantly drawn out of themselves by the overwhelming, the unspeakable, by thrills, stupefaction, ecstasy, dumbness, pure violence, wordless gestures, and which are calculated with the greatest economy and precision to produce effects (so that they make themselves as transparent as possible at this limit of language toward which they hurry, erasing themselves in their writing for the exclusive sovereignty of that which they wish to say and which lies outside of words)–these languages very strangely represent themselves in a slow, meticulous and infinitely extended ceremony. [The language of terror] is of necessity excessive, [as] it is always beyond the limit in relation to itself; it only speaks as a supplement starting from a displacement such that the language from which it separates itself and which it recovers is the one that appears useless and excessive, and that deserves to be expunged; but as a result of the same shift, it sheds, in turn, all ontological weight.

However intriguing, these words could not be applied to all Gothic novels. The language of *The Romance of the Forest* is based on deferral inasmuch as it uses suspense with a certain frequency to keep attention alive, but it is not "beyond the limits" or "excessive". Norton argues that female readers could fully identify with Adeline, who represents a sort of early feminist character. Chard (2009) interprets the initial incident of the carriage, which forces de la Motte and his company to interrupt their flight, as a symbol of romantic escapism. Other critics favour a psychoanalytical reading of the novel. Johnson (1995: 77) considers Adeline "a palpitating provocation of the ethicosexual affectivity of men", although she is a moral agent that ultimately controls every situation. Jane Todd (1989: 266) expresses a different idea and posits that Radcliffe "refuses to accept sexuality overtly", a theory that cannot ultimately convince in the light of the analyses carried out so far, considering Adeline's latent sensuality, which creates tension and desire among male characters.

One of the most interesting literary aspects of the second part of the eighteenth century is linked to the surge in the number of women writers, belonging to different groups and currents. Circles of intellectual women were defined with derogatory nuances, as in Hazlitt's disparaging comments, comparing intellectual women to slimy egg yolk inevitably falling down with dirt, reported by Elisabeth Eger (2010: 206) in her study on the Blue-Stocking group, active between the Age of Reason and Romanticism. Several women were among early Gothic novelists, but critics, notwithstanding their popularity among readers, did not unanimously praise their works. Literary dialogue among contemporary authors was constantly at work, even if it was accompanied by irony and rebuff. Women writers were less praised than ridiculed, and Beckford provides an interesting specimen of the general attitude towards female literature at the turn of the century. An unknown author, called Miss Jacquetta Agneta Mariana Jenks, of Bellegrove Priory in Wales, signed a parody, entitled *Azemia* (1798). The novel was, in reality, Beckford's burlesque response to the excesses of Radcliffean enthusiasm. The masquerade of a woman writer is immoderately sarcastic, and his language's absurd pomposity highlights Beckford's intellectuality mixed with a deep scorn for women writers, as the following passage clearly demonstrates:

The narrator of the adventures of juvenile humanity finds less of labyrinthine involutions in the eccentricities of accumulated improbabilities, less of indescribability in the multifarious camelionity of terraqueous variety, or in the revolutionary scenery of planetary evolution, than dismaying-incomprehensibility in the enfoldings and vicissitudes of the involucrums of the pericardic region. The wildest wonder of imagination, astonishing agglomeration of concatenated rotation, fade into imperceptible invisibility, when opposed to the prevaricating pertinacity, which inoculates perspective projects on what is prohibited, and launches with extended velocity on a chaotic vaguosity of oceanic indistinction, unfathomable, ungovernable and uncontrollable. (*Azemia*: x–xi)

Beckford lampoons Radcliffe, Smith and the Gothic in general, without perhaps realising that the satire could also involve his novel: "In the bosom of the respectable haram of Hamet-beig her father, and in the imperial city of Constantinople, was born and nurtured the beauteous Azemia–educated would be an improper word, for the advantages of education are to the Turkish virgin denied: but Nature had denied none of her most attractive gifts to Azemia" (*Azemia*: 1–2). Azemia is a hopelessly uncultivated beauty. The parodic style of Beckford's pseudo novel reveals his opinion of female characters, namely a mélange of exalting good looks and abysmal ignorance, an idea shared by opinionated critics and literati of the time. The mocking and irreverent tone transforms the text into a caricature of literature as well as of British society. *Azemia* also aimed at ridiculing the clichés of Gothic novels, in which main characters are generally young women in distress. While Walpole had rarely commented on his friends' benevolently ironic accusations of having fathered too many Gothic children, other writers, poets and critics used either irony or their authority to demolish and demonise the influence of Gothic literature, especially the one authored by women. Lewis and Beckford shared a not so latent dislike for women writers, even though they were themselves the object of their contemporaries' negative scrutiny.

Scholars consider Radcliffe's disadvantaged social position as an explanation of her literary outputs, a supposition that is not convincing. Even if Beckford and Lewis, or even Walpole, came from similar privileged situations, their creations were heterogeneous, if not antithetical. Despite several attempts to codify it, the literature of horror tends to reject generalisations. As Clery demonstrates, Radcliffe was struggling daily to fit into the role of the proper woman, afraid that even her most innocent words might be misunderstood or considered inadequate. The definition of a proper woman (Poovey 1985) included all the rigid conventions women had to honour in order to be considered acceptable for society, especially when they decided to go public by writing essays and novels. Men's support, and other women's, was half-hearted at its best with a few exceptions. In 1788, the French philosopher and mathematician Nicolas de Condorcet, a proto-feminist, remarked that every sort of constraint was created for women to better control every sphere of their lives and suffocate their desire for independence–a revolutionary premise for the time. However, his liberal ideas did not have immediate resonance and did not help him when he was guillotined in 1794. While Radcliffe lived in seclusion to defend her respectability, Lewis and Beckford passed from one scandal to the other, both enjoying the affluence of their means, frequently travelling, and launching themselves into adventurous and risky exploits abroad. In 1783, Beckford described his adventures on the Continent in *Dreams, Waking Thoughts and Incidents*, a book of so scandalous a nature that he was forced to burn it because of family pressure. Only a few copies were saved. Beckford changed the book, calling it *Italy, with Sketches of Spain and Portugal* and published it fifty years later in 1833 (Brilli 2006). According to Miles (1995: 8), Radcliffe was a sort of Barbara Cartland of her times, despite the restricted number of works that amounted to five novels during her lifetime, compared to seven-hundred published by Cartland in the twentieth century. Her literary success was not enough: Radcliffe did not dare write after some unpromising reviews of *The Italian* (1797), and apparently lived in seclusion ever after.

Radcliffe's stories had imaginative potential influencing generations of writers. The secluded Louisa Bernini, secretly imprisoned in the dungeons of Mazzini's castle in *A Sicilian Romance,* is at the basis of Agnes's story of life imprisonment, as both characters are believed to be dead, while the fatal passion of the libertine Maria de Vellormo for the young Hippolitus [sic] is reflected in the story of Raymond, who receives the unwanted erotic attentions of the Baroness, Donna Rodolpha. The Marquis of Montalt's decision to abduct Adeline is mirrored in Ambrosio's stratagem to imprison innocent Antonia in a secret place. The ambiguous figures of abbots and abbesses, delineated in both *A Sicilian Romance* and *Udolpho*, are developed in the religious figures in *The Monk*. E. B. Murray (1972: 19) concludes that Radcliffe's imitators "added sex to her lily-white sensationalism and thereby eliminated the Radcliffean delicacy of sentiment, which consistently saved her heroines from a fate worse than death". Todd (1989: 255–256) asserts that Lewis's *The Monk* killed Radcliffe's literary career and forced the "great enchantress" into permanent silence. She even posits that Antonia's rape by Ambrosio was an actual rape of Radcliffe's art by Lewis. Fitzgerald (2003: 49) cites examples of extreme Gothic criticism as well as Todd's conclusions to demonstrate that Lewis's work inspired critics' radicalism as if he had actually performed some of the horrible acts described in his novel.

An Enquiry into the Duties of the Female Sex by Thomas Gisborn, a didactic text providing the rules to follow in the division of the male and female spheres, was published in 1796. It was one of the many conduct books, printed ever since the mid-seventeenth century to control women's behaviour in every aspect of their lives inevitably linked to dominating male figures (Fergusson Ellis 1989). Conduct books betrayed a constant preoccupation with monitoring and censoring incorrect behaviour to make sure that women complied with the social requirements of propriety. Several Gothic female characters, however, tend to avoid social restrictions in a successful way, and without serious consequences for most of them, with the exclusion of unfortunate and/or cruel female characters in Walpole, Dacre and Lewis. In the first scene of Marivaux's light comedy *Game of Love and Chance* (*Jeu de l'Amour et du Hasard* 1730), Silvia is talking to her servant Lisette. Her father has found her a fiancé, but she has some perplexities about tying the knot and becoming a wife. She reveals that, after observing her acquaintances' husbands' bizarre behaviours, infidelities and moody characters, she thinks of rejecting all offers of marriage. Silvia expresses an opinion that was not uncommon among women during the eighteenth century: she is afraid of men's erratic behaviours, generally undetected before marriage, and utters Beatrice's same doubts in Shakespeare's dark comedy, *Much Ado About Nothing* (1599). Susanna Centlivre underlines analogous feelings in Miss Lovely, the main character in the play *A Bold Stroke for a Wife* (1718). Like the fictitious Silvia, Miss Lovely and Beatrice, real-life French playwright and political activist, Olympe de Gouges, guillotined for her exaltation of freedom and women's rights by French revolutionaries (evidently not so keen on the equality of sexes), had rejected a second marriage after becoming a very young widow in the 1760s. She intended to be independent and keep the money from her writings, which she was able to print only after her father's death, showing a need of independence, a feeling that British women writers had experienced starting from the seventeenth century (Carme Font Paz 2018). De Gouges promoted freedom for women in her 1791 *Declaration of the Rights of Women and the Female Citizens*, based on the revolutionary declarations that she found unjust and incomplete, as they did not include women. The French motto of freedom, equality, and brotherhood had ignored the status of women and De Gouges's revolutionary text promoted suffrage for all and equal rights in marriage. A similar opinion to Marivaux's Silvia, Shakespeare's Beatrice, Centlivre's Miss Lovely and Olympe de Gouges, though more drastic, can be found in Mary Wollstonecraft's protagonist's explicit terms in *The Wrongs of Woman* (1792). Maria, the main character, admits that marriage has "bastilled" her for life. The lugubrious castle of the Bastille, a notorious prison, becomes the gloomy metaphor for an unfortunate marriage. The heroine is unjustly kept in a lunatic asylum so that her husband can enjoy her patrimony alone. Her story is Wollstonecraft's demonstration of the dangers inevitably gathering round women's lives.

One of the most important poets in the interregnum between Pope and Wordsworth and one of Radcliffe's poetic mentors, expressed a dissimilar idea when writing about happiness in the household. In "The Garden", a section of the poetic composition *The Task* (1785), the poet exclaims:

> Domestic happiness, thou only bliss
> Of Paradise that has survived the Fall (Cowper: 49)

Cowper's praise of household "bliss" reflect a male viewpoint in sharp contrast with the opinion expressed by both female characters and women writers. Cowper's words show an idealised form of reality, transfigured by a male representation of marriage as a source of harmony and delight. Clery (1995: 125) argues that, according to British legislation, the position of women was not blissful, but rather precarious. Generally excluded from inheritance for economic reasons, if they had the right to inherit a part of the legacy, women could not keep their money and properties long, especially when other male heirs were involved, and they lost everything the moment they got married. Anna Seward's unusual decision to reject marriage has frequently been considered ambiguous by literary critics. She was her parents' only heir and could count on a good income, which allowed her to live at great ease in an elegant mansion surrounded by a vast park. She had a circle of friends, intellectuals, philosophers, and scientists forming an exclusive coterie. Unlike the great majority of the women of the age, she received a private education from her father, which allowed her to become a respected writer, without worrying about couverture. William Blackstone's *Commentaries on The Law of England* (1770) included the feudal norm of couverture, meant for the protection of women, which, however, acquired the nuance of complete control in real life. Chaplin (2004: 127) underlines the strong patriarchal connotation in the words choice: "Blackstone likens English law to an ancient, venerable Gothic castle that simply requires modernization to render it effective in the eighteenth century", revealing a linguistic usage connected with Gothic tropology introduced by Hurd's essay and Walpole's novel and betraying a strong patriarchal stance. Women's status and the difficulties imposed by couverture had an influence on women's writing as well. Worries concerning possessions and marriage are especially highlighted by women writers and early Gothic novelists at the turn of the century. Reeve, Smith, Harley, Wollstonecraft, Radcliffe, Parsons, Roche, Robinson and Austen manifest women's (and also men's) frequent preoccupations linked to financial matters, estates and legacies. Radcliffe adds a particular gloomy alternative to her protagonists living on the continent, where they also face a cruel destiny as recluses in convents. As Ferguson Ellis (1989) and Clery (1995) highlight, Radcliffe's female characters become the unexpected legal heirs of relatives' and benefactors' fortunes, and recover their estates and fortune when stolen by dishonest relatives or criminals. Radcliffe's heroines become extremely rich against all odds and, what is even more interesting, they continue managing their own fortunes even after they are married, an unrealistic legal dream that Radcliffe uses with revolutionary intentions: Julia becomes the heir of a large fortune and also inherits the castle that her brother Ferdinand renounces in *A Sicilian Romance*. In *Udolpho,* Emilie becomes her relatives' only heiress (despite uncles and male cousins), and receives a conspicuous inheritance from the mysterious Laurentini. Ellena de Rosalba recovers her due inheritance and her title after dangerous adventures. Adeline obtains her father's title and her relatives' fortune, the same as Harley's Elwina (*The Castle of Mowbray*), Smith's Emmeline, Parsons's Matilda Weimar, Roche's Madeline, Robinson's Emily and Sabina de Sevrac and *Manfroné*'s Rosalina. Usurpers are punished either by law or by death, and female figures are blessed more by the accumulation of wealth than by requited love, showing how financial independence, which could be easily lost in real life, played a huge part in Gothic narratives.

Interestingly, Radcliffe's tormented characters and their unfortunate fiancés finally celebrate their union at the very end of the stories, when the final page, or rather the final lines, provide scarce details about the couple's future extra-textual conjugal bliss. Female protagonists' tribulations and marriage rejection seem to be Radcliffe's main *topoi*. Julia cannot accept the court of the enamoured Count Hippolitus in *A Sicilian Romance* while her stepmother's machinations aim at getting rid of her rights in the heritance line. *The Italian* features a reluctant Ellena de Rosalba, who rejects Antonio de Vivaldi's court and marriage proposal. Radcliffe's most strong-willed and self-controlled heroine in the catalogue of female characters, Emily, rejects Valancourt's more than once, and her father, St. Aubert, even discourages the young man from courting his daughter, despite his failing health, and makes the same mistake as Elvira in *The Monk*. Once Emily remains orphan of both father and mother, she inexplicably rejects Valancourt's offer of marriage, notwithstanding the innumerable dangers for a girl without couverture. Adeline's situation is even more interesting because she moves in a world populated by masculine figures, who are either potentially dangerous (the minority) or sincerely protective (most of them). Once problems are solved, she refuses marriage. Only in the very last words of the novel does the reader discover that she lives in a château with her husband and children. The continuous deferral of marriage goes hand in hand with a yearning for escapism and independence, which denotes a form of secret female desire and the will to establish one's identity in a patriarchal world (David Owen 2014: 355).

Marriage and imprisonment seem to belong to the same semiotic universe in the Gothic. Milbank (2008: x) identifies the basic female fears in the theme of the "imprisoned woman deprived of her property rights, as well as the maiden endangered with abduction", whereas Eugenia DeLamotte (1990: 29) perceives the constant "fear of violation" related to a primeval angst. On the contrary, according to Johnson (1995: 81–82) this fear has no reason to subsist "because of males' effeminacy caused by vice", an idea that resonates with the series of William Hogarth's paintings of *A Rake's Progress* (1734). Radcliffe's central characters become imperturbably proud vis-à-vis potential violators, but develop an idiosyncrasy for marriage, which is not only a literary device to prolong the action and the narration. Radcliffe's and other Gothic writers' leading characters express a matrimonial reluctance somehow reflecting a social malaise, in which redundant scepticism concerning wedlock is the sign of an unsatisfied need for independence and social recognition.

Further aspects that the early Gothic novels share are ambiguous female figures. The novels by Lee, Harley, Wollstonecraft, Smith, Parsons, Roche and Mary Anne Radcliffe introduce unfortunate female characters, trying to change their situations for the better. Walpole's female characters are submissive, while Lewis's Matilda, Beckford's Nouronihar and Dacre's Victoria in *Zofloya*, who deliberately choose evil, are audacious and hard-hearted. Radcliffe is the most original author among early Gothic novelists because her stories include proactive characters, who not only fight against ruthless male figures but also react against antagonistic females. Her characters are paradoxically more advanced than later representations of women, as for example in Virginia Woolf or James Joyce, in which female characters are either blocked by contingencies or entangled, like Molly Bloom, in their illusion of desire (Didac Pujol 2014).

Radcliffe's young female characters handle the risk of prevarication in a successful manner, despite the overwhelming sense of horror provoked by dangerous events. The figure of the young persecuted woman has sometimes been seen as a form of frustrated female condition, or incestuous desire. DeLamotte (1990) finds analogies between Richardson's *Clarissa* and *The Mysteries of Udolpho*, but the special capacity for self-defence is what makes Radcliffe's female protagonists different from Richardson's and previous novelists' characters. The analysis of women characters in early Gothic involves some important questions concerning their typology. Dacre's Victoria in *Zofloya* is a villainous agent from the beginning to the end of the story. In Radcliffe's and Roche's novels, some female figures show different levels of cruelty, trying to frustrate, damage, or destroy other women. Whereas Madame de la Motte shows indifference and apathy when the heroine (Adeline) is in danger because of her deep jealousy (*The Romance of the Forest*), Madame Cheron selfishly imposes her proud authority on her orphan niece, Emily, in *The Mysteries of Udolpho,* thus creating serious predicaments. Of a more dangerous kind is the corrupt Maria de Vellormo in *A Sicilian Romance*, who is ready to do anything to have her stepdaughters sent to a convent. The "Antigone's situation", presented by Luce Irigaray (1981), describing the woman cut off from society and buried alive, cannot be applied to Radcliffe's main characters, who are proactive agents, intent on facing the world, even though Louisa Bernini *(A Sicilian Romance)* and Countess di Bruno (*The Italian*) embody two examples of forcibly secluded women, who are saved after long sufferings. The darkest example of female character, plotting in the shadow and ready to conspire against Ellena to have her murdered, is *The Italian*'s Marchesa De Vivaldi, one of the most vicious female individuals in Radcliffe's oeuvre. The early Gothic reveals a new perspective on female characters, some of whom represent a problematic and pitiless matriarchy, as dangerous as traditional patriarchy.

A haunting construct that emerges in stories of horror concerning women is the archetype of the mother, whose presence and/or absence and function in the narrative economy, acquires importance in both male and female Gothic novels. Claire Kahane's (1985) paradigm of the "mother as enemy" is interesting to investigate in relation to the novels analysed in this book, although careful distinctions need to be made. In contrast with scholars who detect extreme danger in patriarchal figures, Kahane provocatively posits that male characters do not cause the basic threats for Gothic heroines. In particular, she disagrees with critics who surmise that Gothic horror resides in the fear of potential incest, a theory initiated by Eino Railo's interpretation of male relatives' erotic power in the Gothic (1974). Kahane also questions Leslie Fiedler's definition of the castle as the symbol of paternal and violent authority, interiorised and developed by Ferguson Ellis (1989). Kahane theorises that the mother, even the dead one, is the real cause of tension in young female characters, who struggle for a separate identity trying to escape (many times unsuccessfully) from the maternal imago, dangerously surviving after the parent's death. Kahane opines that mothers, especially in more recent expressions of the Gothic, can be cruel agents, when alive, and maintain their dark nature when they become spectral identities. In Walpole's *Otranto*, Hippolita, a rather neutral persona, incapable of cruelty, even though her passivity indirectly influences her children's destiny, represents one of the few mother figures in the Gothic, who are not potentially hostile. Ignoring her husband's political responsibility, she is dangerously powerless, and cannot prevent Manfred's wrath and ultimate violence. In Beckford as well as in Lewis, mothers are not willing enemies, even though they consciously or unconsciously become dangerous nemeses. If they damage their children, it is because they have misunderstood existential messages. Vathek's mother Carathis is the woman pushing her son to destruction even if she is convinced that he will acquire unlimited power. In *The Monk*, Elvira involuntarily forces her unrecognised son Ambrosio to commit a crime and causes her daughter's cruel destiny. Radcliffe's mother figures are generally absent or irrelevant, whereas Robinson's Emily de Sevrac is good-hearted, but mostly ineffective. Therefore, the mothers described in early Gothic tales do not seem to correspond to Kahane's eternal enemies, but turn into inadequate or inept personifications. The complexity of the mother figure has received scholarly attention: Julia Kristeva's (1982) acknowledges the lack of status as an abjection, which leads mothers to destruction. Ruth Bienstock Anolik (2003: 26–27) notices that the pattern of the "missing mother" contains perils associated to death, imprisonment and abjection, but also considers the non-presence of the mother as a form of proto-independence in the daughter, who acquires a margin of relative freedom and can in this way fight against oppressive forms of patriarchal power. Whereas Walpole's mother figure is excluded from Bienstock Anolik's paradigm, abjection and death suit mother figures in Beckford, Lewis and Dacre, whereas imprisonment seems to be more frequent in Radcliffean contexts.

Nancy Armstrong (1987) considers the mother's role as a "panopticon", a system of strict surveillance, first conceived by eighteenth-century philosopher Jeremy Bentham, who intended to adapt it to buildings such as prisons, schools, hospitals, with the aim of controlling multitudes, otherwise difficult to monitor. However, the idea of a system of organised control does not appear to be compatible with the mother figures encountered in the early Gothic novels. Moreover, the mothers, who try to exert control (Carathis in *Vathek* and Elvira in *The Monk*), cannot fulfil their expectations and are marked by failure. The mother figure means safety, unity and order and is, therefore, the enemy of the "narratable" for Carolyn Dever (1997), which may explain the general lack of mother figures in Radcliffe, Harley, Smith, Roche, and Mary Anne Radcliffe. Radcliffe's Adeline, Emily and, partially, Julia and Ellena de Rosalba represent perfect embodiments of motherless heroines. Adeline, whose dead mother is excluded from the story, experiences, for a short time, the company of a putative motherly figure, Madame de la Motte (rigorously without a name in the entire story), who is dangerously indifferent to her predicament. As a result, the young woman renounces a useless female companionship and decides to act alone.

Whereas it is true that several early Gothic stories abound with violent figures, both males and females, who impose their power in cruel ways, there is one peculiar pattern, which has not been sufficiently scrutinised. Curiously, it can be ascertained in some plots (*Vathek*; *The Romance of the Forest*; *The Monk*): it is the trope of the "missing father". The most explicit and shortest documentation about the protagonist's father is provided in *Vathek*'s first three lines, informing he died prematurely. Antonia's father (*The Monk*) died when still young while he was staying in the West Indies, but the *coup de scène* revealing his real paternity takes place at the very end of the story. Adeline's father is apparently a cruel and despotic man, whose story and function is revealed in the story's unexpected epiphany. Although Carathis becomes too powerful and Elvira is powerless, both end their parable in mishap and are unable to perform their deceased husbands' paternal role. If the risk of persecution and rape are contingent for Adeline, it is because of an indifferent father (who is not her true father) and a disheartened putative figure (de la Motte). Interestingly, real fathers die prematurely in several Gothic novellas without providing the protection, which could avoid distress or tragedy. *Manfroné* contains a further example of potential danger when the main character, Madeline, has to endure innumerable tribulations after her father's death. The figure of the missing father should not be identified with a patriarchal element, but with a positive figure of affection and generosity. Vathek's father created an unlimited kingdom, Ambrosio's dead father could provide wealth, respect and an aristocratic title, Adeline's father is the victim of injustice, but his supernatural, guiding presence is beneficial.

Father figures play a positive role in Francis Lathom's *Midnight Bell* (1798): here Count Cohenburg provides precious teachings even after his death. The case of St. Aubert in *The Mysteries of Udolpho* is apparently complicated, as misleading documents about his conduct are discovered after his death, causing Emily's contingent doubts about his integrity, which dissipate when the story unfolds, confirming the father figure's positive aura. Complicacies multiply in Bentley, Smith, Parsons, Roche, Mary Anne Radcliffe and Dacre when paternal figures are absent or pass away. Present throughout the story, an even more complex figure is Robinson's de Sevrac, who undergoes a series of existential crises that do not allow him to perform his paternal role consistently despite his affectionate character. The originality of the *topos* may lie in the unusual idea of a positive father figure, who is neither conservative nor patriarchal, but complementary and inspiring to female characters. Once this positive presence vanishes, chaos begins if connections with the paternal figure are lost. The novels' missing fathers disappear before or at the beginning of the story and references to them have a deictic value. When they are lost forever, the story tends toward darkness and despair. However, when they can manifest their presence, they have the power to save their children from sorrow and death, as is the case for Adeline and Emily.

If multiple literary sources from the past, especially Antiquity, could be identified in early Gothic novels, which also feature a miscellany of influences from Medieval and Renaissance authors, themes and ideas from eighteenth-century literature have some relevance in their stories. As far as contemporary influences, Gothic novelists' cultural syncretism show how French literature and the Enlightenment also provided abundant material for early Gothic stories. "Beckford seemed very close to Voltaire's purposeful, penetrating, rational irony" (Lonsdale 2008: xxvi), a similitude highlighted by contemporary reviewers, who detected more than one point in common with the French philosopher. Even though some passages in *Vathek* may show analogies with Voltaire's Oriental tales, the similarity is only superficial. In particular, the philosopher's stories show a strong philosophical and didactic impulse, whereas Beckford's final objective is experimentation and aesthetics. Philosophical stories such as Voltaire's *Zadig* (1747) share only some secondary aspects with *Vathek*, which are the Eastern settings, the young protagonists and the plots' supernatural events. Zadig is a prosperous young man of great knowledge, who starts a secret journey to escape from Babylon. He has to undergo many an ordeal before understanding the meaning of life and the importance of providence. Whereas Zadig's adventures make him wiser, Vathek's experiences make him more obnoxious and lead him to damnation. One possible parallel between the two authors can be found in a comic episode in *Vathek*, when the caliph is entertained by many-sided religious figures, worshippers of different creeds, all united in a sort of sacred meeting:

He diverted himself, however, with the multitude of calenders, santons, and dervishes, who were continually coming and going; but especially with the bramins, faquirs, and other enthusiasts [...] Wherever the Caliph directed his course, objects of pity were sure to swarm round him; the blind, the purblind, smarts without noses, damsels without ears, each to extol the munificence of Fakreddin, who, as well as his attendant grey-beards, dealt about, gratis, plasters and cataplasms to all that applied. At noon, a superb corps of cripples made its appearance. (*Vathek*: 60–61)

Henley and Beckford's explanatory note thoroughly describes the different kinds of religious representatives. Beckford's enumeration of funny performances creates the parodic effect, envisaged by Michail Bakhtin, which is also frequently found in Voltaire's narratives. When it comes to religions, strange rites and the various superstitions flowering from them unchain the French philosopher's irony, which is reflected in *Vathek*. Voltaire's criticism of religious exaltation can also be found in *Candide* (1759), in which extreme consequences occur when religious authorities organise an *auto-da-fe*, a human sacrifice, in order to calm God's fury. The entire scene is similar to a huge spectacle, analogous to the emir's religious fair in *Vathek*. However, Voltaire's scene provokes indignation, whereas Beckford is simply looking for colourful narrative effects. In spite of being a religious authority himself, Vathek has a sardonic, superficial attitude, as Beckford's ironic stance is humorous, but it is not meant to be didactic or moralising. On the other hand, Voltaire's deep moral criticism has the specific goal of showing the evils of society.

While Voltaire's irony seem more compatible with Beckford's funny episodes in *Vathek*, a less famous French writer played an important role in the genesis of *The Romance of the Forest*. François Guillaume Ducray-Duminil's novel, *Alexis, ou la Maisonnette dans les bois* (1789), shaped both Smith's and Radcliffe's stories. Abandoned by his father and lost in a forest, Alexis experiences strange events. The analogy between Alexis and Adeline was highlighted by Robert Mayo (1940: 501, 505): "It is probable that to the list of Mrs. Radcliffe's sources for *The Romance of the Forest* there should be added a French Romance, *Alexis* [...] The French story has certain resemblances to Mrs. Radcliffe's novel [and her] imagination owed Ducray a very considerable debt". However, he concluded: "Ducray's scenes of terror were ineptly conceived when measured against the delicate artistry of [Mrs. Radcliffe]". The novel was part of a series of stories for younger readers by the author, the father of the French popular novel, and the roman noir in France, which shares some traits with the Gothic novel. The different, and frequently opposing, explanations of *The Romance of the Forest* make it difficult to unveil sources and envisage a single interpretation of the text. Without following the visionary path of a mystical revelation indicated by Southcott, or the flight from civilisation, influenced by Rousseau's social philosophy, or the image of the heroine as a sexual *agent provocateur* similar to Ariosto's Angelica, it is possible to say that *The Romance of the Forest* is a remarkable novel with a special structure. The nucleus is the kidnapping of Adeline and her strange adventure in Montalt's mansion, which may represent the prologue to a story of perdition and vice in the libertine style. The novel entails an incredibly complex nexus of associations and influences. One of the key characters in the novel, Pierre de la Motte father, takes his name in part from Antoine Houdar de La Motte, a French poet and playwright living at the end of the seventeenth century, whose fables were included in *A Collection of Poems* by Robert Dodsley (1758). Interestingly, as if in a game of literary interconnections, the epigraph of Trapp's poem dedicated to Virgil, which Radcliffe uses to introduce chapter eighteen, is included in Dodsley's collection, which not only shows Radcliffe's knowledge but also seems to confirm the author's awareness of the intertextual value of her novel. Antoine de La Motte composed a play entitled *Amadis de Grèce* (1699), an adaptation of *Amadigi* (1560) by Bernardo Tasso, a Renaissance poet and father to the more famous Torquato. Radcliffe's favourite musician, Handel, made up a magic drama in three acts, *Amadigi di Gaula* (1715) when the composer resided at Burlington House. De La Motte's surname was also related to the "Affair of the Necklace", orchestrated by pseudo Countess Jeanne Valois de La Motte (unrelated to Antoine de La Motte), who tried to procure an inestimable diamond jewel for herself, pretending it was for Queen Marie Antoinette. Even though the latter was unaware of the machinations, and the culprits were found, tried and condemned, the scandal irremediably tainted the French queen's reputation. Cagliostro was initially reputed responsible but later acquitted for lack of evidence against him. Radcliffe's fictional de la Motte's life in Paris is marked by wrong moral choices and inexcusable errors, which he tries to erase with the help of his lawyer, Guyot de Pitaval, who "records the proceedings in the Parliamentary Courts in Paris" (*RF*: 1). De Pitaval is another fictional character based on a real French figure. A former soldier, François Gayot De Pitaval (1673–1743) studied to be a lawyer when he was in his forties. He was a prolific author and became famous for writing accounts of controversial legal cases. Adeline's story resembles Augustine Françoise de Choiseul's plea. She was born to Louise-Gabrielle De La

Baume Le Blanc de la Vallière, a beautiful and promiscuous woman (Louise de la Vallière, her sister, was one of Louis XIV's lovers), and her husband, the old duke César Auguste De Choiseul. Not sure of the girl's paternity, Louise-Gabrielle decided to give Augustine to a friend as a foster child. Both parents died when their daughter was young. After suing her uncle to legitimise her position, Augustine unexpectedly won the case, but she died a few years later. Charlotte Smith was the first to fictionalise De Pitaval's stories in her collection *The Romance of Real Life* published in 1787 (Chard 2009).

Even one of Radcliffe's most supportive biographers, Clara McIntyre, had to admit that there existed a high number of analogies between Smith's work and *The Romance of the Forest*. During his flight, the fugitive gentleman saves Adeline from an obscure destiny, then finds a dark forest and their flight is suspended in the obscure enchantment of the place. Like real-life homonymous Countess, Pierre de la Motte has committed crimes caused by his fall into vice. Therefore, he has to be exiled from society. Adeline's life is threatened and he has a chance to improve his moral character by saving the girl. The refuge that the runaway aristocrat finds in the forest—a place that is enthralling, but at the same time threatening—helps him to keep away from perils and vice. However, other ordeals await him to test his conscience that proves to be weak. The intricate network of cultural and literary influences demonstrates that Radcliffe's sources were heterogenic and complex.

French libertine literature represents an interesting source for Lewis. During his stay in Paris, he likely discovered examples of licentious literature. *Camille et le Souterrain* by Joseph Marsollier (1790) is an example of rescue opera, with a heroine typically in danger: Camille is imprisoned in a dungeon and about to be seduced when she is fortunately saved. A four-act play, *Les Victimes Cloîtrées* (1791) by Boutet de Monvel, is a story of seduction of persecuted virtue by depraved monks during the French Revolution (Sophie Marchand 2011). Interestingly, Lewis mentioned these works in his correspondence, but did not include them in his list of sources in *The Monk*'s prologue. Other works dealing with life in convents and monasteries are Diderot's *La Religieuse* (1780), which Lewis may have seen in the form of a manuscript when he resided in France before its posthumous publication in 1796, and Joseph Fiévée's *Les Rigueurs du Cloître* (1790). A number of anonymous authors published erotic popular novels set in monasteries before or during the Revolution, containing salacious stories of the clergy, and a major focus on erotic adventures with revealing titles, such as *Intrigues Monastiques*; *Amour Encapuchonné*; *Les Tromperies des Prestres*; *Don Bougre*. Erotic texts of adventures in convents had grown in number since the end of the seventeenth century. One of the most popular was *Venus in the Cloister* by Jean Barrin (*Vénus dans le Cloître, ou la Religieuse en Chemise* 1683), translated into English in 1724. The book had been reputed to be excessively scandalous and the British publisher, Edmund Curl, had been arrested and incarcerated. Conversely, the frivolous beginning of *The Monk* may have been taken from the typical incipits in the comedies of Lesage and Marivaux.

A French "fantastique" novel (*roman fantastique*) is of particular interest for the development of *The Monk* and the early Gothic novels. The author, Jacques Cazotte, an eighteenth-century navy officer and member of the Illuminati, first became famous for his playful collection of Oriental tales (*Les Mille et une fadaises* 1742, translated as *One Thousand and one Follies*) imitating the style of *The Arabian Nights*. His bizarre novel, *Le Diable Amoureux* (1772), rendered in 1793 as *The Devil in Love*, was an occult romance, which became his greatest literary success and marked the beginning of supernatural novels in French literature. The story begins when Don Alvaro de Las Maravillas, a Spanish officer in Naples, decides to learn magic to acquire more power, inspired by a fellow-officer, who apparently knows dark rituals. Once the devil is evoked, it takes on different forms of animals until it turns into a male page. The devil's final transformation turns him into the very attractive Biondetta, who repeatedly tries to seduce the supposedly virgin Alvaro. The two quasi-lovers start a pleasant journey, which should allow them to discover secret pleasures. They go to Venice and Paris to enjoy the many distractions offered by the cities of sin, before reaching Spain, where Alvaro's mother should give them permission to marry. As Laurence Porter sagaciously explains, Alvaro undergoes the three different stages of temptation envisaged by Saint Augustine (1978: 5):

The first is *suggestio*, the surprise of the senses attracted by a speciously agreeable object. The second is *delectatio*, the delight of the mind in imagining sins, which we have not yet resolved to commit. It is this phase, which is exploited by the prolonged tease of soft-core pornography. The final phase is the *consensus*, the consent of the will as we actively pursue the object of our desire and engage in sin. Depicting such activities is the business of hard-core pornography like Petronius's *Satyricon*.

Alvaro's sinful phases are mirrored in Ambrosio's story. Whereas Cazotte's story playfully revels in the first two stages of Alvaro's road to temptation, *suggestio* and *delectatio*, exploiting narrative techniques of gallantry and voyeurism, Ambrosio's story rapidly overcomes the first two stages to reach *consensus* and promptly fulfil erotic desire. Cazotte's fantastic events represent an amazingly similar context to Lewis's work, even though the narration is interspersed with elucubrations in the French philosophers' style. This constant musing about the meaning of events is a strong deterrent, helping Don Alvaro to keep the devil and its temptations at large, whereas Ambrosio is irrational and incapable of judiciously considering his situation before falling into a sinful whirlwind. Cazotte's Spanish hero should be a man of the world. However, like Ambrosio, Alvaro has never experienced physical love and needs his strict and religious mother's approval for marriage (and sex). Unlike Ambrosio, he is capable of resisting every form of Biondetta's seduction until the very end of the story, when he apparently succumbs once they arrive in Spain. Biondetta has the same sexual ambiguity as Matilda, first male, then female and her sudden departure, which remains unexplained in Cazotte, recalls Matilda's equally mystifying disappearance in the final pages of *The Monk.* Cazotte's novella abounds in mystery and offers many possible meanings. As Markus Muller (2004: 324) acutely observes, Cazotte did not attribute evil to a transcendental cause, but moved towards its "antropomorphization". The French enlightened author seems to have provided inspiration for not only Lewis but also Beckford and Radcliffe. Cazotte's humorous Oriental stories, his insistence on magic, his strange supernatural evocations in Neapolitan dark vaults and a suspended finale might have played a major role in *Vathek*, *The Monk*, and Radcliffe's *The Italian.* Coincidentally, Radcliffe's last novel features a male protagonist trying to unveil supernatural mysteries within gloomy ruins in Naples. Carlo Testa's (1994) definition of *Le Diable Amoureux* as "the *terminus ab quo* in the history of demonic subgenre" is confirmed by the story's relevant influence on the early Gothic novels and on literary devotees, both French and English, conquered by its complex supernatural allegory.

The sweetness and fine expression in her voice attracted his attention to her figure, which had a distinguished air of delicacy and grace, but her face was concealed in her veil. So much indeed was he fascinated by the voice, that a most painful curiosity was excited as to her countenance, which he fancied must express all the sensibility of character that the modulations of her tone indicated.
(Ann Radcliffe. *The Italian*)

In her article on readers' reactions to Eighteenth-century fiction, based on the philosophical idea of "disinterested sensibility", Fiona Price (2006: 3) highlights what she considers "two of the Gothic's most significant features: its reiteration of emotional excess and its preoccupation with the visual". Before the genesis of the Gothic, analyses of human reactions to situations of great emotional impact were found in the writings of many eighteenth-century thinkers. Shaftesbury's *Characteristicks of Men, Manners, Opinions, and Times* (1713) was a collection of miscellaneous thoughts about the nature of men and women, which he considered guided by innate moral principles, independent from legislations or religious impositions. Influenced by Isaac Newton's scientific studies, David Hume applied an empirical method in the investigation of human psychology. His research became part of *A Treatise of Human Nature: Being an Attempt to Introduce the Experimental Method of Reasoning into Moral Subjects* (1739). Unlike rationalists, who considered reason the major cause behind human actions, Hume argued that passions determine humanity's behaviour. Reinterpreting Shaftesbury's and Hume's ideas, Adam Smith modified his predecessors' definitions and developed his personal reasoning about human sensibility that he considered innate and universal. He published his *Theory of Moral Sentiments* in 1759, in which he analysed the typology of human feelings and passions (1781: 3) that he considered common in every individual:

The emotion which we feel for the misery of others, when we either see it, or are made to conceive it in a very lively manner, that we often derive sorrow from the sorrow of others, is a matter of fact so obvious to require any instances to prove it; for this sentiment, like all other original passions of human nature, is by no means confined to the virtuous and humane, though they perhaps may feel it with the most exquisite sensibility.

The previous texts are some relevant examples of a number of essays on the theme of empathy and sensibility. Lord Kames' *Elements of Criticism* (1761) introduced the theory of the ideal presence (Miles 1999: 10), which also contributed to the primacy of sight and the visual in the Gothic. The discourse on the phenomenology of sensibility and emotional response to particular poignant scenes, whether beautiful or horrifying, includes Burke's fundamental text on the sublime, *A Philosophical Enquiry into the Origins of our Ideas of the Sublime and the Beautiful* (1757). The meditation on terror by John Aikin and his sister Anna Letitia (later known as Barbault), "On the Pleasure derived from Objects of Terror" (1773) was considered the epitome of the theories of the sublime and was to influence writers and the Gothic movement in the decades to come. The visual becomes a general feature of both Gothic and non-Gothic narratives throughout the eighteenth century.

As far as the excesses of emotional distress are concerned, they are not an exclusive prerogative of female writing. Richardson's novels *Pamela* and *Clarissa* provide a clear demonstration, overflowing as they are with expressions of sentimentalism, anguish and torment, even though they are less compelling or passionate compared to Gothic and Romantic extremes, developed a few decades later. Price also analyses a notion adapted from Clara Reeve's definition of "narrative exaggerations", which the first female Gothic author had found in Walpole's *Otranto*. The axioms from which Price develops her ideas, shared by a number of scholars of the Gothic, is that the two features mentioned before (exaltation of the visual and emotional excesses) are mostly Gothic or Romantic, and can generally be found in literary works of the late eighteenth century written by women. Starting from the distinction of the so-called female from the male Gothic, critical literature on horror stories has tended to build an ideal distinction between the two categories, which has recently been questioned. The identification of women's writing as distinguished from male writers, inaugurated by Moers in *Literary Women* (1976) and embraced by Fleenor (1983), among others, represents a lasting aspect of feminist studies. Moers' chapter on

"Female Gothic" was relevant in changing the critical perception of Radcliffe's works, which is supposed to be the prototype of a distinctive female form of writing. However, a number of scholars have rejected the mechanical division between female and male Gothic, as it does not solidly reflect the variety of Gothic works by both male and female writers, written in the decades between the eighteenth and the nineteenth centuries. The female Gothic (or the imitation of the female Gothic as is the case of Francis Lathom, who rigorously intended to apply Radcliffe's canons to his tales of horror) includes women writers generally focused on female characters. Starting with Sophia Lee in 1786 (*The Recess*), passing via Smith, Harley, Wollstonecraft, Burney, Radcliffe, Roche, Parsons, Dacre, and ending with Mary Anne Radcliffe's *Manfroné* (1809), stories are developed around feminine figures, who generally turn out to be positive characters, apart from Dacre's devilish protagonist Victoria (*Zofloya* 1806), Ambrosio's alter ego in the writer's intentions. The featuring of female protagonists was not only a conventional literary choice but also revealed some deeper messages in reaction to the times. Punter and Byron (2009: 278) argue that: "underlying many critical attempts to theorise a female Gothic is the idea that male and female Gothic differ primarily in the ways they represent the relationship of the protagonist to the dominant spaces depicted". By virtue of this mechanical law, male protagonists try to enter some "encompassing" interior, whereas women try to escape from a "confining" interior. This hypothesis, which has been variously maintained since the creation of the phrase "female Gothic", cannot refer to all Gothic stories indifferently. With the exception of the secondary plot concerning Agnes, who is imprisoned in a secret cell of the convent, the major male character, Ambrosio, is the one to be actually captive in *The Monk*: abandoned by his parents at birth, he is inevitably destined to a solitary life enclosed within the dark walls of a lugubrious monastery. Antonia is not segregated and has no need to escape, except in the very last moments of the novel when she is entrapped within a symbolic labyrinth, the monastery's dungeon, which has also entangled Ambrosio.

Reeve's literary stance seems to deny the traditional distinction between male and female Gothic narratives. While recognising the value of Walpole's work, Reeve had openly criticised *Otranto* in the preface to her novel *The Old English Baron* (1778), a Gothic story that was proposed as a balanced alternative to what she considered Walpole's bizarre romance, founded on implausible exaggerations. Walpole's and Reeve's opposing views and techniques may represent a further confirmation of the risks of generalisations when applying gender distinction to Gothic narratives. With her work, Reeve reversed the notion that excesses belonged to female writing by creating a measured Gothic story, in which terror and the supernatural are carefully limited to the essential, both being devices meant to provide a revelation when the story is coming to an end. On the contrary, *The Castle of Otranto* contains several hyperboles and shocking events, the origin of which is unnatural and rarely plausible. The majority of early Gothic authors, whether male or female, seemed to privilege Walpole's narrative example and provoke a wide range of feelings and emotional reactions in readers. In reality, Reeve's balance and measure was too harmonious to be compatible with genuine Gothic descriptions of extreme events, which turned out to be much more popular and satisfy the readers' taste. Apart from Reeve's counterpoise to Walpole's Gothic excess, another aspect defines *The Old English Baron*'s characters and it is their emotional sterility, as the author is more interested in highlighting historical intrigues and past injustice, finally unveiled by a supernatural phenomenon, than enriching her plots with love and passion. Sentimental adventures were excluded from her novel and love only takes a limited space in the plot. Due to her constant preoccupation with narrative proportion, Reeve is probably the only Gothic author to consider sentimental episodes marginal in her plot, an aspect that Lee partially applied to *The Recess* (1786), where the claustrophobic context reproducing Mary Stuart's story in the Elizabethan era is, in reality, a reflection of eighteenth-century female anxieties (Jonathan Dent, 2016). Reeve's dictum was also adopted by Martha Harley. On the contrary, multiple sentimental or passionate plots abound in Walpole, Beckford, Smith, Radcliffe, Roche, Parsons, Lewis, Lathom, Robinson, Mary Anne Radcliffe and Dacre, among others, with no distinction of the writer's gender.

Both male and female Gothic writers show differences as well as analogies: an intriguing customary aspect is their dealing with innocence. A frequent common denominator in early Gothic narratives, innocence in danger, plays an important part in the plots and is generally sexual in nature, even though greed or mere cruelty can be agents of doom for innocent characters. Thus, a number of potential and/or real victims populate every single novel in the early Gothic era. Young women and, less frequently, young men risk facing lustful and violent characters in plots amalgamating terror and strong emotions with high doses of prurient connotations. Different typologies of danger provide a taxonomy of threats to young and innocent characters. Various forms of peril can be represented by an obscure and adverse fate, as in *The Castle of Otranto*, *The Castles of Athlin and Dunbayne*, *The Italian*, *Clermont* and *The*

Midnight Bell. A stolen inheritance or other kinds of dynastic injustice provoke vulnerability and jeopardy, as in *A Sicilian Romance, Emmeline, The Mysteries of Udolpho, The Romance of the Forest, Clermont, The Castle of Wolfenbach, The Castle of Mowbray, an English Romance, Hubert de Sevrac.* Cruel characters' dangerous and forbidden desires become a source of dread, as in *The Castle of Otranto, Vathek, The Castles of Athlin and Dunbayne, The Romance of the Forest, The Castle of Wolfenbach, The Mysteries of Udolpho, The Monk, Clermont, Zofloya* and *Manfroné, or The One-Handed Monk.* Vicissitudes of different kinds occupy a single novel, but the most evident aspect of the Gothic resides in more or less veiled licentious contexts menacing to disrupt innocence irreversibly, a feature that might have been absorbed from the Classics and French libertine literature. Libertine novels introduced different categories of lasciviousness depending on the protagonists' status. In effect, the different social position determined the tone and contents of the story, which could be carnal and thoughtless, or dangerously seductive and doomed to a moral fall. A token of the intellectual audacity of the eighteenth century and a step into modernity (Marine Ganofsky, 2021), French erotic fiction provides wide narrative material for inspiration in the eighteenth century.

Still a teenager, *Otranto*'s Conrad is the first innocent victim of the rising Gothic, whose brutal death shocks the reader at the beginning of the story. The only element to be clear, albeit inexplicable, is the surreal cause of the young character's premature death, which does not imply a crime of passion but a supernatural event prompted by past injustices. It is with female characters that things change: Isabella is a potential victim of Manfred's unrelenting desire, but she astutely avoids danger, whereas Matilda, his daughter, is destined to succumb to his patriarchal violence. *The Monk* features the graphic disruption of innocence of two young female characters, Antonia and Agnes, carried out by Ambrosio, who is himself a primeval victim of devilish agency, embodied by the enigmatic Matilda. A melancholic orphan, quite ignorant of the world, he has been devoted to prayer ever since he was abandoned at the monastery door when still an infant and is now a pious young abbot, suddenly surrounded by strange contingencies orchestrated by cruel demonic entities entangling him in a sinful maze. A naïve champion of moral integrity, he turns into the puppet of a strange destiny, which leads him to his doom. Lured by the lasciviousness proffered by Matilda, he ruins Antonia's innocence and hides the powerless girl in the dungeons of his monastery: "He doubted not, that being beyond the reach of help, cut off from the world and totally in his power, Antonia would comply with his desires. The affection which she had ever exprest for him, warranted this persuasion" (*The Monk*: 377). The images of death and decay he finds inside the sepulchre where he intends to hide his victim do not impair "his resolution to destroy Antonia's honour" (379). Lewis trespasses a limit that no other Gothic author had been able to reach. His female victims can be partially compared to Richardson's tragic Clarissa and De Sade's unfortunate Justine: the former is the victim of a single man's cruelty, whereas the latter undergoes infinite sexual tortures inflicted by several perpetrators, both males and females. Ambrosio's psychological metamorphoses are incomprehensible and disturbing. First an irreprehensible monk, who pitilessly orders Agnes's punishment, he then becomes Matilda's pawn. Infatuated with Antonia, he would like to play the role of a libertine, but he is unable to carry out a convincing form of seduction and relies on magic tools to become the girl's lover, as he is amatorily artless. One of the most risqué scenes in the novel occurs when Ambrosio peers down Antonia through a magic mirror, mingling the common trope of French libertine stories' voyeurism with fairy tale atmospheres (*The Monk*: 271–272):

A confused mixture of colours and images presented themselves to the Friar's eyes, which at length were arranging themselves to their proper places, He beheld in miniature Antonia's lovely form. The scene was a small closet belonging to her apartment. She was undressing to bathe herself. The long tresses of her hair were already bound up. The amorous Monk had full opportunity to observe the voluptuous contours and admirable symmetry of her person. She threw off her last garment, and advancing to the bath prepared for her, She put her foot into the water. It struck cold, and She drew it back again. Though unconscious of being observed, an in-bred sense of modesty induced her to veil her charms; and she stood hesitating upon the brink, in the attitude of the Venus de Medicis. At this moment a tame Linnet flew towards her, nestled its head between her breasts, and nibbled them in wanton play. The smiling Antonia strove in vain to shake off the Bird, and at length raised her hand to drive it from its delightful harbour. Ambrosio could bear no more: His desires were worked up to phrenzy.

The scene contains some interesting iconographic aspects. The object of uncontrollable desire, Antonia represents the metaphor of a complex system of references. She looks like the Classical statue of Venus, thus reiterating the analogy of her persona to a mythological being, and confirming the importance of classical influences in both Lewis's novel and the early Gothic. The image of the bath, which we analyse in the chapter about early Gothic iconographies, also contains an allusion to Boucher's rococo painting entitled *La Toilette de Venus* (1751), which Lewis probably imitates to convey a higher degree of sensuality by means of well-known images (Marnieri 2016). Antonia's nudity is the symbol of a voyeuristic stereotype in libertine literature, but also recalls the Biblical scene of Susan and the Elders, a clear indication of virtue in danger. The young woman embodies the archetype of powerless virtuousness. Ambrosio is not a patriarchal figure imposing his will, but a frustrated sensualist, incapable of fulfilling his desires and rapt in voluptuous thoughts meant to destroy innocence.

Dacre's intriguing novel *Zofloya* (1806), which in the writer's intention should have represented a mirror of *The Monk* featuring a female protagonist, follows the young main character's journey into progressive depravation. After being abandoned by their scandalous mother and mourning their father's death, Victoria and her brother, Leonardo, feel constant discontent, which leads them through a dangerous path. Even though they could improve their situation, they are doomed to adversity. Unlike other female characters in the Gothic, Victoria is willing to adopt profligacy and murder, which makes her antithetical to Gothic heroines. Once she is married to a young and rich aristocrat, Berenza, who tenderly requites her love, Victoria becomes restless. Indifferent to the joys that surround her, she lusts after her husband's brother, Henriquez, and would like to eliminate all the people between them, without realising her passion is not reciprocated. Like Ambrosio, Victoria is apparently seduced and tricked by one of the devil's pitiless intermediaries and carries out ruthless actions to satisfy her lechery. Helped by the ambiguous Zofloya, she kidnaps unsuspicious Lilla, Henriquez's virtuous fiancée, and takes her to a distant cavern where she intends to keep her prisoner:

Lilla opened her eyes. Without being fully restored to sense, she perceived with dismay her situation—she essayed to speak, but could not, and starting up, cast herself despairingly upon her knees, raising her innocent hands in agonised supplication. The motion and noise of the chains caused Victoria to turn her head—she beheld the kneeling defenceless orphan—but she only saw her rival, and pausing while a smile of exulting malice passed over her features, she waved her hand as in derision, and instantly hastened on. As she gained the mouth of the aperture, and retreated from the sight of the wretched girl, who with horror had recognised Victoria, a shrill and piercing scream assailed her ears, but failed to excite in her breast one emotion of pity, for the state in which she had abandoned her. (*Zofloya*: 205)

Wrongly convinced that her unmerciful actions will conquer the reluctant object of her passion, Victoria sacrifices innocence in the cruellest way, but to no avail. Victoria intends to destroy innocence and purity without understanding that in so doing she embraces the horror of crime and is consigned to perdition.

Unlimited viciousness is also shown in a subsequent novel that re-established the traditional Gothic cliché of the persecuted heroine. Published in 1809, the highly inventive *Manfroné, or The One-Handed Monk*, was written by the mysterious Mary Anne Radcliffe (also spelled Mary Ann), identified with at least two possible authors (Norton 2000a), whereas the hypothesis of a pseudonym to attract more readers may not be excluded. The very first lines of *Manfroné* are dense with suspense and extremely shocking, as they apparently show a rape, providentially interrupted by the victim's father and his guards. In the still of night, when beautiful Rosalina is asleep, a mysterious man has entered her room through a hidden passage connecting secret chambers, corridors, and dungeons in the mazy castle, where the young woman lives with her father and servants:

Rosalina started, for at the first glance she imagined the form before her was that of some supernatural visitant: her senses were fast congealing with horror, and the lamp dropped from her trembling hand; but, in a moment after she was terribly convinced of the contrary, for she felt herself seized by a firm grasp, from which she was unable to disengage herself. The lamp, when it fell to the floor was extinguished; and thus, in utter darkness, Rosalina was at the mercy of some unknown assailant, whose base purpose soon became no matter of doubt. (*Manfroné*: 4)

The scene shockingly takes readers by surprise to unchain their feelings of terror and promote their empathy. Early Gothic strategies have been absorbed by the author, who, unlike previous Gothic novelists, does not wait for the plot to evolve, but immediately introduces a daunting context of horror, exploiting the visual by means of the disquieting darkness enveloping horrifying shadows, and provokes intense emotions in the reader. Obscurity is first linked to the supernatural and the shadows moving in the room are perceived as ghosts until the physicality of the firm grasp on Rosalina's arm dissipates any doubt on the nature of the perpetrator, who is not a spiritual entity but a real person instead.

254

Suddenly, Rosalina's "piercing shrieks re-echoed through the vaulted corridors of the castello" (4), and her desperate cries awake her father, who manages to wound the unknown aggressor, but cannot capture him, as the furtive, ghostly figure promptly escapes through an invisible secret passage. The failed rape is just one of the many attempts carried out by mysterious characters to destroy the girl's innocence. Danger is constant and many times Rosalina is on the verge of disaster, but the obscure forces surrounding her do not corrupt her.

However antithetical, Beckford and Radcliffe share unexpected characteristics in their plots, among which we can find the descriptions of strong emotions, and the disruption (either concrete or potential) of innocence. Although the events showing how innocent creatures' lives are dominated by unscrupulous beings are fictional, and stories are set in a vague past, both Beckford and Radcliffe convey ideas that transcend literary invention, as their novels seem to provide clues about the society of their time. Both authors depict dangerous passions that drive some characters' actions and become the cause of their doom. The adolescent heroine in Radcliffe's *The Romance of the Forest,* is introduced a few pages after the beginning of the narration when she is about to lose her life. After refusing to take the veil in Paris, she has been brought to a sordid cottage in the countryside, as some criminals have received the fatal order from her father. Rape and murder are a clear and present danger. The scene transmits extreme distress, as the destiny of an innocent creature is at stake. Adeline is suffocated by despair and horror while the tragic facts unfold directly under the reader's gaze. Even though de la Motte saves her, Adeline later narrates the dramatic event through a new personal perspective, confirming its importance in the economy of the story. If on the one hand, Adeline's innocence transforms her into a potential prey, on the other hand, it provokes strong emotions in both the banditti and the Parisian nobleman. Adeline is aware of her powerlessness in a male-dominated society, which can steal her wealth and titles and exploit her naiveté in many ways. Later in the story, she is kidnapped again, this time by the libertine Montalt, whose actions are dictated by his obscure passion for the young woman:

[T]he door opened, and the Marquis de Montalt appeared. He approached the sofa where Adeline sat, and addressed her, but she heard not his voice–she had fainted. [...] Two young women entered, and, when she began to revive, he left them to prepare her for his reappearance. When Adeline perceived that the Marquis was gone, and that she was in the care of women, her spirits gradually returned, she looked at her attendants, and was surprised to see so much elegance and beauty. Some endeavour she made to interest their pity, but they seemed wholly insensible to her distress, and began to talk of the Marquis in terms of the highest admiration. They assured her it would be her own fault if she was not happy, and advised her to appear so in his presence. It was with the utmost difficulty that Adeline forbore to express her disdain which was rising to her lips, and that she listened to their discourse in silence. But she saw the inconvenience and fruitlessness of opposition. (*RF*: 158)

Montalt acts as a dissolute rake, who not only lives in luxury but also controls a harem of filles de joie, ready to satisfy his commands. Intimately similar to Vathek, he desires Adeline for her beauty and innocence that take him off guard. Radcliffe's originality lies in the choice of an ingenuous character, who finds the strength to preserve her own integrity. In spite of its dangerous contexts, *The Romance of the Forest* does not actually belong to the category of "seduction stories" which "obsessed British writers and readers alike from the Restoration of the Monarchy between 1660 and the end of the Eighteenth Century" (Bowers: 140), even though implicit sensuality plays a remarkable role in the development of Radcliffe's novel. As Bowers argues, "[p]lots featuring coercive heterosexual relations, where questions about force and complicity loom large, recurred in virtually all genres, they were a language that everyone spoke, a focusing point for popular fantasy across social divides". *Pamela* and *Clarissa* were amongst the most popular seduction stories in Great Britain together with French enlightened literature offering a wide range of both dramatic and comedic seduction stories either frivolous, supernatural or tragic. Diderot's facetious *Les Bijoux Indiscrets* (1747) and Cazotte's supernatural *Le Diable Amoureux* (1772) provide remarkable examples. Choderlos de Laclos's *Les Liaisons Dangereuses* (1782), wherein different categories of emotions, passions and sexual intercourses are described in detail, is probably the best example of a record of libertine seductions of innocent victims ending in tragedy. Radcliffe does not, however, envisage a passive heroine doomed to be conquered. Notwithstanding her candour and inexperience, Adeline is no Clarissa. She is conscious of her moral duties and is not intimidated by violence. Although she faces distressing situations, she is resolved to preserve her innocence and avoids other people's deviating passions potentially threatening her life. *The Romance of the Forest*'s author shows a level of originality compared to the literary conventions of seduction stories because Adeline–and Radcliffe's other female characters in general– abandons the victim's role marked by passivity and becomes an action-oriented maker of her own destiny. A strange form of paralysis seems to crystallise the characters' lives in certain contexts (e.g. Adeline's forest; Emily's castle; Ellena's convent). Adeline escapes danger on more than one occasion, despite undergoing a series of ordeals. The young protagonist turns into a courageous being when she runs away from Montalt's trap and escapes from the enchanted forest. Mastering her own destiny and fighting against adverse circumstances, she takes economic, social and moral responsibilities upon herself in order to re-start her life-cycle. Her jeopardised innocence is perfectly preserved.

A few years earlier, Beckford had described ardent desires in the strange story of the hedonistic caliph. Beckford's aesthetic introduction of Vathek's majestic court resembles a Garden of Eden, in which the caliph indulges on all his passions without restraint. The scenes are in sharp contrast with the development of the story, also imbued with a chain of inexplicable situations. Some scenes in *Vathek* offer an example of bucolic calmness derived from classical beauty, but horrible dangers are looming, as a devilish agent, whose identity is a persistent mystery throughout the whole novel (like Matilda's in *The Monk*), destroys a great number of lives. Similar to a monster, the Giaour "had the grin of an Ogre" (*Vathek*: 20), he had "accents more sonorous than thunder" (22). In the end, he becomes a demonic intermediary pretending to satisfy Vathek's appetites. Exploiting Vathek's yearning for the unknown, the repulsive creature has promised the protagonist some magic talismans, but he wants innocent blood in exchange. A group of unsuspicious children are ambiguously stripped naked to show the perfection of their bodies, an aspect that did not go unobserved, and unchained many strictures for the sexual connotations that the scene conveyed. Even though the reader cannot decipher what happens to the children in the Giaour's dark abyss, it is clear that their innocence has been somehow cruelly destroyed. Vathek continues his atrocities and separates Nouronihar and her pre-adolescent fiancé, Gulchenrouz. Like Radcliffe's Adeline and Lewis's Antonia, Nouronihar stands out for her extraordinary beauty and delicate maidenhood, prompting the caliph's uncontrollable infatuation. Even though Vathek's first meeting with Nouronihar resonates with the idealised mode of late medieval love poetry, the context features, in fact, a problematic relationship between an adult and an adolescent. Vathek is enchanted by the delicate countenance of the young princess. The power of the girl unconsciously seducing the caliph is connected to her aura of modesty, which is, however, lost in a few moments. Her young future husband, a sensitive boy in his puberty, whose beauty is obsessively described, is violently sacrificed by Carathis, who rejoices in annihilating his innocence, after performing demonic liturgies, altogether indifferent to the suffering she provokes. Like the giantess Eriphila riding a hideous creature to chase Rinaldo in the seventh canto of Ariosto's *Orlando Furioso*, Carathis starts her journey with an equally horrible creature, as demonic as the Giaour, spreading terror over her land. Unchained and uncontrollable cupidity determines the protagonists' tragic destiny. Unlike the crucial moments in *The Monk*, in which sexuality and violence are described graphically, *Vathek* does not give precise details of the crimes that are perpetrated against innocence, leaving them suspended in imagination. Purity is nevertheless destroyed or tainted without exceptions. Initially a perpetrator, Vathek becomes himself a victim in the end, bedazzled by his lover, a primeval symbol of innocence turned into a merciless woman, anticipating themes of the second generation of Romantic poets.

Although both Beckford and Radcliffe are concerned with uncommon circumstances and in spite of the strong passions shown by a number of characters, their novels appear to be diametrically opposed, as Radcliffe is interested in suspense and unexpected turns of events, while Beckford generally shows other-worldly and improbable contexts. However, the two writers show a common ambiguity. The fervour shown by powerful characters to subjugate weaker creatures and the cruelty against powerless young characters provide clues that go beyond fictional invention to reflect eighteenth-century issues. Parreaux (1960b) and Alexander (1962) identify biographical aspects in *Vathek*, while Norton (1999a, 2000b) and Miles (1995) trace personal details in Radcliffe's works, which supposedly betray experiences of parental and/or adult abuse at a very young age. Beckford's concealment and Radcliffe's scarcity of outstanding personal details provide a limited spectrum of hypotheses. However, the longing for the forbidden and the obsession for innocence, or the constant intrinsic risk of destroying it, dominate their stories and most works by early Gothic novelists. One of the early Gothic points of convergence is the constant danger faced by innocence that can be either preserved (Radcliffe, Walpole, Reeve, Harley, Smith, Roche, Parsons, Lathom, Robinson, Mary Anne Radcliffe) or destroyed (Walpole, Beckford, Lewis, Dacre). The gripping presence of peril dominating multiple pages of early Gothic novels is likely to be connected to real life problematic situations of the period. It is a special focus, linked to social and legal aspects of contemporary society. Even though Beckford's, Radcliffe's and other Gothic authors' novels cannot be included in the category of erotic novels, they are debatable for the dangerous obsessions and moral transgressions that they often feature. The early Gothic indisputably offers many forms of both subconscious and evident sexuality despite an overall ethical stance and the latent moralism of conclusions.

A beguiling common denominator in the early Gothic novels is the mystery surrounding female figures, whose beauty can be felt but often misunderstood. In *Otranto,* Theodore imagines Matilda but cannot observe her because of the obscurity that frequently surrounds them and strange obstacles do not allow him to be with her. On the other hand, the luminous beauty of Nouronihar stupefies Vathek and renders him dreamy and melancholic. The tormenting effect of mysterious beauty in Lewis reaches a superior technical level in *The Monk* episodes concerning Antonia. Her immature but inebriating attractiveness is exacerbated when the veil on her head only partially reveals her harmonious forms, or when she barely covers her naked body while she is secretly observed. A highly allegorical symbol, the trope of the veil is shown with problematic persistence in *The Monk.* Kosofsky Sedgwick (1981: 256) defines the veil as "a physical, a metonymical and a metaphorical object", disconnected from hypocrisy or concealment but "suffused with sexuality" (258). The veil is the basic paradigm of prohibition and sexual desire. When Vathek first meets Nouronihar, she throws jasmine petals at him. He is hypnotised by the perfumes around him emanating from the girl and her companions:

The fragrance diffused from their hair, struck the sense of Vathek, who, in an ecstacy, suspending his repast, said to Bababalouk: 'Are the Peries come down from their spheres? Note her, in particular, whose form is so perfect; venturously running on the brink of the precipice, and turning back her head, as regardless of nothing but the graceful flow of her robe. With what captivating impatience does she contend with the bushes her veil? Could it be her that threw the jasmine at me?' (*Vathek*: 62–63)

Interestingly the beautiful girl is "on the brink of a precipice" like the young victims who were sacrificed in the previous episodes, but she seems to magically avoid danger. Nouronihar's first images are of a girl who is hidden in her silky robe. Her veil together with pleasant fragrances are enough to strike the caliph's senses and seduce him. The image of the veil is iterative in both Radcliffe's and Lewis's stories. Lorenzo de Medina is attracted to Antonia, but he cannot observe her because of the veil hiding her traits on their first meeting. Captured by Ellena's voice, Antonio De Vivaldi is desperate to see her face concealed by a veil in *The Italian*. Ellena as well as Antonia are not only superbly beautiful but they are supreme examples of modesty. On the contrary, the veil, which should hide their features and protect them, acquires a sensual connotation and increases male curiosity, conversely becoming a metaphor of desire. Similar to a veil that covers her features, Matilda's religious garments cover her face, but offer a glimpse of her ivory breast to inflame artless Ambrosio's senses, conveying connotations of mystery and falsity. The meaning of the veil is complex, as it also becomes a carrier of death, a shroud that separates the characters from their impending destiny. The function of the veil covering Laurentini's image in *The Mysteries of Udolpho* is the omen of sinful horror. That the ambiguity of the veil can convey a multiplicity of opposing meanings is confirmed by Jesse Molesworth's (2009) hypothesis, which considers this trope as a symbol of the hymen, the sexual act, and the characters' loss of virginity. Napier (1987: 113–115) identifies the veil as a metaphor of the hypocrisy underlying *The Monk*'s narrative technique, based on the dialectics of irreconcilable features. At first the text seems to declare that the "moral impetus of the novel is that of unmasking, of exposing, and revealing" and although "[t]he resolution of the narrative seems to depend on a process of revelation and unmasking", it is actually developed in parallel with recurrent "images [...] of veiling and distancing" (127). Elisabeth Broadwell (1975) was the first to analyse the meaning of the veil in Radcliffe, identifying it with both chastity and mystery. Reiterated images of the "veil" are also found in *A Sicilian Romance* and *The Romance of the Forest*. Suzanne Greenfield (1992) and Carol Ann Howells (1973) consider the veil as an expression of lesbian desire and interpret the affection between the long lost mother Olivia, segregated in a convent, and the emotional daughter, Ellena, in *The Italian*, as clear signs of sexual attachment. Raymond Mise (1980) reversed the idea and unconvincingly supported the improbable theory of a latent incestuous relationship in *The Romance of the Forest*. He translated Adeline's nightmares and repetitive fainting as a symbol of desire for her father, without clarifying if she feels desire for her real father, whom she has never met and has long been deceased, or if she thinks about her cruel foster father, whom she fears for his brutality. The ambiguity of this supposed secret desire is even greater, as she meets two father figures in her peregrinations, Pierre de la Motte and La Luc, who try to protect her from evil as much as they can. This hypothesis seems to be in total opposition to the heroine's spirit and implausibly distorts her persona.

Mixed with ambiguity, the crimes that are perpetrated, or are narrowly avoided, have strange connotations and are connected with forbidden or even pathological forms of desire accompanied by the will to destroy weaker beings. The reprise of sensual contexts creates an ideal link between the early Gothic and French libertine and anti-clerical literature. As far as erotic publications, the spirit of the century and the need for representation were concerned, Grantham Turner (2005: 216) provides an interesting explanation:

The eighteenth-century novel should be placed within a complex network of clandestine reading, looking, and reporting, demonstrated by an episode in Casanova's memoirs, ostensibly true though drenched in fiction throughout (and written, of course, in French), as if staged for a larger audience. A high-born nun in Murano, known only by the initials 'M.M.', invites him to a secret casino where they browse in, and re-enact, the erotic texts and pictures that line the room—a definitive library of Enlightenment libertinism. In this private space, sex becomes not an expression of intimacy, but a self-conscious performance.

The truthfulness of the episode has not been demonstrated, and there is still a lot of controversy about the story, which was even more complex, as the nun M.M. had another lover, the Abbé Bernis, the French Ambassador in Venice. Apparently, the ambassador had created a casino with two twin rooms divided by a wall decorated with erotic scenes in Rococo style, hiding a series of holes allowing each visitor to observe the other room undisturbed. He supposedly observed his lover making love with Casanova, or together with M.M., he observed Casanova's effusions with one of his mistresses. Casanova's narration increases the sense of suspense because the secret police watches him while he is observed by the Ambassador, who is, at his turn, under surveillance by the French monarchy. The narration offers an interesting interplay of male and female gazes crossing with the enemy's equally voyeuristic eye providing a sort of pornographic panopticon. The visual power of erotic images influence the protagonists of the scene and are an illicit *ékphrasis* promoting unchained sensuality and dissolute sexuality. They confirm the growing importance of the visual in the eighteenth-century. Published in French in the mid-1780s, Casanova's writings were extremely popular and propagated notorious legends around the adventurous Italian libertine.

The insistence of Gothic criticism on genre codification to distinguish the novel from romance probably reveals a need to determine differences in styles as well as in social messages. Pallavicino's scandalous work *La Retorica delle Puttane* (1642) and translated in English as *The Whores' Rhetorick* in 1683, unexpectedly discouraged "the courtesan from reading high-flown Romances because they promote[d] sexual virtue and constancy, recommending instead the cynical comedy and the aphrodisiac Novel" (Grantham Turner: 221). Curiously, the meaning of romance in the seventeenth century was linked to a romantic idea interspersed with fabulous events excluding libertine episodes. On the contrary, the early Gothic showed a predilection for romance, which it transformed by merging various literary ingredients to create a composite form, wherein different nuances of sexuality were included. The Gothic's female characters, living in Medieval Scotland, Spain during the Inquisition, Medieval Italy, Renaissance Italy, early eighteenth-century France and Savoy, or eighteenth-century Naples, reflect in reality the conditions of adolescent orphans in England in the eighteenth century in a period when women's status in society was dangerously unstable. The difficulties that Adeline experiences in *The Romance of the Forest* are realistic and the dangers she faces are concrete, as she has no social status or couverture to preserve her. Any protection she might receive from relatives or strangers is ephemeral, as she has neither parents nor a spouse. Nevertheless, Radcliffe daringly finds a solution that is more than a compromise. What she envisages is an innocent young woman, the potential victim, who can defend herself. Like Emily, Ellena, Madeline, Matilda, Rosalina and many other early Gothic heroines, Adeline overcomes all difficulties and acquires a revolutionary form of conscious independence.

On the contrary, Beckford's hedonistic Vathek is punished because of his crimes, a tragic destiny that he shares with Lewis's Ambrosio, Walpole's Manfred and Dacre's Victoria. Unfortunately, there is no possible redemption for their victims, whose innocence is forever lost. Scholars have frequently taken Beckford's proclivity for pre-adolescent sensuality as evidence of the shady episode involving William Courtenay, 9th Earl of Devon, eight years his junior. The lack of clarity in contemporary reports and the general reluctance to speak about the events that changed the course of Beckford's life (and Courtenay's life as well) do not permit to properly understand what really happened between the two. Apparently, their mutual feeling was strong from the very beginning when Beckford was still an adolescent. After their meeting, Beckford was precautionarily sent to Europe with his tutor Lettice as a chaperon by his severe mother. However, Beckford's behaviour was even more frivolous on the Continent than at home. For this reason, he was talked into settling down and, once back in England, he got married at twenty-three, and it was when his wife was pregnant with their first daughter that he was found by one of his uncles locked in a room with the younger William during a reception in 1784. A number of scholars agree on the fact that some of Beckford's relatives set up the scandal, eager, as they were, to gain his political position in Parliament. However, it is true that Beckford's ambiguity cannot be fundamentally erased. Caliph Vathek's disturbing nonchalance employed to exploit young lives, albeit with grotesque effects, may seriously mirror a concrete situation in real life where the legal system may not have been adequate to prevent abuses towards children, preadolescents and young people.

In his engaging article on a scandalous case, which took place in Venice in 1785, Larry Wolff (2005) interestingly explains how the parameters to judge a sexual crime at the time were altogether different from our twenty-first-centuries social perspectives. A number of transgressions did not have the legal specification they have today. Analysing a trial of a rich Venetian elderly man (Gaetano Franceschini) employing an eight-year-old (Paolina Lozaro) and making her sleep in his bed, Wolff clarifies that (418):

The thick case file offers to the historian of the ancient *regime* one of the most comprehensive explorations of the phenomenon that we today call 'sexual abuse' or 'paedophilia'—for which there were no such clarifying clinical or legal designations in the world of the 1780s. Though the inclinations of Franceschini may have seemed "depraved" to some of his neighbours, including Father Fiorese (the priest that had denounced Franceschini), the absence of any clearly identified concept of sexual abuse meant that even the most comprehensive investigation, seeking to establish the facts of the case, would inevitably find it difficult to assess the legal significance and implications of those facts. The case of Franceschini and Lozaro thus offers insight, at a remarkable level of detail, into contemporary perspectives on sexual relations between adults and children.

Although, as Wolff puts it, "the eighteenth century possessed neither the legal framework nor the conceptual vocabulary" to recognise sexual abuse (436), Franceschini's housekeeper, in her testimony to the tribunal, had declared that she felt "repugnance at cooperating in the sacrifice of an innocent" (420), showing that individual moral sense could not accept the situation, no matter how nebulous the legal system might have been in that respect. Sexual misconducts were not legally defined with clarity. Specific acts, such as adultery, might have had quite serious consequences as in the case of Lorenzo Da Ponte, Mozart's librettist. The Italian artist had risked being involved in tragic consequences for having a liaison with a married woman and had been forced to escape to Vienna to avoid conviction. Moreover, Wolff believes that the libertinism exalted by the supposed paedophile Franceschini was not considered different from the libertinism expressed by a paragon of seduction, such as Casanova, who had apparently a similar penchant to Franceschini's for pubescent and pre-pubescent girls. Casanova's erotic memoirs and De Sade's pornographic stories, respectively published in the 1780s and 1790s, highlight the connection between libertinism and the will to violate innocence. It might be useful to make a distinction: Casanova's autobiography, written in French to reach a wider public, features episodes showing a theatrical quality to entertain and impress the reader, as Grantham Turner has highlighted. On the contrary, De Sade's systematic and violent shattering of innocence in his writings, and particularly in *The 120 Days of Sodom* (1785), *Justine, ou les malheurs de la vertu* (1791), and *Juliette, ou les prospérités du vice* (1797), provides a dialectical and disturbing demonstration of how virtue is sadly ineffectual and useless in a world dominated by opportunism and hypocrisy, wherein success thrives on vice, depravation and crime. De Sade's texts are more philosophical manifestos of ethical paradoxes than genuine novels, in which sex is inevitably accompanied by cruelty, violence and torture.

However different from the Venetian Franceschini, Beckford's scandal with Fontenay is probably difficult to determine from the point of view of our present cultural universe. Gayle Rubin's (1989: 679) explanation, based on Michel Foucault's intuitions in *History of Sexuality*, can help to understand the level of contemporary potential misinterpretations: "In spite of many continuities with ancestral forms, modern sexual arrangements have a distinctive character which sets them apart from pre-existing systems". The great social changes brought about by "industrialization" and "urbanization" in Western Europe and the United States in the nineteenth century modified a variety of aspects of human life, and they "also gave rise to a new sexual system characterised by distinct types of sexual persons, populations, stratification, and political conflict". A peculiar example of the enlightened century divergent perspectives can be found in an unexpected episode of a revered philosopher's life. A few years before the 1780s, Rousseau had interestingly envisaged equality between men and women, respectively represented by the two female protagonists, Julie and Sophie, in his popular philosophical novel, *La Nouvelle Heloise* (1760), which was burnt in protest after its publication because of its ambiguity concerning the protagonists' liaisons, a sort of ménage à trois. The philosopher's pedagogical treatise, *Emile, or on Education*, published in 1762, had introduced the initially rejected idea of respect towards children, who traditionally belonged to the weaker layers of society. The text highlighted the intrinsic innocence of young age and the dangers of a corrupted society, based on injustice. In Wolff's words (432), "*Emile* offered a modern conception of childhood's innocence as something that naturally appertained to the child, and of which the child could only wrongly be deprived". However, Rousseau's autobiographical memoir, *Les Confessions* (1782), revealed a strange circumstance involving the philosopher and one of his friends while they were living in Venice. The two men decided to hire a little girl to keep them company. Although Rousseau candidly confessed he developed fatherly feelings for the child, the peculiar ménage may raise several brows. Concerning Franceschini's confusing case due to the lack of evident sexual abuse in Paolina Lozaro's body, Wolff highlights legal aspects of the time (418, 436):

The legal forum for the prosecution was the unusual Venetian tribunal, *Esecutori contro la Bestemmia*, executors against blasphemy—which had to try to formulate the charges in a way that made sense according to Venetian law. [...] Ultimately, the impossibility of articulating a modern concept of sexual abuse meant that Franceschini's conduct would be prosecuted under the very general rubric of scandal.

Different violations—from cursing to adultery—were all judged by the same tribunal against blasphemy notwithstanding their different characteristics. Moreover, the verdicts that were issued for a multiplicity of scandals were not homogenous. Even Beckford's personal case in real life is probably difficult to determine from the point of view of the present cultural and legal universe. The novel *Vathek* latently introduces problematic crimes against children and describes different forms of immoral passions, potentially connected to paedophilia.

Lewis, who recreated, by modifying and reversing it, Radcliffe's *The Mysteries of Udolpho*, was the Gothic author that took the disruption of innocence to extreme consequences, partially reproducing De Sade's creed, even though no character professes libertinism in *The Monk*, whose protagonist has to turn to magic in order to acquire the power to carry out his wrongs. Like Smith, Roche, Mary Anne Radcliffe, and, in a way, also Walpole, Radcliffe creates female characters that are strong enough to face the sudden twists of fortune, once they are catapulted into real life and, most important, successfully preserve their innocence, whereas Lewis's Antonia, unwillingly, and Ambrosio, willingly, succumb to danger and temptation. Presented as a "male Eve", Ambrosio acts entirely out of lust. The analogy between Ambrosio and the biblical Eve is remarkable in the scene of the serpent in the cloister garden. Williams (1995: 116) claims that his failure is a progressive "feminization" of his character: when he becomes the prey to desire and is imbued with a new sensibility, he is doomed to fail. The discovery of sensuality turns him into a woman, as far as his inner sensations are concerned. His postcoitus frustrations seem to betray a secret queer desire he is unable to express clearly. Williams adds, "The Monk, like the stereotypical female of medieval theology is weak, irrational, carnal [and] his own feminine side" (120) leads him to destitution. *Ambrosio's* carnality reproduces Aristotle's paradigm: evil is directly linked to the female. Ambrosio becomes irrational and emotional–a weakness inversely proportional to Matilda's growing self-control and indifference. In his essay on "Queer Gothic", Haggerty (2008: 389) postulates that Ambrosio's violence and incest are an extreme form of a primeval patriarchal role that he fulfils violently. However, incest was one of the most tragic features in stories of Antiquity, which did not necessarily involve patriarchal modes and which were recreated by Walpole in *The Mysterious Mother* and Robinson in *Vancenza*. Other critics have seen a feminised Ambrosio in contrast with a masculinised Matilda. In particular, Brewer's hypothesis (2001) is similar and specular to Williams's idea (1995) of an emasculated Ambrosio. Williams puts the stress on Ambrosio's excessive sensibility that renders him hysterical, uncontrollable and a victim of desire, whereas Brewer analyses the progressive increase of psychological male characteristics in Matilda that he sees as the prototype of a liberated woman. However, Matilda's liquid identity and innate cruelty cannot actually promote her character as a spokesperson for women, whereas other Gothic female characters become self-assertive and manage to protect their innocence by developing a genuine independent mode, which is exemplary and inspiring. Early Gothic writers transformed and adapted a variety of literary sources. Undervalued and excluded from the cultural mainstream for their narrative choices and their unusual themes, they contributed to remarkable changes in subsequent diegeses. They showed a great degree of originality and introduced romantic atmospheres as well as strange gloomy contexts, filled with mysteries and ambiguities. They featured dangerous emotions in some of their characters, which, in all probability, reflected problematic aspects of society that had not been thoroughly analysed before. They deviated from previous stereotyped patterns oscillating between the powerless victims (Richardson's *Clarissa*) or the unscrupulous women (Defoe's *Moll Flanders*, Cleland's *Fanny Hill*), and introduced ambiguous and threatening situations by filtering them in a subliminal way through stories based on adventure and imagination, with unexpected developments. One element that transpires from their Gothic narratives is the constant menace that any form of innocence has to face. The obsessive threat that is lurking on young and innocent characters is the reflection of a contradictory society that the novelists unconsciously desired to show and, probably, to change. In spite of the new philosophical supremacy of reason and the outstanding technological innovations of the period, obscure and anguishing contexts persisted and re-emerged in a number of works of literature, as the deep self in the unconscious tries to reach awareness. More in-depth analyses of Beckford, Radcliffe, Lewis and other authors active in the decades at the turn of the century could help us discover important clues behind the descriptions of passions and deviations, which were to a certain extent the hidden mirrors of the long eighteenth century's latent contradictions.

So wild, so romantic a spot, seemed rather the work of enchantment, than the earthly habitation of anything mortal! The harmonious warblings of the feathered minstrels; the murmuring sound of intermingling streams; the lulling moans of the confined breezes, amidst the flint-rooted pines that waved their tall heads, rocking their callow tenants in leafy cradles; the verdant glades, here and there opening to the skies, and scattered over with sheep and wild goats; the adjacent hills hanging their dark brows over a vast sheet of quivering water; presented a scene so magnificent, so abstracted from the busy world, that the beholder's heart thrilled with delicious transport, harmonized by the sublime sensations of enchanting melancholy.

(Mary Robinson, *Vancenza, or the Dangers of Credulity*)

Mary Darby Robinson occupies a particular position in the early Gothic panorama. If on the one hand, she was the real precursor and inventor of Romanticism, on the other hand she entered the early Gothic mania with some delay in the 1790s, when quite a large number of works of the genre had already been published. With the exception of Walpole, she was older than all the Gothic writers analysed in this text. Robinson died on 26 December 1800 at forty-three. Her date of birth was probably November 1757, even if she claimed she was born in 1758 in her autobiography, published posthumously. Her daughter, Mary Elisabeth Robinson, co-wrote, completed and published her mother's *Memoirs* in 1801. When Mary Elisabeth decided to publish a tribute collection of Romantic poems in memory of her mother in 1802, she also asked Coleridge for his contribution. The answer she received was harsh and piqued. The poet rebuked Mary's daughter sternly claiming he had a reputation to preserve, and his own children to protect from shame. He claimed that he could not be published together "with those men, who have sold their provocative to vulgar Debauchers, & vicious School boys", such as "Mr. Lewis and Mr. Moore" (Anne Close 2006: 174). Polwhele's violent criticism against women writers may have also had a role in Coleridge's reaction. Women following the ideals of Jacobinism were subject to hoydenism, transfigured as they were into supposedly bad copies of men (Saglia 2009: 731). Maybe Coleridge's rejection was not only due to the risk of vicinity with "a Pander to the Devil" (Close: 187), the notorious author of *The Monk,* as he described Lewis in the same letter. It was not only Polwhele's pitiless critique but it was also the inescapable sense of scandal that was still connected with the glamorous but unfortunate image of Mary Robinson, even after her death. Yet only a few years before Robinson had become Coleridge's complementary poetic voice when, inspired by his lines of *Kubla Kahn*, she wrote a poem dedicated to him, which started a poetic correspondence. As Fulford (1999) explains, in spite of his general rejection of literary women, Coleridge fell under her spell and praised her stimulating and fascinating metre.

Following her mother's advice, who was under the illusion of acquiring economic and financial security, after her estranged husband had forced them to close their school where she was a teacher, young Mary, née Darby, married Thomas Robinson. However, the man did not possess the inheritance that he had boasted about, creating false expectations and preparing a life of misery for Mary. In fact, he was a lazy law student, a gambler and an impenitent womanizer and soon ended up in prison for debts. Mary stayed behind bars for more than a year with him and their little daughter, Mary Elisabeth, born in 1775. She wrote a second collection of poems that Duchess Georgiana Spenser helped her publish while in prison. Meanwhile Mary carried out tasks that her husband was supposed to do instead to get out of prison. Thanks to Garrick's intervention, she started acting in 1776. It was in 1779 that young Prince of Wales fell in love with her when he saw her during a Shakespearian performance. The affair went on for some time after Mary had abandoned her husband. Mary was "the woman famous and infamous in London society as 'Perdita'" (Paula Byrne, 2004: 1). Byrne's biography has the merit of setting several wrong details right about the personal and literary figure of Robinson. Byrne ironically claims that Robinson was a sort of "Madonna of her times" (2). Our world is running fast and even this claim may be considered obsolete a few years later, when social media dominate global communication and different symbols and personalities influence the collective imagination. Certainly, Robinson was an icon during her times and attracted unrelenting interest, even if, as Elisabeth Campbell Denlinger explains (2005) in her essay about literary women in the pre-Victorian era, Robinson's reputation was tainted. However, her persona created constant attention for her remarkable beauty, her elegance, and her rich literary output. Robinson had been a precocious genius. Once her father abandoned her mother and siblings and even before her teen years, she worked as a teacher and started writing poems. Her compositions not only showed her ample classical culture but also evinced her pioneering Romantic spirit, which manifested more than a decade before egotistical poets Wordsworth and Coleridge started their Romantic legend with the publication of the *Lyrical Ballads*. Mary was part of the Della Cruscan poetic exchange (using various nicknames), attracting further attention to her elegant rhyming. She became an appreciated actress, famous for Shakespearian interpretations, and was also a playwright. She dominated the cultural scene in the last two decades of the eighteenth century before her premature death: "From the stage to politics and from the pleasure gardens to the press, Robinson was a prominent player in many cultural arenas of late-eighteenth-century London. As a fashion icon, she popularized the latest Parisian designs, which were then carefully reported in magazines and imitated by other women and aspiring leaders of taste" (Saglia 2009: 718). Newspapers and magazines of the time dedicated considerable space to Robinson's appearances and her creativity in fashion novelties. The *Morning Herald*, the *Morning Chronicle,* the *London Chronicle* and the *Lady's Magazine*, in particular, kept the public, especially "the votaries of Venus", constantly informed about Robinson (Gamer and Robinson 2008: 223–224). At the zenith of her beauty, before the illness struck her badly leaving her partially paralysed–maybe because of a serious infection she had contracted during a miscarriage–she was described as "a superior Splendour" casting shadows on all the "other Beauties" in one of the frequent panegyrics dedicated to her by the *Morning Herald* between 1782 and 1783 (221). Robinson was a Romantic poetess, imbued with classical, medieval and renaissance knowledge, a literary woman and an intellectual preoccupied with the status of women and a fashion icon dominating the London scene. Her activity was tenacious considering that she was a playwright, a socialite, a poet, a novelist, a translator, a journalist and an essayist before her death, caused by a series of illnesses troubling great part of her adult life. "The theatre not only provided the central vehicle for Robinson's transformation of herself from actress to icon, but also governed her metamorphosis in the late 1780s from icon to poet" (220).

Robinson was known as "Perdita" (Byrne 2004; Gamer and Robinson 2008) and "The English Sappho" (Judith Pascoe 1997), as she had mostly expressed herself through drama and poetry in the 1770s and the 1780s when a further change took place in the 1790s. Robinson started writing novels, a choice probably dictated by a series of reasons. First, there were unending financial necessities, as was the case with Charlotte Smith, Eliza Parsons and many other writers. Another element was probably the desire to emulate the most successful Gothic author of the decade. Ann Radcliffe's early successes with romances full of mysteries and supernatural atmospheres probably pushed Robinson to try her hand in gloomy and adventurous stories. A third factor was her contact with Godwin and Wollstonecraft's circle, which inspired her for their use of the novel as a means to propagate ideas on politics, society and philosophy. The Gothic genre was a problematic literary field, which became even more disturbing to critics in the hands of Robinson. "The threatening intersection of a sexually notorious woman like Robinson and a genre which was often perceived as of pandering to the lowest public taste incited particularly charged critical response"(Close: 174). Robinson's first Gothic novel was *Vancenza; or, the Dangers of Credulity* (1792), a tragic story of incestuous love that may have attracted the attention of Lewis before writing *The Monk*, as the main character, Elvira, falls in love with her half-brother without knowing his real origins. Once Elvira discovers the truth, she cannot cope with shame and the story ends tragically, reproducing a classical mould of a disastrous destiny. Robinson's subsequent Gothic effort was *Hubert de Sevrac. A Romance of the Eighteenth Century*, published in 1796 (Henceforth *Sevrac* in quotations). However similar to previous Gothic novels, her romance *Hubert de Sevrac* introduces peculiarities, which are worth exploring. This section includes various aspects of this novel and aims to demonstrate how Robinson was indebted to a number of authors, among whom Radcliffe, for the Gothic atmosphere, and Godwin, Wollstonecraft and Enlightened philosophers for the social ideas frequently accompanying an intricate and, sometimes, confusing plot. Despite her imitation of famous novels, Robinson detached herself from her predecessors and created a sort of problematic Gothic with the publication of *Hubert de Sevrac*, which is only partly a mirror of the Radcliffean romance and mostly a strange combination of genres and styles. Whereas the tragic *Vancenza* had received positive reviews and was reprinted several times, *Hubert de Sevrac* was not as successful as Robinson's previous Gothic novel. *Vancenza* perfectly fits in the more traditional Radcliffean canon of a Gothic story and differs from Robinson's next Gothic publication highlighting how chameleonic and changeable Robinson could be in her ample literary efforts.

271

The story of *Sevrac* is quite strange and the plot gradually becomes more complex, making it difficult for the reader to follow the events. The novel starts in 1792 when the dangerous clangour of the revolutionaries becomes more threatening. The incipit is similar to Radcliffe's *The Romance of the Forest* (1791), as a husband and his wife arrive at the Castle of Montnoir in Lombardy, after escaping from Paris. Marquis Hubert de Sevrac and his sweet wife Emily are forced to abandon their properties in Paris because of the dangerous turn the Revolution has taken. They travel with their adolescent daughter Sabina and their faithful companion and surrogate paternal figure, the old Abbé Le Blanc. Via a very short flashback, we discover that, forced to wear peasants' clothes, they escaped through the French countryside and reached Italy in disguise. Interestingly and contrary to what many scholars think (Close 2006), France is not the setting of the action, which takes place entirely in Italy. Indeed, the main characters are on French soil only in the short summary of their journey in the first two pages of the three-volume novel, and the country is sporadically mentioned when some analepses briefly describe the life of de Sevrac and other aristocrats in Versailles, or when some mystery from the past is unveiled about the main character. The devastation and the horror of the revolution are not the only causes of sorrow that occupy the minds of de Sevrac and his wife. In marrying at quite a young age, they contravened to their respective parents' desires for religious reasons. Emily de Sevrac, a British protestant, defies her parents' authority and is disinherited. De Sevrac faces his Catholic father's ire and undergoes a similar punishment, as his furious parent leaves the greatest part of his patrimony to his servant's son, the greedy and hypocrite Ravillon, who now possesses the greatest part of de Sevrac's inheritance and all his domains in Italy, between Lombardy and Tuscany. The stay in Lombardy marks the beginning of a chain of unfortunate events forcing the characters to face scary and dangerous situations and become itinerant on the Italian peninsula.

The revolutionary theme receives a great attention in the story. Socio-political meditations constellate the narration from the very beginning in the manner of essays and tales created by the French philosophers of the Enlightenment. An otherwise silent and passive character, de Sevrac's daughter Sabina becomes vocal when it comes to social injustice. During her father's unmotivated imprisonment for murder in Milan, she claims that every prisoner has the right to be informed of his crime and have the possibility of defending himself. Her speech reflects the ideas of Beccaria's *An Essay on Crimes and Punishments* (1764), which highlighted the potential injustice of ill-treatment of prisoners, especially when they turned out to be innocent (as we the saw in the introductory chapter). When Sabina is exploring a "cimetière" where she thinks their travel companion, the young English aristocrat St Clair, is buried, she is taken by a deep discomfort. She not only grieves for (apparently) lost love but she becomes melancholic when she notices the striking differences in the tombs. She speaks to a venerable monk and expresses her profound sadness when she observes simple graves with no ornament. Her sadness becomes even deeper when she thinks of rich mausoleums bought with gold to glorify the memory of their powerful owners (*Sevrac* II: 122). Even when they are finally distant from the revolution and free to explore the country that provides refuge, the de Sevrac family is the prey of anguish and melancholy. They cannot forget their present misery, which is even more acute when they see the cruel Ravillon enjoying the prosperity and social recognition from which they are excluded. Interestingly, in her frequent interventions on the matter, Sabina would like to understand what could have prevented the Revolution. In the following passage, she expresses her disappointment for her superficial feelings in the past that revealed her lack of awareness concerning social problems:

"Alas!" exclaimed Mademoiselle de Sevrac, "these are scenes of which I had not the most faint idea! Little did I think when I beheld the splendours of Versailles, the brilliant circle, the illuminated ballroom, and sumptuous banquet! That the poor and houseless peasants were exposed to all the storms of Heaven, unpitied and defenceless! We never talked of them the season, whose severity pinches the child of nature, was to us a season of festive luxury!" Monsieur de Sevrac wished to divert her mind from the objects which seemed to fix its attention, at the same moment that he admired its sensibility. He endeavoured to speak of inequality as a matter of political utility; and wished her to believe that the sorrows of life were impartially distributed, only varying in their forms, and adapted to the mental strength of the sufferer. (*Sevrac* II: 84)

However trustworthy, the justification provided by de Sevrac is weak and more metaphysical than political or social. Sabina continues ruminating about the false image that literature frequently conveys. In an appealing metaliterary discourse, Sabina goes against the precepts promoted by David Hume in his *Inquiry concerning the Principles of Morals* (1751), encouraging a sort of censorship that aimed at eliminating every toil and difficulty in the description of poor people's labour, as we saw in the chapter dedicated to Radcliffe. Sabina disapproves of idealised literature showing idyllic images of peasants working happily in the middle of nature. "She had read of the happy peasants, books had portrayed them as the gayest and most contented of the human race, the mountain swain, the village maid, were represented by the pages of romances, as enjoying a life of rural bliss, heightened by the beautiful simplicity of guileless manners" (*Sevrac* II: 85). Sabina's words criticise the pastoral and idealised visions of peasants she found in her readings and she compares these stories with her real life observations. It was Radcliffe, who, among other eighteenth-century authors, following Hume's dictum and inspired by James Thomson's poems and Virgil's *Georgics*, had depicted the happy life of simple people. Unlike Radcliffe, Robinson shows emaciated and tired peasants in rags, starving and tired because of their hard toil, which is just necessary for survival, amplifying Gray's sad observations in his *Elegy written in a Country Churchyard* (1751). Robinson's differences from Radcliffe are clear as far politics is concerned, especially because the former is vocal about social injustice, whereas the latter tends to omit social observations and criticism. Later, Sabina and her father discuss the validity of laws. The girl exclaims, "Laws, that owned no code, but in the bosom of a despot, were the mere mockery of freedom" (*Sevrac* II: 150), evincing a deep knowledge of Montesquieu's *Spirit of the Laws* (1748). The Gothic that Robinson creates is different from contemporary early Gothic novelists as far as politics is concerned. First, Robinson chooses the present as the setting for her romance and she does not need Radcliffe's and other Gothic writers' escapism to other epochs to create adventurous stories. The second difference is that Robinson clearly mentions the historical context and describes its horrors. Both Gothic and contemporary authors are busy describing dreadful and dangerous events, but the French Revolution is carefully avoided in Gothic novels (and also non-Gothic) that generally prefer to describe indefinite political unrest, if any, set in a distant and blurred past. One of the few exceptions was Charlotte Smith, who daringly supported the French Revolution in her epistolary novel *Desmond* (1792), which made her a literary *persona non grata* in the Francophobic England of the 1790s. Thirdly, Robinson unveils the deep hypocrisy of hiding the dire reality that lower classes face in late eighteenth-century society.

Wollstonecraft was in Paris in the fatal years between 1791 and 1794. She witnessed the progressive increase in violence and the events that brought about the absolute power of the Jacobins, replacing the moderate Girondins. Jacobins intended to guillotine anybody who was supposedly a conspirator or an anti-revolutionary. Wollstonecraft had seen several friends die without clear accusations and had written about the atrocities she had observed. Reacting to Edmund Burke's *Reflections on the Revolution in France* (1790), Wollstonecraft had initially exalted the revolution in *A Vindication of the Rights of Men* (1790). She had later widened her analysis in *A Vindication of the Rights of Woman* (1794), as she had realised—like the French Olympe de Gouges—that even in revolutionary times the importance of women in society was still dramatically ignored. Wollstonecraft modified her opinions on the Revolution after her stay in France. Robinson had been in France in the years preceding the Revolution and, like Sabina, she had been charmed by the scintillating world of Versailles. She wrote a monody in honour of Marie Antoinette after the French Queen's tragic death, recalling the days of her happiness. The Queen's ill-fated end deeply saddened her, proving that she was not that ferocious maenad that Polwhele had described. Robinson's preoccupation was with social justice and with the recognition of equal rights for women in society. Even though Polwhele or other vehement critics considered her works full of Jacobin sympathies—a theory embraced by Brewer (2006), they did not understand the modernity of Robinson's vision of a better world. The adolescent Sabina represents Mary's spokesperson. Her naïve desire for an equal society reflects Robinson's inner hope.

Robinson's romance contains a further feature, which reveals the male character's complications represented by his problematic melancholy, anxiety and instability. The fact that Thomas Warton and David Hume, among others, praise melancholy in their prose and poetry reiterating the charm of this state of the soul in the eighteenth century—a feeling extensively described by Burton in the previous century—is likely to have created a general psychological propensity towards this feeling of sadness for its special aura of aristocratic superiority. However, such perplexing aspects as excessive melancholy, anxiety and instability in a male personality are debatable. These flaws seem to be compatible with the opinions of Marivaux's Silvia and Shakespeare's Beatrice that we mentioned in the chapter about Gothic miscellanea. Centlivre expressed a similar idea *A Bold Stroke for a Wife* (1718). In the play, "The heroine Miss Lovely lacks social and sexual agency, calling on outside forces to save her from personal distress and decide her marriage options. [...] Centlivre sought to depict the injustices of a marriage system in which women like Miss Lovely are sacrificed to an overpowering patriarchal structure" (Gamer and Robinson: 237). De Sevrac, like St Clair and other male characters in Gothic stories, seems to reproduce the strangeness detected by the female characters mentioned above. An elegant and refined aristocrat in his thirties, charming and of beautiful aspect, de Sevrac is a "generous and benevolent" man. He does not appear to be a patriarchal figure. Despite all his many good qualities, he progressively reveals a series of flaws. Even though he loves his wife tenderly and wants to protect his only daughter Sabina at the cost of his life, he betrays a series of strange behaviours. Apart from ending up in front of several judges and risking death penalty twice, unjustly accused of robbery, abduction and murder because of his precipitate behaviour, when de Sevrac is acquitted for being absolutely innocent, he strangely develops a series of idiosyncrasies that leave his wife and daughter baffled and powerless. De Sevrac commits several *faux pas* revealing a serious degree of ineptitude. The most evident is when he abandons his wife and daughter with the hideous servant Dufango and his equally horrible mother in the gloomy castle of Montnoir to go and stay in Milan with guileful Ravillon, who is moreover constantly plotting against him. The reason is that he becomes anxious and frantic in the castle of Montnoir thinking about his sorrows and the clash with his father before the old man's death. He is taken by anxiety when walking in the obscure thick forest surrounding the castle, but the situation degenerates in Milan where countess Monteleoni falls for him and Ravillon is furious with jealousy, provoking de Sevrac to challenge him in a duel. Then, when the family is forced to escape and hide in Bologna, he puts his life in peril again to follow the mysterious Marianna every night, as he feels a telepathic connection with the young woman. He even enters her house more than once and here discovers a mysterious youth mortally wounded. The family becomes itinerant again to reach Florence. They decide to stop and settle in a beautiful cottage, which they call Chateau-neuf, surrounded by a picturesque countryside and sublime mountains between Bologna and Florence, in which they could settle indefinitely. For the umpteenth time, de Sevrac causes havoc, as a strange form of angry paroxysm takes hold of him, as he thinks his daughter intends to elope with their new travel companion, the handsome young British aristocrat St Clair. This represents one of de Sevrac's strange fixations, considering that St Clair was instrumental in saving him while imprisoned in Milan. When Sabina disappears, he does not realise that the dangerous abbot Palerma (Ravillon's relative) forcefully keeps the girl prisoner in his monastery from dawn until night. De Sevrac searches fields and hills for St Clair like a lunatic. After being set free, Sabina's obstinate and incomprehensible silence concerning the episode and St Clair's sudden departure increase his state of anxiety and he decides to follow deceitful Palerma's treacherous suggestions without understanding the danger they imply. Notwithstanding the relatively happy situation while living in Chateau-neuf, de Sevrac cannot find peace:

Madame de Sevrac continued to ascend the mountain, notwithstanding the increasing storm, impelled by affection, and anxious for the safety of the unfortunate being, whom fate had condemned to buffet with the tempest, all inferior considerations vanished; she stood for some moments within a few paces of the Marquis, before he perceived she was near him: the vacant fixture of his eyes bespoke the state of his mind; and his ghastly smile when Sabina embraced him, augmented their fears that his intellects were disordered. (*Sevrac* II: 28)

Whereas in most early Gothic stories, the father is an absent figure and his heirs, generally women, have to face innumerable predicaments alone, in this case the paternal figure is present but ineffectual. He does not show patriarchal attitudes, but he acts in a questionable and almost paranoid way, doubting of the good faith of certain characters and blindly trusting dangerous individuals. He frequently sees dangers when there is none, but is unaware of the machinations that his enemies organise. When he finally understands that Palerma is plotting Sabina's abduction to force her into marrying Arnaut, Ravillon's covetous son, he tries to stop the nocturnal ambush. His disorganised intervention causes the fatal wounding of good friar Evangelista, who had been protecting Sabina, and he inadvertently wounds somebody that he identifies as St Clair. His anxiety and sense of guilt almost turn him into a deranged man. His difficult state forces the family to move from place to place. First to a poor farm, then to many locations in Florence, where they waste their remaining money after being robbed during one of their peregrinations. Always escaping from his enemies in the Tuscan city and risking imprisonment again, de Sevrac and his family further move southward along the peninsula until they reach Naples where many plots are unveiled and the truth revealed. Interestingly, the young and fascinating St Clair shares some strange attitudes with de Sevrac. Like him, he is attracted to wild and sublime landscapes that make him sadly contemplative and his mood becomes changeable for no reason. Equally changeable are his affection and love for Sabina. In effect, he seems to succumb to libertinism and erotic adventures once he is alone in Florence after ambiguously promising eternal love—however platonic—to Sabina. Moreover, he conceals some mysteries that are unveiled only in the grand finale. The characters of de Sevrac (and of St Clair for that matter) seem to embody partially negative figures of men, like the ones rejected by Silvia, Beatrice, Miss Lovely, and frequently present in early Gothic stories. They are unpredictable and at the same time incapable of facing difficulties. Despite being an educated aristocrat characterised by good looks and capable of deep affection, de

Sevrac is in a constant state of crisis ranging from melancholy to anxiety, deep agitation and frenzy. Like other masculine figures, he is not a villain, but he is particularly awkward and complex. On his part, St Clair, who shares many traits with de Sevrac, does not appear to be downright reliable. These ambiguous male figures may be a token of some negative characteristics of men in the society of late eighteenth century Britain and Europe that Robinson, either consciously or unconsciously, wanted to display realistically.

Mothers may have tense relationships with daughters in more recent Gothic stories, whereas their absence is frequent in early Gothic romances, revealing a series of problems that Rogers analyses in *Matrophobic Gothic* (2007), which do not seem to pertain to Robinson's novel. Unlike her contemporaries, Robinson makes a different choice and preserves the figure of the mother in her novel. However, both de Sevrac mother and daughter are characterised by silence, omissions and aphasia. Emily de Sevrac does not acquire the role of a surveillant or a "panopticon" (Armstrong 1987). According to Dever (1997), the mother cannot subsist in the Gothic because her presence means protection, which may explain the general lack of mother figures in early Gothic stories—with some exceptions: Hippolita, the passive mother figure Walpole's *The Castle of Otranto*, and the inadequate figures of Carathis (*Vathek*) and Elvira (*The Monk*). Radcliffe's main characters are always motherless heroines. Even if Emily de Sevrac, does not correspond to Kahane's (1985) figure of the cruel mother, or to the other clichés described by Armstrong and Dever, she is not an effective figure and is seldom able to solve situations or protect her daughter. Robinson's decision to maintain both the fatherly and motherly figures is unusual. One may think that the presence of both parents should prevent prevarications and dangers, which on the contrary multiply in the story. The situation in *Hubert de Sevrac* is quite different and challenges previous and contemporary gothic stories. The figure of the mother is not contrary to the "narratable", as Dever (1997) claims, but is as powerless as the figure the father. Emily de Sevrac does not exert a "strict surveillance" and is generally silent. She demonstrates her affection and support with her mimics and proxemics but does not frequently express herself. When the situation she faces becomes unbearable, she cries or she "shrieks", a verb that seems to be suitable to her delicate character. She has the best intentions, but she is not able to help her husband or protect her daughter. One blatant example is when she decides to visit a solitary convent with her daughter in the countryside near Lake Albano. The place is picturesque, but is surrounded by a vast, luxuriant forest, which becomes threatening after darkness, as it may hide many dangers. The two women are lost in a pleasant dialogue with the kind abbess and realise evening has fallen when it is too late. Crossing the cheerless forest in darkness, they are attacked by the inevitable banditti and Sabina is kidnapped once again, thus demonstrating her mother's unreliability.

For all her harangues in favour of her unfortunate father and her many speeches on social injustice, Sabina remains unnervingly silent on all other occasions, especially the most dramatic ones. She seems to suffer from a generalized form of aphasia. Sabina's Gothic aura lies in the fact that she is in constant danger of prevarication and death. What is completely unclear is why she never involves her parents in her predicaments notwithstanding their proximity. While her parents have to face a trial in Milan, Sabina is violently abducted and taken back to Montnoir where a young priest is going to celebrate her unwanted marriage to Arnaut Ravillon. Only a series of fortuitous circumstances help her escape and join her parents. However, she never mentions that dramatic episode to neither of them. She continues with her obstinate silence even when a thief enters her room stealing important objects or when an apparent ghost disturbs her sleep and forces her to pronounce a solemn oath. Instead of confirming the innocent nature of her relationship with St Clair, she remains mute causing a fit of rage in her father, who systematically misunderstands her reticence. The most disquieting situation is when she is held captive in Abbot Palerma's lugubrious monastery and she does not reveal the inexplicable events happening there. On their part, her parents are surprisingly naïve concerning the situation, more worried as they are about the possible liaison between St Clair and their daughter than of abbot Palerma's unjustifiable and potentially dangerous actions. A sort of conspiracy of silence involve other characters. When talking to Padre Francesco in the "cimetière", Sabina infers that the anonymous tomb must belong to St Clair without any tangible proof and starts mourning obsessively without verifying her hypothesis. The unsaid becomes more important than the pronounced words. When de Sevrac tries to understand how the young person in the unnamed tomb died, he takes Padre Francesco's few words as a reproach to him and presumes a series of improbable events that risk deranging his mind, as he is convinced that he committed an atrocious murder. Robinson is in this sense the opposite of Radcliffe, whose loquacious main characters express their feelings and frequently analyse the situations in dialogues or interior monologues. The lack of clear communication and the constant verbal omissions could potentially turn Robinson's romance into a tragedy. Another strange aspect characterising Sabina is that despite her beauty and innocence, the girl does not possess the sensuality of other Gothic female characters. Even the topos of the "veil" that we frequently see in all Gothic stories is not present here. When Sabina meets St Clair, she immediately falls for him and often misunderstands his simple actions as expressions of his love for her. The erotic tension provoked for example by Radcliffe's Adeline, Walpole's Matilda, Beckford's Nouronihar and the majority of Gothic heroines is totally absent in *Hubert de Sevrac*. Sabina can attract interest as long as she can guarantee a conspicuous fortune to her abductors. She is more frequently at risk of being murdered than of being seduced, as her death would mean the assurance of a complete inheritance for the Ravillon family.

It is not clear whether it was a simple narrative choice to define certain features of both her male and female characters or whether Robinson wanted to describe the dangers of ingenuity and its potentially tragic consequences for both sexes. Considering the divergence with most Gothic romances, in which parents are missing, it may be plausible to claim that, by preserving the figures of parents, Robinson wanted to describe social dangers and "the severity of fortune" (*Sevrac* I: 6). Her pessimism highlights the inevitable precariousness of existence, to which all individuals are inexorably subject.

Robinson applies Gothic iconographies of danger to her story: like Radcliffe, she describes Gothic mansions and picturesque landscapes. The Burkean sublime attracts all characters basically pure at heart, especially if it is represented by extreme natural events or scary situations conveying a sense of horror. The peculiarity of this Gothic novel is the architectural variety of buildings and dwellings where the de Sevrac family resides, or which they visit in the different phases of the story. The gloomy and haunted castle of Montnoir in Milan, the splendidly furnished but equally haunted residence Vall'ombrosa in Florence, the mazy prison in Milan, the beautiful house (dubbed Chateau-neuf) in Pianoro near Bologna, Palerma's gloomy monastery facing the Apennines, Briancour's labyrinthlike mansion in Cortona—with innumerable hidden chambers—plus a range of mysterious houses, cottages, taverns and inns are examples of a sort of Baroque superabundance that Robinson seems to favour. Apparently, Robinson is not interested in providing a single mythical location for the story and differs from the majority of Gothic writers, who tend to choose an iconic building, in which gloom, mystery and the supernatural dominate, as we can infer by simply analysing the titles of early Gothic novels. However, the castle of Montnoir occupies a special place in the narrative economy of *Hubert de Sevrac*. With its sombre rooms, mysterious recesses, traces of murders, supernatural events and the lush, dark forest surrounding its walls–where dangers lurk and crimes are committed–Montnoir has the function to inaugurate the Gothic side of the story from the very first pages. Inevitably, castles, monasteries and other architectures are surrounded by a strange nature, which is picturesque, but more frequently sublime and fearsome. The Gothic dyad of castle and forest is present in the story and has a strongly evocative function. Both inside and outside a sublime atmosphere attracts and terrorizes the protagonists according to the Burkean ideal of the delightful horror.

The novel showcases many iconic Gothic and Romantic moments when unpredictable and frightful storms show their horrifying power. When sailing between Naples and Caprea (Capri), a violent storm surprises the group on board the ship:

The weather was beautifully serene, the sea was only ruffled by breezes, sufficient to waft the vessel over the waves: but towards midnight a fresh gale sprung up, which in the course of an hour, augmented to a tempest. The thunder rolled in rattling peals; the lightning, darting through the black and suffocating atmosphere, at intervals illumined the deck, and presented the sea foaming and bounding with terrific fury. [...] [T]he elemental strife grew louder, and the bursting clouds cast forth-incessant shafts of fire, which directed their mazy courses in every direction. (*Sevrac* III: 270)

The description becomes even more engaging when the waves shake the ship, alarming the crew and the people on board, "The vessel at length became ungovernable, rocking from side to side as the wind fell; or plunging with the resistless waves, which one minute swelled to the sky, and the next seemed to divide in liquid mountains" (270–271). The watery element turns into a torment and a source of horror with its majestic and destructive force. Nature is in turmoil and dreadful Mount Vesuvius abruptly explodes with a formidable eruption of fire: "[...] on a sudden they beheld a column of fire bursting from the crater of Vesuvius, and hurling forth its burning entrails, as if to compete the horrors of the tumultuous scene! The bright red flame presented a terrible contrast to the blue coruscations which flashed around them; and wherever the eye turned it encountered some new object, to appal the soul and quell its resolution" (271). The eruptions of Vesuvius, being highly spectacular, were frequently the object of painters reproducing sublimity in nature. Wright of Derby's several canvas showing whirlwinds of smoke, fire and lava spitting out of Vesuvius' caldera became a sublime representation of fear and horror embodied by a volcano. Even though it is not clear whether he witnessed a dramatic eruption during his stay in Naples in 1774, Wright of Derby may have observed several pyroclastic flows, as Vesuvius was frequently active and violently erupted at least six times during the eighteenth century, according to the Volcanic Observatory (*Osservatorio Vesuviano*). One of his many views of the Neapolitan volcano, now at the Tate Gallery in London, (*Vesuvius in Eruption, with a View over the Islands in the Bay of Naples*, ca. 1775) emphasizes the nocturnal atmosphere, where the pearly light of the moon contrasts with the reddish nuances reflected in the clouds over the explosion. This particular painting may have represented a genuine inspiration. If we consider Robinson's literal description of the event, however, we might find the iconographic equivalent in a painting created by the Scottish expat Jacob More, now at the National Galleries of Scotland, which may be dated 1781 thanks to a letter of the artist's art dealer, James Irvine. The great "column of fire" can be admired in the painting conveying the "wild horrors of Vesuvius" (*Sevrac* III: 219). In this case, the identification of the iconographic source may be vague, while on other occasions Robinson is more explicit in the declaration of her pictorial sources.

Robinson reiterates the motif of the tempest. Frequent storms shatter nature and the main characters alike from the onset of the story when "the fury of the elements" overtook de Sevrac and his family during their flight (*Sevrac* I: 11). A dreadful storm starts when they have settled in a farm near a graveyard (the "cimetière") before reaching Florence. After the storm, a strong wind batters the valley. The horrible nocturnal scene agitates de Sevrac and his wife, as they have lost Sabina. When they finally find her, they are in front of an appalling scene:

When [father Francesco] saw him stop at the cimetière, he hastened forward, and reached the gate as the Marquis advanced among the heaps of mould, where he perceived the white dress of Mademoiselle de Sevrac: he rushed towards her, and beheld a sight that almost annihilated him with horror! She was sitting by the side of the stranger's grave, her arms encircling the little cross, and her eyes raised towards the clouds that passed over the valley. Her hair hung over her shoulders to her waist, partly covering her bosom which was drenched by the midnight tempest, her cheek was pale, and her hand almost petrified; she had laid her cloak upon the grave, as if to guard it from the storm; and fixed, like the image of despair, seemed wholly insensible of everything that approached her. (*Sevrac* II: 172–173)

The episode combines Gothic and Romantic aspects. The gloomy images of the "cimetière" and the terrifying tempest are Gothic clichés, while the unfortunate passion uniting lovers even after death is a symbol of Romanticism. The scene represents one of the several tragic moments when despair almost maddens the characters. Curiously, generally sensible characters able to rationalise in an enlightened way fall into an abyss of despair. Sabina, de Sevrac and St Clair alternate moments of lucidity and sensibility with strange attitudes, which make them seem lunatic. What is even stranger in this particular extract is that Sabina is almost driven crazy mourning over an anonymous tomb, but she never saw the person buried inside. If on the one hand the context tends to be macabre according to the tradition of the Gothic, on the other hand an unexpected subterranean sense of irony is present. The quasi-sardonic context becomes evident when we discover that St Clair is perfectly well, enjoying his libertine phase in Florence. This coup de scene is compatible with narrative choices in Walpole, Beckford and Lewis and their tendency towards pastiche. Robinson seems to be experimenting and trying to create her specific Gothic trait, syncretising different styles and sources.

Robinson is very circumstantial about the places in the Northern area of the peninsula, which the de Sevrac family visits. Unlike Radcliffe's nebulous hints to painters such as Rosa, Poussin, Claude and Piranesi, which have pushed scholars to look for her visual sources, Robinson openly mentions her bibliographic and visual reference. The two volumes by John Smith—published in 1792 and containing extensive images and maps of Italian territories—offered interesting and concrete visualisations of mythical locations that had indefinitely been exploited and vaguely described by early Gothic writers. Robinson cites Smith's works in her novel more than once in the first volume (*Sevrac* I: 234). The de Sevrac arrive in Lombardy, then proceed to Emilia Romagna, Tuscany, Latium, Umbria and Campania and they visit a great number of towns (Milan, Bologna, Florence, Siena, Cortona, Perugia, Roma, Naples and Capri) and different villages and picturesque places in-between, which are rendered with a Radcliffean touch, as in the following description:

The scenery would, to minds at ease, have afforded the most sublime of contemplative pleasure. Rich and variegated plantations of vines and olives; distant forest of oak and cork trees; beautiful valleys; the vast lake of Perugia; with a grand perspective of Apennine above Apennine, piercing the blue expanse, and seeming to blend with the horizon as far as the confines of Sienna, while the wavy irregularity of the stupendous eminences enclosed a tract of scenery, scarcely to be equalled, not to be delineated. The sun rose on one of those mornings of Spring, which harmonize and re-animate all the beauties of nature! The breezes were soft and refreshing; the verdure glowing and luxuriant, and the sky, brightly blue and uniformly unclouded. (*Sevrac* III: 28–29)

Notwithstanding Robinson's personal Gothic tones and choices, Radcliffe's influence remains strong throughout the novel. In effect, Radcliffe's representations of nature are much longer and detailed, whereas Robinson has a tendency to be more telegraphic in her descriptions of landscape–even compared to her first Gothic work, *Vancenza*–privileging theatrical actions, sudden fears and a state of constant suspense in both rural and urban contexts. Despite its brevity, the passage we have just read contains themes dear to Radcliffe and her special love for bucolic scenes taken from Virgil. The fresh and verdant effect of spring on nature can be found in the Virgilian *Georgics*, in Thomson's T*he Seasons* (1730) and in Radcliffe's central novels. A further explicit homage to Radcliffe and to Virgil can be detected when de Sevrac seeks protection from banditti behind "a venerable tree" (II: 199) or when lovers in distress "turn to venerable trees" for consolation (*Sevrac* III: 214). In her diary as well as in her central novels, Radcliffe describes trees with extreme accuracy, following the example of Virgil in *The Georgics*. The phrase "venerable trees", frequently adopted by Radcliffe, is a narrative mannerism betraying the inevitable narrative power of the "Great Enchantress" (Miles 1995) on both her contemporaries and Robinson, even though the latter appears to be in search of a personal Gothic style.

One essential moment shows Robinson's poetic strength and her special taste for Romanticism, which contribute to a dark Gothic setting, imbued with suspense and horror. Kidnapped by fiendish Ravillon to be married to his evil son, Sabine is alone in Montnoir. Despite the peril, she courageously (or recklessly) explores the place:

She found herself surrounded by a deep and terrifying gloom that made her start from her seat, fearful and trembling. She was proceeding towards the doors, when her feet were arrested by an indistinct humming in the adjoining apartments. [...] She then opened the door of the saloon: a sepulchral silence prevailed round the dreary building. The only ray that directed her steps was that of the rising moon which cast a dim side light over one half of the chateau. Sabina, struck with the peculiar stillness and solemnity of everything round her, stood for a time motionless, with her eyes fixed on the immensity of air, illumined by the pale lustre of that planet, which has ever been soothing to romantic minds. (*Sevrac* I: 153–154)

The prevalence of sibilant sounds ("sepulchral silence", "stillness", "solemnity"), highlighted by the frequent alliterations, gives an onomatopoeic value to the narration, which makes the reader hear Sabina's soft steps. The words also have a strong evocative power underlining the solitude of Sabina and the tantalising suspense of her dire situation. Robinson adds her special poetic mastery to her peculiar Gothic.

Nemeses are the great protagonists of late eighteenth-centuries dark romances. The early Gothic novel is characterised by the enigmatic figure of a villain occasionally assisted by some other cruel characters, intent on persecuting innocent characters. Robinson's choice in *Hubert de Sevrac* is quite different. The first pages introduce Ravillon, who is supposed to be the main antagonist and is described as "the grand spring in the vast machine of villainy" (*Sevrac* II: 211). However, the figures of enemies seem to multiply in the course of the story and de Sevrac has to face endless dangers. There is a sort of criminal network of people from every social layer, working relentlessly to destroy de Sevrac and force his daughter into an undesired marriage. It is as if a form of maddening choral cruelty, exacerbated by de Sevrac's inability to detect hypocrisy and malice, surrounds him and his entourage. Ravillon intends to maintain his possessions and acquire Sabina's inheritance as well. He is a Machiavellian figure in constant fear of losing the wealth he has dishonestly and violently inherited (a fact unknown to de Sevrac), as it may go to the legitimate owner if his son dies. The parvenu Ravillon and his son Arnaud plot incessantly and are ready to kill if Sabina rejects their plans. Their hideous servants Dufango and his mother help them in their scheme. The deceitful Abbot Palerma wants to instil fear in Sabina and keeps her segregated in a monastery, which is full of mysteries and horrors, engulfed as it is with centuries of dark superstition. The apparently amicable but disingenuous Florentine lawyer Lupo secretly machinates to destroy de Sevrac and is almost successful. Ravillon's mercenaries and banditti attack de Sevrac and his wife and daughter on various occasions. By means of a change of identity and a fatal ruse, Ravillon, who intimately desires to be Sevrac's doppelganger, finds a tragic destiny. However, he has an ally, an arch-cruel and shadowy character, who conceives the most brutal conspiracy to destroy de Sevrac's reputation and peace of mind. Marquis Briancour has carried out his cabal ever since his designated victim was an appreciated young man at the French court. No motivation is provided for Briancour's lasting and devastating hate for de Sevrac, as the reader discovers the man's existence indirectly through de Sevrac's words, who is unaware of how far his former friend has gone to ruin him. Briancour has used all the darkest means at his disposal to set up the destruction of the de Sevrac family. He has committed an infinity of crimes and managed to put the blame on de Sevrac. Unlike Ravillon, Briancour appears for just a few moments in the story and the reader cannot visualise or understand this character, who, like a puppeteer, has deceptively manoeuvred the greatest parts of the incidents in the plot.

This stylistic choice is quite dubious, as it is particularly confusing for readers. Robinson probably considered the network of organised crime more plausible and realistic than a single figure of an omnipresent villain, like in Radcliffe and other Gothicists, who is constantly informed, spies on every character and repositions quickly in the story, following every move of his victims. On the one hand, this unusual literary decision makes the Gothic story more theatrical with innumerable coups de scene. On the other hand, the flow of events tends towards the picaresque for its constant change of frame and context. Evil characters do not have the psychological depth they possess in other early Gothic novels and Robinson herself remains sometimes entangled in the excess of her creativity, as many characters start narrative threads that are later abandoned without sufficient explanation.

Although Robinson's Gothic technique is unusual, her influences betray a Radcliffean mode. The most relevant peculiarity is her use of the dialogue and the sudden and frequent change of scene. The levels of theatricality in the novel are quite high and they resonate with Robinson's experiences in the 1780s as an actress, a playwright and a theatre-goer (Gamer and Robinson: 241). Like in Radcliffe, she introduces her chapters using lines taken from drama and poetry. Her epigraphs, mostly dedicated to Shakespeare, show the importance of drama in her novel. Many parts in the story seem to be scenes taken from a play, especially when they abruptly change, introducing different settings. Robinson instilled Shakespearean elements in de Sevrac because of his unresolved and traumatic conflict with a father that he would like to admire and honour despite obscure elements enclosing his persona. Other epigraphs are taken from eighteenth-century poets and in particular from graveyard poets with whom Robinson shares gloomy nocturnal settings and a deep sense of melancholy.

We have seen that the plot is complex. If the novel could be transposed into a film in the present days, it would probably become a television series of several episodes and many seasons for all the twists and turns it contains. Compared to Robinson, Radcliffe generally provides a more extended analysis of her characters and appears to have a more organised development of plots. It may seem that Robinson has a tendency to improvise situations and accumulate tensions and actions to the detriment of consistency. Echoes of Radcliffe constellate the novel. It is clear that Radcliffe is Robinson's role model when she describes picturesque landscapes or when her characters are subjugated by sublime settings, which have a remarkable influence especially on male characters, which is Robinson's peculiarity. She also imitates Radcliffe in organising a series of infinite predicaments for the young heroine. Robinson does not forget to include the usual intellectualism that many characters in Radcliffe manifest, especially when it comes to reading the Classics and Italian poets. When Sabina and her mother explore the immense and sombre library in Montnoir, they come across volumes by Ariosto (*Sevrac* I: 50). An attentive reader would immediately recognise the analogy with Radcliffe, who spends pages idolising this particular author and even reproducing some of his literary contexts in her stories. However, Robinson chooses an ironic trick to create an alternative to a Radcliffean cliché. The volumes of Ariosto in Montnoir library are mockingly fake, as they hide a device to enter a secret recess in the castle. Now it is the turn of Lee's suggestions because the hidden place conceals terrible secrets. Using the title of Lee's story is a strategy for Robinson so that she can convey a sense of mystery and violence and create a thin red line with other Gothic writers. After exploring the dim chamber hardly illuminated by a small "latticed window" (*Sevrac* I: 51), mother and daughter make a terrible discovery: a bloody poniard appears in a closet and a strange voice is heard talking threateningly to the two women, suggesting the very first introduction to the supernatural in the narration. As far as the supernatural is concerned, if Radcliffe was criticised for apparently rationalising and elucidating mysterious events, Robinson does not clarify if they are part of the uncanny, or if they are the results of human artifice.

On a different occasion and, coincidentally, towards the end of the story de Sevrac and some friends are escorted by some guards to Briancour's castle in Cortona, near Perugia, to unveil horrible crimes. At the entrance of the menacing building, they see huge statues representing horrid creatures that recall the entrance to Eblis in *Vathek* and are a clear hint at Dante's *Inferno*. In Florence, de Sevrac finds books by Dante and Metastasio, two authors he appreciates. Dante has been admired in various epochs for his chilling descriptions of the netherworld and, as Saglia (2006) demonstrates, the medieval poet represented a vast catalogue of direful images for the Gothicists and the Romantics. One of the greatest voices of the Middle Ages, the attraction Dante exerts on poets and writers in the course of centuries is undeniable and the early Gothic and Romanticism frequently borrow images from his inventive *Comedy*. Robinson confirms in this way other Gothic authors' tendency. Mentioning the librettist and poet Metastasio is unusual, and Robinson is the first to include this poet, who had a great influence on the second part of the eighteenth century with his rich production of melodrama *serio* and, even if he chronologically belonged to the period of the Enlightenment, he betrays a Romantic sensibility. Robinson knows all the works of her predecessors and consistently plays with intertextuality and at the same time fills the story with her personal touch.

Intertextuality is at play in various themes. An interesting philosophical echo of *Vathek* lies in a Lucretian pessimistic statement pronounced by St Clair about the unhappiness of the human condition, which recalls the parable of Beckford's hero:

Man is but an unreasonable creature, with all his boasted intellect. Even the prodigality of fortune will not satisfy him. The attained is sure to satiate; while that which is unattainable, perpetually excites his hopes and cherishes his inquietude. [...] [I]n this short scene of existence, something is to be sought after beyond the mere gratification of the senses. We are to look for social enjoyments; connections that charm without benumbing the faculties; and mental delights, harmonized by the soft touches of taste and sensibility. (*Sevrac* III: 218–219)

The tragedy of Vathek resides in his insatiable desires, which are typical of greedy men observed by Lucretius in his *Nature of Things*. What St Clair preaches is a form of balance and moderation, which could be welcome if it did not sound contradictory and even hypocritical. He has not only enjoyed the extremes of passions and libertinism in Florence but has also been on the limit of temptation with Sabina de Sevrac, which makes him more similar to the male character in William Hogarth's *Mariage a la Mode* (1744) than to a wise philosopher, considering that he turns out to be, however regretfully, a married man. Another important topic in *Hubert de Sevrac* is the hereditary and financial issue, and the ensuing anguish, humiliation and difficulties that disinherited characters have to endure. Starting with Walpole and proceeding up to Radcliffe, Roche, Lewis and many other early Gothic writers, losing one's right to inheritance is the beginning of tribulation and social exclusion regardless of gender. Women are certainly more exposed to danger, but Robinson intends to show that despite coverture, i.e. the protection of a father and/or a husband, they can face indifference, greed and violence if they lose their legal inheritance. Theodore should be a king in *The Castle of Otranto* (1764), but he is a peasant instead and is in danger unless his title is recognised. The same happens to Reeve's male protagonist in *The Old English Baron* (1777), who is humiliated and oppressed. It is necessary for de Sevrac to progressively dismantle Ravillon's system of lies, a pursuit that is rather more fortuitous than planned. Finally, also Abbé Le Blanc has his moment of short-lived glory in the plot. An otherwise passive character, frequently forgotten by the very same Robinson, the good and venerable Abbé manages to be at Emily's mother deathbed. Before the Countess dies in his arms, he obtains a reconciliation between the dying woman and her daughter, and Emily's inheritance is restored together with the one from de Sevrac's father, which is the best conclusion a Gothic romance may offer.

The critical response to *Hubert de Sevrac* was not positive. Coleridge's review did not express appreciation (Close: 174). An author that Robinson adored and considered a friend and a mentor, Wollstonecraft was tepid in her appraisal and did not seem to reciprocate Robinson's affection and esteem. She considered Robinson a perfect imitator of Radcliffe, "still the characters are so imperfectly sketched, the incidents so unconnected, the changes of scene so frequent, that interest is seldom excited, and curiosity flags" (*The Analytical Review*. 1796. XXV: 523). Robinson's frantic production of novels and essays during the last four years of her life seem to be a desperate attempt to fight with time and illness. *Hubert de Sevrac* betrays a hasty, and sometimes careless, writing, which is nevertheless enticing. Robinson's literary output also mirrors her intention to reach a wider public and obtain that economic stability that frequently lacked in her life, alternating with short periods of financial successes. Despite the remarkable number of works and an extended autobiography, Robinson shares Radcliffe's destiny. Like Radcliffe, she was the victim of oblivion for more than a century, but has progressively started to attract critical interest and some monographies have rendered her justice in the last few decades, highlighting her special character and rich literary creations. Ashley Cross (2017), who wrote a relevant biography, recognises the importance of Robinson in the development of Romanticism and her pioneering role in the creation of a new form of poetry, rich in imagination and enriched with constant classical hints. Her Gothic production contains traces of her classical knowledge, which is evident in *Vancenza*, and only suggested in *Hubert de Sevrac*.

The immortal image of Mary Robinson can be found in Joshua Reynolds's portrait dated 1783, a token of "thoughtfulness, introspection, wistfulness [...]", her head turned away towards the distance to recall her famous Perdita character (Byrne: 233). She is "looking into a stormy sea" (Gamer and Robinson: 241), an enchanting heroine observing the tempest lingering on her beautiful but difficult life that began in the style of Charles Dickens's *David Copperfield*: "If the *Memoirs* is to be believed, even the weather contributed to the atmosphere of foreboding on the night of her birth. 'I have often heard my mother say that a more stormy hour she never remembered. The wind whistled round the dark pinnacles of the minster tower, and the rain beat in torrents against the casements of her chamber'. 'Through life,' Mary continued, 'the tempest has followed my footsteps'" (Byrne: 8–9). This gloomy introduction to her birth and life represents the Gothic and Romantic essence of Robinson's unique character.

Early Gothic Iconographies: From Classical to Rococo through
Renaissance

The Romantics of the eighteenth and nineteenth century were
fascinated by the savage grandeur, horror, and sublimity that
they saw in Salvator Rosa's works.
(Richard W. Wallace, "The Genius of Salvator Rosa")

Richard Wilson caught the tone and character of Italian scenery
and stepped his spirit in its splendor. His landscapes are fanned
with the pure air, warmed with the glowing suns, filled with the
ruined temples, and sparkling with the wooded streams and
tranquil lakes of that classic region.
("Richard Wilson: The Landscape Painter"
The Illustrated Magazine of Art)

The process of etching, in which the artist draws with a stylus
on the varnished surface of the copperplate (rather than
working with an engraving burin *into* the copper itself) allows
the acid to produce soft, delicate, spidery, even painterly
effects with the printer's ink.
(Richard Wendort, "Piranesi's Double Ruin")

The Gothic absorbed the notion of the visual foreshown in works by Burke,
Hume and other thinkers of the epoch. Iconographies more or less hidden
in Gothic stories, apart from the ones we have already analysed in
previous chapters, are worth examining for the richness of their
suggestions. Early Gothic writers, especially Walpole and Beckford, were
art lovers and they poured their noticeable knowledge into their stories,
which have a remarkable visual appeal. Radcliffe specialised in word-
painting but also recognised the impact of painters she frequently
mentioned in her stories to reiterate their importance. Lewis was more
reluctant and, as with his literary sources, did not clearly acknowledge
artistic sources, even though he mentioned famous pieces of art to

compare to his beautiful female characters. We saw how grottoes and their representations in Teniers the Younger, Rosa da Tivoli and Renaissance gardens might have provided images for *The Castle of Otranto*. Foreshortening, *quadratura* and *anamorphosis* were technical innovations (re)introduced by Italian Renaissance and Seventeen-Century painters to create illusions and fake perspectives, or provide the impression of a space other, a different dimension expanding beyond the limits of a fresco or a picture. Ancient artists knew several techniques, as the works of Antiquity and the mosaics in Pompeii, among others, demonstrate. These various kinds of trompe l'oeil–to which the National Gallery of Art in Washington dedicated an impressive exhibition "Deception and Illusions" in 2002–were meant to create an interaction between the viewers, their space and the representation within the frame. With his strange episode of the spirit coming out of a frame to interact directly with "real" characters in the story, Walpole was creating a further illusion inherited from the Old Masters. A painting dated 1470 by Francesco Benaglio of Verona shows an old and ghostlike *Saint Jerome* about to step out of the painting, as if quitting the desert where the holy man had been experiencing tremendous visions. The image seems to provide a model to Walpole and his fearsome story, which not only brought about a new idea of romance and started the Gothic trend but also provided visual strength.

Like Walpole, Beckford was an art lover and collector throughout his life. Cozens, his drawing-master, "was the most important influence on his youth" (Alexander: 13) after his father. Born in Russia to a shipbuilder and an Englishwoman, Cozens travelled to Italy where he met Claude-Joseph Vernet. He worked in the French painter's studio in Rome. When he moved to England, he worked at Eton and taught painting techniques to various aristocratic children. He opportunistically disappeared from Beckford's life when the Courtenay scandal broke out. He had developed a landscape drawing technique, which, as John Sena clarifies (1973: 212–213), was based on "blots". The painter expanded these patches of colour until they became clearer images: "Beckford was thoroughly familiar with Cozens' theory and style of painting. The artist probably employed the same principles and techniques in teaching Beckford to paint that he later suggested in a *New Method of Assisting the Invention in Drawing Original Compositions of Landscape* (1785) for all aspiring landscape painters to follow". Cozens was instrumental in the development of young Beckford's imagination. He introduced his son to young William and they were travel companions during Beckford's several visits to the Continent. Cozens later introduced Beckford to Vernet, the renowned French landscape painter, who had lived in Italy for more than twenty years. Beckford met Vernet when he was twenty-three and the French painter realized that he was already a genuine connoisseur of art in spite of his young age. Following his father's example, Beckford acquired masterpieces of various Dutch, French and Italian masters that were kept at Fonthill for his personal enjoyment during the long years of his solitary life, apparently "surrounded by catamites", as Norton reports in "The Fool of Fonthill". The National Gallery in London now owns many paintings that belonged to his collections (Gerald Reitlinger 1961). The catalogue of masterpieces at Fonthill Abbey, sold at the 1823 auction, contains an impressive variety of authors and paintings of all epochs, without mentioning artefacts, furniture and precious objects. Beckford had constant incentives for his inventiveness by simply observing his collection. Looking up the names in the auction catalogue list can give a sense of what a majestic and rich palace Beckford inhabited. It was an art lover's paradise: Brueghel, Sebastiano del Piombo, Guercino, Carracci, Correggio, Paolo Veronese, Canaletto, Domenichino, Claude, Salvator Rosa, Poussin, Robert Hubert, Cima da Conegliano, Raphael, Luca Signorelli, Andrea Mantegna, Perugino, Leonardo da Vinci, Louis Le Nain, Teniers, Velázquez, Hans Holbein, Rubens, Van Eyck, Greuze, Rembrandt, Murillo, Watteau, Bronzino, Bassano, Ruisdael, Bellini, Albrecht Dürer, Wilson, Palma, Van der Meer, Andrea del Sarto, and Gainsborough were among the celebrated artists he owned in a collection formed by a myriad paintings, drawings, and miniatures. The collection also included Jacques Callot's Baroque drawings and prints. Beyond the traditional rendering of landscapes and naturalist characters, Callot was famous for depicting strange and deformed creatures, which inspired Beckford to delineate the hideous Giaour and other grotesque elements in *Vathek*.

The extraordinary *mise en scène* for his coming of age organized by de Louthenbourg (Alexander: 78) was impressed in his mind, as the event had given him a sense of absolute happiness that he could not feel any more for the rest of his life. One of Vathek's palaces offer clear traces of de Louthenbourg's influence. The place "named *The Delight for the Eye* or *The Support of Memory,* was an entire enchantment. [...] Here the well-managed perspective attracted the sight; there the magic of optics agreeably deceived" (*Vathek*: 2). In a note written on 9 December 1838, more than sixty years later, Beckford still recalled the phantasmagorical celebration that he described as if it had happened a few days before. He had a strange sense of time and frequently joked about his age in his correspondence. Alexander reveals that after he turned eighty, while conversing with his daughters, he humorously observed that death had probably forgotten about him. With William Wordsworth's and Mary Shelley's exceptions, Beckford outlived the majority of Gothic writers and Romantic poets active between the end of the eighteenth century and the beginning of the nineteenth century. In his later years, Beckford still remembered the reproduction of a classical temple in an oak-grove, lit "by a continuous glow of saffron-coloured flame". The atmosphere was magic but also strange because the "throng assembled before [the temple] looked dark and devilish by contrast" (Alexander: 79–80). Beauty always seemed to have a gloomy counterpart for Beckford. In fact, a series of bonfires had been set up in the garden in remembrance of "Troy and Hector's funeral". The majestic event, to which he contributed with a series of suggestions, showed some aspects that are traceable in his literary works. Beckford included classical elements and he mixed them to Gothic imagery and Romantic sensibility, as it is possible to infer from the following words:

Delightful indeed were these romantic wanderings; delightful the straying about this little interior world of exclusive happiness, surrounded by lovely Beings in all the freshness of their early bloom, so fitted to enjoy it. Here, nothing was dull or vapid; here, nothing resembled in the least the common forms and usages, the *train train* and routine of fashionable existence [and] even the uniform splendour of gilded roofs was partially obscured by the vapour of wood aloes, ascending in wreaths [...]. I still feel warm and irradiated by the recollection of that strange and necromantic light which Louthenbourg had thrown over what absolutely appeared a realm of Fairy, or rather perhaps a Demon Temple deep beneath the earth, set apart for tremendous mysteries. (Alexander: 81)

De Louthenbourg's elaborate sound-and-light show had unchained Beckford's fantasy. A vast range of sources may have given life to the variety of images in *Vathek*. Some beautiful landscapes in the novel are romantic, but their vagueness does not provide clues for analogies. A medley of landscape artists' picturesque panoramas, from George Lambert to Richard Wilson, Thomas Gainsborough and Wright of Derby could have inspired images for *Vathek*. Some passages of the novel feature placid landscapes. In one bucolic scene, the caliph and the caravan from Samarah have stopped to rest: Beckford has slowed down his nonchalant narration to offer a quiet pastoral moment, full of classical tones. The description seems to be a reproduction of George Lambert's *Pastoral Scene* painted in 1744. Lambert was one of the few painters who had never been on the Grand Tour, but he had interiorised Rosa and

Lorrain's style and created an appreciated method of landscape painting. He reproduced Oriental landscapes and was a renowned painter of theatre sceneries, a detail that Beckford certainly noticed. The author may have used Lambert's quiet natural settings with shepherds and white flocks as an interlude between the paroxysms of Vathek's agitated actions. Wright of Derby was the unsurpassed British master of romantic *chiaroscuro,* the technique that he had perfected during his stay in Rome. In 1784, he created one of his most famous masterpieces, *Dovedale by Moonlight.* It represents a valley traversed by a river and surrounded by luxuriant woods suffused with an enchanting whitish gleam, which was followed by the equally dramatic *Peak District Landscape,* created after 1785, in which the moon is still semi-hidden behind some trees, conveying a sense of mystery and Burkean sublime (Elisabeth E. Barker 2009: 176). Beckford seems to reproduce these images in his nocturnal scenes. Some undertakings in *Vathek* occur during the night that can be full of horror, "uncommonly dark", traversed by a "pestilential blast" when Carathis dominates the scene. On the contrary, the night conveys a sense of languor and mildness when Vathek is gratifying his hedonist ego: "during these occurrences, the moon arose, the wind subsided, and the evening became [...] serene and inviting" (*Vathek*: 69). The temporal proximity of the writing of *Vathek* and Wright of Derby's paintings, together with Beckford's curious interest for every artistic production old and new might support the analogy between the novel's night scenes and Wright of Derby's famous canvases, which also influenced Radcliffe's nocturnal sketches.

The progression of Vathek's strange parable, with his colourful seraglio, his eunuchs and all his servants begins as an optimistic enterprise full of merriment and expectation. The caliph goes on a mythical quest and the atmosphere is peaceful; devastating storms and strange events are still distant. Despite some distinctions, it is possible to find visual similarities between Beckford's apparently blissful journey and Antoine Watteau's rococo atmosphere in *Embarkation for Cythera* also known as *The Pilgrimage to the Isle of Cythera* (1717). Watteau was dominant in Beckford family's art collection and is frequently present in *Vathek* in the writer's delineation of variegated assemblies. Watteau's painting merges Oriental images with classical mythology, embellished by rococo imagination. However, the meaning of the representation remains mysterious. Women and men join in a joyful expedition to the land of love, accompanied by playful cupids. It is not clear if they are leaving for their distant destination or getting ready to return to their place of origin. When asked about the painting's significance, Watteau never clarified the message that the painting was to transmit. In a similar way, Vathek's light-hearted subjects enthusiastically pursue his colourful wanderings without really understanding the sense of the events happening around them. Children take part to the adventure as well, but despite all gaiety, the majority is doomed to find a tragic destiny. A destiny that is shared by the caliph and his beautiful companion. When they arrive at the mysterious palace of doom, they find a terrifying ensemble of "death-like stillness" surrounding "the ruins of an immense palace" (*Vathek*: 107–108). Piranesi's fictitious architectural structures seem to dominate Beckford's elaboration of the infernal context at the entrance to the lugubrious but majestic subterranean world, in which all characters are to be prisoners forever. Many etchings could have provided the inspiration, but two in particular seem to have a link to the scene. Made between the 1740s and the 1750s, they are respectively: *Part of the Subterranean Cellar of the Capitoline Hill* (Piranesi II: 409) and *The Interiors of the Baths of Sallust* (Piranesi II: 419). The former corresponds to a special view of a labyrinthine subterranean construction and the latter is a majestic entrance to hypogean thermal springs. Both etchings convey ideas of obscurity and mystery within majestic places hidden underground. In the end, when fatal punishment strikes the protagonists, they lose hope and their faces are deformed by infinite torment (*Vathek*: 119). The characters of Adam and Eve majestically summarize despair in Masaccio's painting describing *The Expulsion from the Garden of Eden* (1425) and seem to anticipate Vathek's iconography of hopelessness.

Compared to Walpole and Beckford, Lewis's artistic influences are less evident. Even if he does not share the hypothesis, Maurice Lévy (1995) reports that Lewis's earlier critics and biographers, such as Summers, Varma and Peck, justified his dark imagery as a consequence of the fearful impressions he had received when he was a child. The images he observed largely affected him while he was reading his mother's book *Saducismus Triumphatus* (1681) by Joseph Glanvill (also spelled as Glanvil, as per the *Encyclopaedia Britannica*). The horrid representation of the devil in the book might have marked his fervid imagination. On the contrary, Lévy conjectures that various sources and different events spurred Lewis's imagination. Baron Wilson (I: 28) describes Lewis's visits to a sombre castle, Stanstead Hall, owned by one of his powerful relatives on his mother's side when he was a child. She posits that the place must have left a lasting impression on young Matthew's imagination, as his two sisters corroborate in their correspondence. His sister Sophia remembered that the majestic building had affected their imagination while they were children, particularly because one wing of the castle was thought to be haunted (Baron Wilson I: 62). This represents an interesting anecdote, but it is not enough to determine the sources *The Monk*'s cryptography. Baron Wilson also writes that Lewis had a special predilection "for the picturesque" (II, 113).

Unlike the novels that had preceded it, the iconography of *The Monk* concentrated more on characters than on landscapes. Lewis's descriptions of nature are limited to the essential but the sporadic sections in which nature is present are particularly important. Even though Lewis had not been to Italy yet, he probably had a satisfactory knowledge of Italian literature and art. Italian painters, who created images of beauty representing either people, places or nature in the seventeenth and the eighteenth century, such as Artemisia Gentileschi, Rosa, Guardi and Canaletto, were widely known and greatly appreciated in Britain. The highly acclaimed Claude and Poussin had spent most of their life in Italy, an aspect that clearly emerged in their works. Piranesi was highly esteemed in Britain and was appointed honorary member of *The Royal Society of Antiquaries*. British painters, such as Wilson and Reynolds and the expat Cozens spent time in Italy to learn different techniques. They often painted Italian monuments and landscapes, reproduced and admired in other countries. Notwithstanding the importance of the visual arts and the dissemination of Italian art in Britain, tracing the sources of Lewis's fiction is more complicated than in Walpole, Beckford or Radcliffe, whose iconographies have a more recognisable matrix.

The historical dynamics of the period can help us determine the impact of the visual arts, and in particular, of Italian art, which was remarkably strong in Britain. Charles P. Brand (1957: 138) demonstrates that there was "a flood of Italian art" coming to England during the French Revolution and the Napoleonic Wars. This phenomenon was due to a series of reasons. The first one was that French noblemen's art collections had been ravaged and sold (when not destroyed) during the Revolution. After the Revolution, many confiscated aristocrats' paintings ended up being sold in Britain. The second is that Italian aristocracy, frightened by the effects of French Revolution and in anticipation of possible spreading of revolts, preferred to "sell their art-treasures rather than risk having them plundered". The third reason is that British ships sometimes intercepted French ships carrying art works. All of this contributed to an important art market dominated by British art collectors. Then there was a huge market dedicated to the reproduction of famous paintings by known painters. Robert Sayer was a publisher specialised in maps and prints, who made large copies of engravings and etchings of famous painters of the day—in particular, he reproduced paintings by a German expat, who had established his residence in England after a long stay in Rome and became his friend and associate. In spite of being a popular artist and one of the most famous portraitists among Royal families during the second half of the eighteenth century, Johan Zoffany has been overlooked until recently. Penelope Treadwell's (2009) and Martin Postle's (2012) biographies highlight the importance of the visual production of this artist, including his informal portraits of the Royal Family and theatrical scenes with famous actors of the time. His *Tribuna of The Uffizi,* now in The Windsor Royal Collection, dates back to the 1770s. It shows major masterpieces of the recently inaugurated Florentine Museum in a single painting. The so-called "gallery paintings", introduced by Dutch artists in the seventeenth century, had turned into forms of encyclopaedic representations *à la mode* in the eighteenth century. Gallery paintings showed the opulence and luxury of museums, merchants and collectors, but they also had a didactic and informative role for displaying foreign forms of art.

Lewis may have discovered paintings thanks to his various journeys or by observing engravings, prints and reproductions. His love of music seemed more evident than his interest in art, less discernible than in other Gothicists. However, there are in particular three images in the novel that capture the attention for their strong iconographic effect. The most vivid one is the image of the solitary mountains, which are the setting for the protagonist's final tragic moments. A work by Domenico Veneziano, made around 1445, displays a sort of anticipation of the contrast between the wretched monk and the arid landscape surrounding him before he loses his senses. Veneziano's scene shows a semi-naked Saint John, whose body is antithetical with the whitish mountains in his solitary wandering through the desert. The figure of the saint is unusual, as explained in the catalogue of the Washington National Gallery of Art. The image "is classical in appearance [...], but it is a fusion of pagan and Christian ideas". The naked body of the young man represents the classical canon, while the sharp peaks still recall a Gothic context. The description provided by Lewis has a strong resemblance with the painting: "The disorder of his imagination was increased by the wildness of the surrounding scenery; by the gloomy Caverns and steep rocks, raising above each other, and dividing the passing clouds; solitary clusters of Trees scattered here and there" (*The Monk*: 439). The Renaissance image anticipates the saint's future suffering and represents a further analogy with the final context in *The Monk*, even though Ambrosio's path will not sanctify him. The images of mountains and deserts were common in the Renaissance and later on. They were an iconographic inheritance from Pliny and his *Natural History*, in Latin *Naturalis Historia*, written between 77 and 79 CE, before the devastating eruption of Vesuvius took his life. Like other Latin scholars, Sarah Blake McHam (2013) posits the importance of Pliny the Elder's encyclopaedic work on nature for visual arts. Langmuir (1996: 113) supports the hypothesis that Pliny's descriptions of deserts influenced painters from the late Gothic to the Renaissance, such as Giovanni di Paolo, Adam Elsheimer and many others.

The second relevant image in *The Monk* is the beautiful Madonna painting, which provokes Ambrosio's strange emotional state. When Matilda, the doppelganger of the Madonna painting, threatens to stab herself, she uncovers her bosom:

The weapon's point rested upon her left breast: And Oh! That was such a breast! The Moon-beams darting full upon it, enabled the monk to observe its dazzling whiteness. His eyes dwelt with insatiable avidity upon the beauteous Orb. A sensation till then unknown filled his heart with a mixture of anxiety and delight. (*The Monk*: 65)

Some scholars posited that Lewis had Rafael's painting in mind, called *Madonna del Cardellino* (1506), or *Madonna with a Goldfinch*. However, there is no possible resemblance between the Renaissance artist and Lewis's description. Ambrosio mentions the Madonna's beautiful "snowy bosom" (41). However, Rafael's image does not portray this detail. Paintings of the Virgin did not generally show her breast except in images dedicated to the *Virgo Lactans*, known in English as the nursing Madonna, whose iconography apparently started with St. Bernard's miracle, who received nourishment as well as sacred knowledge from a portrait of Mary. Although few mediaeval representations remain, Renaissance and Baroque painters produced various examples of breastfeeding scenes. They united charitable providence with the glorification of the female body. A famous female painter known for her sensual nursing Madonnas is Artemisia Gentileschi, who became well-known during the seventeenth century for her original technique. Her beautiful nursing Madonnas are both ethereal and earthly since they convey ideas of divinity and sensuality at the same time. Artemisia's rape at a very young age surface in her works, in which the clash between male and female characters has dramatic tones. She was internationally popular and Charles I invited her to spend some years in Britain (Tiziana Agnati 2001: 37–42). Artemisia's Madonnas may represent a source for Lewis. One painting dated c.1500, *Madonna Litta*, attributed to Leonardo da Vinci seems the most suitable to represent Ambrosio's mysterious image: it features a delicate Madonna with child showing her right breast. Jan Gossart provided a Flemish version of the scene in a painting of the *Madonna and Child* dated 1527. Her gaze seems to move outside the painting while she is showing her right naked breast, but not in the act of breastfeeding. Her golden ringlets falling down her shoulder recall both Matilda's and Antonia's hair. The French Jean Fouquet portrayed a stylised and self-assured *Madonna* in 1452. What is surprising is the ivory colour of her skin, which recalls the colour "white" in Lewis's descriptions of the beautiful protagonists. Fouquet's Madonna is not breastfeeding, but simply looking at her child and showing her left breast. Even if similarities exist between several representations of naked Madonnas and Ambrosio's *ékphrasis*, they provide only partially convincing analogies. In all probability, Lewis observed images of sacred breastfeeding either in art galleries or in collections of etchings and engravings, but he remained vague on purpose.

The novel offers a third episode endowed with strong visual power that we saw in the previous chapter about endangered innocence. It is amongst the most abhorred by prudish critics, who saw an excess of sensuous exaltation in it. It confirms a sort of iconographic dualism in Lewis, divided between religious icons and mythological representations. Thanks to Matilda's mysterious present, a magic mirror, which has similar attributes to Ariosto's bewitched ring, Ambrosio can secretly spy on Antonia. Antonia is described as a Medicean Venus at the beginning of the story (*The Monk*: 9). Both Antonia and Matilda are characterized by a special aura, which is connected with classical canons of beauty. Antonia is not only compared to a Medicean Venus but she is also defined as a mythical wood nymph "an Hamadryad" (*The Monk*: 9). In this particular context of nudity, the monk can observe Antonia taking a bath and joyfully playing with a little bird (*The Monk*: 271), reproducing the pose of the Venus de Medici.

The Medicean Venus is a Roman marble copy of a Greek statue (dating circa 150 BCE) in the Galleria degli Uffizi in Florence from the collection of the Medici family (McEvoy note 9, 444). Following the fashion of imitation of Antiquity, the Venus de Medici was probably the most widely reproduced form of female beauty—in painting and sculpture—during the eighteenth century. By providing paradigms of classical perfection, modest attitude and sensuality at the same time, the famous sculpture of Venus attracted sensualists like Lord Bryon, who dedicated her some lines in *Childe Harold Pilgrimage* (1812). The statue also intrigued a moralist writer such as Maria Edgeworth, who could not help taking the Medicean Venus as a token of fashion and harmony in her 1801 novel *Belinda* (Olivia Ferguson 2018). An amateur painter and etcher, the renowned art expert

Claude-Henry Watelet introduced the picturesque in France in his *Essai sur les Jardins* (1774) based on James Thomas Whately's *Observations on Modern Gardening* (1770). Watelet described the *Venus de Medici* as an example of perfect proportion in his poem *L'Art de Peindre* (1760). A copy of the Medicean Venus, who seems to seduce Lewis's imagination insistently, as her image is more than once compared to Antonia's physicality, could be admired at the *Royal Academy* in London. The collection, established in 1761, included an unknown artist's copy of the Venus de Medici. The Duke of Gloucester donated the art-piece in 1779, therefore Lewis may have had several opportunities to admire the statue and not only observe it in gallery paintings of the Uffizi. However scandalous it may be, Antonia's bathing image reproduces an iconographic Rococo stereotype, in which the playful nudity of gods or humans is portrayed in a bucolic and serene atmosphere. Fashionable French court painter François Boucher was the master of these delicately licentious scenes. His paintings, frescoes and decorations were an example of the recently developed *"petit gout"* (Rossi Pinelli 1997: 6), dominant in France and then in Europe during the eighteenth century, in contrast with the traditional majestic historical (and/or religious) taste. The similarity between Boucher's bucolic scene, describing *La Toilette de Venus* (1751), now at the New York Metropolitan Museum of Art, and Antonia's unconsciously erotic bath is remarkable. Young Lewis might have admired Boucher, Watteau and other popular Rococo painters while in Paris or thanks to their frequent reproductions. Boucher produced frescoes, paintings and drawings in large quantities and cooperated with Etienne Maurice Falconet, the director of Sèvres Porcelain Company, sending him sketches and drawings. His friend, the etcher and engraver Gilles Demarteau, reproduced many of his paintings and drawings (Rossi Pinelli 1997: 49) thus creating an even greater visibility for his art.

In parallel with literary sources, we may assume that Lewis absorbed iconographic influences, which he inserted into his novel. The works by painters, engravers, illustrators, draughtsman and topographers such as Thomas Hearne, William Watts and Jacob Schnebbelie reproduced monuments, archaeological sites, ruins and landscapes as well as famous paintings. Picturesque theorist Gilpin was a watercolourist and published the images of the locations he had visited, thus spreading the fashion of the picturesque among his contemporaries (Lévy 213). The dissemination of engravings, etchings and illustrations was enhanced by printing through a number of publishers. Cultural societies, among which *The Royal Society of Antiquaries* of London, were instrumental in their large diffusion and consequent accessibility to a wider public. Bookshops, such as the *Temple of the Muses* owned by the bookseller and publisher James Lackington, further contributed to the discovery and propagation of visual arts reproducing an enormous variety of places, either real or imaginary.

Discerning the inspirational iconography in Radcliffe's stories is complicated for a certain vagueness that characterizes her innumerable descriptions of geographies and architectures. Some critics do not think her descriptions correspond to real places. Being an art lover and connoisseur, she might have taken inspiration from visual arts more than from real territories. A number of British painters, illustrators and architects reproduced distant landscapes, especially Italian ones that they had created during their artistic apprenticeships and cultural exchanges in Italy. Wright of Derby and Wilson amply copied sceneries of the places where they long sojourned, contributing to picturesque visions of Italy and the South of the Continent. The etching made from one of Wilson's scenes (1778), in the *Royal Academy,* is entitled *Solitude* and features a thick luxuriant forest, where different kinds of trees can be admired and their reflection creates a liquid forest in the crystal clear water of a lake. Two small characters are in the foreground, apparently reading. The atmosphere is serene and recalls the forest described in Radcliffe's novel, *The Romance of the Forest.* Terry Castle (1995) finds that Radcliffe's landscapes are scattered with interior images that became equivalent to ghostly presences. Jayne Lewis (2006: 377–379) borrows ideas from Aline Grant's 1952 biography of Radcliffe and emphasises that the writer's "characters move through canvases" she probably saw "with her husband during visits to the *Royal Academy*". She adds that Radcliffe, by using quite a limited spectrum of colours, often exploited indefinite images to turn her panoramas into vague landscapes filtered by haze. Radcliffe could have observed a number of etchings and engravings at the *Royal Academy*, which included original versions and copies from famous painters and engravers such as Piranesi, Poussin, Gaspar Dughet, Hubert Robert, Lorrain and Wilson. Dughet, Poussin's brother-in-law, who was born in Italy and lived there his whole life, "was enamoured of untamed nature, which he painted from life in a manner more realistic and less laden with symbols than the grandiose and pantheistic nature of his brother-in-law" (Pierre Rosenberg and Marc Fumaroli 1982: 162). Dughet was highly appreciated and often imitated, thus it was difficult to distinguish the original from the imitation. His paintings were in great fashion in eighteenth-century Britain and were frequently reproduced in black and white etchings and engravings. His landscapes are luxuriant and nature is the dominant aspect surrounding mythological or pastoral beings in the technique of *staffage*, which was widely used by both Lorrain and Poussin. The painting attributed to Dughet (which can be admired at the National Trust Collections) depicts a *Landscape with a Storm*. The colours of the rich foliage and the cloudy sky are transfigured by the violence of the storm. Trees are blown by a furious wind. Dangerous lightning appears through the dark dismal clouds. Some small figures in the foreground show their distress while they proceed with difficulty along the path. The atmosphere is in contrast with the early peaceful moments that Adeline, de la Motte and his wife enjoy, protected by a benevolent nature, and is related to the fearful moments when a horrible storm has unchained, accompanying Montalt and de la Motte's fatal meeting with its disheartening sounds. An appreciated painter mostly famous for his historical and mythological representations, Poussin's landscapes and *staffage* technique tend to reproduce the seventeenth-century Dutch mode in landscape. However, he added a special touch of luminosity in his panoramic descriptions. One of his paintings of the *Garden of Eden*, entitled *Spring*, could well represent a bucolic scenery in Radcliffe's novel:

The first tender tints of morning now appeared on the verge of the horizon, stealing upon the darkness—so pure, so fine, so ethereal it seemed as if Heaven was opening to the view. [...] Meanwhile in the east, become more vivid, darting a trembling lustre far around, till a ruddy glow, which fired all the part of the Heavens, announced the rising sun. At first, a small line of inconceivable splendour emerged on the horizon, which, quickly expanding, the sun appeared in all his glory, unveiling the whole face of nature, vivifying every colour of the landscape, and sprinkling the dewy earth with glittering light. The low and gentle responses of birds, awakened by the morning ray, now broke the silence of the hour. (*RF*: 22)

Salvator Rosa's sublime scenes show an alluring but threatening Nature. He influenced Radcliffe's darkest narrations of beautiful sublime and latent horror. The sources of Radcliffe's eidetic imagery may be as innumerable as possible, but she gives some clues when she openly declares her admiration for Rosa, Correggio, Poussin and Claude paintings. One tranquil scene by Salvator Rosa (*Mercury, Argos and Io*) shows a peaceful landscape. It depicts, however, a tragic story from *The Metamorphoses*. Images of anguish in the abbey ruins may be found in Piranesi's etchings. Greatly appreciated by a British group of painters and architects during their stays in Rome, he sent several copies of his works to the *Society of Antiquaries*. His labyrinthine *Ruins of Maecenas' Villa* and the ruins of *Castello dell' Acqua Giulia* could respectively represent an

303

inspiration for the abbey in *The Romance of the Forest*. On a visit to Belvedere house in 1805, Radcliffe noted in her diary the different styles of the mansion: "the Grecian portico", "The French grey stucco" (Talfourd: 64) and enumerated some of the most important paintings that she was able to admire. She mentions the Italian Canaletto, the English Reynolds, the Dutch Rembrandt and Teniers, and "an exquisite *Campagna di Roma* by Claude". Talfourd introduces Radcliffe's description of the painting and highlights her deep appreciation of art (Talfourd: 64–65):

The sight of this picture imparted much of the luxurious repose and satisfaction, which we derive from contemplating the finest scenes of Nature. Here was the port, as well as the painter, touching the imagination and making you see more than the picture contained. You saw the real light of the sun, you breathed the air of the country, you felt all the circumstances of a luxurious climate on the most serene and beautiful landscape; and, the mind being thus softened, you almost fancied you heard Italian music on the air–the music of Paisiello; and such, doubtless, were the scenes that inspired [Claude].

Radcliffe's awareness of visual arts is akin to aesthetic appreciation in Walpole, Beckford and Robinson. These writers seem much more sensitive to the attraction of iconographies and artistic images than Lewis. Lewis and the majority of early Gothic novelists do not indulge in the description of nature or places and do not seem to be interested in special iconographies. One of the few exceptions is Lewis's allegorical *ékphrasis* connected with the dramatic development in the plot that we analysed in the chapter dedicated to *The Monk*. Critics have frequently tried to identify the sources of Radcliffe's imaginings in travel and tourist literature. Radcliffe's descriptions of Venice in *Udolpho* unchained a sequel of hypotheses and a hunt for literary sources. Lévy (1995: 248) asserts that her inspiration came from artists such as Canaletto, Guardi, Tiepolo and Longhi. Although it is difficult to identify the literary sources for the vast descriptions in her novels, whether of distant geographies, luxuriant landscapes, horrid mansions or sublime ruins, it is possible to surmise that she was able to apply a personal syncretism of various authors and artists that she blended to create a form of visual-writing, which she inherited from the masters of colours. Among the prerogatives they shared, major early Gothic authors used vivid representations recalling numerous iconographies belonging to Antiquity, the Renaissance, the Baroque and the Rococo. The remarkable visual power of their narrations highlights the artistic, literary and encyclopaedic value of their creations.

Afterword: The Gothic's Forbidden and Abiding Fascination

Madeline locked the door after her with a trembling hand, and involuntarily shuddered as she turned from it at finding herself alone in a chamber so gloomy, and so remote from everyone as her present was. Her spirits were too much agitated, in consequence of her conversation to Agatha, to permit her to sleep; and even if inclined to do so, she could not think of reposing on a bed where she had so lately seen the corpse of her friend; whenever she glanced at it, it was with a kind of terror, as if she almost expected to have beheld again upon it the same ghastly figure.
(Regina Maria Roche. *Clermont*)

The dawn of the new century was inaugurated by the growing dominance of Romantic poets, who conquered the public's admiration, even though the Gothic continued to prosper. However, the early Gothic novelists, who had created sensational novels just a few decades before, did not, or could not, publish anymore, or if they did, their publications could no longer obtain the popularity of their previous works. Walpole had passed away, Beckford continued travelling and dedicating himself to his architectural dreams while Lewis became more interested in drama, ballads and folklore before abandoning literature once he got his father's inheritance. Radcliffe's obstinate silence until her death in 1823 remains shrouded in mystery in consideration of the astronomical amount of money she left, which she could not have exclusively gained through her five novels. Lathom, Roche and Dacre, who eagerly filled the void left by the afore-mentioned authors, dominated the first decade of the nineteenth century. An ideal compendium of early Gothic clichés, Mary Anne Radcliffe's *Manfroné or the One-Handed Monk* (1809) seems to mark the completion of an ideal first era of the early Gothic in prose, with its complex plots and subplots, uncertain authorship, the writer's mystery-inspiring name, the affrighting and evocative title and the desire to create suspense in every page. *Manfroné* does not, however, include those special forms of artistic, literary and cultural syncretism—typical of Walpole, Beckford, Radcliffe and Lewis—or their sensibility for Antiquity and authors of the past, which is generally lost in imitators of mainstream early Gothic novelists we have analysed here. It is evident that major Gothic writers' use of Classical models and renowned authors of the past aimed at lofty results and cultural recognition. Robinson stands someway in-between original Gothicists and their imitators because she inserted few classical themes in her Gothic romances. She probably did not need them to acquire grandeur in producing Gothic stories, as she had used the inspiration from Classical, Medieval and Renaissance authors extensively in her accomplished poetic collections.

The second generation of Romantic poets, Byron, Shelley and Keats, notwithstanding their Romantic self-fashioning celebrations, created dismal stories that were evident re-elaborations of Gothic themes and effects, in which violence seemed to be a recurring factor (Joan Curbet Soler, 2003). Keats's narrative poems oscillated between descriptions of innocent victims and *femmes fatales.* An example of the former typology, *Isabella and the Pot of Basil* (1818), depicts the supernatural story of two lovers' tragic destiny, inspired by Boccaccio's novella in the *Decameron* about Lisabetta da Messina, victimised by her murderous brothers. *Lamia* and *La Belle Dame sans Merci* are paradigms of the latter, i.e. the cruel and mysterious woman destroying her lover. The title character, *Lamia* (1819), is a harmful daemon in the form of a serpent, ominously falling in love with a human. The story is an ill-fated love, originally found in the play *Peace* by Aristophanes (421 BCE) and in *Life of Apollonius of Tyana*, written by Philostratus between the second and the third century CE, and included in Burton's *Anatomy of Melancholy* (1621). *La belle Dame sans Merci* (1820) imitates a dark poem by the French medieval Alain Chartier, about a knight enslaved by an ethereal damsel, who is in reality a destructive, supernatural temptress. These Romantic works confirm their Gothic spirit in adopting the tendency of the early Gothic novels to exploit Classical, Medieval and Renaissance sources to show images of horror together with the cyclic destruction of innocence.

Two years before tragically dying at sea, Lewis was in Geneva, meeting with Madame de Stael and working with Byron in Villa Diodati in 1816 (David Ellis, 2011). In June of the same year, during the famous "sunless summer", Byron, Shelley, Mary Shelley and John Polidori decided to undergo phantasmagorical experiences that altered their states after the group had abundantly libated liquor and absinthe in honour of the Muses to magnify sensitivity and increase fear before immersing in the reading of horrid Gothic stories (Hogle 2015). The eventful experiment has been represented in a number of memoirs, essays and films, the most graphic of which is Ken Russell's *Gothic* (1986). Following their bizarre ordeal, all the participants created works of terror, among which Byron's *Manfred* (1817) and Shelley's *The Cenci* (1819), thus continuing the Gothic tradition of supernatural horror. Polidori's novella *The Vampire* (1819) not only inspired Victorian novels and Bram Stoker's *Dracula* (1899) but was also at the origin of the long-lasting iconography of the vampire, exploited in multiple literary and media forms. The most recent progenies of vampires still play an important role in the collective imaginary, as a concourse of television series, novels and films demonstrate. *The Twilight Saga*, 2005–2011; *True Blood*, 2009–2014; *The Vampire Diaries*, 2009–2017 are some examples of a successful trend, which had been preceded by the teen supernatural drama *Buffy, The Vampire Slayer* (1997–2003), a vampire saga featuring a sacrificial teenager, ready to immolate herself like the heroines of Antiquity to save her peers (Tania Evans 2018). An enemy of vampires at first, Buffy is involved in the intriguing tale of fatal love between humans and supernatural creatures.

Mary Shelley's *Frankenstein* (1818) was a gloomy story featuring a complex narrative technique and a pseudo Gothic theme, which, like the vampire, has never ceased to be part of the collective imagination with its disquieting notion of monstrosity. Many critics do not consider it a Gothic novel for its undefined supernatural context and its preoccupation with the ethics of science (Michael Nicholson, 2020). In fact, M. Shelley's story contravenes the Gothic trend, as it is written by a woman and mostly features male characters in search of the inscrutable, metaphysical meaning of life and death. The novel is generally considered the formal conclusion of the early Gothic, sometimes in association with the peculiar *Melmoth the Wanderer* (1820), wherein the Irish playwright Maturin seems to reinterpret the Faustian myth through different phases–recalling the stations of the Way of Sorrows–and explore moral values through the uncanny. In fact, more than the conclusion of the Gothic, *Frankenstein* and *The Vampire* seem to incarnate the beginning of a new phase in this literary genre.

Even if its end had been decreed, the Gothic genre found the way to persist and proliferate across the majestic wave of Romanticism. It also manifested unexpectedly in works of literature that were far from Gothic, as the Italian Alessandro Manzoni's novel attests. Italian Romanticism was belated in Italy and, when it timidly flourished, it was more preoccupied with history and the movements of national independence –known as *Risorgimento* –than lyrical expressions of one's feelings. The stories of

Carbonari giving their lives for the birth of a Nation were considered more Romantic than other topics. Walter Scott's historical novels were taken as an important example, in a period of violent struggles for national identity and bloody wars of independence against the reigns of foreign powers on the Italian soil. A great admirer of Scott's works, Manzoni published the historical novel *The Betrothed* (1827–1840), *I Promessi Sposi*, which he set in the past when the Spaniards dominated the Italian Peninsula. His story, however, covertly criticised the abhorred and ruthless Austro-Hungarian dominion. Cesare Beccaria's grandson, Manzoni grew up in a richly literary and intellectual environment and was fluent in both French and Italian. French authors were the most important point of reference for Italian culture and French translations generally filtered English literature. As Mary Ambrose clarifies (1972: 74), "in translating Scott the French headed the Italians by several years" and Scott cult in Italy was well established by the 1820s thanks to French translations of his works. A French librettist had discovered Scott's *The Lady of the Lake* and passed it to Gioachino Rossini. Influenced by Scott, the Italian musician composed *La Donna del Lago*, a great success that premiered in 1819. The delay in translating into Italian was due to a series of factors, such as the political division of the land limiting communication, the suffocating censorship imposed by foreign rulers and the traditional prevalence of French studies over other languages. Whereas Scott's influence was universally considered evident in Manzoni as a form of literary pride, no relation with other British authors has been disclosed so far. However, some episodes in *The Betrothed*, a story that takes place in Lombardy between Lake Como and Milan, bear a curious resemblance to occurrences in *The Italian* and other novels by Radcliffe, a coincidence that scholars seem to have overlooked. A brutal Spanish aristocrat, who intends to seduce the young, innocent Lucia, orders his henchmen to kidnap her—an event mirroring the almost identical incident in *The Romance of the Forest*. *The Italian*'s Ellena is forcefully brought to a stony-hearted abbess, who seems to provide the source for Manzoni's murderous nun of Monza. Nostalgic passages, in which Emily and Ellena salute the beautiful landscape they are about to abandon is also reproduced in *The Betrothed*. Radcliffe was not translated into Italian until the end of the nineteenth-century. However, her novels were amply available in French (Rogers 1994; 1996). If we consider Manzoni's French cultural roots, his long stay in Paris and his perfect knowledge of the language, besides thoroughly studying Scott, we can infer that he likely read Radcliffe's stories in widely known French translations. However, he never acknowledged her influence, even though, being an avid and curious reader, he probably read Radcliffe's novels and had a chance to peruse Scott's essays on British novelists, which included Radcliffe, The strange case of unexpected cultural echoes in *The Betrothed* containing early Gothic themes and techniques should be further investigated. The analogies demonstrate the pervasiveness of Gothic novels, however imperceptible, which enrich English and European narratives in the nineteenth century, which also resurfaced in American masterpieces by Edgar Allan Poe, Nathaniel Hawthorne and Herman Melville among others. While imitating the Romantics was evidently a form of cultural and literary privilege, avowing influences belonging to supposedly inferior literary works might have damaged the self-aggrandising opportunism of mainstream authors both in Great Britain and abroad. Gothic authors were generally ignored or harshly denigrated, but their images and ideas were absorbed, stolen and plagiarised in the Victorian Age and subsequent periods.

The invention of cinematography gave new vigour to the Gothic, as films could materialise the highly imaginative and visual characteristics of the Gothic, evident since its rise into the literary panorama (David Punter 2019; Sara Martín Alegre 2002). The early Gothic novelists played with the notion of genre from the inception, an aspect that made them apt to be imitated and at the same time gave them an aura of modernity. Elena Sottilotta (2017: 2) rightly observes, "the adaptability of the Gothic and its tendency to surpass the verbal margins of literature is determined by the intrinsic intertextual and intermedial quality of this genre". Early Gothic patterns of horror could translate the existential anguish, and their thematic inventions could be adapted to different literary works in various periods. Their open finales, waiting for other images and worlds to originate from them, were a symbol of modernity that found a fertile place in disparate forms of literature and visual arts. After being institutionalised by critical re-interpretations and re-evaluations in the recent decades, the Gothic has become so complex and diversified that "an overarching definition becomes problematic and even undesirable" (Xavier Aldana Reyes, 2018). Two extremely popular television series featuring preternatural contexts provide incontrovertible evidence of the difficulty of cataloguing contemporary Gothic: *Supernatural* (2005–2021) and *Lucifer* (2016–2021) both involve the uncanny presence of devilish creatures, but a univocal definition of their nature cannot be applied to their plots. The two series have several points of convergence, in which terror sometimes mingles with irony, romance and eroticism. However, the former investigates all forms of hair-raising urban legends, inexplicable horrors and the inescapable dichotomy of good and evil frequently leading to tragic outcomes. On the contrary, the latter generally features a light-hearted and humorous perspective, in which agents of evil can paradoxically metamorphose into bringers of goodness. In the series, the devil does not take the form of Cazotte's Biondetta and is at the antipodes of his medieval Dantesque description in *The Comedy*. He is a handsome Armani-clad hedonistic womanizer, cooperating with LAPD to solve hideous crimes thanks to his deep knowledge of the human soul.

The merit of the early Gothic is elemental and its complex mysteries and constructions still offer material for research. The narratives and the iconographies of the early Gothic are intense and mystifying and show deeper associations with a multiplicity of images of different literary and artistic periods. An enigmatic Renaissance painting inspired by Lucretian axioms (Stephen J. Campbell 2003), *The Tempest* (1508) by Giorgione, is the quintessential representation of mystery, in which a threatening storm is menacing a tranquil landscape. In the background, a lightning in the moonlight illuminates a ghostly Gothic castle. A man is standing on the left with his enigmatic gaze, which could inspire either protection or menace. He beholds a beautiful naked woman taking care of a child, looking at the viewer with mysterious eyes. She could be a victim, but her arcane, imperceptible smile conveys her inner strength. Danger seems to be lingering in the atmosphere, but its enigma is unsolved and still offers many possible interpretations. The painting contains all the *topoi* of the early Gothic novels.

Another painting, Salvator Rosa's *Mercury, Argos and Io* (1653), set in an extensive and luxuriant landscape entrusts a latent meaning connected to the Gothic. It represents a serene, dense forest. However, tragedy loiters over the scene in spite of its soothing peacefulness: Mercury is about to kill the dangerous Argos to free Io, one of Jupiter's lovers turned into a heifer, punished by incensed and revengeful Juno. Both Giorgione's and Rosa's paintings seem to enclose the narrative tropes of Gothic stories with all their mysteries, their tragedies and their delightful horrors.

If you have a garden and a library, you have everything you need
(Cicero. "To Varro". *Ad familiares*)

311

1753. *The Adventurer* 92, Saturday, September 22, 1753 (by Samuel Johnson): 68–76.

1783. Rev. of *Orlando Furioso* trans. by John Hoole. *The English Review. Or an Abstract of English and Foreign Literature.* Vol. II. London: J. Murray: 171–176.

1786. Rev. of *Vathek. A New Review.* June IX: 410–412; Rev. of *Vathek. A New Review.* July X: 33–39.

1786. Rev. of *Vathek. The European Magazine.* August X: 102–104.

1786. Rev. of *Vathek. The English Review* .September VIII: 180–184.

1787. Rev. of Beckford's *Vathek. The Monthly Review.* May LXXVI: 450.

1788. Rev. of Polwhele's Translation of Theocritus. *The Monthly Review* 78: 309 and 350.

1792. Rev. of *the Romance of the Forest. The English Review* 20. London: Printed for J. Murray, 352.

1794. *The Lady's Magazine. Entertaining Companion for the Fair Sex, appropriately solely for their Use and Amusement.* Vol XXIV. London: G.G. and J. Robinson.

1796. *The Analytical Review. History of Literature, Domestic and Foreign.* XXIV. London: J. Johnson, 403.

1796. *The Analytical Review. History of Literature, Domestic and Foreign.* XXV. London: J. Johnson, 523.

1818. *The Tickler. Monthly Compendium of Good Things in Prose and Verse.* I.1 (December). London: J. White, 2–3.

1822. [1713]. *The Guardian.* "The Story of Santon Barsisa" in *The Guardian* 148 (31 August 1713). *A New Edition, Carefully Revised in Two Volumes, with Prefaces Historical and Biographical by A. Chalmers.* Vol. II. London: Stereotype Edition: 296–300.

1823. *Catalogue of the well-selected and valuable Collection of Gallery and Cabinet Paintings by Ancient and Modern Masters. Pictures and Miniatures at Fonthill Abbey.* London: Phillips Son & Neale.

1832. *A Catalogue of the Classic Contents of Strawberry Hill by Horace Walpole.* London: Smith and Robins.

1891. [1711]. "The Vision of Mirzah" by Joseph Addison. 159, September 1st 1711. *The Spectator. A New Edition reproducing the original Text*

both as first issued and as corrected by its Authors. Introduction,
Notes, and Index by Henry Morley. Vol. I. London: George Routledge
and Sons.

2023. Osservatorio Vesuviano, Italian National Institute of Geophysics and
Volcanology. *Summary of the Eruptive History of Mount Vesuvius*.
Web.

Addison, Joseph. 1837. *The Works of Joseph Addison complete in three
Volumes, embracing the whole of The Spectator etc.* Vol III. New York:
Harper and Brothers.

-- 1996. [1712]. "Pleasures of Imagination". *Spectator* 412. 23 June 1712
in A. Ashfield and P. De Bolla (Eds.). *The Sublime: A Reader in British
Eighteenth-Century Aesthetic Theory*. CUP, 62–69.

Aers, David, Jonathan Cook and David Punter (Eds.) 1981. *Romanticism
and Ideology. Studies in English Writing 1765–1830*. London:
Routledge and Kegan Paul.

Agnati, Tiziana. 2001. *Artemisia Gentileschi*. Firenze: Giunti.

Alali, Ahmed. (2014). "William Beckford's *Vathek*: A Call for
Reassessment". *Research on Humanities and Social Sciences* 4. 28: 77–
82.

Aldana Reyes, Xavier. 2018. "The Contemporary Gothic". *Literature*
26.09.2018: OUP. Web.

Alexander, Boyd. 1962. *England's Wealthiest Son: A Study of William
Beckford*. London: Centaur Press.

Ambrose, Mary. 1972. "*La Donna del Lago*: The First Italian Translations of
Scott". *The Modern Language Review* 67.1: 74–82.

Anderson, Howard. 2008. "Note on *The Monk*" OUP, xxxii–xxxiv.

Appelbaum, Stanley. 2004. Introduction, Notes and Translation of *The
Sorrow of Young Werther*, by J. W. Goethe. New York: Dover
Publications.

Ariosto, Ludovico. 1556. [1516] *Orlando Furioso*. A cura di Girolamo
Ruscelli e Giouambattista Pigna. Venetia: Vincenzo Valgrisi.

-- 1816. [1516] *Orlando Furioso* (Translated. by John Hoole). Six Vols.
Philadelphia: Henry Hudson.

-- 1858. [1516] *Orlando Furioso* (Translated. by William S. Rose). 2
Vols. London: Henry G. Bohn, York Street Covent Garden.

-- 1970. [1516] *Orlando Furioso*. A cura di Piero Nardi. Milano:
Mondadori.

Armstrong, Nancy. 1987. *Desire and Domestic Fiction: A Political History
of the Novel*. OUP.

Arnaud, Pierre. 1976. *Ann Radcliffe et le fantastique. Essai de
Psychobiographie*. Paris: Aubier Montaigne.

Austen, Jane.1992 [1815]. *Emma*. Ware: Wordsworth Editions.

-- 2006. [1817]. *Northanger Abbey*. London: Penguin Books.

Backscheider, Paula R. and Catherine Ingrassia (Eds.) 2005. *Eighteenth-Century English Novel and Culture*. Malden (MA), London, Victoria: Blackwell.

Baker, Eric. 2007. "Lucretius in the European Enlightenment" in S. Gillespie and P. Hardie (Eds.). *The Cambridge Companion to Lucretius*. CUP, 274–288.

Baker, Samuel. 2014. "Ann Radcliffe beyond the Grave: *Gaston de Blondeville* (1826)" in D. Townshend and A. Wright (Eds.). *Ann Radcliffe, Romanticism, and the Gothic*. CUP, 168–182.

Baldick, Chris and Robert Mighall. 2000. "Gothic Criticism" in David Punter (Ed.). *A Companion to the Gothic*. Oxford: Blackwell, 209–228.

Ballaster, Ros. 2005a. *Fabulous Orient. Fictions of the East in England 1662–1785*. OUP.

-- 2005b. "Narrative Transmigrations: The Oriental Tale and the Novel in Eighteenth Century Britain" in Paula Backscheider and Catherine Ingrassia (Eds.). *Eighteenth-Century English Novel and Culture*. Malden (MA), London, Victoria: Blackwell, 75–95.

Barbieri, Giovanni. 1791. *The Life of Joseph Balsamo, commonly called Count Cagliostro*. London: C. & C. Kearsley.

Barker, Elisabeth E. (2009). "Joseph Wright of Derby's Moonlight Landscape in Cologne". *Wallraf-Richartz Jahrbuch*. 70: 175–194.

Baron Wilson, Margaret. 1839. *The Life and Correspondence of M.G. Lewis, with many pieces of Prose and Verse, never before published*. 2 Vols. London: Henry Colburn Publisher.

Bates, Richard. 2005. "Italian Literature" in S. Gillespie and D. Hopkins (Eds.). *The Oxford History of Literary Translation in English: 1660–1790*. Vol. III. OUP, 395–405.

Batey, Mavis. 2005. "The Pleasures of the Imagination: Addison's Influence on Early Landscape Gardens". *Garden History* 33. 2: 189–209.

Battaglia, Beatrice. 2008. *Paesaggi e Misteri. Riscoprire Ann Radcliffe*. Napoli: Liguori.

Baudelaire, Charles. 1999. [1857]. *Les Fleurs du mal*. Paris: Livre de Poche.

[Beccaria, Cesare]. 1775. [1764]. *An Essay on Crimes and* Punishments, (Translated from French and attributed to Voltaire). London: Ed. for F. Newbery.

[Beckford, William]. 1797. *Azemia. Novel Interspersed with Pieces of Poetry*. Jaqueta A. M. Jenks. Two Vols. London: Sampson Low.

Beckford, William. 1834. *Italy: with sketches of Spain and Portugal.* Vol I. London: Richard Bentley.

-- 1838. *Biographical Memoirs of Extraordinary Painters.* London: Richard Bentley.

-- 2008. [1786]. *Vathek.* Edited by Roger Lonsdale. OUP.

Beniscelli, Alberto (Ed.). 1997. *Naturale e Artificiale in Scena nel Secondo Settecento.* Roma: Bulzoni.

Bessler, John. 2014. *The Birth of American Law: an Italian Philosopher and the American Revolution.* Durham: Carolina Academic Press.

Bienstock Anolik, Ruth. 2003. "The Missing Mother". *Modern Language Studies* 33. 1/2: 24–43.

Black, Jeremy. 1992. *The British Abroad: The Grand Tour in the Eighteenth Century.* Stroud, Gloucestershire: Alan Sutton.

-- 2003. *Italy and the Grand Tour.* New Haven CT: Yale University Press.

Blake McHam, Sarah. 2013. *Pliny and the Artistic Culture of the Italian Renaissance.* New Haven: Yale University Press.

Boccaccio. 1974. [1350]. *Decameron.* 2 Vols. Milano: Garzanti.

Boccassini, Daniela. (1997). "Love Magic and Storytelling in Boiardo's *Orlando Innamorato*: the Dragontina Episode". *Forum Italicum Supplement*: 35–59.

Boiardo, Matteo Maria. 1823. [1483]. *The Orlando Innamorato* (Translated into prose from the Italian of Francesco Berni by William Stuart Rose). Edinburgh and London: W. Blackwood and T. Cadell.

Botting, Fred. 1993. "Power in the Darkness. Heterotopia, Literature, and Gothic Labyrinths". *Genre* 26: 253–282.

-- 1995. *Gothic.* London and New York: Routledge.

-- 2008. *Limits of Horror, Technologies, Bodies, Gothic.* Manchester University Press.

Bowers, Toni. 2004. "Representing Resistance: British Seduction Stories, 1660–1800" in Paula Backscheider and Catherine Ingrassia (Eds.). *Eighteenth-Century English Novel and Culture.* Malden (MA), London, Victoria: Blackwell, 140–163.

Boyd, Henry. 1802. *Divine Comedy by Dante.* Translation by Henry Boyd. Three Vols. (*Inferno, Purgatorio, Paradiso*). London: Cadell and Davies.

Brand, Charles Peter. 1957. *Italy and the English Romantics. The Italianate Fashion in Early Nineteenth* Century. CUP.

Braund, Susanna. 2013. "The Ghost in Seneca in Renaissance Drama" in Emma Buckley and Martin Dinter (Eds.). *A Companion to the Neronian Age.* Oxford: Blackwell.

Brewer, William D. 2001. "Transgendering in Matthew Lewis's *The Monk*". *Gothic Studies* 6.2: 192–207.

-- 2006. "The French Revolution as a Romance: Mary Robinson's *Hubert de Sevrac*". *Papers on Language & Literature* 42.2: 115–149.

Brilli, Attilio. 2006. *Viaggio in Italia. Storia di una Grande Tradizione Culturale*. Bologna: il Mulino.

Broadwell, Elisabeth P. 1975. "The Veil Image in Ann Radcliffe's *The Italian*". *South Atlantic Bulletin* 40. 4: 76–97.

Brontë, Anne. 1994. [1848]. *The Tenant of Wildfell Hall*. Ware: Wordsworth Classics.

Brontë, Emily. 1995. [1848]. *Wuthering Heights*. OUP.

Brooks, Peter. 2004. [1973]. "Virtue and Terror: *The Monk*". In Fred Botting and Dale Townshend (Eds.). *Gothic. Critical Concepts on Literary and Cultural Studies*. Vol. II. London and New York: Routledge, 191–203.

Brown, Sarah Annes. 2012. "Science Fiction and Classical Reception in Contemporary Women's Writing". *Classical Reception Journal* 4. 2: 209–223.

Brydone, Patrick. 1773. *A Tour through Sicily and Malta*. London: for W. Strahan, and T. Cadell.

Burke, Edmund. 1782. [1757]. *A Philosophical Enquiry into the Origins of our Ideas on the Sublime and the Beautiful*. London: Ed. for J. Dodsley.

Butler, Marilyn. 1981. *Romantics, Rebels, & Reactionaries. English Literature and its Background 1760–1830*. OUP.

Burton Robert. 1836. [1621]. *The Anatomy of Melancholy. What it is: With all the Kinds, Causes, Symptoms, Prognostickes, and Several Cures of it. In Three Maine Partitions with their several Sections, Members, and Subsections. Philosophically, Medicinally, Historically, Opened and Cut Up*. London: printed for B. Blake.

Byrne, Paula. 2004. *Perdita: The Literary, Theatrical. Scandalous Life of Mary Robinson*. New York: Harper-Collins.

Byron, George Gordon (Lord). 1980. *The Complete Poetical Works*. Edited by Jerome McGann. Oxford: Clarendon Press.

Byron, Glennis and David Punter (Eds.). 1999. *Spectral Readings. Towards a Gothic Geography*. London: MacMillan Press.

Campbell D., Elizabeth. 2005. *Before Victoria: Extraordinary Women of the British Romantic Era*. New York: Columbia University Press.

Campbell, Stephen J. 2003. "Giorgione's *Tempest*, *Studiolo* Culture, and the Renaissance Lucretius". *Renaissance Quarterly* 56. 2: 299–332.

Castle, Terry. 1995. *The Female Thermometer: Eighteenth Century Culture and the Invention of the Uncanny*. OUP.

-- 2004. "The Spectralization of the Other" in *The Mysteries of Udolpho*" in Fred Botting and Dale Townshend (Eds.). *Gothic: Critical Concepts in*

Literary and Cultural Studies. Vol. II. London and New York: Routledge, 80–104.

Catullus. 1867. [First Century BCE]. *The Poems of Valerius Catullus*. Edited by James Cranstoun. Edinburgh: William P. Nimmo.

Cazotte, Jacques. 1960. [1772]. *Le Diable Amoureux: Roman fantastique*. Paris: Le Terrain Vague.

Cavallaro, Dani. 2002. *The Gothic Vision. Three Centuries of Horror, Terror, and Fear*. London and New York: Continuum.

Ceram C. W. 1994. [1949]. *Gods, Graves & Scholars. The Story of Archaeology*. New York: Wings Books.

Chalker, John. 1969. *The English Georgic. A Study in the Development of a Form*. London: Routledge and Kegan Paul.

Chaplin, Sue. 2004. *Law, Sensibility and the Sublime in Eighteenth-Century Fiction. Speaking of Dread*. Aldershot and Burlington, VT: Ashgate.

-- 2011. *Gothic Literature. Texts, Contexts, Connections*. London: York Press.

Chapman, Guy. 1952. *Beckford*. London: Rupert Hart-Davis.

Chard, Chloe. 2009. Introduction and Notes to *The Romance of the Forest*, by Ann Radcliffe. OUP, vii–xxv.

Châtel, Laurent. 2013. "Re-orienting William Beckford: Transmission, Translation, and Continuation of the Thousand and One Nights" in Philip F. Kennedy and Marina Warner (Eds.). *Scheherazade's Children: Global Encounters with the Arabian Nights*. New York University Press, 53–69.

Chew, Samuel Claggett. 1967. [1948]. *A Literary History of England. Nineteenth Century and after: 1789–1939*. Vol. IV. London: Routledge & Kegan Paul.

Choné, Paulette (et al.). 2001. *L'Age d'or du Nocturne*. Paris: Gallimard.

Cleland, John. 1985. [1749] *Fanny Hill or the Memories of a Woman of Pleasure*. London: Penguin Popular Classics.

Clery, E. J. 1995. *The Rise of Supernatural Fiction, 1762–1800*. CUP.

-- 1998a. Introduction and Notes to *The Castle of Otranto*, by Horace Walpole. OUP, vii–xxxviii.

-- 1998b. Introduction and Notes to *The Italian,* by Ann Radcliffe. Oxford University Press, vii–xxxi.

Close, Anne. 2006. "Notorious Mary Robinson and the Gothic". *Gothic Studies* 6. 3: 172–191.

Coleridge, Samuel Taylor. 1797. Review of *The Monk,* by Matthew G. Lewis. *Critical Review* 19 (1797): 194–200.

Cooke, Arthur L. 1951. "Some Side Lights on the Theory of Gothic Romance". *Modern Language Quarterly* 12. 4: 429–436.

Cooper, L. Andrew. 2001 "Gothic Threats. The Role of Danger in the Critical Evaluation of *The Monk* and *The Mysteries of Udolpho*". *Gothic Studies* 8. 2: 18–34.

Copley, Stephen and Peter Garside (Eds.) 2010. *The Politics of the Picturesque. Literature, Landscape and Aesthetics since 1770.* CUP.

Coral Escolá, Jordi. 2007. "Vengeance is Yours: Reclaiming the Social Bond in *The Spanish Tragedy* and *Titus Andronicus*". *Atlantis* 29. 2: 59–72.

Cosgrove, Denis and Stephen Daniels. 2000. *The Iconography of Landscape.* CUP.

Cowper, William. 1875. [1785]. *The Task*. Edited by Henry Thomas Griffith. Vol. II. Oxford: Clarendon Press.

Craig, Randall. 1984. "Beckford's Inversion of Romance in *Vathek*". *Orbis Litterarum* 39. 2: 95–106.

Crisafulli, Edoardo. 2001. "The Divine Comedy. La Commedia" in Olive Classe (Ed.). *Encyclopaedia of Literary Translation into English.* Vol. 1. A-L. London and Chicago: Fitzroy Dearborn Publishers.

Cross, Ashley. 2017. *Mary Robinson and the Genesis of Romanticism. Literary Dialogue and Debts 1784–1821.* New York: Routledge.

Curbet Soler, Joan. 2003. "Hallelujah to Your Dying Screams of Torture. Representations of Ritual Violence in English and Spanish Romanticism" in Avril Homer (Ed.). *European Gothic. A Spirited Exchange 1760–1960.* Manchester University Press, 161–182.

Curran, L. C. (1978). "Rape and Rape Victims in *The Metamorphoses*". *Arethusa* II 1. 2: 213–241.

Dacre, Charlotte. 2008. [1806]. *Zofloya, or the Moor of Venice.* Oxford World Classics.

Daiches, David. 1960. *A Critical History of English Literature.* Two Vols. London: Secker and Warburg.

Dakers, Caroline (Ed.). 2018. *Fonthill Recovered. A Cultural History.* London College UP.

Daniels, Stephen. 2000. "The Political Iconography of Woodland in later Georgian England" in Denis Cosgrove and Stephen Daniels (Eds.). *The Iconography of Landscape.* Cambridge University Press, 43–82.

Dante. 1802. [1320]. *Paradiso* (Translated by Henry Boyd), Vol. III. London: printed by A. Strahan for T. Cadell Jun and W. Davies.

-- 1892. [1320] *Inferno* (Translated. by Charles Eliot Norton). Boston and NY; Cambridge: Houghton, Mifflin and Company; The Riverside Press.

-- 1897 [1320]. *The Divine Comedy.* (Translated by Henry F. Cary and Dante Gabriel Rossetti). Edited by Levi Oscar Kuhns. New York, Boston: T.Y. Crowell and Company.

-- 1999 [1320] *Commedia. Inferno, Purgatorio. Paradiso.* Italian English Version. The Princeton Dante Project. University of Princeton. Web.

-- 2000 [1320] *The Inferno of Dante.* (Translated by Robert Pinsky). English Italian Version. New York: Ferrar, Starus and Giroux.

Davis Paul. 2005. "Didactic Poetry" in S. Gillespie and D. Hopkins (Eds.). *The Oxford History of Literary Translation in English 1660–1790.* Vol. III. OUP, 191–203.

Deacy Susan and Karen Pierce (Eds.). 2002. *Rape in Antiquity: Sexual Violence in the Greek and Roman Worlds.* London: Gerald Duckworth.

De Quincey, Thomas. 1960. [1821]. *Confessions of an English Opium-Eater.* OUP.

De Sade, (Marquis) Donatien A.F. 1878 [1800]. *Idée sur les Romans.* Paris: Edouard Rouveyre.

DeLamotte, Eugenia. 1990. *The Perils of the Night.* OUP.

Demata, Massimiliano. 2006. "Italy and the Gothic". *Gothic Studies,* 8.1: 1–8.

Dennis, John. 1693. *Miscellanies in Verse and Prose.* London: James Knapton.

Dent, Jonathan. 2004. "Contested Pasts: David Hume, Horace Walpole, and the Emergence of Gothic Fiction". *Gothic Studies* 14. 1: 21–33.

-- 2016. *Sinister Histories: Gothic Novels and Representations of the Past, from Horace Walpole to Mary Wollstonecraft.* Manchester: University Scholarship Online.

Derrida, Jacques. 1980. "The Law of Genre". (Translated by Avital Ronell). *Critical Inquiry* 7.1. On Narrative: 55–81.

Desmet, Christie and Anne Williams. 2009. "Introduction" in Christie Desmet and Anne Williams (Eds.). *Shakespearean Gothic.* Cardiff: University of Wales Press.

Dever, Carolyn. 1997. *Death and the Mother from Dickens to Freud: Victorian Fiction and the Anxiety of Origins.* CUP.

Dickens, Charles. 2003. [1859]. *A Tale of Two Cities.* London: Penguin Books.

Diderot, Denis. 2000. [1796]. *La religieuse.* Paris: Le Livre de Poche.

-- 1749. *Les Bijoux Indiscrets, or the Indiscreet Toys.* Vol. II. London (Tobago): Ed. for Pierrot Ragout, sold by R. Freeman near S. Paul's.

Dixon Hunt, John. 1989. [1976]. *The Figure in the Landscape.* Baltimore and London: Johns Hopkins University Press.

Doody, Margaret. 1977. "Deserts, Ruins and Troubled. Waters. Female Dreams in Fiction and in the Development of the Gothic Novel". *Genre* 10: 529–572.

Doran, Robert. 2015. *The Theory of the Sublime from Longinus to Kant.* CUP.

Doyle, Barry. 2004. "Freud and the Schizoid Ambrosio. Determining Desire in *The Monk"*. *Gothic Studies* 2. 1: 61–69.

Drake, Nathan. 1798. *Literary Hours. On Sketches Critical and Narrative.* London: T. Cadell and W. Davies.

Dryden, John. 1697. *Georgics* in *The Works of Virgil.* Translated into English Verse by Mr Dryden. Vol. I. London: Jacob Tonson.

-- 1700. *Fables Ancient and Modern;* Translated into Verse from Homer, Ovid, Boccace & Chaucer, with Original Poems. London: Jacob Tonson.

Duff, William. 1978. [1767]. *An Essay on Original Genius: and its Various Modes of Exertion in Philosophy and the Fine Arts, particularly in Poetry.* Delmar, NY: Scholars Facsimiles and Res.

Duncan, Ian. 1992. *Modern Romance and Transformations of the Novel. The Gothic, Scott, Dickens.* CUP.

Durant, David. 1982. "Ann Radcliffe and the Conservative Gothic". *Studies in English Literature 1500–1900. Restoration and Eighteenth Century* 22. 3: 519–530.

Dussinger, John A. 1990. "Madness and Lust in the Age of Sensibility" in Syndy McMillen Conger (Ed.). *Sensibility in Transformation. Creative Resistance to Sentiment from the Augustans to the Romantics.* London and Toronto: Associated. University Presses, 86–96.

Eagleton, Terry. 2004. *The English Novel: An Introduction.* Oxford: Wiley-Blackwell.

Eco, Umberto. 1976. *Opera Aperta. Forma e Indeterminazione nella Poetica Contemporanea.* Milano, Bompiani.

-- 2001. *Experiences in Translation.* Toronto University Press.

-- 2004. *Mouse or Rat: Translation as Negotiation.* London: Phoenix.

-- 2014. *Storia delle Terre e dei Luoghi Leggendari.* Milano: Bompiani.

Eger, Elisabeth. 2010. *Bluestockings: Women of Reason between the Enlightenment and Romanticism.* London: Palgrave Macmillan.

Eliot, Thomas Sterne. 1923. *"Book Reviews: Ulysses, Order, and Myth".* The Dial 75. 5: 481–483.

Ellis, David. 2011. *Byron in Geneva. That Summer of 1816.* Liverpool University Press.

Ellis, Markman. 2000. *The History of Gothic Fiction.* Edinburgh University Press.

Euripides. 1902. [428–405 BCE]. *Hippolytus, The Bacchae* (Translated by Gilbert Murray). Vol. III. NY and London: Longmans, Green and Co.

Euripides. 1910. [413 BCE]. *Electra. The Plays of Euripides.* Vol. I. London and New York: J. M. Dent & Sons, 159–198.

Evans, Tania. 2018. "Sacrificial Shadows: Tragic Greek Heroines Reinvented for Television in *Buffy the Vampire Slayer* and *Game of Thrones*. Locating Classical Receptions on Screen". Web.

Favret, Mary. 1994. *Romantic Correspondence. Women, Politics and the Fiction of Letters.* CUP.

Ferguson Ellis, Kate. 1989. *The Contested. Castle. Gothic Novels and the Subversion of Domestic Ideology.* Urbana and Chicago: University of Illinois Press.

Ferguson Olivia. 2018. "Venus in Chains: Slavery, Connoisseurship, and Masculinity in *The Monk*". *Gothic Studies* 20.1–2: 29–43.

Fitzgerald, Lauren. 2003. "Crime, Punishment, Criticism. The Monk as Prolepsis". *Gothic Studies* 5.1: 43–54.

-- 2008. "The Gothic Villain and Vilification of the Plagiarist. The Case of *The Castle Spectre*". *Gothic Studies* 7.1: 1–13.

Fleenor, Juliann (Ed.). 1983. *The Female Gothic.* Montreal: Eden Press.

Fleming, John V. 2013. *The Dark Side of the Enlightenment. Wizards, Alchemists, and Spiritual Seekers in the Age of Reason.* London and New York: W. W. Norton and Company.

Folsom, K. James. 1964. "Beckford's *Vathek* and the Tradition of Oriental Satire". *Criticism* 6. 1. Article 5: 53–60.

Font Paz, Carme. 2018. "Writing for Patronage or Patronage for Writing? Two Case Studies in Seventeenth-Century and Post Restoration Women's Poetry in Britain" in Carme Font Paz and Nina Geerdink (Eds.). *Economic Imperatives for Women's Writing in Early Modern Britain.* Leiden: Brill, 97–123.

Foucault, Michel. 1977. *Language, Counter-Memory, Practice. Selected Essays and Interviews.* (Translated by D. F. Bouchard and S. Simon). Edited by D. F. Bouchard. Ithaca, NY: Cornell University Press.

France, Peter. 2005. "Voltaire and Rousseau. French Literature" in S. Gillespie and D. Hopkins (Eds.). *The Oxford History of Literary Translation in English.1660-1790.* Vol. III. OUP, 381–393.

Frank, Frederick. 1990. "The Gothic *Vathek*: the Problem of Genre Resolved" in K. W. Graham (Ed.). *'Vathek' and the Escape from Time.* New York: AMS Press, 157–172.

-- 2005. *Guide to the Gothic III: an annotated. Bibliography of Criticism 1994–2003.* Lanham, Md, Oxford: Scarecrow Press.

Frye, Lowell T. 1996. "Romancing the Past. Walter Scott and Thomas Carlyle". *Carlyle Studies Annual* 16. Special Issue: Carlyle at 200. Lectures II: 37–49.

Frye, Northrop. 1963. *Fables of Identities. Studies in Poetic Mythology.* NY: Harcourt, Brace and World.

Fulford, Tim. 1996. *Landscape, Liberty and Authority*. CUP.

-- 1999. "Mary Robinson and the Abyssinian Maid: Coleridge's Muses and Feminist Criticism". *Romanticism on the Net*. Issue 13.

Fusillo, Massimo. 2012. *Feticci*. Bologna: il Mulino.

Gallaway, W.F. Jr. 1940. "The Conservative Attitude toward Fiction. 1770–1830". *PMLA* 55. 4: 1041–1059.

Galli della Loggia, Ernesto. 1998. *L'identità italiana*. Bologna: il Mulino.

Galperin, William and Susan Wolfson. 1997. "The Romantic Century". *Romantic Circles*. Web.

Gamer, Michael. 1999a. "Authors in Effect: Lewis, Scott and the Gothic Drama". *ELH* 66. 4: 831–861.

-- 1999b. "Genres for the Prosecution: Pornography and the Gothic". *PMLA* 115. 5: 1043–1054.

-- 2000. *Romanticism and the Gothic Genre. Reception and Canon Formation*. CUP.

-- 2001. "Gothic Fiction and Romantic Writing in Britain" in J. Hogle (Ed.). *The Cambridge Companion to Gothic Fiction*. CUP, 85–104.

Gamer, Michael and Terry F. Robinson. 2009. "Mary Robinson and the Dramatic Art of the Comeback". *Studies in Romanticism* 48. 2: 219–256.

Ganofsky, Marine. 2021. "The Libertine Novel" in Adam Watt (Ed.). *The Cambridge History of the Novel in French*. CUP.

Garrett, John. 1992. "Ending in Infinity: William Beckford's Arabian Tale". *Eighteenth Century Fiction* 5. 1: 15–34.

Garside, Peter, James Raven, Rainer Schöwerling, (Eds.). 2000. *The English Novel 1770–1829. A Bibliographical Survey of Prose Fiction published in the British Isles*. OUP.

Gill, Russ. 2003. "The Author in the Novel: creating Beckford in *Vathek*". *Eighteenth Century-Fiction* 15. 2: 241–254.

Gillespie, Stuart and David Hopkins (Eds.). 2005. *The Oxford History of Literary Translation in English: 1660–1790*. Vol. III. OUP.

Gillespie, Stuart. 2011. *English Translation and Classical Reception. Towards a New Literary History*. Malden, Oxford: Wiley-Blackwell.

-- 2005. "The Developing Corpus of Literary Translation" in S. Gillespie and D. Hopkins (Eds.). *The Oxford History of Literary Translation in English: 1660–1790*. Vol. III. OUP, 123–146.

Gilpin, William. 1808. [1771]. *Observations on Several Parts of England, particularly the Mountains and Lakes of Cumberland and Westmoreland, relative chiefly to Picturesque Beauty*. London: printed for T. Cadell and W. Davies.

Glitz, Rudolph. 2013. "A Case of Authorial Emendation in Matthew Lewis's *The Monk". ANG* 26. 1: 24–26.

Godwin, William. 2005. [1794]. *Caleb Williams.* London: Penguin Classics.

Goethe, Johann Wolfgang, von. 2004. [1774]. *The Sorrows of Young Werther.* Edited and Translated by Stanley Appelbaum. New York: Dover Publications.

-- 1970. [1816]. *Italian Journey 1786–1788.* (Translated by W.H. Auden and E. Mayer). London: Penguin Books.

Goldsmith, Oliver. 1881. [1765]. *The Traveller.* NY: Clark and Maynard.

Graham, Kenneth W. 1972. "Beckford's *Vathek.* A Study in Ironic Dissonance". *Criticism* 14. 3: 243–252.

-- 1975. "*Vathek* in English and French". *Studies in Bibliography* 28: 153–166.

-- 1990 (Ed.). "*Vathek" and the Escape from Time. Bicentenary Revaluations.* New York: AMS.

Grant Aline. 1951. *Ann Radcliffe. A Biography.* Denver: Alan Swallow.

Grantham Turner, James. 2005. "The Erotics of the Novel" in Paula Backscheider and Catherine Ingrassia (Eds.). *Eighteenth-Century English Novel and Culture.* Malden (MA), London, Victoria: Blackwell, 214–234.

Greenblatt, Stephen. 2011. *The Swerve. How the Renaissance began.* London: The Bobley Head.

Greenfield, Suzanne C. 1992. "Veiled Desire: Mother-Daughter Love and Sexual Imagery in Ann Radcliffe's *The Italian". The Eighteenth Century* 33. 1: 73–89.

Gregory, William Harry (Ed.). 1898. *The Beckford Family. Reminiscences of Fonthill Abbey and Lansdown Tower.* London: Simpkin, Marshall, Hamilton, Kent and Co. Lts.

Griffin Wolff, Cynthia. 1979. "The Radcliffean Gothic Model: A Form for Feminine Sexuality". *Modern Language Studies* 9.3, *Eighteenth-Century Literature*: 99–113.

Groom, Nick. 2008. "Romantic Poetry and Antiquity" in J. Chandler and M. N. McLane (Eds.). *The Cambridge Companion to British Romantic Poetry.* CUP.

-- 2016. Introduction, Select Bibliography, Chronology, Explanatory Notes to *The Monk,* by M. G. Lewis. OUP, vii–xxxix.

-- 2017. Intr. and Notes to *The Italian,* by Ann Radcliffe. OUP, ix–xl.

Haggerty, George E. 1989. *Gothic Fiction/Gothic Form.* University Park and London: Pennsylvania State University Press.

-- 2008. "Queer Gothic" in Paula Backscheider and Catherine Ingrassia (Eds.). *A Companion to the Eighteenth-Century Novel and Culture*. Oxford: Wiley-Blackwell, 383–397.

Hall, James. 1813. [1797]. *Essay on the Origin, History, and Principles of Gothic Architecture*. London: Ed. by W. Bulmer for J. Murray, J. Taylor, and W. Blackwood.

Hammond, Paul. 2001. "Dryden, Milton and Lucretius". *The Seventeenth Century* 16. 1: 158–176.

Handa, Rumiko and James Potter (Eds.). 2011. *Conjuring the Real. The Role of Architecture in Eighteenth- and Nineteenth-Century Fiction*. Lincoln and London: University of Nebraska Press.

Hardie, Alex. 2020. "The Epilogue to the *Georgics* and Virgil's Nurturing Bees". *Vergil* 66: 35–67.

Hardie, Philip. 2002. *Ovid's Poetics of Illusion*. CUP.

Harrison, Stephen (Ed.). 2007. *The Cambridge Companion to Horace*. CUP.

Henderson Lizanne. 2016. *Witchcraft and Folk Belief in the Age of Enlightenment. Scotland 1670–1740*. London: Palgrave Macmillan.

Hirsch, Eric. 1995. "Landscape between Place and Space" in Eric Hirsch and Michael O'Hanlon (Eds.). *The Anthropology of Landscape*. Oxford: Clarendon Press, 1–28.

Hofman, Amos. 1993. "Opinion, Illusion, and The Illusion of Opinion: Barruel's Theory of Conspiracy". *Eighteenth-Century Studies* 27. 1 (Autumn): 27–60.

Hogle, Jerrold (Ed.). 2001. *The Cambridge Companion to Gothic Fiction*. CUP.

-- 2004. "The Restless Labyrinth. Cryptonomy in the Gothic Novel" in F. Botting and D. Townshend (Eds.). *Gothic. Critical Concepts in Literary and Cultural Studies*. Vol. I. London and NY: Routledge, 145–166.

-- 2015. "Gothic and Second-Generation Romanticism: Byron, Shelley, Polidori and Mary Shelley" in A. Wright and D. Townshend (Eds.). *Romantic Gothic*. CUP, 112–128.

Holes, Clive. 2005. "The Birth of Orientalism: Sir William Jones" in S. Gillespie and D. Hopkins (Eds.). *The Oxford History of Literary Translation in English. 1660–1790*. Vol. III. OUP, 443–445.

Home, Lord Kames, Henry. 1881. [1761]. *Elements of Criticism*. New York: Published by F. J. Huntington.

Hopkins, David. 2007. "The English Voices of Lucretius: Lucy Hutchinson to John Mason Good" in S. Gillespie and P. Hardie (Eds.). *The Cambridge Companion to Lucretius*. CUP, 254–273.

Howard, Jacqueline. 1994. *Reading Gothic Fiction: A Bakhtinian Approach*. Oxford: Clarendon Press.

-- 2009. Introduction and Notes to *The Mysteries of Udolpho. A Romance*, by Ann Radcliffe. London: Penguin Books, vii–xxvi.

Howells, Coral Ann. 1973. *Love, Mystery, and Misery: Feeling in Gothic Fiction*. London: Athlone Press.

Hume, David. 1957. [1751]. *An Inquiry Concerning The Principles of Morals*. Upper Saddle River NJ: Prentice Hall.

-- 1904. [1741]. *Essays Moral, Political and Literary*. London: Grant Richards.

-- 1874. [1739]. *A Treatise of Human Nature: Being an Attempt to Introduce the Experimental Method of Reasoning into Moral Subjects and Dialogues Concerning Natural Religion*. Two Vols. London: Longmans, Green & Co.

Hume, Robert. 1969. "Gothic versus Romantic: A Revaluation of the Gothic Novel". *PMLA* 84. 2: 282–290.

Hunt, Leigh. 1846. *Stories of the Italian Poets: being a Summary in Prose of the Poems of Dante, Pulci, Boiardo, Ariosto, Tasso; with Comments throughout*. New York: Wiley and Putnam.

Hurd, Richard. 1776. [1762]. "Letters on Chivalry and Romance" in *Moral and Political Dialogues*. Vol III. London: printed for T. Cadell.

Irigaray, Luce. 1981. *Le corps à corps avec la mère*. Montréal: Editions de la Pleine Lune.

Irwin, Robert. 2010. *The Arabian Nights. A Companion*. London: Tauris Paperbacks.

Jackson, Hazelle. 2001. *Shell Houses and Grottoes*. London: Bloomsbury.

Johnson, Claudia L. 1995. *Equivocal Beings. Politics, Gender, and Sentimentality in the 1790s. Wollstonecraft, Radcliffe, Burney, Austen*. University of Chicago Press.

-- 2008. "The Novel and the Romantic Century 1750–1850". *European Romantic Review* 11. 1: 12–20.

Johnson, Samuel. 1757. *The Works of Samuel Johnson, LL.D.* Vol. IX. London: Ed. for J. Buckland, G. Rivington & Sons.

Jones, William. 1807. [1771]. "The Seven Fountains" in *The Works of Sir William Jones*. Edited by Lord Teignmouth. Vol. X. London: J. Stockdale & J. Walker, 231–250.

Jung, Sandro. 2010a. "Sensibility, the Servant and Comedy in Radcliffe's *The Mysteries of Udolpho*". *Gothic Studies* 12. 1: 1–12.

-- 2010b. "Visual Interpretations and Illustrations of Thomson's *The Seasons*". *Eighteenth-Century Life* 34. 2: 23–64.

-- 2011. "The Architectural Design of Beckford's *Vathek*". *Eighteenth-Century Fiction* 24. 2: 301–323.

Kahane, Claire. 1985. "The Gothic Mirror" in Shirley Nelson Garner, Claire Kahane, Madelon Sprengnether (Eds.). *The (M)Other Tongue: Essays in Feminist Psychoanalytic Interpretation*. Ithaca: Cornell University Press, 334–351.

Kavanagh, Julia. 1862. *English Women of Letters: Biographical Sketches*. Leipzig: Bernhard Tauschnitz.

Kennedy, Deborah. 2001. "The ruined abbey in the eighteenth century". *Philological Quarterly* 80. 4: 501–523.

Kennedy, Emmet. 1989. *A Cultural History of the French Revolution*. New Haven and London: Yale University Press.

Kewes, Paulina. 2005. "Classical Greek and Latin Literature. Drama" in S. Gillespie and D. Hopkins (Eds.). *The Oxford History of Literary Translation in English: 1660–1790*. Vol. III. OUP, 241–252.

Kiely, Robert. 1972. *The Romantic Novel in England*. Cambridge: Harvard UP.

Kilgour, Maggie. 1995. *The Rise of the Gothic Novel*. London and New York: Routledge.

Kliger, Samuel. 1952. *The Goths of England. A Study in Seventeenth and Eighteenth Century Thought*. Harvard University Press.

Knox, Vicesimus. 1779. *Essays Moral and Literary*. London: Edward and Charles Dilly.

Knox-Shaw, Peter. 1995. "*Vathek* and 'The Seven Fountains' by Sir William Jones". *Notes and Queries* 42. 1: 75–76.

Kosofsky Sedgwick, Eve. 1980. *The Coherence of Gothic Conventions*. New York, London: Methuen.

-- 1981. "The Character in the Veil: Imagery of the Surface in the Gothic Novel". *PMLA* 96. 2: 255–270.

Kristeva, Julia. 1982. *Powers of Horror: An Essay on Abjection*. Trans. Leon S. Roudiez. New York: Columbia University Press.

Kuhns, Oscar. 1899. "Dante's Influence on English Poetry in the Nineteenth Century". *Modern Language Notes* 14. 6: 176–186.

Laclos, Choderlos (de). 1972 [1782]. *Les Liaisons Dangereuses*. Paris: Gallimard.

Lamb, Susan. 2009. *Bringing Travel Home to England. Tourism, Gender and Imaginative Literature in the Eighteenth Century*. Newark: University of Delaware Press.

Lathom, Francis. 2007. [1798]. *The Midnight Bell*. Richmond, Virginia: Valancourt Books.

Langmuir, Erika. 1996. *The National Gallery Companion Guide*. London: National Gallery Publications.

Lee, Sophia. 2000. [1783]. *The Recess*. Lexington: Kentucky University Press.

Lefkowitz, Mary. 1993. "Seduction and Rape in Greek Myth" in Angeliki E. Laiou (Ed.). *Consent and Coercion to Sex and Marriage in Ancient and Medieval Societies*. Washington D.C.: Dumbarton Oaks, 17–37.

Lepre, Aurelio e Claudia Petraccone. 2008. *Storia d'Italia. Dall'Unità ad oggi*. Bologna: il Mulino.

Lévy, Maurice. 1995. *Le Roman "Gothique" Anglais. 1764–1824*. Paris: Albin Michel.

Lewis, Jayne Elisabeth. 2006. "No Colour of Language. Radcliffe's Aesthetic Unbound". *Eighteenth Century Studies. New Feminist Aesthetics* 39. 33: 377–390.

Lewis, Matthew Gregory. 2008. [1796]. *The Monk*. Edited by Howard Anderson. Introduction and Notes by Emma McEvoy. OUP.

Lewis, Wilmarth Sheldon. 1969. Introduction and Notes in *The Castle of Otranto*, by Horace Walpole. OUP, vii-xvi.

Lieber Gerson, Paula. 1986. *Abbot Suger and Saint Denis. A Symposium*. New York: Metropolitan Museum of Art.

Lilley, James. 2013. "Studies in Uniquity: Horace Walpole's Singular Collection". *ELH* 80. 1: 93–124.

Lipking, Lawrence. 1992. "Inventing the Eighteenth Centuries: A Long View" in Leo Damrosch (Ed.). *The Profession of Eighteenth-Century Literature: Reflections on an Institution*. Madison, WI: University of Wisconsin Press, 7–25.

Locke, John. 1764. (1693). *Some Thoughts Concerning Edu*cation. London: printed for A. Millar, etc.

Longinus, Dionysus. 1743. [1st Century ME]. *On the Sublime*. Translated from the Greek, with notes and Observations by William Smith. London: published for B. Dodd at the Bible and Key.

Longueil, Alfred. E. 1923. "The Word 'Gothic' in Eighteenth Century Criticism". *Modern Language Notes* 38. 8: 453–460.

Lonsdale, Roger. 2008. Introduction and Notes to *Vathek*, by William Beckford. OUP, vii-xliii.

Loretelli Annamaria. 2017. "The First English Translation of Cesare Beccaria's *On Crimes and Punishments*. Uncovering the Editorial and Political Contexts". Open Access: Università degli Studi di Firenze. Web.

Lucretius, Titus Carus. 1743. [circa 55 BCE]. *On the Nature of Things: in six Books. Illustrated with proper and useful Notes. Adorned with copperplates, curiously engraved by Guernier, and others*. Two Vols. Edited by

John Adams. London: Ed. for Daniel Browne at the Black Swan without the Temple-Bar.

Lucrezio. 2012. [I century BCE]. *La Natura*. Latin Italian Versions. A cura di Francesco Giancotti. Milano: Garzanti.

MacCarthy, Bridget. 1994. [1947]. *The Female Pen. Women Writers and Novelists 1621–1818*. New York University Press.

Macdonald, David Lorne. 2000. *Monk Lewis. A Critical Biography*. University of Toronto Press.

-- 2006. "A Dreadful, Dreadful Dream. Transvaluation, Realization, and Literalization of *Clarissa* in *The Monk*". *Gothic Studies* 6. 2: 157–175.

Machiavelli, Nicolò, 2019 [1513]. *The Prince*. CUP.

Mack, Robert. 2005. *"The Arabian Nights' Entertainment* and Other 'Oriental' Tales" in S. Gillespie, D. Hopkins (Eds.). *The Oxford History of Literary Translation in English: 1660–1790*. Vol. III. OUP, 470–476.

Mack, Ruth. 2009. *Literary Historicity: Literature and Historical Experience in Eighteenth-Century Britain*. Stanford University Press.

Mack Smith, Denis. 1997. *Modern Italy. A Political History*. London: Yale University Press.

Macpherson, James. 1790–96. [1765]. *The Poems of Ossian*. Two Vols. Dublin: Ed. for J. Moore.

MacVay, Anne. 1948."Dante's Strange Treatment of Vergil". *The Classical Journal*. 43. 4: 233–234.

Madoff, Mark. 1979. "The Useful Myth of Gothic Ancestry". *Studies in Eighteenth-Century Culture* 8: 337–350.

Marivaux, Pierre. 1980 [1730] *Le Jeu de l'Amour et du Hasard*. Paris: Bordas.

Marchand, Sophie. 2011. *Monvel. Les Victimes Cloîtrées*. London: Modern Humanities Research Association.

Marnieri, Maria Teresa. 2016. *Critical and Iconographic Reinterpretations of Three Early Gothic Novels*. Doctoral Dissertation. Universitat Autònoma de Barcelona.

Martín Alegre, Sara. 2002. *Monstruos al Final del Milenio*. Madrid: Imágica.

[Mathias, James]. 1799. [1798].*The Shade of Alexander Pope on the Banks of the Thames. A Satirical Poem with Notes*. London: Printed for T. Becket, Pall Mall.

-- 1801. [1794]. *The Pursuits of Literature. A Satirical Poem in Four Dialogues with Notes*. London: Printed for T. Becket, Pall Mall.

Matthews, Joseph Chesley. 1957. "Doctor Oliver Wendell Holmes and Dante". *Italica* 34. 3: 127–136.

Maxwell, Richard. 2003. Introduction and Notes to *A Tale of Two Cities*, by Charles Dickens. London: Penguin Books, ix-lii.

Mayo, Robert. 1941. "Ann Radcliffe and Ducray-Duminil". *Modern Language Review* 36: 501–505.

McEvoy, Emma. 2008. Introduction and Notes to *The Monk*, by Matthew Lewis. O.U.P., vii–xl.

McIntyre, Clara Frances. 1920. *Ann Radcliffe in Relation to her Time*. New Haven: Yale University Press.

-- 1921. "Were the 'Gothic Novels' Gothic?" *PMLA* 36: 644–667.

McKean, James. 2020. "The Gothic Gaze. The Perception of the Ruined Abbey and Anti-Catholicism in the Long Eighteenth Century". Stirling University Thesis. Web.

McMillen Conger, Syndy (Ed.). 1990. *Sensibility in Transformation. Creative Resistance to Sentiment from the Augustans to the Romantics*. London and Toronto: Associated University Presses.

Melville, Lewis [Benjamin, Lewis Saul] (Ed.). 1910. *The Life and Letters of William Beckford, of Fonthill*. London: William Heinemann.

Milbank, Alison. 2008. Introduction and Notes to *A Sicilian Romance*, by Ann Radcliffe. OUP, ix–xxix.

-- 2014. "Ways of seeing in Ann Radcliffe's early Fiction": *The Castle of Athlin and Dunbayne* (1789) and *A Sicilian Romance* (1790) in D. Townshend and A Wright (Eds.). *Ann Radcliffe, Romanticism, and the Gothic*. CUP, 85–99.

Miles, Robert. 1993. *Gothic Writing. 1750–1820. A Genealogy*. London and New York: Routledge.

-- 1995. *Ann Radcliffe. The Great Enchantress*. Manchester UP.

-- 1999. "The Eye of Power. Ideal Presence and Gothic Romance". *Gothic Studies*. 1: 1–21.

-- 2000. "Ann Radcliffe and Matthew Lewis" in David Punter (Ed.). *A Companion to the Gothic*. Oxford: Blackwell, 41–57.

Mise, Raymond. 1980. *Gothic Heroine and the Nature of the Gothic Novel*. New York: Arno Press.

Mitchell, Sebastian, 2013. *Visions of Britain, 1730–1830*. London: Palgrave-Macmillan.

Moers, Ellen. 1976. *Literary Women*. Garden City NY: Doubleday.

Molesworth, Jesse M. 2009. "Syllepsis, Mimesis, Simulacrum: *The Monk* and the Grammar of Authenticity". *Criticism* 51. 5: 401–423.

Montanari, Massimo. 2002. *Storia medievale*. Bari: Laterza.

Moore, John. 1790. *Zeluco. Various Views of Human Nature, Taken from Life and Manners Foreign and Domestic*. Vol. I. London: A. Strahan and T. Cadell.

Moore, Dafydd. 2016. "A Comparison Similar to This: *Ossian* and the Forms of Antiquity". *Journal for Eighteenth-Century Studies* 39. 2: 171–182.

Morris, David. 1985. "Gothic Sublimity". *New Literary History* 16. 2: 299–319.

Morrissey, Lee. 1999. *From the Temple to the Castle. An Architectural History of British Literature 1660–1760*. Charlottesville and London: University of Virginia.

Muller, Markus. 2004. "From Parody to Paradox: Jacques Cazotte and the Emergence of the Fantastic". *Journal of the Fantastic in the Arts* 15. 4 (60): 320–345.

Munday, Michael. 1982. "The Novel and its Critics in the early Nineteenth Century". *Philology* 79. 2: 205–226.

Murray, Douglas. 1991. "Classical Myth in Richardson's *Clarissa*: Ovid revised" *ECF* 3. 2: 112–124.

Murray, E.B. 1972. *Ann Radcliffe*. New York: Twayne.

Napier, Elisabeth. 1987. *The Failure of Gothic. Problems of Disjunction in an Eighteenth Century Literary Form*. Oxford: Clarendon Press.

National Gallery of Art, Washington. The Collection. "Domenico Veneziano, Saint John in the Desert (1445–1450)". Web.

National Galleries of Scotland. nationalgalleries.org. Web.

Nicholson, Michael. 2020. "A Singular Experiment: *Frankenstein's* Creature and the Nature of Scientific Community". *Science Fiction Studies* 47. 1: 1–29.

Norton, Rictor. 1999a. "The Fool of Fonthill", *Gay and Literature History*. Web.

-- 1999b. *Mistress of Udolpho. The Life of Ann Radcliffe*. London and New York: Leicester University Press.

-- 2000a. "Mary Anne Radcliffe. *Manfroné*" in *Gothic Readings. 1764–1840*. Web.

-- 2000b. "A Visit to Fonthill". *The Great Queers of History*. Web.

Noske, Frits. 1981. "Sound and Sentiment: the Function of Music in the Gothic Novel". In *Music & Letters* 62. 2: 162–175.

O'Gorman, Frank. 1997. *The Long Eighteenth Century: British Political and Social History. 1688–1832*. London: Arnold.

O'Gorman, Frank and Lia Guerra (Eds.). 2013. *The Centre and the Margins in Eighteenth-century British and Italian Culture*. Newcastle upon Tyne: Cambridge Scholars Publications.

Oldmixon, John. 1728. *The Arts of Logick and Rhetorick. Interpreted and Explained by the Learned and Judicious Critick Father Bouhours.*

London: Ed. for John Clark and Richard Hett, John Pemberton, Richard Ford, and John Gray.

Oliphant, Margaret. 1883. *The Literary History of England in the End of the Eighteenth and the Beginning of the Nineteenth Century.* Vol. II. New York: Macmillan and Co.

Oliver, John Walter. 1932. *The Life of William Beckford.* OUP.

Ovid. 1844. [8 CE]. *Metamorphoses.* Translated by Dryden, Pope, Congreve, Addison, et al. Two Vols. NY: Harper Brothers.

Ovid. 1931. [circa 25–16 BCE]. *Heroides and Amores.* With English Translation. Ed. by Grant Showerman. London: William Heinemann.

Ovidio. 2012. [8 CE]. *Metamorfosi.* Two Vols. Latin Italian Version. Milano: Garzanti.

Owen, David. 2014. "(Mal)Interpretando el deseo femenino: control e independencia de la mujer en el siglo XVIII (Samuel Richardson, *Clarissa*)" in Joan Curbet Soler (Ed.). *Figuras del deseo femenino.* Madrid: Catédra, 317–360.

Pallavicino, Ferrante. 1683. [1673]. *The Whores Rhetorick Calculated to the Meridian of London.* London: printed for George Shell in Stone-Cutter-Street in Shoe-Laine.

-- 1673. *La Rettorica delle Puttane. Composta conforme li precetti di Cipriano.* Stampata in Villafranca.

Panizzi, Antonio. 1830. *Orlando Innamorato di Boiardo: Orlando Furioso di Ariosto: with an Essay on the Romantic Narrative Poetry of the Italians.* London: William Pickering.

Parreaux, André. 1960a. *The Publication of "The Monk". A Literary Event 1796–1798.* Paris: Didier.

-- 1960b. *William Beckford. Auteur de "Vathek" (1760–1844). Etude de la création littéraire.* Paris: A.G. Nizet.

Pascoe, Judith. 1997. *Romantic Theatricality. Gender, Poetry, and Spectatorship.* Ithaca: Cornell UP.

Pursglove, Glyn and Karina Williamson. (2005). "Prose Fiction and Fable" in S. Gillespie and D. Hopkins (Eds.). *The Oxford History of Literary Translation in English: 1660–1790.* Vol. III. OUP, 291–307.

Paulson, Ronald. 1981. "Gothic Fiction and the French Revolution", *English Literary History* 48. 3: 532–554.

Peck, Louis F. 1961. *A Life of Matthew G. Lewis.* Cambridge: Harvard UP.

Pennington, Montagu. 1807. *Memoirs of the Life of Mrs. Elisabeth Carter, with a New Edition of Her Poems.* London: Ed. for F.C. and J. Rivington.

Perkins, Pam. 2006. "John Moore, Ann Radcliffe and the Gothic Vision of Italy". *Gothic Studies* 8. 1: 35–51.

Piozzi [Thrale], Hester Lynch. 1861. *Autobiography, Letters and Literary Remains of Mrs. Piozzi Thrale*. Edited by A. Hayward. Two Vols. London: Longman, Green, and Roberts.

Piranesi, Giovanni Battista. 2011. *The Complete Works*. Edited by Luigi Ficacci. Two Vols. Köln: Taschen.

Pocock, J. G. A. 1976. "Between Machiavelli and Hume: Gibbon as Civic Humanist and Philosophical Historian". *Daedalus* 105. 3: 153–169.

Polwhele, Richard. 1800. [1798]. *The Unsex'd Females. A Poem addressed to the Author of the Pursuits of Literature*. New York: William Cobbett.

Poovey, Mary. 1979. "Ideology and *The Mysteries of Udolpho*". *Criticism* 21. 4: 307–330.

-- 1985. *The Proper Lady and the Woman Writer*. Chicago UP.

Porter, Lawrence. 1978. The Seductive Satan of Cazotte's *Le Diable Amoureux. L'Esprit Créateur* 18. 2. *The Occult in Literature*: 3–12.

Pope, Alexander. 1966. [1693]. "Eloisa to Abelard" in *Poetical Works*. OUP.

Postle, Martin. 2012. *Johann Zoffany. RA: Society Observed*. London: Royal Academy.

Price, Fiona. 2006. "Myself creating what I saw. The Morality of the Spectator in Eighteenth-Century Gothic". *Gothic Studies* 8.2: 1–17.

Price Martin. 1969. "The Sublime Poem: Picture and Powers". *Yale Review* 58: 194–213.

Propertius. 1916. [I Century BCE]. *Elegies*. Edited by H. E. Butler. London: Heinemann.

Prosperi, Valentina. 2007. "Lucretius in the English Renaissance" in S. Gillespie and P. Hardie (Eds.). *The Cambridge Companion to Lucretius*. CUP, 214–226.

Priestman, Martin. 2007. "Lucretius in Romantic and Victorian Britain" in S. Gillespie and P. Hardie (Eds.). *The Cambridge Companion to Lucretius*. CUP, 289–305.

Pujol, Didac. 2014. "Molly Bloom. La Mirada que fragmenta" in Joan Curbet Soler (Ed.). *Figuras del Deseo Femenino*. Madrid: Cátedra, 531–570.

Puletti, Ruggero. 2000. *La storia occulta. Il Pendolo di Foucault di Umberto Eco*. Manduria: Lacaita.

Punter, David. 1996. *The Literature of Terror. A History of Gothic Fictions from 1765 to the Present Day*. London and NY: Longman.

-- 2000. *A Companion to the Gothic*. Oxford: Blackwell.

-- 2010. "The Picturesque and the Sublime: Two Worldscapes" in S. Copley and P. Garside (Eds.). *The Politics of the Picturesque. Literature, Landscape and Aesthetics since 1770*. CUP, 220–239.

-- 2012. (Ed.). *A New Companion to the Gothic*. Oxford: Blackwell.

-- 2019. *The Edinburgh Companion to Gothic and the Arts*. Edinburgh University Press.

Punter, David and Glennis Byron (Eds.). 2009. *The Gothic*. Oxford: Blackwell.

Quignard, Pascal. 2015. [2007]. *The Sexual Night*. (Translated by Chris Turner). London, New York: Seagull Books.

Radcliffe, Ann. 1826. "On the Supernatural in Poetry". *New Monthly Magazine* 16: 145–152.

-- 1833. [1826]. *Gaston de Blondeville, A Romance; St. Alban's Abbey, a Metrical Tale, with various Poetical Pieces. To which is prefixed a Memoir of the Authoress with Extracts from Her Private Journals.* Vol. I. London: Henry Colburn, R. Bentley, New Burlington Street.

-- 1998. [1789]. *A Sicilian Romance*. Edited by Alison Milbank. OUP.

-- 2001. [1794]. *The Mysteries of Udolpho. A Romance.* Edited by Jaqueline Howard. London: Penguin Books.

-- 2008. [1797]. *The Italian.* Edited by Fredrick Garber. Introduction and Notes by E. J. Clery. OUP.

-- 2009. [1791]. *The Romance of the Forest.* Edited by Chloe Chard. OUP.

-- 2017. [1797]. *The Italian.* Edited by Frederick Gerber. Revision, Introduction and Notes by Nick Groom. OUP.

Radcliffe, Mary Anne. 2007. (1809). *Manfroné; or The One-Handed. Monk.* Kansas City: Valancourt Books.

Railo, Eino. 1974. [1927]. *The Haunted. Castle: A Study of the Elements of English Romanticism.* NY: Gordon Press.

Redding, Cyrus (Ed.). 1859. *The Memoirs of William Beckford of Fonthill.* 2 Vols. London: C.J. Skeet.

Reeve, Clara. 1778. *The Old English Baron. A Gothic Story.* London: Ed. for Edward and Charles Dilly.

Reitlinger, Gerald. 1961. *The Economics of Taste: The Rise and the Fall of Picture Price 1760-1960.* London: Barrie and Rockliff.

Richardson, Samuel. 1985. [1748]. *Clarissa, or, the History of a Young Lady.* London: Penguin Classics.

-- 2001 [1740]. *Pamela, or Virtue Rewarded.* OUP.

Ricco Renato e Susanna Villari. 2016. "Francesco Robortello in Librum Aristotelis de Arte Poetica Explicationis". *Studi Giraldiani. Letteratura e Teatro* 2. Web.

Rintoul, Suzanne. 2005. "Gothic Anxieties. Struggling with a Definition". *Eighteenth Century Fiction* 17. 4: 701–709.

Rix, Robert W. 2014. "Gothic Gothicism. Norse Terror in the Late Eighteenth to the Early Nineteenth Centuries". *Gothic Studies* 13. 1: 1–20.

Roberts, Adam and Eric Robertson. 1996. "The Giaour's Sabre. A Reading of Beckford's *Vathek*". *Studies in Romanticism* 35. 2: 199–211.

Robinson, Douglas. 2011. *Translation and the Problem of Sway.* Amsterdam and Philadelphia: John Benjamin Publishing Company.

Robinson, Mary. 1824. *The Poetical Works of the Late Mrs. Mary Robinson.* London: Jones Company.

-- 1792. *Vancenza, or The Dangers Of Credulity.* Two Vols. London: Mr. Bell at the British Library.

-- 1796. Hubert de Sevrac. A Romance of the Eighteenth Century. Three Vols. London: Hookham and Carpenter, Old Bond Street.

Robinson, Mary and Mary Elisabeth Robinson. 1895. [1801]. *The Memoirs of Mary Robinson.* Introduction and Notes by J. Fitzgerald Molloy. London: Gibbins and Company, Ltd.

Roche, Regina Maria. 2005. [1798]. *Clermont.* Richmond, Virginia: Valancourt Books.

Rogers, Deborah (Ed.). 1994. *The Critical Response to Ann Radcliffe.* Westport and London: Greenwood Press.

-- 1996. *Ann Radcliffe: A Bio-Bibliography.* Westport CT: Greenwood Press.

-- 2007. *The Matrophobic Gothic and its Legacy. Sacrificing Mothers in the Novel and in Popular Culture.* New York: Peter Lang.

Rosati, Gianpiero. 1983. *Narciso e Pigmalione: illusione e spettacolo nelle Metamorfosi di Ovidio.* Firenze: Sansoni.

Roscoe, William. 1806. [1795]. *Life of Lorenzo de Medici, Called the Magnificent.* Three Vols. London: printed by J. M'Creery, for T. Cadell and W. Davies.

Rosenberg, Pierre and Marc Fumaroli. 1982. *France in the Golden Age: Seventeenth-Century French Paintings in American Collections.* New York: Met Publications.

Ross, Deborah. 1991. *The Excellence of Falsehood. Romance, Realism and Women's Contribution to the Novel.* Lexington: University of Kentucky Press.

Rossi Pinelli, Orietta. 2004. *Piranesi.* Firenze: Giunti.

-- 1997. *Boucher.* Firenze: Giunti.

Rounce, Adam. 2007. "Housing the Alien. Translation in the Long Eighteenth Century". *Modern Philology* 105. 2: 326–336.

Rousseau, George Sebastian. 1991. *Perilous Enlightenment: Pre- and Post-Modern Discourse: Sexual, Historical.* Manchester University Press.

Rousseau, Jean Jacques. 1967 [1776]. *Julie ou la Nouvelle Héloïse*. Chronologie et introduction par M. Launay. Paris: Garnier Flammarion.

Rubin, Gayle. 1989. "Sexual Transformations" in Julie Rivkin and Michael Ryan (Eds.). *Literary Theory: An Anthology*. Malden and Oxford: Blackwell, 679–689.

Saglia, Diego. 2002. "William Beckford's 'Sparks of Orientalism' and the Material Discursive Orient of British Romanticism". *Textual Practice* 16: 75–92.

-- 2006. "From Gothic Italy to Italy as Gothic Archive: Italian Narratives and the Late Romantic Metrical Tale". *Gothic Studies* 8. 1: 73–90.

-- 2009. "Commerce, Luxury, and Identity in Mary Robinson's *Memoirs*". *Studies in English Literature 1500–1900*. Restoration and Eighteenth Century. 49. 3: 717–736.

Sambrook, James. 1972. Introduction and Notes to *The Seasons* and *The Castle of Indolence*, by J. Thomson. Oxford: Clarendon Press, ix–xxvii.

Sandner, David. 2011. *Critical Discourses of the Fantastic, 1712–1831*. Farnham: Ashgate.

Schama, Simon. 1995. *Landscape and Memory*. London: Fontana Press.

Schroeder, Natalie. 1980. "*The Mysteries of Udolpho* and *Clermont*. The Radcliffean Encroachment on the Art of Regina Maria Roche". *Studies in the Novel* 12: 131–143.

Schulz, Dieter. 1973. "Novel, Romance, and Popular Fiction in the First Half of the Eighteenth Century". *Studies in Philology* 70. 1: 77–91.

Scott, Walter. 1826. "Mrs. Radcliffe". *Life of the Novelists*. Vol. II. Zwickau: Brothers Schuman, 38–101.

-- 1847. *The Complete Works of Sir Walter Scott with a Biography and His Last Additions and Illustrations*. Vol III. Philadelphia: Carey and Hart.

-- 1890. *The Journal of Sir Walter Scott*. Two Vols. From the Original Manuscript at Abbotsford. The Literary Network.

Sena, John. 1973. "The Landscape of *Vathek* and the Paintings of Alexander Cozens". *Etudes Anglaises* 26. 2: 212–215.

Seneca. 2001. [I century CE]. *Thyestes*. (Translated by Caryl Churchill). London: Nick Hern Books.

Shaftesbury, Earl of, Anthony. 1773 [1713]. *Characteristicks of Men, Manners, Opinions, Times*. Three Vols. Birmingham: John Baskerville.

Shelley, Percy B. 1887 [1821] "A Defence of Poetry" in *Essays and Letters*. Edited by Ernest Rhys. London: Walter Scott.

Sikes, Edward Ernest. 1936. *Lucretius: Poet and Philosopher*. CUP.

Sills, Kenneth C. M. 1905. "References to Dante in Seventeenth-Century English Literature". *Modern Philology* 3. 1: 99–116.

Siskin, Clifford. 1988. *The Historicity of Romantic Discourse.* OUP.

Smith, Adam. 2005. [1776]. *An Inquiry into the Nature and Cause of the Wealth of Nations.* Edited by Jim Manis. Hazelton PA: Electronic Classics Series, PSU.

-- 1781. [1759]. *The Theory of Moral Sentiments.* London: Printed for Strahan, J. & F. Rivington.

Smith, Charlotte. 1794. *The Banished. Man.* London: Printed for T. Cadell and W. Davis.

Smith, John. 1792. *Select Views of Italy with Topographical and Historical Descriptions.* London: printed by T. Chapman

Sodeman, Melissa.2012. "Sophia Lee's Historical Sensibility". *Modern Philology* 110. 2: 253–272.

Sottilotti, Emma. (2017). "Re-Imagining the Gothic in Contemporary Serialised Media". *Crossway Journal* 1. Web.

Sowerby, Robin. 2005. "Epic" in S. Gillespie and D. Hopkins (Eds.). *The Oxford History of Literary Translation in English: 1660–1790.* Vol. III. OUP, 149–170.

Spencer, Jane. 1989. *The Rise of the Woman Novelist: From Aphra Behn to Jane Austen.* Oxford: Blackwell.

Spiegelman, Willard. 1985. "Some Lucretian Elements in Wordsworth". *Comparative Literature* 37. 1: 27–49.

Stableford, Brian. (2009). *Gothic Grotesques. Essays on Fantastic Literature.* Rockville, MD: Wildside Press.

Sterne, Laurence. 1979. [1768]. *A Sentimental Journey through France and Italy.* London: Penguin.

Stewart, David. (1996). "Political Ruins. Gothic Sham Ruins and the '45" *Journal of the Society of Architectural Historians* 55. 4: 400–411.

Stone, John. 2012. "Seventeenth-Century Jurisprudence and Eighteenth-Century Lexicography: Sources for Johnson's Notion of Authority" in Anne McDermott (Ed.). *The Eighteenth Century* (Ashgate Critical Essays on Early English Lexicographers, Vol. 5). Farnham: Ashgate.

Summers, Montague. 1969. [1938]. *The Gothic Quest: A History of the Gothic Novel.* London: Fortune Press.

Swinburne, Henry. 1790. *Travels in the Two Sicilies.* Vol. IV. London: J. Nichols for T. Cadell and O. Elmsly.

Swindells, Julia and David F. Taylor (Eds.). 2014. *The Oxford Handbook of Georgian Theatre. 1737–1832.* OUP.

Syer, Kathrine. 2014. *Wagner's Visions. Poetry, Politics and the Psyche in the Operas through Die Walkirie.* Rochester University Press.

Talfourd, Thomas Noon. 1826. "Memoirs of the Life and Writings of Mrs. Radcliffe" in Ann Radcliffe, *Gaston de Blondeville, or the Court of Henry III*. Vol. I. London: H. Colbourn, 3–132.

Tarrant, Richard. 2007. "Ancient Receptions of Horace" in S. Harrison (Ed.). *The Cambridge Companion to Horace*. CUP, 277–290.

Tate Gallery. tate.org.uk. Web.

Thackeray, John. 1992. "Christopher Pitt, Joseph Warton, and Virgil". *Review of English Studies* 43. 171: 329–346.

Testa, Carlo. 1994. "Review: *The Devil in Love* by Jacques Cazotte: Stephen Sartarelli". *Nineteenth-Century French Studies* 22. 3–4: 539–541.

Thomson, James. 1972. [1730/1748]. *The Seasons. The Castle of Indolence*. Oxford: Clarendon Press.

Tibullus. 1720. [I century BCE]. *Works of Tibullus. Containing his Four Books of Elegies*. Edited and Translated by Mr. Hart. London: by T. Sharpe for W. Newton.

Tissol, Garth. 2005. "Ovid" in S. Gillespie and D. Hopkins (Eds.). *The Oxford History of Literary Translation in English: 1660–1790*. Vol. III. OUP, 204–216.

Todd, Janet. 1989. *The Sign of Angelica. Women, Writing, and Fiction 1660–1800*. London: Virago Press.

Tollebeek, Jo. 2001. "Renaissance and 'Fossilization': Michelet, Burckhardt, Huizinga". *Renaissance Studies* 15. 3: 354–366.

Tompkins Joyce M. S. 1969. *The Popular Novel in England: 1770–1800*. London: Methuen.

Tonin, Raffaella. 2010. "*Dei delitti e delle pene* di Cesare Beccaria in Spagnolo". *Intralinea. Translation Journal*. 12. Web.

Treadwell, Penelope. 2009. *Johan Zoffany: Artist and Adventurer*. London: Paul Holberton Publishing.

Varela-Portas Orduña, Juan. 2019. "Nei limiti della immaginazione (II): l'ultima iniziazione alla luce attraverso tre similitudini analitiche ('Paradiso' XXX 46-99)". *Tenzone* 20: 221–260.

Varma, Devendra P. 1966. *The Gothic Flame: being a History of the Gothic Novel in England: its Origins, Efflorescence, Disintegration, and Residuary Influences*. New York: Russell & Russell.

Vasari, Giorgio. 1897. [1550]. *Lives of the most eminent Painters, Sculptors, and Architects*. Edited by J. P. Richter. Six Volumes. London: George Bell and Sons.

Venuti, Lawrence. 1993. "Translations as Cultural Politics: Regimes of Domestication in English". *Textual Practice* 7: 208–223.

Virgil. 1830. [I Century BCE]. *The Eclogues* (Translated by Wrangham). *The Georgics* (Translated by Sotheby). *The Aeneid* (Translated by Dryden). Vol. 1. London: A. J. Valpy, M.A. Henry Colburn and Richard Bentley.
-- (Publii Virgilii Maronis). 1849.. [I Century BCE]. *Georgica.* Montreal: Armour and Ramsay.
Virgilio. 2013. [I BCE] *Georgiche.* G. B. Conte (Ed.). Traduzione e note di A. Barchiesi. Latino/Italiano. Milano: Mondadori.
Voltaire. 1966. [1747]. "Zadig". *Romans et Contes.* Paris : Garnier-Flammarion, 29–85.
-- 1966. [1759] "Candide ou l'Optimisme". *Romans et Contes.* Paris: Garnier-Flammarion, 179–259.
Von Klenze, Camillo. 1907. *The Interpretation of Italy during the last two Centuries; a Contribution to the Study of Goethe's "Italienische Reise".* Chicago University Press.
Wagner, Corinna. 2012 "The Dream of a Transparent Body. Identity, Science and the Gothic Novel". *Gothic Studies* 14. 1: 74–92.
Wallace, Miriam. 2009. "Enlightened. Romanticism or Romantic Enlightenment?" in Miriam Wallace (Ed.). *Enlightening Romanticism, Romancing the Enlightenment. British Novels from 1750 to 1832.* Farnham and Burlington VT: Ashgate, 1–20.
Walmsley, Peter. 2009. "The Melancholy Briton: Enlightenment Source of the Gothic" in Miriam Wallace (Ed.). *Enlightening Romanticism, Romancing the Enlightenment. British Novels from 1750 to 1832.* Farnham and Burlington VT: Ashgate, 39–53.
Walpole, Horace. 1982. [1764]. *The Castle of Otranto. A Gothic Story.* Edited by Joseph Reed. Introduction and Notes by W. S. Lewis. Oxford Paperbacks.
-- 1871. [1771]. *Anecdotes of Painting in England.* London: Alexander Murray, 30, Queen Square. W.C.
Warner, Marina. 2002. *Fantastic Metamorphoses, Other Worlds. Ways of telling the Self.* OUP.
Warton, Thomas. 1969. [1754]. *Observations on the Faerie Queene of Spenser.* Two Vols. New York: Haskell House Publishers.
Watelet, Claude-Henri de. 1760. *L'Art de Peindre. Avec des réflexions sur les différentes parties de la peinture.* Paris: Guerin & Delatour.
Watt, Ian. 1987. [1957]. *The Rise of the Novel: Studies in Richardson, Defoe, and Fielding.* London: The Hogarth Press.
Watt, James. 1999. *Contesting the Gothic: Fiction, Genre and Cultural Conflict, 1764-1832.* CUP.

Weiskel, Thomas. 1986. *The Romantic Sublime: Studies in the Structure and Psychology of Transcendence.* Baltimore and London: The Johns Hopkins University Press.

Wendort Richard. 2001. "Piranesi's Double Ruin". *Eighteenth Century Studies* 34. 2. *Antiquarians, Connoisseurs, and Collectors*: 161–180.

West, Shearer. 2014. "Manufacturing Spectacle" in J. Swindells and D. F. Taylor (Eds.). *The Oxford Handbook of Georgian Theatre. 1737–1832.* OUP, 286–303.

Westover, Paul. 2012. "On Ideal Presence" in *Necromanticism. Travelling to meet the Dead 1750–1860.* Palgrave Studies in the Enlightenment, Romanticism and Cultures of Print book series. London: Palgrave Macmillan, 17–30.

Whale, John. 2010. "Romantics, Explorers and Picturesque Travellers" in S. Copley and P. Garside (Eds.). *The Politics of the Picturesque. Literature, Landscape and Aesthetics since 1770.* CUP, 175–195.

Whatley, John. 2003. "Introduction of Cult-like and Occult Undertakings". *Gothic Studies* 5. 1: 1–10.

Whatley, Thomas. 2016. [1770]. *Observations on Modern Gardening. An Eighteenth-Century Study of the English Landscape Garden.* Woodbridge: The Boydell Press.

Wickman, Matthew. 2005. "Terror's Abduction of Experience: a Gothic History". *The Yale Journal of Criticism* 18. 1: 179–206.

Wiesenfarth, Joseph. 1988. *Gothic Manners and the Classic English Novel.* Madison: University of Wisconsin Press.

Wieten, Alida Alberdina S. 1926. *Ann Radcliffe. Her Relation toward Romanticism.* Amsterdam: H. J. Paris.

Williams, Anne. 1995. *Art of Darkness. A Poetics of Gothic.* University of Chicago Press.

-- 2006. "Horace in Sicily: Discovering a Gothic Imagination". *Gothic Studies* 8. 1: 22–34.

Williams Raymond. 1983. [1958]. *Culture and Society. 1780–1950.* New York: Columbia University Press.

Wilson, Edmund. 1944. "A Treatise on the Tales of Horror". *New Yorker,* 27th May: 67–73.

Wilson, Penelope. 2005. "Lyric, Pastoral, and Elegy" in S. Gillespie and D. Hopkins (Eds.). *The Oxford History of Literary Translation in English: 1660–1790.* Vol. III. OUP, 173–190.

Winkelmann, Johann Joachim. 1850. [1764]. *The History of Ancient Art Translated from the German of John Winkelmann by Giles Henry Lodge.* London: John Chapman, 142, Strand.

Wolff, Larry. 2005. "Deprived. Inclinations. Libertines and Children in Casanova's Venice". *Eighteenth Century Studies* 38. 3: 417–440.

Wollstonecraft, Mary. 1989. [1792]. *Maria: Or, The Wrongs of Woman.* OUP.

Wordsworth, William and Samuel Taylor Coleridge. 1961. [1798–1805]. *The Lyrical Ballads.* Introduction and Notes by George Sampson. London: Methuen & Co.

Wu, Ya-feng. 2009. "Blazoning the Paired Tableaux: *The Mysteries of Udolpho* and *The Monk*". *Journal of Humanities* 27: 1–32.

Yeager, Stephen. (2019). "Gothic Palaeography and the Preface to the First Edition of *The Castle of Otranto*". 21. 2: 145–158.

Printed in Great Britain
by Amazon

32571809R00195